Further praise for

ETHAN ALLEN

"The definitive biography of the frontier hero and founder of Vermont. . . . Authoritative, vivid. . . . Colorful, well-written and nuanced."
—*Kirkus Reviews*, starred review

"Randall incorporates a wealth of research and colorful detail into an absorbing, well-paced narrative that highlights Allen's distinctively American energies—and contradictions."
—*Publishers Weekly*, starred review

"Willard Sterne Randall has provided for us a long overdue biography of this first hero produced by the American Revolution."
—James A. Percoco, *Washington Independent Review of Books*

"Randall has penned a balanced and exciting study of the original Green Mountain Boy and the roiling times in which he lived."
—Ron Soodalter, HistoryNet.com

"Willard Sterne Randall has few equals as a writer. A careful and meticulous historian and an esteemed biographer, Randall has marshaled his many talents to produce the definitive biography of Ethan Allen, one of the most fascinating figures in the founding of the American nation. . . . A must-read."
—John Ferling, author of *Independence*

"This is a powerful story about an essential and little-understood figure in American history. Willard Randall writes with grace and insight, and *Ethan Allen* is an engaging biography."

—Jon Meacham, author of *American Lion*

"This is the first full biography of Ethan Allen in half a century, and the only one to render him a psychologically complicated, fully flawed hero of the American Revolution."

—Joseph J. Ellis, author of *Founding Brothers* and *American Sphinx*

ETHAN ALLEN

Other Works by Willard Sterne Randall

Alexander Hamilton: A Life

George Washington: A Life

Thomas Jefferson: A Life

Benedict Arnold: Patriot and Traitor

A Little Revenge: Benjamin Franklin and His Son

Building Six: The Tragedy at Bridesburg
(with Stephen D. Solomon)

Founding City (with David R. Boldt)

Thomas Chittenden's Town (with Nancy Nahra)

American Lives (with Nancy Nahra)

Forgotten Americans (with Nancy Nahra)

Willard Sterne Randall

ETHAN ALLEN

HIS LIFE AND TIMES

W. W. NORTON & COMPANY

NEW YORK ❋ LONDON

Frontispiece: Ethan Allen demands the surrender of Fort Ticonderoga.
(Courtesy of Fort Ticonderoga Museum)

For information about permission to reproduce
selections from this book, write to Permissions,
W. W. Norton & Company, Inc.,
500 Fifth Avenue, New York, NY 10110

For information about special discounts for bulk purchases,
please contact W. W. Norton Special Sales at
specialsales@wwnorton.com or 800-233-4830

Manufacturing by RR Donnelley, Harrisonburg
Book design by Ellen Cipriano
Production manager: Anna Oler

Library of Congress Cataloging-in-Publication Data

Randall, Willard Sterne.
Ethan Allen : his life and times / Willard Sterne Randall. — 1st ed.
p. cm.
Includes bibliographical references and index.
ISBN 978-0-393-07665-3 (hardcover)
1. Allen, Ethan, 1738–1789. 2. Soldiers—United States—Biography.
3. United States—History—Revolution, 1775–1783—Biography.
4. Vermont—History—Revolution, 1775–1783. 5. Fort Ticonderoga
(N.Y.)—Capture, 1775. 6. Vermont—Militia—Biography.
7. Vermont—History—To 1791. I. Title.
E207.A4R36 2011
973.3'31092—dc22
[B]
2011007522

ISBN 978-0-393-34229-1 pbk.

W. W. Norton & Company, Inc.
500 Fifth Avenue, New York, N.Y. 10110
www.wwnorton.com

W. W. Norton & Company Ltd.
Castle House, 75/76 Wells Street, London W1T 3QT

1 2 3 4 5 6 7 8 9 0

To Nan and Lucy
close editors
and to
John W. Heisse Jr.
close friend

CONTENTS

PART THREE ▪ "NO DAMNED ARNOLD"

PROLOGUE

WHAT MAKES THE STORY of Ethan Allen endure so prominently in American history? There have been very few books about him—only one credible biography in nearly half a century—yet his own narrative as a prisoner of war has remained in print for more than two centuries.

Some sixty editions alone came off the presses before the Civil War. His legacy was especially dominant during our nation's defining battle between the North and the South, when thousands of Green Mountain Boys, tracing their lineage to the regiment Ethan Allen formed during the American Revolution, streamed down from their hill farms. In fact, per capita, twice as many Vermonters as men from any other Union state joined the fight against slavery, an institutional evil that never had been tolerated in a state where iconoclastic traditions have always been distinguishing features.

Like Vermont, the nation's first independent republic, Ethan

Allen bore scant resemblance to his fellow founding fathers, so little that he, even in his own lifetime, became a myth, part of a folklore that people handed down, as if to arrive at a truth that somehow validated them. And, like a myth, the fable of Ethan Allen spread in many different ways. Invariably, his story, over the centuries, became the myth of the first famous frontiersman, ineluctably pulled toward the newest frontier. As the frontier spread west, so did his myth. The hero of the New England frontier came to represent not just the yearnings of disenfranchised Yankees but invariably the struggles of generations of frontiersmen who lamented, some more raucously than others, that the voices of Washington's established politicians failed to respond to their distinct needs.

In the nineteenth century, a young nation without much of a past demanded such mythic tales, while today, as we appear mired in a new state of spiritual malaise, we seem to cling to such myths to shield us from that which may be more unvarnished than we want to know. Yet now, still at the beginning of the twenty-first century, it feels imperative to me, as a historian and biographer, to examine these legends and to separate myth from self-serving fiction. Nevertheless, in this new biographical evaluation, it remains paramount that we not exclude those voices that have been generally excluded, for often their insights are of great historical significance.

While Ethan Allen embodied the virtues and vices of the nation's founding fathers more colorfully than any of his more venerated and aristocratic counterparts, he is frequently defined by a single night in 1775 when he led a daring predawn attack on Fort Ticonderoga, a British fortress in northern New York. Yet, as the man who virtually hand-carved the state of Vermont into the Union, Allen was an enigmatic and highly charismatic product of the American frontier, blessed with an extraordinary intellect if also with a hot-tempered propensity for action.

To delve more deeply into his character and achievements, it is now possible, with the help of an ever-increasing number of Internet links, to mine databases that extend the use of fragile documents in archives, to examine long-neglected records in the United States, England, and Canada, and to consult the personal papers of other Revolutionary War–era figures, both friends and enemies. Widening the scope of my research beyond the borders of Vermont, I have attempted as well to shed new light on Allen's brutal treatment as a prisoner of war of the British, a sustained period of his life that has not always interested more popular historians. At the same time, I have also concentrated on his intrigues as a frontier politician and as a progenitor of guerrilla warfare in undefined colonial borderlands. A so-called Robin Hood in the eyes of many dispossessed Green Mountain settlers, Allen also, and unabashedly so, aggrandized the holdings of his family, a fact that is generally glossed over in previous accounts. He emerges here not only as a public-spirited leader but as a self-interested individual as well, often no less rapacious than his archenemies, the New York land barons of the Hudson and Mohawk valleys.

As aware as Benjamin Franklin about the need to burnish his popular image, as concerned as Jefferson, though in a more folksy way, to define his legacy, Allen projects himself as a populist frontier philosopher on horseback. His copious newspaper writings and pamphleteering first brought him to the attention of other New England radicals, making him their choice, with the help of his legion of Green Mountain Boys, to lead the first American offensive of the Revolutionary War. Allen's sometimes embellished prisoner-of-war narrative established him, after Tom Paine, as the second-best-selling author of the Revolution, influencing Enlightenment thinkers ranging from Paine himself to Madison. A speculator in business and war, Allen also evolved into a homespun pundit who translated his rational explorations into often impetuous action. His final testament was to take the Scottish Enlightenment philosopher John Locke's "state of nature," simply lop off "of nature," and make a new state—Vermont, whose distinct ideology would come to reflect a parallel and potent voice in American political history.

ETHAN ALLEN

Royal Governor Benning Wentworth of New Hampshire.
(New Hampshire Archives)

PART ONE

---※---

"THE MOST UNWEARIED PAINS"

1.

"A Sincere Passion for Liberty"

❋

IN THE STORM-TOSSED hours since midnight, only two waterlogged workboats had managed to cross the narrow neck of wind-whipped Lake Champlain. Just eighty-nine of Ethan Allen's Green Mountain Boys had been able to get from the tree-shrouded shore of Vermont to the steep protuberance of New York less than a mile away. Now the protective darkness was fading as a white morning fog cast a faint glow on the massing rebels. Soon that would burn off, exposing Allen's amateur assault force to British sentinels patrolling Fort Ticonderoga's looming ramparts. All night, Allen had waited for more commandeered vessels to arrive, for more of the two thousand men he'd promised he could muster for the attack, but by five o'clock on the morning of May 10, he realized he could wait no longer. Without even the two hundred chosen men waiting to join him from their hiding place behind a screen of spruces on the Vermont shore, he would have to assault the most formidable British fortress in the American colonies.

Only two weeks earlier the shocking news had reached Ethan Allen that the first shots of the American Revolution had been fired. Reports wrapped in rumors of massacre had spread like a crown fire over the forests and mountains of New England. Initially, few details could be confirmed, but at least one conclusion was indisputable: on April 19, 1775, in a deadly clash of arms between Massachusetts militia and British regulars in the outskirts of Boston, a decade of ideological ferment and partisan protests over England's fumbling attempts to formulate imperial policies had finally turned into open rebellion.

The announcement of the birth of the United States at Lexington and Concord quickly reached the thousands of transplanted New Englanders on the Vermont frontier. From the minutemen on the village green of Henry Wadsworth Longfellow's Lexington to Ralph Waldo Emerson's "shot heard round the world" at the "rude bridge that arched the flood" in Concord, the strands of patriotic embroidery were already being laced from town to town by the volunteer couriers of Massachusetts' revolutionary movement.

Acrid blue clouds of musket smoke still hung over the bayoneted corpses of the Revolution's first casualties when the Massachusetts Provincial Congress, in hiding in Watertown, summoned its most trusted courier, twenty-three-year-old Israel Bissell, and handed him a single document. Bissell was to ride west first to Springfield, on the Connecticut River, then south as far as New York City, spreading the news of the British invasion. At every town, he was to obtain the countersignature of the chairman of the Committee of Safety to this missive:

Wed. morning near 10 of the Clock

Watertown,

To all friends of American liberty: let it be known that this morning before break of day a British brigade consisting of about 1000 or 1200 men landed at Phips farm at Cambridge and marched to Lexington where they found a company of our colony militia in arms, upon whom they fired without any provocation and killed six men and wounded four others. By an express from Boston we find another brigade are now upon their march from Boston supposed to be about 1,000. The bearer, Israel Bissell, is charged to alarm the country, and all persons are desired to furnish him with fresh horses, as they may be needed. I have spoken with several who have seen the dead and wounded.[1]

Recent historical research, however, suggests that the British raid was no surprise. The forewarned Patriots had prepared carefully to confront and eagerly exploit it. For ten years, radical Bostonians, self-described Patriots, had clashed sporadically with British colonial officials. In a town of 16,000, a garrison of 4,000 British troops seemed powerless to enforce the tax levies and new trade restrictions emanating from Parliament in London. As American protests against British rule and occupation escalated, the Patriots sometimes responded with excruciatingly painful and invariably fatal tarring and feathering of British sympathizers but more commonly with a torrent of propaganda in a pamphlet war between Patriot and Loyalist apologists.

In the year before the clashes at Lexington and Concord, a network of thirty "observers" coordinated by the Boston Committee of Safety provided intelligence of British movements. Alerted by postriders led by Paul Revere, townspeople all over the

Bay Colony stood silently, sullenly by, watching while columns of the detested Redcoats, locally styled "bloody lobsterbacks," sortied from Boston to seize the colony's supplies of gunpowder and weapons from magazines in Charlestown, Cambridge, and Salem. In September of 1774, some 40,000 alarmed New England militia, many of them combat-seasoned veterans of the French and Indian War, mobilized when British troops marched out from Boston to Medford and Charlestown to seize the colony's militia depots. Some militiamen, primed to fight raw British recruits, rode or marched one hundred miles or more that day from every direction, only to turn back in disappointment when they learned that, since the British had drawn no blood, there was no legitimate provocation to shoot them. In December of 1774, 2,000 British regulars marched to the coastal port of Portsmouth to seize New Hampshire's gunpowder, but Revere had already warned the local Sons of Liberty, who seized the powder. In February of 1775, 150 troops marched again, this time to Salem, but a crowd blocked the road and raised the drawbridge leading to the powder stores in the harbor. In March, the month before the Battle of Lexington, when Lord Percy rode out at the head of some 3,000 regulars, on a march out into the countryside, postriders sounded their tocsins, and, as thousands of militia turned out, Percy turned back. In effect, the Patriots of Massachusetts had successfully blockaded the British inside Boston.

THE JUSTIFIABLY NERVOUS British commander in chief in America at the moment was Sir Thomas Gage, and he refused to launch an unauthorized attack on the recalcitrant revolutionaries. A sober, persistent man, the aristocratic Gage, the second son of an English viscount, had been nicknamed "Honest Tom" by American provincial troops who had served under him in the French and Indian War because of his habitual caution, perhaps a product of his propensity for being wounded. He had sustained serious wounds in the British debacle against the French at Fontenoy, again while blindly leading the vanguard of General Edward Braddock's army into a forest ambush at the Monongahela and then was wounded somewhat less seriously in a foolhardy British frontal attack on the entrenched French in the unfinished Fort Ticonderoga on July 8, 1758. In the space of an afternoon, more than 3,000 British troops perished. The next year, the French, carrying out a scorched-earth strategy as they retreated toward Canada, blew up their prized fortresses around Lake Champlain. The conquering British spent upwards of £4 million to rebuild them. The costly British failure at Ticonderoga made martyrs of the dead, heroes of its survivors. For Ethan Allen even to think of desecrating this shrine to British valor would have horrified and undoubtedly outraged Gage.

A COMMANDING FIGURE in his forest green greatcoat and sheared beaver tricorn hat, the thirty-seven-year-old Ethan Allen, described by a contemporary as a "robust, large-boned man," had served for five years as colonel commandant of his creation, the Green Mountain Boys, the largest paramilitary force in North America. He founded the volunteer militia regiment to defend some twenty-nine frontier settlements between Lake Champlain and the Connecticut River in a border war over conflicting land grants made by royal officials in New Hampshire and New York. For five years, Allen systematically and with remarkably little bloodshed thwarted the Crown officials in the provincial capital of New York City who claimed that New Hampshire had no right to have sold settlers some three million acres of hardwood forests in the Green Mountains. Consequently, New York declared that the thousands of frontier settlers who held New Hampshire deeds were squatters, subject to eviction. New York based its claim on a century-old charter granted by King Charles II stating that New York extended east to the Connecticut River; New Hampshire, on the fact that it had built forts and protected the territory from the French. (Until the American Revolution, Vermont did not actually exist.)

Frustrated by pro forma eviction orders issued after cursory hearings in a New York court composed of corrupt lawyers and wealthy Hudson Valley land speculators, Ethan Allen, at the behest of selectmen in Vermont settlements, organized and trained a regiment of settlers. With his vigilant militiamen, Allen was able to intercept and repeatedly repulse sheriff's posses attempting to seize frontier homesteads for resale by New York's royal officials to major land speculators and high-ranking British military officers. So successful were Allen and the Green Mountain Boys in their turn at evicting New York magistrates and posses from Vermont that, little more than a year before Allen's expedition against the Lake Champlain forts, the New York Provincial Assembly, dominated by major landholders, passed seven acts declaring Allen and five of his officers outlaws. New York's royal governor, Sir William Tryon, posted a hefty £100 reward for Allen's capture and decreed a sentence of death, summary execution to take place without the nicety of a trial by jury.

Like so many immigrants then and since, the man who founded and defended what became the state of Vermont left behind half a life of boom and bust. Ethan Allen was well over six feet tall, a rarity in eighteenth-century America. As a Puritan, he possessed the upbringing of a genteel Puritan family. One of eight children of a town-founding farmer, Allen was largely self-educated; his only formal schooling was eight months of classics and mathematics he imbibed at seventeen to prepare him for a

Yale College education that never materialized. His relatives and in-laws included prosperous merchants, ministers, a miller, and the owners of extensive landholdings. Several had attended Yale at a time when to attend college at all was the privilege of a high echelon of colonists. While Allen frequently wielded biblical quotations to his advantage, he abjured organized religion: in fact, the Pope he admired was a poet named Alexander. The disputatious Allen wrote fluidly and copiously, spelling out in widely read newspaper articles and book-length pamphlets the plight of the smallholder on the frontier who was being victimized by a feudal English legal system that favored the landed aristocracy and granted few rights to the British yeoman class transplanting itself en masse to find refuge in the backcountry forests of America.

Dark-miened, thick-bodied, and rugged from years of grueling work as a farmer, as a working partner in Connecticut's first successful iron foundry, and as a professional hunter, Allen had grown wealthy in his twenties yet impoverished in his thirties. Outspoken in the face of New England's rigid theocracy, he had been "read out" of Puritan-dominated towns in Massachusetts and Connecticut. His use of profane language in the workplace made laborers love him and clergy and magistrates prosecute him. Refusing to tolerate corrupt business practices, he used bullwhip and bare knuckles when he felt he was being exploited by the tight-knit commercial society of New England towns. In order to support a large family, he spent winters hunting alone in the Green Mountains, exploring the uncharted land recently evacuated by the French and their Indian allies. Each spring, he brought back hides to family businesses—a tannery, a factory for manufacturing buckskin clothing, a general store in Connecticut. Forming the Onion River Land Company (known widely as the Ethan Allen Land Company), he purchased large tracts of rich hardwood wilderness, often on credit, and then sold small parcels

for modest sums to impecunious families who became his loyal
followers in the Green Mountain Boys.

To FULLY APPRECIATE what motivated Allen, one must
examine the political and economic currents that so dramatically
transformed the colonies in the dozen years following the end
of hostilities between the British and the French. For most of
the years since the French surrender in 1763, the commander in
chief of all British forces in North America was General Gage.
He recovered from his war wounds sufficiently to marry Margaret Kemble, a beautiful American heiress. The daughter of
wealthy New Brunswick, New Jersey, Loyalists, she was related
to the aristocratic Livingston family of Hudson Valley land
barons, archenemies of Ethan Allen and the Vermont settlers.
Because of his heroism under fire, Gage became a favorite of King
George III, who personally promoted him and sought his advice
on America. His status at court brought him considerable riches,
including 18,000 valuable acres in Oneida County, New York, a
large tract in New Brunswick now called Gagetown, and a West
Indian plantation yielding an income of £600 annually. Gage's
vested interest in America may help to explain his desire, not
shared by all of his countrymen, to keep the peace in Boston, a
feat that would prove beyond his, or perhaps anyone's, abilities.
He was repeatedly caught off guard by the town's Patriots. After
the Peace of Paris ended the French and Indian War in 1763,
England faced a crushing war debt, heavy taxes at home, and the
expense of supporting a large army in America. As a worldwide
postwar depression set in, Parliament chose this inopportune
moment to pass the American Revenue Act, the first law ever
enacted for the specific purpose of raising money in its colonies
for the Crown. The law extended an existing duty on molasses, a

staple produced in Boston from West Indian sugar, and imposed new import duties that affected almost every American: on non-British textiles, coffee, indigo, and Madeira and Canary Islands wines. It also banned the import of French wines and foreign rum and doubled the duties on goods imported from other countries or their colonies. The list of goods that Americans could export only to the mother country or her colonies was expanded to include iron, hides, whale fins, raw silk, potash, and pearl ash, promising to stifle nascent American industry. When Parliament also decreed that it would for the first time strictly enforce the higher imposts, Samuel Adams, a malt brewer and lawyer whose father's fortune had been wiped out by British currency regulations, foresaw the consequences of taxing of American colonists without granting them representative seats in the House of Commons. He regarded new royal regulations as the resounding tocsin of an alarming parliamentary infringement of colonial rights:

> If our trade may be taxed, why not our lands? Why not the product of our lands and everything we possess or make use of? This we apprehend annihilates our charter rights to govern and tax ourselves. It strikes at our British privileges which, as we have never forfeited them, we hold in common with our fellow subjects who are natives of Britain. If taxes are laid upon us in any shape without our having a legal representation where they are laid, are we not reduced from the character of free subjects to the miserable status of tributary slaves?[2]

Perversely, Parliament responded to initial American objections by imposing the Stamp Tax, which required almost all Americans to pay a sizable tax on paper, as the English had for almost a century. Items taxed included bills of lading, dice and playing cards, mortgages and liquor licenses, printed pamphlets, newsprint and newspaper advertisements, almanacs, calendars, surveying documents, and college diplomas. At a time when cash was sparse and unemployment high, the taxes had to be paid in silver or gold. Some were outrageously steep. The stamp for a college diploma cost £4 (equivalent to about $600 in 2010) at a time when half the students at Harvard were studying for the ministry on scholarships. But the burden fell heaviest on lawyers, printers, tavern owners, merchants, and shipowners, broadening the base of opposition to growing parliamentary power. Merchants, lawyers, and sailors rioted all up and down the Atlantic seaboard. All the lawyers in New Jersey refused to conduct any business requiring the obnoxious stamps, which put a stop on all legal business in the colony. In Boston, crowds chased the stamp commissioner through the streets, sacked the home of the royal governor, and literally pulled it down with blocks and tackles as he escaped out a window. The Boston town meeting denounced taxation without representation in Parliament and proposed intercolonial action. The colony's House of Representatives authorized forming a committee of correspondence to coordinate protests with other colonies. In August of 1764, America's first trade boycott materialized. Boston merchants agreed to forgo importing English lace and ruffles, and the town's mechanics followed suit by pledging to wear only leather work clothes made in Massachusetts.

Gage wrote home to the ministry in London, "I have never been more at a loss." To him, it was obvious that the protests were well organized:

The plan of the people of property is to raise the lower class to prevent the execution of the Law. . . . The lawyers are the source from which these clamors have flowed. . . .

[M]erchants in general, assembly men, magistrates, &c have been united in this plan of riots, and without the influence and instigation of these the inferior people would have been quiet. . . . The sailors who are the only people who may be properly styled Mob, are entirely at the command of the Merchants who employ them.[3]

As the protests intensified, Gage rotated his forces from frontier posts to build up a garrison at Boston: by late 1768, into a town of 16,000 he injected 4,000 Redcoats. Gage chose his troops unwisely, as the historian David Hackett Fischer points out, selecting "for that difficult assignment the 29th Foot, a regiment notorious for poor discipline, hot-tempered officers, and repeated violent clashes with civilians in Canada and New York." Among these troops were the men who shot and killed six protesters in the so-called Boston Massacre of 1770. As the home government "yielded by bits" to unpopular demands, Gage's attitude stiffened. In 1772, he wrote to his superiors in London, "Democracy is too prevalent in America, and claims the greatest attention to prevent its increase." New England's laws were bizarre, the people litigious. "Every man studies law, and interprets the laws to suit his purposes." An important element in the problem, Gage grew convinced, was the abundance of cheap land. "The people themselves have gradually retired from the coast" and "are, already, almost out of reach of Law and Government."[4]

AFTER AN INTERVAL of relative calm, some 7,000 Bostonians gathered at Old South Church on December 16, 1773, to protest the arrival of three shiploads of tea by the British East India Company, a monopoly that was undercutting prices charged by

Boston merchants. That night, somewhere between 30 and 130 Sons of Liberty, thinly disguised as Mohawk Indians, boarded the ships and dumped 342 lacquered Chinese chests of the hated cargo into the harbor. (The ships and their cargoes were the investments of £1,000-a-share stockholders in the East India Company, many of them members of Parliament; its consignees were the sons of the royal governor.) Gage was on home leave in England when reports reached him. King George summoned him and solicited his advice. Gage had come to despise town meetings as "democraticall despotism." As early as 1770, he had urged the king and his councillors to annihilate Massachusetts's royal charter and abolish town meetings: "No peace will ever be established in that province, till the King nominates his council, and appoints the magistrates, and all town-meetings are absolutely abolished; whilst those meetings exist the people will be kept in a perpetual heat."[5]

The Boston Tea Party convinced the king that Gage's assessment was correct: he ordered his first minister, Lord North, to push through Parliament a set of Coercive Acts. When Gage, now the royal governor as well as commander in chief, returned to Boston, he promulgated what Bostonians called the Intolerable Acts. Henceforth, town meetings could be called only with his permission. The king would henceforth appoint an executive council that effectively stripped the general assembly of its crucial taxing and spending authority. All judges would be appointed and paid by the Crown. Until Bostonians repaid the East India Company the £10,000 value of the tea, Parliament had effectively cut off all trade by land and sea with the port town. Perhaps even more devastating, Parliament rescinded Massachusetts' fishing rights in the Atlantic. On June 1, 1774, the Port Act took effect, and normal business came to a standstill. Other colonies kept Bostonians supplied, driving donated flocks of sheep and herds of pigs across the narrow neck connecting Boston and the mainland—between British cannon.

In the months that followed, Gage encountered unabated resistance during raids on nearby powder magazines as he attempted to disarm the colonists. The situation was growing out of hand. Early in 1775, he wrote to London for further instructions. In Massachusetts, each town that tense winter was organizing crack units of seventy rapid-response minutemen to turn out on a moment's notice. The resistance movement not only was spreading throughout New England but was winning growing sympathy in other colonies, especially among the merchant class. In Connecticut, the general assembly commissioned two new independent military companies, each recruited, outfitted, and paid by wealthy shipowners. In coastal Norwich, Benedict Arnold, owner of thirteen merchant ships and a thriving apothecary and luxury goods store, received the assembly's commission as captain of the Second Connecticut Foot Guards, recruited Yale College students, and outfitted them in scarlet. Connecticut also coined six new regiments of militia, upwards of 6,000 men in a colony of 100,000 citizens. The Connecticut Assembly dispatched fast ships to the Caribbean to purchase weapons and gunpowder and ordered all militia to train for twelve days, double the normal term of service, before May 1, 1775, paying them six shillings a day, double the wages of a skilled artisan. In March 1775, a purge of leaders of old militia units, including any suspected of being Loyalists, swept a dozen top officers from their posts. Invariably, their offices went to the most radical Patriots, the Sons of Liberty. Intimidated by Patriot crowds, more than 1,100 Loyalists from all over New England fled that winter from their homes into Boston, seeking British protection.

. . .

ON APRIL 14, 1775, as drilling militia practiced the manual of arms on town greens, General Gage opened fresh orders from Lord Dartmouth, the colonial secretary. Gage now received authorization to march into the countryside, as he had requested, "with large detachments to secure obedience through every part of it." Both Massachusetts and Connecticut were to be stripped of their seventeenth-century royal charters, and Boston's radical leaders, preferably Samuel Adams and John Hancock, were to be arrested and shipped in irons to London to be tried for high treason. What actually occurred only four days later quickly became shrouded in folklore and would be transformed into a story that has been repeated from poet, parent, and teacher to child and new citizen ever since. It was a cool, windy day. At three o'clock on the morning of April 19, seven hundred handpicked British light infantry and grenadier guards marched to the south end of Boston Commons and boarded launches from the men-of-war that took them up the Charles River to Cambridge. There they stepped off, without rations or bedrolls, for what they expected to be a twelve-mile sortie to Lexington, where, according to Loyalist informants, the Patriots were known to be stockpiling munitions. At first light, Major John Pitcairn and the British advance guard rounded a bend in the Great Road where it approached Lexington Green and discovered a crowd of several hundred Patriots, including seventy militiamen formed in two neat ranks. It instantly struck Pitcairn that the Minutemen were not posted where they could fire from behind cover but were out in the open, in daylight, exposed within a hundred yards—the maximum range of the British muskets—away from the road the British would have to follow to Concord. For several days in the preceding week, Samuel Adams and John Hancock had been guests at Hancock's childhood home, now the parsonage of the Reverend Jonas Clark, the political as well as the spiritual leader of Lexington.

Adams apparently already knew of British plans to march on Lexington and Concord. Many historians believe that his informant was the wife of the British commander. David Hackett Fischer writes that "it was none other than Margaret Kemble Gage, the American wife of General Gage . . . [who] had long felt cruelly divided by the growing rift between Britain and America." Mrs. Gage reputedly informed her close personal friend Dr. Joseph Warren, the president of the Massachusetts Provincial Congress, that her husband's troops planned to raid armories in Lexington and Concord: her warning led to Paul Revere's famous ride. In fact, Gage himself suspected his wife and shipped her off to his estate in England to avoid further embarrassment.[6]

According to Gage's personal papers, the British commander had his own spy close to Adams: Dr. Benjamin Church, a Harvard-educated poet and a member of the Massachusetts Provincial Congress, the extralegal governing arm of the radical movement. Dr. Church, hedging his bets to be on the winning side of the struggle, was reporting the intimate details of the radicals' meetings and passing along his acute analyses of the revolutionaries' moods and problems to the British commander through one of his mistresses. Church had told General Gage that Samuel Adams was under intense pressure because of the adverse effects to trade that the closing of the Boston port had and was receiving only tepid support from other colonies. Adams, according to Church, worried that the Patriot cause was losing momentum and needed a fresh infusion of martyrs.

Informed by Samuel Adams and Hancock of the imminent British attack, Captain John Parker, leader of the Lexington militiamen, summoned his men at midnight. The majority of the men decided that they did not want to try to obstruct the British march. Captain Parker reported their decision to Parson Clark, Hancock, and Adams. Whatever arguments Hancock and

Samuel Adams mustered to persuade Parker to overrule his men, he reassembled the militiamen three hours later, just before dawn and ordered them to form up on the green.

MAJOR PITCAIRN WOULD always insist he gave his men positive orders not to fire unless fired upon. Later, he told an American prisoner of war that he did not see who fired first. According to the written account of his prison interview, which was passed on many years later to the Reverend Ezra Stiles, by then the president of Yale College, the British major rode up to the militiamen and ordered them to disperse. When they did not immediately heed his command, they crossed an invisible line that made them rebels in arms against the king. Wheeling his horse and giving a command to his men to surround and disarm the militiamen, Pitcairn saw a gun in the hands of "a peasant" behind a stone wall "flash in the pan without going off." Then two or three more guns, also being fired from cover, went off. Instantly, without orders, "a promiscuous, uncommanded but general Fire took place," which Pitcairn later insisted he could not stop even when he swung his sword downward, the signal to cease firing. Pitcairn's official report to General Gage is more nuanced and self-serving:

> I gave directions to the troops to move forward, but on no account to fire or even attempt it without orders. When I arrived at the end of the village, I observed drawn up upon a green near 200 of the rebels, and when I came within about 100 yards of them, they began to file off toward some stone walls on our right flank. The light infantry, observing this, ran after them. I instantly called to the soldiers not to fire but to surround and disarm them and after sev-

eral repetitions of those positive orders to the men not to fire etc., some of the rebels who had jumped over the wall fired four or five shots at the soldiers, which wounded a man of the Tenth [Regiment], and my horse was wounded in two places. . . . At the same time several shots were fired from a Meeting House on our left. Upon this, without any order or regularity the light infantry began scattered fire and continued in that situation for some little time, contrary to the repeated orders of both me and the officers that were present.[7]

When the British firing stopped, eight Americans lay dead and ten more, badly wounded, were carried to nearby houses as the British regrouped for the march to Concord. Among them was Captain Parker. After he fell wounded by a musket ball, a British soldier ran him through with a bayonet. He survived.

DOGTROTTING THE FIVE miles from Lexington to Concord, the British vanguard encountered unexpected resistance from hundreds of Patriots who refused to retreat when the two forces fired across Concord's North Bridge. Guided by Loyalists, the grenadiers battered down doors with the brass-jacketed butts of their heavy muskets in their precisely targeted quest for concealed weapons and munitions. Dragging terrified families into the street, the grenadiers ransacked and looted houses, shooting and bayoneting anyone who resisted. One squad of grenadiers uncovered a pair of ancient cannon, one of them capable of lobbing 24-pound cannonballs down on British ships at anchor in Boston Bay. The soldiers sheared off the guns' trunions, making it impossible to mount and fire the cannon. Able to evacuate most of their munitions to the ponds and basements of nearby farms, the Patriot leaders had left the vital cannon buried, thinking they were hidden well enough. The British raiding parties, more importantly, failed to ferret out their principal targets, John Hancock and Samuel Adams, who had escaped to nearby Woburn and were hiding in the cellar of a Puritan parsonage.

ANY VENEER OF civility between occupiers and colonists vanished within the span of a week, replaced by a savagery formerly ascribed only to Indians. As the British column reformed to countermarch to Boston, a swelling mass of well-officered militia galled them from rooftops, firing accurately out of windows, from trees, from behind stone walls. Moving rings of skirmishers continually surrounded the retreating Redcoats, firing into their thinning ranks, sometimes with long guns meant for duck gunning. By the time the regulars reached Metonomy, they were responding savagely to any resistance by individual householders. Giving no quarter at defended buildings, they put to death everyone they found inside. They did not spare noncombatants. More than one hundred bullet holes riddled one tavern where the proprietor, his wife, and two topers were found bayoneted, their skulls crushed. The Redcoats carried away anything they could fit into a knapsack, even communion silver. In a bloodlust saturnalia, marauding British soldiers set fire to the buildings and slaughtered livestock. One young boy responded to the carnage by running out and scalping a wounded Redcoat with a hatchet and hacking off his ears.

In all, seventy-three British soldiers died and two hundred more were critically wounded before they managed, reinforced by a brigade of one thousand regulars belatedly sent from Boston to relieve them, to fight their way back to the launches they'd left bobbing in the Charles River and the protection of the cannon on

British men-of-war. Overnight, more militia poured in from all over New England. Militia officers trained by the British in the French and Indian War laid out siege lines and organized work parties to build a thin line of earthworks from Roxbury all the way north through Cambridge and east to Chelsea on the north shore of the Mystic River. The morning after the battles, John Adams left his home in Braintree and rode along the makeshift American lines, concluding that "the Die was cast, the Rubicon crossed."[8]

For a dozen increasingly confrontational years before it boiled over on a mild spring morning, the clash between the British imperial government and its American colonists had been simmering. In London, the neophyte architects of the first British Empire seemed capable only of designing legislation and administrative policies that provoked American protests, which, in turn, precipitated ever more repressive—and equally unenforceable—British edicts. Now, in the long-awaited days of springtime, a mass of twenty thousand infuriated New England militiamen abandoned their farms, their shops, and their shipyards and rushed to avenge years of British arrogance, escalating taxation, and overbearing government regulation.

AT HIS PLANTATION atop Monticello overlooking Charlottesville, the thirty-two-year-old lawyer Thomas Jefferson, a newly elected delegate to the Continental Congress, lamented that force, not wisdom, was prevailing. Jefferson was sending off a gift of three cases of Madeira that had aged for eight years in his wine cave to his close friend William Small, the Scottish-born professor at William and Mary College who had taught him how to write and to reason. Small had returned to the British Isles just as the imperial crisis erupted. Saddened, Jefferson wrote a letter he

assumed would he opened and read by British officials before it
reached his mentor:

> We have received the unhappy news of an action of consid-
> erable magnitude between the king's troops and our breth-
> ren in Boston, in which it is said 500 of the former with
> Earl Piercy are slain. That such an action has happened
> is undoubted, tho' perhaps the circumstances may not
> yet have reached us with truth. This accident has cut off
> our last hopes of reconciliation, and a phrenzy of revenge
> seems to have seized all ranks of people.

Jefferson blamed the "accident" at Lexington and Concord on
Lord North, the anti-American first minister to King George III
and England's principal policymaker. Instead of attempting to
reconcile British and colonial American leaders, Jefferson decried
Lord North's "blowing up the flames as we find him doing in
every speech and public declaration":

> This may perhaps be intended to intimidate into acquies-
> cence, but the effect has been most unfortunately other-
> wise. A little knolege of human nature and attention to
> it's ordinary workings might have foreseen that the spir-
> its of the people here were in a state in which they were
> more likely to be provoked than frightened by haughty
> deportment.[9]

AT HIS HEADQUARTERS on the ground floor of the sprawling, square, unpainted Catamount Tavern on the poplar-canopied
Post Road in Bennington, Ethan Allen was huddling with the
chairmen of Committees of Safety from surrounding towns

and officers of the Green Mountain Boys, when an express rider breathlessly handed him the first report of Lexington and Concord. Anger quickly turned to exhilaration as Allen and his adherents set to work formulating a strategy that he believed would not only aid the Patriot cause but thrust him to the fore-front of the struggle. By mustering his regiment of nearly two thousand frontiersmen—the largest paramilitary force in colonial America—which he had trained and disciplined through four years of armed resistance to royal officials in New York, Allen believed he could quickly seize control of the strategic British fortresses dominating Lake Champlain and forward hundreds of cannon to the primitively armed Patriots investing Boston.

From his base at the northwest corner of New England, Allen could also see the strategic importance of occupying the British forts controlling Lake Champlain. The 116-mile-long lake drove a wedge between the Adirondack Mountains of New York and the Green Mountains. At either end and in the middle, the British maintained decaying forts built on the sites of former French settle-ments but now garrisoned collectively by a meager sixty Redcoats and their families. From an advanced base at Fort Ticonderoga, at the foot of the lake, Allen envisaged a lightning summer inva-sion of weakly defended Quebec Province that could make it the fourteenth state of a new North American union before the British could send reinforcements from faraway England.

Strategically inclined, Allen believed that the lake forts had to be seized before they could be reinforced by British Redcoats based in Montreal and before an opposing force of Loyalist mili-tiamen, many of them Scottish Highlanders combat-seasoned in the French and Indian War, could be mobilized by New York's royal government to reinforce the forts. One leading Loyalist was Allen's erstwhile mentor, Colonel Philip Skene, a Scottish veteran who had built blockhouses on his 30,000-acre forest manor just ten miles south of Lake Champlain. There, his family, his slaves, and the workers in his sawmills and shipyard had prepared to defend his manor with cannons and with his own armed schooner, *Betsey*. As Allen prepared his attack on Fort Ticonderoga, he thought that Colonel Skene was still on the high seas returning from England with instructions to raise a regiment of Loyalist troops to hold the forts. In fact, Skene's ship was being blown off course and, instead of anchoring in safety in New York harbor, landed in Philadelphia where a jeering crowd of Patriots escorted him to the city jail.

To Allen, seizing the key Champlain forts at Ticonderoga and Crown Point was an inevitable preemptive act. He later wrote that he was not one to cower and wait for the British and their Indian auxiliaries to descend from Montreal and attack the scattered settlements around the mountain lake and in the Green Mountains. Acting in secret, Allen decided he could trust only his younger brother Heman, a respected Connecticut merchant and captain in the Green Mountain Boys, to ride south to the Connecticut capital at Hartford and deliver his strategic plan to Patriot leaders assembling there.

SOME THREE HUNDRED miles to the south, Benjamin Franklin, a Pennsylvania delegate to the Second Continental Congress, woke to the cacophony of Pennsylvania German farmers and their families unloading their Conestoga wagons and setting up their wares in the covered shed bisecting Philadelphia's Market Street. Having returned only days before from failed peace negotiations in London, Franklin wrote to a friend in Parliament his initial reaction to Lexington and Concord:

You will have heard before this reaches you of the Commencement of Civil War; the end of it perhaps neither myself, nor you, who are much younger, will live to see. I find here all Ranks of People in Arms, disciplining themselves Morning & Evening, and am informed that the firmest Union prevails throughout North America.[10]

At nine o'clock the morning of the attack on Fort Ticonderoga, delegates from nine provinces, from as far away as New Hampshire and Georgia, took their places in the Pennsylvania State House on Chestnut Street around each colony's green baize-covered table. They were summoned by the peal of a great bronze London-forged bell, ironically cast a quarter century earlier to celebrate American liberties. In the largest and most ornate building in colonial America, delegates sent by extralegal congresses of nine of the chain of thirteen Atlantic-rim British provinces settled into tall Windsor side chairs and prepared to debate for the third summer season. They were to decide, they now knew, what response, if any, they would collectively make to the disastrous British onslaught. After two years of inconclusive arguments, the First Continental Congress had adjourned in stalemate, sending only an obsequious olive-branch petition off to colonial officials in London, a feeble protest against the catalog of increasingly stringent British policies. No reply came from Whitehall Palace. Lord Dartmouth, the secretary of state for North America, had slid Congress's petition, unread, under the bottom of a pile of eighty-five petitions of grievance from all over the nascent British Empire.

A majority of congressional delegates still clung to the hope that reconciliation with the mother country was possible, that all grievances could be assuaged short of military action. That first divided Congress could not even agree to establish a committee on defense, much less consider an offensive such as the Lake Champlain campaign. Until he learned of the fighting at

Boston, the recent immigrant Thomas Paine, editor of Franklin's *Pennsylvania Magazine*, considered the argument between colonies and England "a kind of lawsuit," but the brutality of the British raids in Massachusetts made him reject "the hardened, sullen-tempered Pharoah of England forever."[11] When George Washington received the electrifying news at Mount Vernon, the Virginia congressional delegate wrote to a friend, "The once-happy and peaceful plains of America are either to be drenched in blood or inhabited by slaves. Sad alterative! But can a virtuous man hesitate in his choice?"[12] Brevetted a British army brigadier after five years of combat in the recent French and Indian War, Washington was the only delegate to ride from his Philadelphia boardinghouse to the Second Continental Congress wearing his full military regalia. As late as May 16, 1775, six days after Ethan Allen and his Green Mountain Boys attacked Fort Ticonderoga, the delegates in Philadelphia were still passing a resolution declaring that "Congress had nothing else in mind but the defense of the colonies."[13]

WHEN THE POSTRIDER Israel Bissell reached New Haven at noon two and a half days after the British marched into Lexington, the Connecticut seaport's leading smuggler, Benedict Arnold, rounded up sixty-three members of his Second Connecticut Company of Foot and ordered them to pack their kits and be ready to march early the next morning. At dawn on April 22, Arnold and his uniformed militiamen surrounded the tavern where New Haven's selectmen had begun debating the grim news. At gunpoint, Arnold, son-in-law of New Haven's sheriff, demanded the keys to the town's powder magazine. Seizing ammunition, Arnold and his huzzah-ing volunteers stepped off briskly north toward Boston, a streak of scarlet against the bare spring landscape. They soon encountered Samuel Holden Parsons, colonel of the New London County militia and a member of the Connecticut General Assembly's committee of correspondence. Returning from leading the militia of Connecticut's largest port to the American lines outside Boston, Parsons was hurrying to Hartford to an emergency meeting of Connecticut's principal Patriots. He paused long enough to bemoan the inherent weakness of the American forces in the face of an inevitable British counterattack. Without artillery, he told Arnold, the 15,000 to 20,000 massed militia would be helpless.

Parsons and Connecticut radicals knew Benedict Arnold as a fifth-generation New Englander, a patrician descended from Rhode Island's longest-serving governor. Married to the daughter of the sheriff of New Haven County, Arnold owned thirteen merchant ships. He had grown rich smuggling luxury goods from the Caribbean, but he was heavily in debt to London merchants. The leader of the 10,000 member Sons of Liberty, he had personally and quite publicly flogged a crewman who informed customs officers of his illicit cargo. Arnold now told Colonel Parsons that he knew just where to find hundreds of serviceable cannon: the French had buried them or left them intact around the Lake Champlain forts when they retreated to Canada fifteen years earlier. The British forts, he added, were garrisoned only by corporals' guards. As Arnold resumed his brisk march toward Boston, Parsons galloped to Hartford, arriving just as Governor Jonathan Trumbull convened an emergency joint meeting of the Connecticut Committee of Correspondence and the Hartford Committee of Safety. Massachusetts' congressional delegation had arrived by fast sloop down the Connecticut River from Springfield. Samuel Adams, the Harvard-educated firebrand of Boston's Patriots, whose father's fortune had been ruined by British currency regulations, and Colonel John Hancock, scion of Boston's wealthiest

commercial dynasty and chairman of the Massachusetts Committee of Safety, had just come ashore exhausted after a sleepless week on the run. They had planned to ride south to the Continental Congress in Hancock's comfortable carriage, stopping to pick up the other delegates—John Adams, Thomas Cushing, and Robert Treat Paine—en route, but they were spirited from their Woburn hiding place by an escort of armed Massachusetts militiamen the fifty miles to Worcester, where they waited a nerve-racking five days for the other delegates before sailing to hastily arranged clandestine meetings at Hartford and New Haven.

The Connecticut contingent at the Hartford conference included some of the wealthiest and most powerful leaders of that colony. All of them were financially interested in westward expansion, blocked by royal decree for the past dozen years from a greater share of the fabulously valuable fur trade that New Englanders had expected to take over from the French but that they now saw coming under the control of British merchants. Parsons, head of the militia of the colony's principal port, was a major land speculator, as were Silas Deane and Christopher Leffingwell, who had represented Connecticut in the First Continental Congress. Leffingwell's family had founded Norwich, and he was the patriarch of a flourishing family network of agricultural and mercantile businesses, including the manufacture of paper, a scarce commodity at the time, and the production of chocolates. It was Leffingwell who bankrolled Arnold's march to Boston and paid his men. He was the captain of the Norwich Light Infantry, a cavalry unit composed of businessmen and their clerks. An organizer of early protests against British trade restrictions, he had openly opposed the Stamp Act and served on the seaport's Committee of Safety.

Silas Deane, secretary of the assembly's Committee of Correspondence, was a blacksmith's son from Groton who became a lawyer and married wealthily twice. His second wife was the granddaughter of Gurdon Saltonstall, former governor of Connecticut. Deane, who would become the Continental Congress's first diplomatic representative in France a short time later, had a reputation of being clever, opportunistic, and amoral, in part because of dealings connected with the estate of his first wife and questionable real estate dealings. He was a prime mover in the Susquehannah Company of Pennsylvania, a frontier land-developing scheme in which Ethan Allen's father was an original investor. The colony's leading expansionist, Deane was in politics closely allied with Governor Trumbull.

Without waiting for authorization from Congress or the Connecticut General Assembly, Trumbull, the only royal governor who became a revolutionary governor, agreed with the Adamses, Hancock, and the other committeemen that they must act swiftly to buttress the New England army. John Adams described the chaotic conditions along the makeshift Patriot lines and seconded Parsons's assessment of how woefully insubstantial they were. By meeting's end, the Connecticut committeemen decided to "borrow" £3,000 (about $450,000 today) on their personal security from the colony's treasury to finance an expedition to seize Fort Ticonderoga, Fort Amherst, and their vital cannon.

To BENEDICT ARNOLD's intelligence about the trove of French cannon around Lake Champlain and Ethan Allen's offer to put at their disposal the Green Mountain Boys, the Adamses and Hancock added another precipitant for the lightning strike at the king's forts. For months, the Massachusetts Provincial Congress had been receiving secret reports from John Brown, a Pittsfield lawyer and Arnold's cousin acting as the secret emissary of its Committee of Safety (aka Samuel Adams) to Montreal's mercantile community. According to Brown, a cousin of Arnold's, many Canadians, both English and French, were eager to make common cause with the Americans. A quick capture of the British forts would yield a unique opportunity to remove a far greater threat. A thrust up Lake Champlain into Quebec Province would make it possible to seize control of the poorly defended province before the British could implement a new form of government that, in the eyes of the Puritan Patriots gathered at Hartford, endangered New England's very culture and economy. Among Americans angered by the Coercive Acts, which had closed the port of Boston, New England Puritans in particular seethed at the passage of the Quebec Act of 1774, which would take effect in only a few days, on May 1, 1775. The act would more than double the size of Quebec Province, extending its boundaries to the Ohio River and the Mississippi (roughly the American Midwest). Even more egregious from the standpoint of Protestant New England, it guaranteed religious toleration for Catholics and preserved the ancient feudal system of the French.

The act was the handiwork of the French-speaking Sir Guy Carleton, governor-general of Quebec Province. Despite persistent opposition in the House of Commons, Carleton had managed finally to prevail through powerful connections at the English court, including the Duke of Richmond, the secretary of state for the Northern Department, effectively the man in charge of all the American colonies. Carleton had won parliamentary support for the controversial bill by maintaining that it would keep the conquered French Canadians peaceful by honoring their traditions and their religion. Carleton paid little heed to the consternation of some three thousand New England merchants and traders who had flocked into Quebec Province after the 1763 Treaty of Paris to harvest the wheat of the rich 750-mile-long St. Lawrence Valley and had a monopoly on the lucrative trade with the Indians in beaver pelts coveted by fashionable gentlemen in Europe. Carleton made no secret that he despised what he considered the money-grubbing New England Yankees. He privately feared their struggle for increasingly radical democracy, and he had worked for years to thwart it.

The secret blueprint for Canadian government that Carleton had written and personally taken to London to see through Parliament would create not only a vastly enlarged colony but one entirely different from any other British American province. Fiercely resisted and long bottled up in parliamentary committee, the act finally passed by a four-to-one majority in the wake of the Boston Tea Party. Many Americans saw it as a reprisal for the Boston Sons of Liberty's December 1773 raid, organized and led by Samuel Adams as a protest against the force-feeding of English tea. The Quebec Act, by extending Quebec Province beyond its former borders, annexed to the Canadian province the uncharted western territories granted by the charters of Connecticut, Massachusetts, and Virginia in their early seventeenth-century charters, thus blocking their westward expansion and interdicting land speculation. It also created a single-house legislature appointed by the king to advise the royal governor, himself also a Crown appointee, eliminating the lower house elected by the people and its taxing power. It preserved French civil law, including land-tenure law, and abolished English law courts, habeas corpus, and trial by jury, the bedrock of English liberties dating back to Magna Carta in 1215. The Quebec Act, widely regarded as embodying a model of the form of government the British wished to impose on their other colonies, by granting religious toleration to Catholics, as one noted Jesuit archivist in Quebec put it, gave "permission to Roman Catholics to enjoy the free exercise of their religion and to their clergy to receive from their parishes their accustomed dues and rights." But as Reverend

Stiles warned from his pulpit, the Quebec Act established the "Romish Church and IDOLATRY." Establishment Catholicism, pervasively feared in the colonies, meant that, for the first time since the Reformation, there would soon be in British territory Catholic bishops supported by the tithing of the crops and the incomes of all citizens.[14]

THE ODIOUS QUEBEC ACT took effect on May 1, 1775, before the news of Lexington and Concord reached Montreal. That morning, a crowd gathered in the Place d'Armes, at Montreal's center. Overnight, the bust of King George III had been smeared with a coat of black paint and a rosary of potatoes and a black cross draped around its neck. On the cross was the inscription "Behold the Pope of Canada, or the English Fool." Indignant British officers offered a £50 reward for the culprit. A young Jewish merchant, David Solebury Franks, would later admit it was his handiwork. The next day, a French merchant told bystanders that the proper reward for such an insult was hanging. At that, young Franks punched the Frenchman, as another merchant, named Salomon, shouted that it must have been done by a French Canadian. When a Frenchman reported that it was more likely a Jew, Salomon punched him in the face. British soldiers seized both Franks and Salomon.[15]

In Protestant New England, the injection of this incendiary religious issue brought together politicians and clergy to drum up support for armed resistance to British reforms. Within a month of the signing of the Quebec Act, the Reverend Peter Whitney, pastor of the Church of Christ in Northborough, Massachusetts, protested the presence of a popish bishop and Catholic priests in neighboring Quebec as "not safe for any Protestant government."[16] The Reverend Samuel Sherwood of Fairfield, Connecticut, warned parishioners they were on the point of being deprived of "the liberty of our conscience" and that New England should unite against the British government's new policy. Such sermons were printed for wide distribution. In New Haven, Stiles called the Quebec Act the outstanding grievance against the British government. Protest against the act was incorporated into the most radical Massachusetts document, the Suffolk Resolves, drafted by Dr. Joseph Warren, president of the Massachusetts Provincial Congress, and adopted by the Boston town meeting. The resolves, rushed to Philadelpia and adopted at the end of the First Continental Congress, characterized the new Canadian charter as "dangerous in an extreme degree to the Protestant religion and to the civil rights and liberties of all America. As men and Protestant Christians, we are indispensably obliged to take all the measures for our security . . . to acquaint ourselves with the art of war as soon as possible."[17]

WITH THE FULL Connecticut Assembly in adjournment, neither the Connecticut Committee of Correspondence nor the Hartford Committee of Safety had any right to authorize a military expedition against any territory, let alone other British colonies. The Patriot committeemen certainly knew that it would be an illegal act of war and that the instigators of such an attack would undoubtedly be branded traitors. If they were discovered, they could be arrested and transported—in chains, of course—to England where they would surely be hanged and drawn and quartered in London. Yet Connecticut's revolutionary leaders considered themselves bound in common cause with Massachusetts' Patriots, who, they believed, had without provocation been attacked by British troops. Brushing aside their law books, the Patriot leaders of Connecticut and Massachusetts summoned Heman Allen into the tavern meeting room the afternoon of April 28. Silas Deane handed Heman the committee's lethal instructions: Ethan Allen was to muster the Green Mountain Boys without delay and seize Fort Ticonderoga and Crown Point and aim their guns toward Boston. A dispatch sent by Colonel James Easton, a Pittsfield, Massachusetts, tavern keeper and captain in the Berkshire County militia, to a friend who had joined the siege of Boston, reported that, several hours later, "a number of gentlemen" from Connecticut had just passed through Pittsfield to join an attack on Ticonderoga to be led by Allen:

> The expedition has been carried on with the utmost secrecy, as they are in hopes of taking those forts by surprise. . . . The plan was concerted at *Hartford* last *Saturday* by the Governour [John Trumbull] and [his] Council, Colonel *Hancock*, and Mr. *Adams*, and others from our Province being present. . . . We earnestly pray for success to this important expedition, as the taking [of] those places would afford us a key to all *Canada*.[18]

ON THE AFTERNOON of April 30, less than a week after Ethan Allen had first been informed of the carnage outside Boston, three mud-spattered riders galloped up to the Catamount Tavern, the unofficial capitol of pre-revolutionary Vermont, with an answer. Inside, their muskets slouched against the walls of the tavern's main room, a few score Green Mountain Boys were laughing and sipping on tankards of the house specialty, Stonewall, a potent punch made of hard cider laced with rum. Heman Allen, a successful Connecticut merchant, a captain in the Boys, and Ethan's partner in Vermont's leading land company, shouldered his way through the entrance, marked by a crudely lettered sign, "Council

Room." There he found his one-year-older brother, resplendent in his calf-length, forest green, gold-epauletted colonel commandant's uniform huddling with his fellow officers. Heman had ridden all night over slippery roads with Captains Edward Mott and Noah Phelps, veterans of the French and Indian War, to bring Ethan a commission and orders from Hartford. Indeed, as he had proposed, the Boys were to attack the Lake Champlain forts and speed their precious cannon toward Boston. Heman gave the hushed crowd more details of the heavy fighting. For the first time, many of the Boys learned that the makeshift New England army would be helpless to withstand a British counterattack without state-of-the-art artillery.

Consequently, Heman told his brother that Massachusetts and Connecticut Patriot leaders were commissioning him a colonel in the Connecticut militia and placing him in command of the Green Mountain Boys. They were to seize the cannon in two of the king's forts on the New York shore, at Fort Ticonderoga and at Fort Amherst, twelve miles north at Crown Point. Ethan Allen could have refused to carry out a treasonous invasion of one British province, New York, on the dubious authority of an illegal assemblage of rebels from two other provinces not even sanctioned by a divided Continental Congress. But Allen needed little prodding. He later wrote in his 1779 memoir that his selection for the mission "thoroughly electrified" him. "Ever since I arrived to a state of manhood, and acquainted myself with the general history of mankind, I have felt a sincere passion for liberty." The blood shed at Lexington and Concord was to him the first "systematical and bloody attempt" by the British to "enslave America" and made him determined to risk a traitor's death, fully realizing that to accept Connecticut's commission to attack the king's forts was a blatant act of treason under English law.[19]

Sending couriers north and south, Ethan Allen recruited in

less than two weeks an advance force of 300 frontiersmen from the hills of western Massachusetts, Connecticut, and present-day Vermont as hundreds more slogged through mud-season roads to join him. After years of successfully rebuffing New York sheriffs and posses, Allen believed that he could count on—from a population of 8,800—as many as 2,000 armed and trained frontiersmen, to join the expedition. Turning out for the attack on Fort Ticonderoga was a motley crew: wealthy and poor farmers; hunters and trappers; a lawyer and a tavern owner; town clerks and storekeepers; a poet; a recent Yale College graduate; three African Americans; new immigrants from Scotland, England, and Ireland; a future congressman; and six of Ethan Allen's brothers and cousins. They arrived on the Champlain shore in their work clothes or in buckskin hunting shirts made by their wives, sisters, or mothers. In linsey-woolsey, fustian or plush, in wool stockings, moccasins or rude boots, in prized beaver hats or bearskin caps, in calico or silk waistcoats, they pelted down from their hill farms and from river towns to join Allen at the staging area at Hand's Cove in Shoreham, where, after a two-day march from Bennington, Allen had set up his headquarters in Paul Moore's farmhouse.

ONLY HOURS BEFORE the attack had to begin, the arrival of Benedict Arnold, bearing a freshly minted Massachusetts colonel's commission, almost dashed Allen's plan. All spit and polish, Arnold had marched his Connecticut Second Company of Foot to Cambridge, where, because of their impeccable martial appearance and red uniforms, they were asked to make up the guard of honor that escorted the body of the sole British officer slain at Concord to British headquarters. Arnold then informed the Massachusetts Provincial Congress of the number and disposition of cannon in the Lake Champlain forts. The Massachusetts congress, unaware that Connecticut had already commissioned Allen for the task, commissioned Arnold a Massachusetts colonel and ordered him to dash west, recruiting enough men to seize the vital cannon as he went.

After overtaking Allen on the Vermont shore opposite Ticonderoga, the imperious Arnold was demanding that Allen turn over command of the Green Mountain Boys and all other recruits to him. The two men faced off in front of the Boys in a field at Shoreham on May 9. At first, Allen, nearly a head taller than Arnold, seemed to cave in before Arnold's ramrod-straight physical presence, but it was only an act. Allen knew that he had no more and no less legal authority than Arnold. But he also knew that the Green Mountain Boys around him, clutching their guns, would follow only his orders. He had successfully wielded de facto authority in the forests for four years. He did not intend to relinquish it now, much less to a bombastic elitist like Arnold. In a loud, mocking voice, Allen announced that Colonel Arnold would henceforth command the Boys. If they followed Arnold, their pay would be the same two dollars a day.

Allen's uncharacteristically unassuming tone sent a signal to his men. Without a word, they silently drifted to the edges of the clearing and stacked their guns. To a man, the Boys refused to fight under anyone but the officers they had already elected. If they could not have Ethan Allen as their leader, they would club their muskets over their shoulders and march home. Arnold had no choice but to back down. Then Allen's demeanor suddenly changed. He now proposed a joint command, with Allen leading the Boys and any Connecticut troops, and Arnold commanding any soldiers who showed up from Massachusetts. As a token of reconciliation, Allen lent Arnold a short brass blunderbuss. The hair-triggered Arnold had ridden off to war without a gun.

On his arrival at Shoreham three days earlier, Allen was confident that it would be relatively easy to enter and seize one of the strongest British fortresses in North America by surprise. Nevertheless, he dispatched two veteran officers, Connecticut Captains Noah Phelps and Ezra Hickok, to stroll into the fort and pass themselves off as a pair of fur trappers coming down from the hills to have their long, unkempt beards and matted hair trimmed by the fort's barber. Once inside, they had time to note the laxity of the sentinels, the poor condition of the walls, and the fort's strengths and weak spots. Because he had so often been there, Allen knew that all sorts of people on the New York–Vermont frontier—hunters, trappers, and fur traders, merchants, farmers, and Indians—wandered in and out of the fort. Indeed, Phelps and Hickok returned to report that the fort's main gates were no longer locked at night. Somebody even said that the keys had long ago been lost. Fortuitously, Allen's spies had also discovered that the British garrison was made up of forty-six regulars with their wives and children and two officers and learned that reinforcement by the Twenty-sixth Regiment of Foot from Montreal was imminent.

THE BRITISH GARRISON inside Fort Ticonderoga had no reason to expect Vermonters to assault a Crown fortress on New York soil, in part because that province's royal government had officially and expressly forbidden any such raid. Unlike New Englanders, the majority of New Yorkers, not only the wealthy landowners, were at this time loyal to the Crown, and New York was no Massachusetts. In addition, the First Continental Congress had resolved that on no account should colonists molest the garrisons of British forts. As long as the British did not construct any new fortifications or impede the free passage of citizens, the Redcoats should be allowed to occupy their barracks peaceably. A hundred miles south in New York City, the conservative provincial congress of New York, meeting in City Hall on Broadway, had interpreted this to mean that the people should not confiscate any military property belonging to the British Crown.

Ticonderoga's garrison had not yet learned that fighting had broken out far to the east, outside Boston, that hundreds of British regulars had been killed or wounded, that a state of rebellion existed. Military dispatches or mail of any type did not travel quickly or directly from Boston west over the mountains to Lake Champlain. The news that fighting had erupted nearly a month earlier had to be sent by Royal Navy courier aboard a man-of-war first from Boston north to Halifax, Nova Scotia, where it was forwarded the long reach around eastern Canada and then south, up the St. Lawrence River to Quebec. There it had to be transferred to a supply ship that sailed only periodically from Quebec to Montreal, where the British officer in charge had to countersign it and write his own orders to be put aboard another vessel that had to carry it south along the Richelieu River to St. Jean in southern Quebec Province.

After receiving a written communiqué two months earlier from the British commander in chief, Sir Thomas Gage in Boston, Ticonderoga's commandant, Captain William Delaplace, had asked Sir Guy Carleton, governor-general of Quebec, for reinforcements. The first of those left Canada on April 12. A second squad of ten, under Lieutenant Jocelyn Feltham, arrived on April 29, but those troops did not know about Lexington and Concord. On May 10, the communiqué describing the bloody battle outside Boston was aboard the Royal Navy sloop of war *George*, tied up at a dock at St. Jean-sur-Richelieu, just inside Quebec Province and nearly 125 miles away from Fort Ticonderoga. However, that ship would sail for Ticonderoga any day now. With it would undoubtedly come more British reinforcements and skillful resistance.

Even without reinforcements from the Montreal garrison, the veteran British detachment inside the heavily armed fort could be expected to put up a fight. If they could hold out until several hundred more regulars arrived, the American capture of Fort Ticonderoga and its vital cannon would be virtually impossible. If Ethan Allen and the Green Mountain Boys succeeded, they would be renowned as the first heroes of the American Revolution. If they failed, they would either be killed or be shipped off to England to be hanged and drawn and quartered. Undoubtedly, Allen calculated the risk of failure against success in resolving a dozen years of claims, counterclaims, and armed clashes between neighboring colonies over the ownership of hundreds of thousands of acres of richly forested lands, a struggle that he now believed would be, at this opportune moment, subsumed into a general American rebellion against what he perceived to be every colony's common oppressor, England.

LATE THE AFTERNOON of May 9, Allen lined up the Boys in a light rain and, in his distinctive country preacher voice, as was his custom and their accustomed lot, gave them a speech that he hoped would inspire them. Four years later, in his popular wartime memoir, he recalled having told the Boys that by undertaking the perilous mission "conceived at Hartford," they were carrying out an "important expedition . . . to provide us a key to all Canada," for a century and a half the base for French and Indian attacks on New England's frontier settlements:

> Friends and fellow soldiers, you have, for a number of years past, been a scourge and terror to arbitrary power. Your valour has been famed abroad. . . . I now propose to advance before you, and in person conduct you through the

wicket-gate; for we must this morning either quit our pre-
tensions to valour, or possess ourselves of this fortress in a
few minutes; and, in as much as it is a desperate attempt,
which none but the bravest of men dare undertake, I do
not urge it on any contrary to his will.[20]

By sunset, three hundred men chafed at Hand's Cove, anxiously waiting for boats to be rounded up by detachments Allen
had sent north, along the lake toward Crown Point and south
to Skene's plantation. But six hours later, as the wind whipped
the lake into whitecaps, there still were no boats. A fierce storm
lashed the lake half the night, nearly wrecking the expedition.
When it died down, there was barely enough time to ferry a fraction of the force over to the New York shore before daybreak.
What Allen wouldn't learn for several days was that Captain
Samuel Herrick and the thirty men he'd sent to seize Skenesborough couldn't find the schooner Allen was relying on, because
it was cruising a hundred miles farther up the lake, delivering
grain and iron from the manor to the British garrison at St. Jean
in Quebec Province. Another detachment Allen had sent north,
under Captain Asa Douglass, could locate only a single thirty-
three-foot scow sailed by a terrified young black slave along the
shore near Crown Point. Douglass told the slave he wanted to pay
him to take him and his men hunting. The lumbering workboat
finally tacked into Hand's Cove at three in the morning on May
10. As Allen and his first chosen men clambered aboard, the sky
to the east was already turning gray against the black silhouettes
of the mountains. The scow wallowed in the choppy water under
the weight of so many men and their guns, nearly sinking into
the heaving lake. Water sloshed over the gunwales. At that time
of year, the water temperature rarely reaches forty-five degrees.
The lugsail was useless: in the high wind, it would capsize the

unwieldy, overloaded boat. Squall-whipped water drenched the novice oarsmen, blinding them. It took a nerve-racking hour and a half for the scow to make the one-mile crossing and return for more men. After a second slow crossing, only eighty-three shivering men had reached the New York shore.

By first light the next morning, the unlikely duo of Ethan Allen and Benedict Arnold were jumping side by side out of the wallowing boats just north of Willow Point, scarcely a quarter mile from the fort, leading the Boys silently past the unguarded eastern redoubt, the shoreline outer works of the fort. The ghostly column of frontiersmen hugged the wall of the unguarded waterfront redoubt, then hurried up the steep slope two hundred yards toward the looming granite walls of the main, star-shaped fortress. At five, with the sun about to rise and only a third of his scratch army—and none of their supplies—on the right side of lake, Allen whispered "Let's go" to Benedict Arnold and, making the prearranged pass-along signal, three owl hoots, launched the first offensive military action in the history of the United States.[21]

2.

"The Roughest Township
in Connecticut"

※

ALL HIS LIFE, ETHAN ALLEN would be immersed in turmoil in a New England roiling with religious controversy. At the time of his birth, on January 31, 1738, in the Berkshire Mountains frontier town of Litchfield, more than a century had elapsed since the first Puritans had emigrated from England, arriving on the run from condemnation to be burned at the stake as heretics. Yet the clergy of another state church, the Congregationalists, were still attempting to control every facet of government and society in the new England. Generations of Allen's forebears had refused to conform to any established state religion. The Allens had abandoned their comfortable ancestral homes to follow the apocalyptic preachings of a messianic Puritan, the founding father of Connecticut, Thomas Hooker.

A Cambridge-educated son of the steward to a nobleman, Hooker enjoyed the patronage of Sir Francis Drake, famed for vanquishing the Spanish Armada. Appointed to a living in

Surrey within Drake's gift, Hooker ministered to the spiritual needs of Drake's wife. At her death, he moved to East Anglia, where he became the leading Puritan social and political critic of decadent Stuart England, warning the nation of God's displeasure over "unthankfulness and carelessness." When King Charles I untethered his chief inquisitor, Archbishop William Laud, authorizing his "thorough" policy of "root and branch" destruction of all religious dissent from the Church of England, a defiant Hooker fled to Holland. He then led the Dorchester Company, better known as Mr. Hooker's Company, to the new Massachusetts Bay Colony.

Ethan Allen's great-great-grandfather Samuel and his brothers Thomas and Matthew were among Hooker's congregants emigrating from Colchester in lowland Essex. They first appear in Massachusetts records for 1632, only three years after the mass migration of Puritans and the creation of the Massachusetts Bay Colony. The Allen brothers and their wives, their children and their cousins, crowded onto a three-masted bark with their livestock, pots, pans, featherbeds, and Bibles. Dumped on the inhospitable Massachusetts shore, they fashioned their own open boat and sailed it up the Charles River to their allocated land in Newtowne (now Cambridge), by land a twenty-five-mile journey from Boston over a terrible road through wolf-infested forests. There the Reverend Hooker established a congregation-based community and preached preparationist theology: the religious conversion demanded by the Puritans, Hooker held, came not in a moment of blinding insight but in distinct and observable stages. For the next hundred years, this was to be Puritan orthodoxy, and all the Allens adhered to it.

It took only four years for the Allens to grow discontented in Massachusetts. Finding their allotments of land, producing little more than a harvest of rocks inadequate and totally unsuitable for cultivation or grazing, they were unwilling to settle for mere subsistence farming after all the sacrifices of emigration. Stories of fertile land and riches of beaver pelts drifted back from the Connecticut River valley. New Englanders were jealous of the Dutch fur trade to their south, as the historian Eric Jay Dolin points out. In the first of a series of clashes that would drive the Dutch from the eastern seaboard, English settlers began sweeping into the Connecticut Valley. The Reverend Hooker and his entire congregation sold their lands to the next boatload of unwitting immigrants, knocked the clay of Massachusetts off their boots, and followed a trail over the mountains to found Hartford on a high bluff over the Connecticut River flanked by broad, fertile floodplains. Among the first families in the region, most of the Allens remained in Connecticut, which Hooker soon organized under a royal charter after a crisis in Puritanism nearly wrecked the Puritan polity.[1]

THE ROOTS OF Ethan Allen's lifelong struggle for freedom of expression lie, in fact, in the story of Anne Hutchinson, the first American feminist, the first American to stand trial in defense of liberty of conscience and, effectively, the founding mother of two colonies, Rhode Island and Connecticut. Her trial induced many early Puritans to leave Massachusetts to find more freedom in these neighboring colonies. In a celebrated ecclesiastical trial that would have profound ramifications for Allen more than a century later, some thirty Puritan ministers met in a synod in Newtowne, Massachusetts, in August 1637 to denounce as error and heresy a popular movement called antinomianism: any departure from the customary, or orthodox, Puritan way. Hooker was called back from Connecticut to preside. Boston Puritans were split into two camps. The antinomians espoused a covenant of grace, insisting that divine grace was sufficient and good works unnecessary for salvation, a view popular among wealthier Bostonians. Orthodox Puritans adhered to the covenant of works, which held that good works were necessary to "prepare" for salvation. Among devotees to the covenant of grace were the colony's governor, the head of its militia, and many merchants, as many as eighty of them gathering each week to hear Anne Marbury Hutchinson, a popular midwife, herbalist, and the mother of fourteen healthy children, expound on the day's sermons.

Anne's father, Sir Francis Marbury, a distinguished Anglican preacher who loudly denounced the lazy, uneducated clergy of the Church of England, was twice tried in church courts by the "self-seeking, soul-murdering" bishops. At times the only voice crying for reforms in the state church, he was stripped of his living and confined under virtual house arrest through much of Anne's childhood, affording him ample time to educate his daughter as a son. On her mother's side a kinswoman of the playwright John Dryden, Anne spent more time reading than sewing in an age when female literacy in England was higher than ever before or until the nineteenth century. She learned to be a midwife, a figure respected by other women.

In London, Hutchinson first imbibed the ideas of familism, a radical sect that preached direct communication between each individual, male and female, and God. Holding that the spirit was superior to the Bible, familists, many of them women, preached that women and men could return to the innocence that preceded the Fall, advocated the election of the clergy by the people, and put reason above ritual. Its teachings could not have been more opposed to Puritan orthodoxy, for they rejected the bedrock Calvinist doctrine of predestination, which precluded individual free will and original sin and which denounced Eve and blamed women for all sin. London women took active roles in the Puritan movement, and some two hundred were hauled before Laud's Star Chamber ecclesiastical courts, suffering heavy fines and imprisonment for, among other things, keeping secret the locations of clandestine Puritan printing presses. The rapid spread of this radical agenda by women preachers brought intensifying persecution by the state church. In January 1620, only months before the Pilgrims gave up hope of returning to England from exile in Holland and crowded onto the *Mayflower*, the bishop of London told all his clergy to preach vehemently against the insolence of women and to condemn their "wearing of broad-brimmed hats, pointed doublets, hair cut short or shorn" and their carrying of daggers and swords. One Londoner recorded, "Our pulpits ring continually of the insolence of women."[2]

From almost the moment she stepped on board the *Griffin* bound for Boston, Anne Hutchinson spoke her mind, perhaps feeling she was safely away from the inhibiting atmosphere of England's church spies. She quickly incurred the wrath of two ministers aboard. One reported immediately on landing to authorities that she had confided "that she had never had any great thing done about her but it was revealed to her beforehand." To claim that she communicated directly with God through revelation was heretical enough: that a *woman* claimed direct contact with God smacked of witchcraft. Denouncing one of the preachers for his five-hour, nonstop shipboard sermons, especially his constant belittling of women, Hutchinson began to hold meetings for women.[3]

Arriving in Boston, she was shocked at "the meanness of the place," a flat, swampy backwater town of crowded, unpaved streets with pigs rooting in the filth, its hundred-odd houses dominated by a square, barnlike meetinghouse. A tribunal of four ministers headed by Lieutenant Governor Thomas Dudley after a five-hour hearing was "satisfied that she held nothing different from us." For the next two years, the Hutchinsons were busy building and furnishing a spacious wattle-and-daub house right across the street from former Governor John Winthrop, leader of the Puritan migration, as Hutchinson built a practice as one of the town's four midwives. She began to hold weekly meetings for women in her capacious parlor, where she explained her pastor's sermons. As more eager listeners thronged her house, she added a second weekly session attended by as many as eighty men and women, oblivious to the fact that she had come under the scrutiny of spies who were reporting each sermon to Winthrop, once again elected governor.[4]

"From these gatherings a murmur of discontent began to be heard," writes the historian Alan Heimert, as she criticized all but a few of Boston's clergy. By January 1637, "with remarkable speed and partisan ferocity, a cleavage in the entire colony was beginning to form around Hutchinson's leadership." On a fast day called to restore harmony, her brother-in-law, the Reverend John Wheelwright, stepped forward from the congregation and, according to Governor Winthrop, "stirred up the people against [the magistrates and ministers] with much bitterness and vehemency." Wheelwright criticized anyone following the orthodox covenant of works, the whole Puritan belief that good works were necessary to "prepare" for salvation and that God's will could be fathomed only from the pages of the Bible. Wheelwright, like Hutchinson, espoused a covenant of grace, which was based on personal intervention and revelation from God that could not be earned by good works. At the core of Hutchinson's critique of the clergy was her growing conviction that something was being lost in Boston, that the piety of the clergy and their congregations had cooled, that preaching and devotion had become mechanical, little more than a system of obligations with social rewards.[5]

How damaging this set of beliefs could be to the stability of clergy-dominated society of Massachusetts struck Governor Winthrop, who could see who was coming in and out of her home meetings: not only ordinary citizens but wealthy merchants, disgruntled with Puritan restrictions on trade and profits, and the head of the militia. As many as eighty auditors routinely jammed the house, including members of congregations who trekked long distances from all over the colony to see and hear this bold woman speak out against the black-robed, all-male power structure. Just as theocratic officials in two New England colonies would later decry Ethan Allen's outspoken freethinking, Governor Winthrop accused Hutchinson of "being one of those who have troubled the peace of the commonwealth and the church." As the historian Edmund Morgan has put it, "More was at stake here than the welfare of the Boston church."[6] The English historian Lawrence Stone saw the crisis as a threat to the very foundations of New England society:

> Both the role-model for the self-reliant woman and the religious theory to break the bonds of patriarchy were first supplied by the indomitable Anne Hutchinson. . . . If the individual conscience were the only test for law and obedience and if Grace were conferred equally by God on members of either sex, this idea, if carried to its logical extreme, could wreck the deferential social system of the seventeenth century, not only in Church and State, but also in the family.

As in many revivalist movements, the most numerous and enthusiastic supporters of Anne Hutchinson, Stone noted, were women. Her women devotees complained publicly that "men usurp over their wives and keep them in servile subjection," while

Winthrop and the orthodox clergy worried that, by luring women away from the family church, the movement was causing "division between husband and wife." Hutchinson particularly disturbed lay and clerical authorities in Massachusetts because they foresaw the overthrow of the conventional relationship between the sexes, demanding equality between men and "silly women laden with their lusts."[7]

In the summer of 1637, Governor Winthrop summoned the colony's General Court, which, except for the governor and lieutenant governor, was made up of Puritan clergy. The court compliantly issued an order forbidding anyone to entertain strangers for more than three weeks without permission of the magistrates. Intended as a precedent in cases where free speech threatened to undermine the authority of the clergy, the court order was essentially pointed at new immigrants from England whose views accorded with Mrs. Hutchinson's. The new edict became America's first immigrant-screening law, aimed at stifling religious dissent. Then, on August 30, Reverend Thomas Hooker, called back from Hartford, presided as ministers converged from all over Massachusetts and Connecticut, a convocation of ecclesiastical ravens picking over morsels of the Old Testament in twenty-four days of parsing orthodox Puritan doctrines to flesh out for each other the implications of eighty-two "errors in conduct and belief" that witnesses testified were coming from Anne Hutchinson's house.[8]

Its collective mind already made up that she must be silenced, the General Court, when it reconvened on November 12, summoned the forty-six-year-old, five months pregnant Hutchinson on charges of sedition and heresy. In actuality, she stood accused of presuming to teach men. The trial, moved away from her followers in Boston to an unheated barn in rural Newtowne in winter when the trek over icy roads was all but impossible, marked a fitting conclusion to 1637, the year when Puritan New England lost its innocence. Massachusetts troops had used the excuse of the murder of a fur trader to destroy the main stronghold of the Pequot Indians near coastal Stonington, Connecticut. Combining with forces from Plymouth and Connecticut, they slaughtered the escaping remnants of the tribe near New Haven and opened the way for mass immigration into Connecticut.

Some two hundred clergy and farmers crowded into the frigid barn to see Anne Hutchinson, dressed in black, escorted in and told to stand facing the bench, a long table at which gowned and bewigged court officials, mostly clergy, sat flanking Winthrop. Among the judges were the six witnesses, all orthodox clergy. Only the judges had foot warmers with hot coals inside. Standing and parrying the governor's questions for seven uninterrupted hours with a devastating mix of nerve, wit, logic, and unshakable knowledge of the Bible, Hutchinson reduced the lawyer Winthrop to exasperated outbursts. "We do not mean to discourse with those of your sex," harrumphed Winthrop, adding, "We are your judges and not you ours." The grilling stopped only at night when the pregnant defendant fainted after not being allowed to sit, eat, drink, or leave the courtroom for natural relief all day. The next day, she nearly set off a riot when she insisted that all the witnesses against her were the same clergy. The case against her collapsing, Winthrop and the panel withdrew the charges.[9]

In her moment of unqualified triumph, Hutchinson blurted out that she had known from a revelation at the outset of her trial that she would prevail. She went further: "And see this scripture fulfilled this day in mine eyes. . . . Take heed what ye go about to do unto me. . . . God will ruin you and your posterity and this whole state." Disbelieving what he had heard, Winthrop asked Hutchinson how she knew "that it was God that did reveal these things." Condemning herself under the colony's biblical law against claiming immediate divine revelation, Anne replied, "by the voice of his own spirit to my soul." Deliberating only briefly, the court voted ten to three that Anne's words were sufficient grounds to convict her of heresy. Winthrop ordered her placed under arrest and imprisoned in Newtowne. The Reverend Hugh Peter, her most vociferous critic on the all-clergy jury, roundly denounced Anne: "You have rather been a husband than a wife, and a preacher than a hearer and a magistrate than a subject."[10]

Twelve days after her sentencing, her husband and the head of militia along with fifty-nine Bostonians and seventeen others from surrounding towns who had frequented her meetings were stripped of their guns, powder, lead, and right to vote. Held under house arrest in Newtowne until spring, Anne Hutchinson refused to recant. Excommunicated, she was ordered to leave the colony. "The movement collapsed," wrote Stone. "Church, state, and male domination in the family were successfully restored in Massachusetts." With twenty loyal followers, Hutchinson traveled sixty miles by horse to Aquidneck, Rhode Island, where she resumed preaching. Thomas Hooker, who sat silently in the audience in the barn in Newtowne throughout her ordeal, came away thoroughly shaken by the heavy-handed verdict of his fellow clerics.[11]

Returning to Hartford, Hooker fashioned a form of government remarkably more liberal than the Bay Colony's. On May 31, 1638, undoubtedly with members of the extended Allen family in their pews, Hooker delivered a sermon in the new meetinghouse in Hartford. He promised that the citizens of this new colony would be able to choose their own governors, their own magistrates, and their own ministers. When Connecticut's first General Court convened later that year, it accepted Hooker's liberal blueprint. By ratifying the Fundamental Orders, the colony's charter, the new government guaranteed that the choice of public magistrates would belong to the people and that those who had the power to appoint magistrates could also limit their power. A star chamber proceeding such as the trial of Anne Hutchinson, all too reminiscent of the ecclesiastical tyranny of England that New Englanders had fled, would be impossible in Connecticut. From the outset, Connecticut considered itself more democratic than Massachusetts. Tellingly, Connecticut's pioneering constitution did not require Puritan church membership to vote. The Allens and their progeny thrived under this, the first written American constitution.

BY THE TIME Ethan Allen, a fifth-generation American, was born exactly a century later, Connecticut had become the most overcrowded and, arguably, the most contentious British colony in America. Like the colony itself, the Allens were a restless if not disputatious lot. Each generation pulled up stakes and moved in search of more arable land if not a brighter world, almost invariably beyond the edge of settlement. As soon as they helped plant a new settlement, they seemed to feel intolerably hemmed in. For example, after only a few years in Hartford, still not satisfied, Samuel Allen, Ethan Allen's great-great-grandfather, packed his wife, Ann, and their infant son, Nehemiah, into the family oxcart and moved again. This time, they cleared a new farm in Windsor, on the northwestern Connecticut frontier. Each move meant felling trees, clearing land, building a rudimentary house, growing sufficient crops, and raising enough livestock not only to feed themselves but to barter for other necessities in a largely cashless society.

The next generation moved on yet again, to the northwestern Berkshire Mountains, for the moment on the cusp of Puritan settlement. Pursuing the rapidly receding New England frontier, moving first northward, then westward, the Allens filled their larders by becoming expert hunters and trappers. In winter, much like their closest neighbors, the Indians, they covered themselves with the pelts of deer, beaver, and bear. Their way of life lacked even the smallest conveniences of medieval England and was brutally hard, relieved only by the thrice weekly compulsory gatherings at the nearest Congregational meetinghouse and the staple ceremonies of Puritan communal life—sermons and funerals, baptisms and marriages.

The Allens usually prospered, but not always. Ethan Allen's grandfather, the second American Samuel, inherited an established farm in Northampton, Massachusetts, from a childless cousin. Leaving Connecticut, he moved his family north to it. But he was not content with the hard work of farming. He managed to lose much of his wealth and all of his energy in a series of bad speculations in land. Fortunately, he had married an enterprising cousin, Mercy Wright. She possessed the qualities he lacked. After running up heavy debts and auctioning off most of the family farm to pay them or face imprisonment, Samuel in 1705 sold what remained of the farm to his younger brother, Joseph. Samuel and Mercy headed north again, this time up the Connecticut River to Deerfield, on the Massachusetts frontier. It was a good year to buy land there. Few people wanted it. One year earlier, during Queen Anne's War between the English and the French empires, in a pattern of intercolonial depredations that was to become all too familiar, French-led Abenaki Indians from the St. Lawrence Valley of Quebec had devastated Deerfield. They killed thirty-eight settlers and took more than one hundred hostages back to their base near Montreal. Ironically, it was the great Deerfield raid that provided Samuel and Mercy Allen the opportunity to recoup their lost status. By ignoring the ever-present danger of further attacks, and carving out a prosperous new farm amid the ruins around them, they were able to sell their Deerfield holdings at a profit when peace resumed on the frontier. This time, breaking their own pattern, they moved south, back to Connecticut, to buy a proprietor's share in yet another newly laid-out town, called Coventry. In 1713, after seventy-five years of cutting down its forests, depopulating its wildlife, and building new communities along its coast and rivers, Connecticut was auctioning off the last remnants of its wilderness.

WITH SAMUEL ALLEN's death in 1718, Mercy Allen finally became free to make sensible decisions. She established an Allen tradition by refusing to break up the family, as was customary, and apprentice out her six children. Instead, she put them to work on the farm. Eight years later, a group of speculators formed a land company and paid the last band of Pootatuch Indians £15 sterling for the site of Litchfield on the latest frontier in the Berkshire foothills. Mercy Allen had saved up enough money to buy a proprietor's share in the new town. A share, usually about 350 acres but sometimes as much as 500 acres, gave her a town lot and forested upland that yielded enough timber for a house, a barn, fences, and firewood. Girdling and felling the hardwood trees, grubbing out the stumps to make pastureland, Mercy and her sons and daughters built a gambrel-roofed cottage. That he would one day inherit it as the firstborn son under the law of primogeniture did not hold her only grown son, Nehemiah, however. More than hard work, the years of constant dread of Indian attacks persuaded him to flee Litchfield during a scare in 1723.

With her five younger children, Mercy hung on. Ethan Allen often heard how his grandmother helped defend Litchfield, taking her turn with the men building the town fort and standing watch. Mercy was not afraid of Indian attacks, backbreaking work, or a male-dominated society. By the time she died, in 1728, she had earned a place among the most prosperous one-quarter of Litchfield County landowners, accumulating enough of an estate in the ten years since her husband's death to provide sufficient land for a prosperous farm for each of her sons or a dowry that allowed each daughter to marry into another prosperous family and remain in the same social class.

When Mercy Wright Allen died, her youngest son, nineteen-year-old Joseph, inherited one-third of her estate. It was mostly uncleared, hilly land, but the Allens had become established in a prosperous Puritan community in what was to become the county seat and trading center of northwestern Connecticut. Joseph Allen's religious heritage entitled him to a place in New England's upper class. According to the Calvinist form of Puritanism then prevalent in New England, the Allens were considered visible saints, predestined for salvation simply because of their descent from the founding Puritans of New England. Someone who took seriously active participation in Congregational affairs, Joseph Allen was as conservative by nature as his father hadn't been. Only nine when his father died, Joseph waited nine years after his mother's death before, at age twenty-seven, he married his fiancée, Mary Baker. By then, the couple had cleared enough land one mile south of the Litchfield meetinghouse to establish a seventy-two-acre farm—an enormous amount in an age before mechanization, forty acres of it under cultivation by ox, plow, and hoe. Over the next thirteen years, Mary Baker Allen gave birth to eight children. All of them survived to adulthood, extremely rare at the time. Even with such a large family, Joseph and Mary were able to put aside enough money to buy an additional five hundred acres of woodland and to invest in a proprietor's share in a Connecticut company speculating in land on the New York–Pennsylvania frontier.

Fittingly, the name they chose for their firstborn child was Ethan, a Hebrew word meaning strong. Perhaps with names like Joseph and Mary, they could consider only biblical names, but names were terribly important to the Puritans. They knew the Bible so well that they were able to make conversational points and legal arguments with well-known quotations from Scripture. Joseph and Mary, like so many couples of their generation, could sit down and turn the well-worn pages of the family Bible until they found the aptest Old Testament name for each of their newborn children. It is entirely possible that, as the firstborn son, Ethan Allen was destined to be his devout father's tithe to the church, to study for the clergy and become a Puritan minister. Even before Ethan's birth, relatives and in-laws were educated for the clergy at Yale College, in New Haven, where they prepared to take their places among the governing elite of the state church of New England.

Ethan's parents—and anyone else who cared to—could find Ethan's name in the Old Testament book of First Chronicles, chapter 19, verse 16, where King David, the first king of the Jews, "spoke to the leaders of the Levites," the priestly class, telling them to appoint singers and musical instrumentalists. The Old Testament Ethan produced the loud sounds of brass cymbals and sang "by lifting up the voice with joy." Accordingly, Ethan Allen's well-tempered instrument would turn out to be his trumpeting voice, a voice he took joy in sounding in countless orations as a military and political leader. Joseph and Mary Allen gave all six of their sons names with militant and authoritative biblical resonances. Heman, Heber, Levi, Zimri, and Ira all bore the Old Testament names of heroes celebrated in passages about battles and leadership. But by the time their youngest child was born, Joseph had become so disenchanted with the constant religious discord in New England that he abandoned the Puritan faith altogether, returning to the Church of England of his ancestors. Emblematic of his about-face, he gave his last-born child the distinctly un-Puritan name of Lucy, which means light, itself soon to become a term of contention as religious conflict rent the colony.

How many of these decisions Ethan Allen's mother made is difficult to ascertain, but all of the Allens for generations had shared the Puritan belief that the family was the fundamental unit of society. They believed in greater mutual affection than was common among their English forebears. Husbands and wives were supposed to be "two sweet friends," but while women were given the responsibility of the spiritual instruction and home-schooling of their children, the family remained a "little commonwealth" with the husband as its absolute ruler.[12]

ETHAN ALLEN WAS scarcely two years old and toddling around the gambrel-roofed Allen cottage when America's first major religious revival movement swept over New England, cleaving virtually every town and congregation into warring factions and creating discord that affected Allen for the rest of his life. It dislodged his family from its comfortable life in Litchfield and launched it on a quest for serenity in a frontier wilderness. Early one autumn morning in 1740, a dust-covered messenger spurred his horse north through the Connecticut River valley. Passing fields of newly stacked hay, the rider yelled from his foaming horse to farmers, "George Whitefield is coming! George Whitefield is coming!"

For more than a month, since the young Oxford-educated Anglican priest had landed in America, thousands of New Englanders of all ages had been thronging meetinghouses to see and hear this charismatic English evangelist. In his glistening white cassock and long blond hair, Whitefield brought to stump-studded clearings a fiery gospel of redemption, his quivering, powerful voice holding thousands spellbound. Against the landscape of a season of drought, Whitefield pranced on horseback from town to town trailing a folding pulpit on a second horse and, invariably, a jubilant, hymn-singing entourage of enthusiastic young people rarely seen in church before his arrival.

Crowds flocked to hear his emotional sermons all the way down the Atlantic seaboard from the Congregational meetinghouse of Newport, Rhode Island, to an open-field sermon in Savannah, Georgia, where Anglican clergy barred him from their pulpits. In Boston, so many people packed into Brattle Street Church that its gallery tore away, crushing to death five of the faithful. Farmers and their families rode and hiked long distances. One Connecticut Yankee farmer described in his spiritual diary what it was like that day as Whitefield headed for Hartford. Nathan Cole was bringing in his meager harvest when the dun-colored rider pelted past him.

"I was born," he began, "and born again. . . . I was in my field at work. I dropped my tool that I had in my hand and ran home to my wife, telling her to make ready quickly to go and hear Mr. Whitefield." Running to harness his horse, "fearing that [he] should be too late," Cole hoisted his wife up on their horse behind him and rode "as fast as [he] thought the horse could bear. When the horse got much out of breath, [he] would get down." Cole ran alongside until he was "much out of breath and mounted [his] horse again." Running as if they were fleeing for their lives, the Coles covered twelve miles in an hour. The fields around them were deserted.

At a rise overlooking the Connecticut River, Cole stared down in wonder:

I saw before me a cloud of fog arising. I first thought it came from the great river, but as I came nearer the road I heard a noise of horses' feet. . . . I could see men and horses slipping along . . . like shadows. . . . Scarcely a horse [was] more than his length behind another, all of a lather and foam with sweat, their breath rolling out of their nostrils at every jump. Every horse seemed to go with all his might to carry his rider to hear news from heaven. . . . It made me tremble to see the sight. . . .

For Connecticut farmers like the Coles who rarely saw more than a few hundred people gathered together, the spectacle of "three or four thousand people" crowded around the white-spired Congregational Church of Hartford was astonishing. Everything "seemed to be struggling for life." The Reverend Mister Whitefield, his white robes contrasting with the dark-garbed Puritans around him, "looked almost angelical." As Whitefield's words resounded over the valley, farmers, shopkeepers, their wives, and children started to sway. Evangelical, open-field preaching and the American tradition of revivalism was being born.[13]

To the multitudes he mesmerized, Whitefield promised a new, more spiritual understanding of Christianity. He tried to reconcile the traditional Calvinist teachings on original sin and predestination for salvation with eighteenth-century experience. His preaching aligned with the writings of his strongest theological supporter, the Reverend Jonathan Edwards of Northampton, Massachusetts. Edwards, in his most famous work, *Freedom of the Will*—whose full title was *Enquiry into the Modern Prevailing Notions of the Freedom of the Will Which Is Supposed to Be Essential to Moral Agency, Virtue and Vice, Reward and Punishment, Praise and Blame*—defended Calvinism's bedrock doctrine of predestination: people were inclined either by God or were sinful by nature; people's choices in life depended on their characters. Edwards wrote copiously on the psychology of religion, focusing on how people behaved during intense religious experiences. He tried to exclude anyone from receiving Holy Communion, one of the privileges reserved for the elect, who, even though they were born with the hereditary right to baptism, did not undergo a conversion experience. Like Whitefield, Edwards refuted the Calvinist dictum that it was possible and necessary to prepare for salvation. The grace of God, they agreed, came suddenly, as Whitefield put it, like the dawn.

AN EVANGELICAL MOVEMENT that would have a profound impact on migration to New England's backcountry swept the coastal towns of British America, leaving a powerful impression on future revolutionaries. As Americans congregated beyond the confines of their churches in large numbers for the first time, the future revolutionary Benjamin Franklin, a Philadelphia journalist who contributed to eight churches but usually attended none, was skeptical when he read reports in New England newspapers forwarded to him. In his *Autobiography*, he recalled that he reluctantly attended Whitefield's first open-air sermon in the city of 15,000 largely because he disbelieved estimates of the size of the crowds published by his fellow scriveners:

> He had a loud and clear voice and articulated his words and sentences so perfectly that he might be heard and understood at a great distance, especially as his auditors, however numerous, observed the most exact silence. He preached one evening from the top of the court house steps, which are in the middle of Market Street, and on the west side of Second Street. Both streets were filled with his hearers to a considerable distance. Being among the hindmost in Market Street, I had the curiosity to learn how far he could

be heard by retiring backward down the street towards the river and I found his voice distinct till I came near Front Street, when some noise in that street obscured it.

Franklin improvised a method for counting the crowd. Imagining Whitefield's listeners "in a semicircle, of which my distance being the radius," he allowed two square feet for each auditor: "I computed that he might well be heard by more than thirty thousand; this reconciled me to the newspaper accounts of his having preached to 25,000 in the fields." Characteristically, Franklin noted that Whitefield "made large collections."

Franklin's *Autobiography* further shows the shift in the clergy's view of the revival movement that had burgeoned since Whitefield first landed in Lewes, Delaware, in 1739. By the time Whitefield returned to Philadelphia for a third visit, in 1742, the clergy had "taken a dislike to him," Franklin noted, and "soon refused him their pulpits." Whitefield was "obliged to preach in the fields":

> The multitudes of all sects and denominations that attended his sermons were enormous, and it was a matter of speculation to me, who was one of their number, to observe the extraordinary influence of his oratory on his hearers, and how much they admired and respected him, notwithstanding his common abuse of them by assuring them they were naturally "half beasts and half devils." It was wonderful to see the change soon made in the manners of our inhabitants, from being thoughtless or indifferent about religion, it seemed as if all the world were growing religious, so that one could not walk through the town in an evening without hearing psalms sung in different families of every street.

Between Whitefield's tours de force, half a dozen disciples drew crowds so large that no building in Philadelphia could have accommodated them. Franklin and his junto of friends decided to build "a house to meet in" so that Whitefield and other visitors would not remain subject "to the inclemencies" of Philadelphia's weather. Their fund-raising campaign rapidly yielded enough money for the construction of a building "100 feet long and 70 feet broad, about the size of Westminster Hall" in London. Franklin chaired a board of trustees who pledged that the building would be available "for the use of any preacher of any persuasion, so that even if the mufti of Constantinople were to send a missionary to preach Mohammedism to us, he would find a pulpit at his service." The edifice, erected near the corner of Fourth and Arch streets abutting the city's commons, eventually became the Academy and College of Philadelphia, forerunner of the University of Pennsylvania. The foundations of two other colleges arose from Great Awakening evangelism: Princeton University and Dartmouth College, where Ethan Allen would one day publish some of his most important work.[14]

FOR A GENERATION before George Whitefield's first American tour, revival movements had sporadically sprung up in New England, sputtered, and quickly died out. Increasingly, clergy looked down from their pulpits at a sea of white hair. In colonies chartered a century earlier as havens from persecution in England, young people by the mid-eighteenth century had no memory of such tribulations. Few bothered to go to church, only to writhe through the turgid three-hour exigeses of Old Testament texts. Just half a dozen years before Whitefield's first American crusade, the young theologian Jonathan Edwards had attempted to launch a revival movement in Northampton, Massachusetts. Farmers began to trickle back into Edwards's church, drawn by his oft-repeated hallmark sermon, "Sinners in the Hands of an Angry God." Edwards spellbound his listeners. They were dangling by a thread over the flames of hell, and they would be "Damned! Damned! Damned!" unless they repented and were born again.[15]

Publicly supporting Whitefield's crusade, Edwards invited him to preach in his church and helped organize his peregrinations. Before the revival movement, wrote Edwards, Christianity in New England was in a "cold, dead state," and he included the clergy in the postmortem. While anathema to orthodox Puritanism, the enthusiasm displayed by followers of the Great Awakeners, Edwards contended, was proof it was the work of God, the resulting tumult only to be expected. In the wake of Whitefield's first visit in 1740, half a dozen "itinerant preachers," as disapproving establishment clergy called them, began to traverse New England every summer, all summer, most of them taking the pulpit in Northampton with Edwards's blessing. At first, moderate clergy opened their church doors, but more conservative ministers barred them—not that they could have held the crowds anyway. The leading Boston divine, the Reverend Charles Chauncy of First Church, began to shadow the revivalists on their rounds, a self-appointed grand inquisitor who interviewed scores of clergymen and took their affidavits, which he published as unsigned reports in the Boston press:

Their main Design in preaching, seems not so much to inform Men's judgments, as to *terrify* and *affright* their Imagination; by *awful Words* and *frightful Representations*, to set the Congregation into hideous Shrieks and Outcries. . . . In every Place where they come, they represent that God is doing *extraordinary* Things in other Places and that they are some of the last hardened Wretches that stand out; that this is the last Call that ever they are likely to have; that they are now hanging over the Pit of Destruc-

tion and just ready, this Moment, to fall into it; that Hellfire now flashes in their Faces; and that the Devil now
stands just ready to seize them, and carry them to Hell.

Chauncy's words seem specifically to echo Jonathan Edwards's
oft-delivered "Sinners in the Hands of an Angry God."

Contrasted with that of the sedate, unemotional sermons
Chauncy and other orthodox Puritans preached, the scene at an
awakening was truly shocking:

> They will oftentimes repeat the awful Words, "Damnd!
> Damnd! Damnd! Damned!" This frequently frights their
> tender mothers and sets them to screaming [which] by
> degrees spreads over a great part of the congregation. Forty,
> fifty or a hundred of them screaming all together makes
> such an awful and hideous noise as will make a man's hair
> stand on end. Some will faint away, some will fall upon the
> floor, wallow and foam. Some will rend off their caps, hand-
> kerchiefs and other clothes, tear their hair down about their
> ears and seem perfectly bereaved of their reason.[16]

WHAT BROUGHT THE five-year-long outpouring of religious
enthusiasm to a crisis in New England seems to have been the
tumultuous visit of one of the more charismatic evangelical
preachers, the Yale-educated James Davenport (whose great-
great-grandfather had accompanied the Allens to America), to
New London on May 6, 1743. Ever since he had heard George
Whitefield preaching during his 1740 visit, Davenport, an evangelical Pied Piper of a sort, had traversed New England each
summer, leading ever-growing parades of enthusiastic young
followers as they sang through the streets. When the Hartford

sheriff arrested him in the summer of 1742 under the new Connecticut anti-itinerant law, a large crowd surrounded the sheriff's deputies and the town jail and demanded that Davenport be released, then escorted him to a ship that helped him to escape. In 1743, he returned intent on launching a seminary—he called it the Shepherd's Tent—to train other New Light evangelists.

Arriving by sloop at New London from his parish in Southold, Long Island, that Sabbath afternoon, Davenport joined his hymn-singing disciples on the town dock and worked them into such a frenzy, the *Boston Evening Post* reported, that townspeople "ran to see if Murder or some other Mischief was not about to be done." The *Post*'s correspondent wrote that he witnessed Davenport and his followers gathered around a huge bonfire, and casting into the flames such classics of Puritan theology as the sermons of the famed seventeenth-century Boston divine Increase Mather as they sang "Hallehuahs and Gloria Patri over the Pile."[17]

The next day, Davenport paraded his coterie back to the pier for an assault on material possessions. This time the jubilant crowd pitched into the flames "wigs, cloaks and breeches, Hoods, Gowns, Rings, Jewels and Necklaces," anything that reminded them of "the world." When Davenport peeled off and cast into the bonfire his "plush breeches," one young woman, horrified, retrieved them and flung them back at Davenport. The newspaper publicity perhaps as much as the event itself proved intolerable to New London's clergy and magistrates. Davenport escaped across the sound to Long Island, while the New London sheriff rounded up his devotees and jailed them until they went on trial for disorderly conduct. Davenport prudently never returned: he had already been arrested twice in Boston, where a jury found him non compos mentis and ordered him jailed for twenty days.[18]

• • •

BY THE TIME Ethan Allen turned five years old, anxious black-robed clerics representing congregations from all over Connecticut were gathering in a convention in Hartford and admonishing the Puritan faithful to ignore "those screechings, cryings-out, faintings and convulsions." In 1742, the Connecticut General Assembly summoned the colony's ministers (at taxpayers' expense) to discuss "the unhappy misunderstandings and divisions" caused by the revivals. Since communications were so primitive and newspapers so few, and then limited to the larger coastal towns, the clergy relied for evidence on affidavits gathered by the Reverend Chauncy and published in his angry, three-hundred-plus-page denunciation, *Seasonable Thoughts on the Present State of Religion in New-England.* Chauncy, the pastor of Boston's elite First Church, had vested himself in the mantle of gladiator to slay the beastly Great Awakenings in response to Jonathan Edwards's 1742 publication of a stout defense of the "great and general awakening" of Whitefield's school of energetic, classless evangelism entitled *Some Thoughts concerning the Revival of Religion in New England.* (Today, Edwards would probably be an Evangelical Lutheran; Whitefield's success inspired the brothers John and Charles Wesley to adopt open-field preaching as the principal tool of the Methodists, the offshoot of the Church of England they christened soon afterward.)

Indeed, Chauncy's inquisition of Great Awakening preachers arguably was the response of those New Englanders who were entrenched in power in an aristocracy of church leaders, merchants, and politicians, not unlike the heavy-handed response of baronial New York landowners to rebellious tenant farmers along the Vermont frontier. Just who commissioned the costly printing of Chauncy's *Seasonable Thoughts* becomes evident in its opening page-after-page subscription list. As he stalked the itinerant preachers from town to town and interviewed the irate clergy in the Awakeners' wake, Chauncy appears to have taken orders and collected cash to pay the printer. The leadership class of New England lined up to support Chauncy's counterattack on the nascent democratic stirrings of the Great Awakening.

Paying for up to six copies each, subscribers included the governors and lieutenant governors of Massachusetts, Connecticut, and Rhode Island, the president of Harvard College and the rector of Yale, eighteen judges, fifty-four wealthy merchants, the collector of customs of Boston, captains of Royal Navy ships, several sheriffs, lawyers, major landowners, and one hundred fifty-one prominent Congregational clergymen, the pastors of the vast majority of New England's Puritan churches. Chauncy noted that still more subscriptions were pouring in even as he had to rush off to the printer in time for the clergy convention, which he blanketed with tomes. The names of many of the clergy whose testimony and cash he had solicited town by town appear on the subscription list.

Copiously detailing the "bad and dangerous" things perpetrated by the open-field evangelists, Chauncy made it clear that he considered few offenses more egregious than their impertinence. "Upon what *Warrant*, either from *Scripture* or *Reason*," he demanded, did Davenport cross over from his church at Southold, Long Island, and go "about Preaching from one *Province* and *Parish* to another where the Gospel was already being preach'd?" Davenport obviously had too "*high an Opinion* of his own *Gifts*" and was too fond of the "*popular Applauses* every where heaped on him." But Chauncy knew that other New England clerics were also annoyed by the evangelists' ability to wring coins out of tight-clenched Yankee fists: "No one . . . , besides himself, can tell the *Amount* of the *Presents*, he received in this Town [Boston]."

The whole notion of preaching anywhere but in a consecrated Congregational church was high on Chauncy's list of objections.

That the free-spirited evangelists had "preached sometimes in private houses, sometimes in a bar, sometimes in the open air" was held against them with no mention that their crowds sometimes swelled to as many as 25,000, as Benjamin Franklin had calculated. By this time, the newspaper publisher Franklin was contributing to the turnout by running notices of Whitefield's impending visits in journals he printed up and down the Atlantic coast and growing wealthy by printing the sermons in fast-selling books. Underlying Chauncy's cavils and possibly explaining the "who's who" of subscribers to his volume of indictments was something he had earlier written for the *Boston Evening Post*. Most of the separatists were "idle or ignorant persons and those of the lowest rank," chiefly "young and illiterate"—and predominantly female.

Summing up, after 366 pages, his condemnation of the Great Awakening, Charles Chauncy declared,

Good Order is the Strength and Beauty of the World. ———The Prosperity both of *Church* and *State* depends very much upon it. And can there be Order, where Men transgress the Limits of their Station, and intermeddle in the business of others? . . . The only effectual Method, under God, for the Redress of *general Evils*, is, for *every one* to be faithful, in doing what is *proper* for him in his *own Place*.[19]

Finding the Reverend Chauncy's arguments against itinerant preaching and the commotion it was causing in staid New England compelling and the visits of wandering evangelists "inconvenient," the Connecticut General Assembly, on the overwhelming recommendation of the Connecticut clergy convention, enacted laws that outlawed open-field and itinerant preaching on pain of fine and imprisonment. The act further forbade preaching in other clergymen's churches without the pastors' and their con-

gregations' express consent. It entirely banned preaching by anyone except trained and ordained clergy. But it was already too
late to reverse the effects of the revival movement in many towns.
In Norwich, Connecticut, for instance, where Benedict Arnold
toddled down the aisle of First Church to the front pew of his
mother's distinguished family, the New Lights, as the separatists began to call themselves, skirted the new law by moving into
a dilapidated, boarded-up old meetinghouse. The town minister
appealed to the legislature to pass yet another law to enforce the
town's church taxes. The legislature obliged him. The sheriff
arrested the separatist preacher and held him in jail, a local pigpen, for twenty days. When a widow in her eighties refused to pay
her church tax, she, too, was arrested. Over her protest, the town
magistrate, her son-in-law Samuel Huntington, a future governor
of Connecticut and signer of the Declaration of Independence,
paid the fine for her for the next twenty-five years.

EPHEMERAL AS IT SEEMED, the Great Awakening was
America's first major revolution, the climax of what the historian
of religion Alan Heimert has called "the most prodigious era of
sermonizing in American history":

> Perhaps above all the Awakening brought an end to the
> regional and tribal consciousness that had been so mani-
> fest throughout New England's first century. However one
> defines it . . . the Awakening, and the controversy between
> Edwards and his mighty "rationalist" opponent Charles
> Chauncy, shifted the focus away from the nature of God to
> the nature of man. . . . [A]nother epoch had opened for the
> mind of New England and all America. . . .[20]

In a widespread rebellion against the established theocratic order in New England, born-again Puritans formed some three hundred breakaway churches in as many towns. They dared to refuse to pay taxes for the existing Congregational meetinghouses and their ministers, in the face of fines, arrest, and new laws dictated by clergymen supporting one another in dissent from these laws. Although it lasted only five years before it was officially suppressed, this incipient social revolution ignited a long fuse that, a generation later, would help to trigger a more lasting political revolution.

For public officials in one British colony in 1775 to raise troops in another to attack English forts in a third province would have been unthinkable only a few decades earlier, before a gradual political transformation was triggered by the convergence of religious and social upheaval in Connecticut. By the onset of the Great Awakening of the 1740s, a majority of Connecticut's citizens believed they had no voice in secular or church government. A shrinking percentage of Congregationalists, often the propertied descendants of the founding Puritan families of each town, made their wishes known through their church elders and ministers and then through the ministerial consociations, which in turn influenced the general assembly, which passed and enforced laws. Individual dissent was all but useless, and political parties were nonexistent in a system that invoked the authority of God and state. Seeking freedom from the coastal aristocracy, many began to move west, in search of a more democratic form of participatory government.

But the Great Awakening contained elements of both a social revolution and a religious revolution that led to major political changes as well. When the Awakened, many of them young and from the lower and middling classes, broke with officially established congregations to form separatist churches and call themselves New Lights, conservatives such as Joseph Allen of Litchfield became known as Old Lights and were proud of it. Everyone in a town, and eventually in the entire colony, knew who went to which church and on which side of the great rift everyone else stood.

When New Lights refused to pay the taxes customarily collected from everyone to support the town minister, it was the first widespread tax resistance in America, fully ten years before the Stamp Act crisis. Reasserting themselves, the Old Lights had attempted to outlaw the Great Awakening by passing and rigorously enforcing laws against itinerant preaching. But this only touched a nerve among some of the elders: to ban the use of churches for revivals and to arrest preachers sounded too much like persecution. Increasingly, when sheriffs and magistrates did the bidding of Old Light ministers, angry crowds intervened, protesting that church and state were too closely linked. Many of the elite withdrew from Congregational churches and joined the New Lights. Open resistance to the stringent new anti-itinerant laws shocked Old Lights, who feared that the spirit of rebellion had gone beyond any specific statute. Old Lights like Charles Chauncey castigated New Lights as enemies of order and government who were plotting, as Benjamin Gale worried to Jared Ingersoll, "a great change in the civil government."[21]

The religious revolution took on more of a political form in the 1750s, nearly two decades before Ethan Allen would coalesce similar men into his Green Mountain Boy movement. The New Lights believed that to suppress their religious revival was to fight against God. Gradually, an opposition political party composed of New Lights grew up in the Connecticut General Assembly and began to object to every bill that represented the commingling of church and state. Becoming known as the New Light Party, it included men from distinguished families. By the 1760s, New Lights had taken control of the general assembly and led the colony's opposition to the Stamp Act. They were able, through the often illegal activities of the Sons of Liberty, to intimidate their political opposition. During the Stamp Act crisis, they would raise a thousand veterans of the French and Indian War and successfully pressure the newly appointed royal stamp commissioners in every colony to resign.

The changes the New Lights demanded in government were as fundamental as those in religion. While the Old Light Party of the 1760s wanted colonial government to become more responsive to the economic needs of the people through established channels with England, thus giving the people a stronger reason to obey and respect authority, the New Lights rejected this appeal to rational self-interest and insisted that nothing short of a complete political conversion experience—similar to what they required in church—should take place in government. They demanded repentance for past political sins and a new and inspirited political engagement to purge and rectify the flaws of government and society. Increasingly, they came to regard themselves as chained to a mother country that was old and corrupt. Just as the Great Awakening called on people to take a more active role in their religious communities, the political movement among the Awakened called on citizens to take action politically. The Great Awakening and the Stamp Act protests were linked in a twenty-five-year process that led up to the American Revolution. Many of the Awakened churchgoers who had never had a role in church or state found a voice in government by the end of the Stamp Act crisis in 1766. Many would join subsequent protests against new British tax policies that fell heavily on cash-strapped colonists not only in the coastal mercantile towns but on the frontier, where many of the Allen family's commercial activities became illegal.

The political shake-up went as high as the Connecticut state-house, where the governor was called to account by the New Lights for refusing to convene the assembly to discuss the Stamp Act. In the first elections after the Stamp Act crisis, they defeated the Old Lights. The New Light leader Jonathan Trumbull became lieutenant governor. Trumbull's social credentials were impeccable: his wife was a direct descendant of the Reverend John Robinson, spiritual leader of the Pilgrim migration on the *Mayflower*. Three years later, Trumbull became the first New Light to be elected Connecticut's governor. The New Light victory was complete and enduring. Trumbull would remain in office throughout the entire revolutionary era, becoming one of the most vigorous prosecutors of the revolutionary movement and the man who unlocked the treasury of Connecticut to "borrow" the funds to pay for Ethan Allen's attack on Fort Ticonderoga.

The New Light movement and the Stamp Act crisis combined to produce new leaders who could orchestrate political action. In 1765, fully ten years before the British attack on Lexington and Concord, Ezra Stiles, then the professor of moral philosophy at Yale, wrote that three-fourths of the men in Connecticut were "ready to take up arms for their liberties." One estimate was that upward of ten thousand men had joined the Sons of Liberty, whose influence gradually swept from eastern seaport towns west onto the New England frontier.[22]

FOR ETHAN'S FATHER, Joseph, the Great Awakening proved a nightmare. When the New Lights became the majority in Litchfield's Congregational meetinghouse, they declared the town minister "unconverted." While the Reverend Timothy Collins did not subscribe to Charles Chauncy's counterrevolutionary volume, he was branded by the New Light majority in Litchfield as "unconverted" because he would not adopt the New Lights' style of evangelical preaching and public hymn singing. The New Lights loudly insisted that Old Light moderates like the Reverend Collins and the Allens either had to admit to spiritual deficiency and undergo a public conversion experience in the aisle of the church at Sabbath services or be refused communion, and thus accept a diminished status in the church and in the community. All his life, Joseph Allen had conformed to the orthodox covenant of works, taking seriously its doctrine of redemption by actively performing charitable deeds. He did not subscribe to the possibility of a thunderclap conversion, the bedrock doctrine of the covenant of grace espoused by the Great Awakeners.

The historian Edmund Morgan has written that "this conversion experience, required for full membership in a church, was nothing short of orgasmic, a possession of the soul so physical that it required carnal metaphors to describe it." In sermons,

the most common metaphor for Christ was the bridegroom. What He did for believers was what bridegrooms did for brides, and ministers did not hesitate to use the word "impregnate" to describe it. Every true believer longed "for the kisses of Christ's mouth, not for a single kisse, but for kisse upon kisse." Church services were the "marriage bed," and "a maid affected with the love of her beloved, is not satisfied without the enjoyment of the marriage-bed."[23]

To submit to what he considered the self-righteous demands of the New Lights, to agree to what seemed to him the superfluous suffering of a public humiliation, was an ordeal Joseph Allen refused to endure; he found it intolerable to accept what he considered a diminution in status. He refused to be born-again publicly. Once before, the Allens had migrated to the American frontier to escape religious discrimination, and a precedent had already been established. In 1739, he decided he had to leave Litchfield as the spiritual as well as the civil leader of this new Allen family pilgrimage. Once again, the Allens moved to the edge of settlement, to mountainous northwestern Connecticut, where they founded a new town, Cornwall. The Reverend Timothy Dwight, later the president of Yale, limned this sketch of the frontier town's raw setting:

> *The God of Nature, from his boundless store,*
> *Threw Cornwall into heaps and did no more.*

Dwight, who traveled all over Connecticut over the years, went on to note that Cornwall was "generally considered as the roughest township" in Connecticut. This relocation later had a profound impact on the young Ethan. It was in this new setting that Joseph Allen prayed there would at last be true freedom of religion.

3.

"I Experienced
Great Advantages"

✵

AS A BOY, ETHAN ALLEN learned how to sculpt a frontier town from nothing but a forest. When the boy was only one, his father, Joseph Allen, then thirty-four, took his family into the wilderness, inspiring fifty staunchly Old Light families to follow him over the next four years and buy land in a newly surveyed township twenty miles to the northwest of Litchfield. His timing, that year of 1739, was fortuitous. Two years before, the Connecticut General Assembly had taken steps to sell off the last ungranted public lands at auction, creating seven new townships in the colony's rugged northwest corner. Joseph Allen traveled to Fairfield for the land auction. Moving quickly when he decided to move at all, he bought a proprietor's share, roughly 350 acres, in the newly laid-out township of Cornwall on the east bank of the Housatonic River. Joseph Allen's leadership ability, his talent for getting people to cooperate and work hard for the common good, would not be lost on the boy.

In fact, the Allens were among the first settlers actually to move to this remote, mountainous corner of the colony and begin to lay out their upland farm in the Litchfield hills overlooking a small central valley. While the valley itself would have made a more logical townsite, Joseph Allen decided they would have to avoid its heavy stand of primeval pines, which would make land clearing all but impossible. Eschewing the typical New England layout of a town planted around a Congregational church, he chose land according to its fertility; other settlers followed his example in taking up farmland scattered through the township according to soil quality. Joseph Allen blazed trees around a hillside lot and began to build what would take years to turn into a comfortable home. Guiding the oxen that pulled the family belongings in carts the twenty-mile uphill trek from Litchfield, Joseph strode along, occasionally cracking the bullwhip. Mary sat on a pillion, a sort of pillow lashed to the horse behind the saddle, holding one-year-old Ethan. With them came their two cows, the minimum to provide milk, butter, and cheese, and two pigs that would give them enough bacon and chops for the first winter. Exactly what else the Allens brought beside livestock is hard to reconstruct, but the animals were taxable property so there is a record of them.

Carving a new community out of the wilderness required someone who could inspire collective effort. Teams of men wielding heavy axes had to chop down towering trees of uniform diameter. The settlers had to wait until the ground was frozen hard enough for the oxen to drag the logs through the woods to the site chosen for the cabin. Working together, the new neighbors then dovetailed the logs together, covered the walls with temporary roofs made of slabs of bark, caulked the cracks with clumps of moss, and covered the window holes with oiled paper.

As soon as enough land was free of rocks, the townspeople communally planted the first crop: enough hay to feed the livestock, corn for the pigs, an acre of winter wheat to make themselves bread. Piling up the rocks into long, low stacks, they divided their fields.

For many settlers, those first few years in Cornwall brought a crude awakening. Until they had cleared enough forest to build a proper house, they lived in small cabins. The cabin stayed smoky from the kettles and the spits sizzling in the stone fireplace. At night, the family climbed a ladder to the loft where a featherbed of goose down, the prize of a bride's trousseau, rewarded parents after a backbreaking day. For the children, more often the bed was a sack stuffed with straw. The most valuable possessions were the farm animals. Until a barn could be built, often a year or two later, the cows, horses, oxen, and even the pigs needed to be brought inside on the coldest winter nights to keep them from freezing to death. The animals took over the ground floor; the humans crowded into the loft overhead. If the first year's harvest was good, the next winter the family could look forward to having a small shed or barn attached to the cabin so that the animals would have separate sleeping accommodations.

Turning rocky Cornwall into a self-sufficient community of hill farms proved especially challenging. The soil was thin and poor. There was no grazing land at first, not until enough of the walnut, elm, pine, hemlock, and maple trees were felled that grass could sprout. There was little cash and, at first, no market to sell their surplus crops—little to look forward to but an indefinite term of hardscrabble, subsistence farming, the terrain making it almost impossible to export surplus crops. To feed the oxen, cows, and pigs required sixteen bushels of corn and about five tons of hay annually. Animal and man had to forage, the cows and pigs

searching for nuts that fell from the trees. To feed their growing family, the Allens would have to clear more land every year.
When there were four family members, they needed to harvest
sixty bushels of wheat alone to be able to bake enough bread, at
least triple that when there were eight children, several of them
teenage boys. To put enough meat on the table, in addition to
game from the forest and fish from the river, they had to slaughter
at least one 500-pound hog a year and a steer to yield some beef.
Out of each sack of corn they harvested, the miller, a twenty-five-
mile round trip away, had to be paid one-twelfth of whatever he
ground and bagged.

Just to subsist, their family having grown to ten people,
Joseph and Mary Allen had to clear, plow, and sow half the
year. To clothe all those people, Joseph, taking his son Ethan
along as soon as he could be useful, hunted and trapped much
of the rest of the year. Every man in the valley had to be his
own carpenter, mason, blacksmith, and harness maker. All year
long, Mary Allen spent any waking hour not needed for cooking in making and mending clothing. Cloth was the scarcest
and most valuable commodity on the frontier. Families had to
fashion their own garb. Mary raised flax in the kitchen garden to strip and boil and pound and weave into linens. A typical Connecticut woman knitted twenty pairs of socks a year:
to make the yarn, she had to card, twist, and spin the wool her
husband had shorn. Itinerant peddlers occasionally came to a
larger town, seldom to the sparsely populated frontier hamlets.
In England, where there were weekly markets in shire towns,
a farm family could sell goods or barter surplus crops, hides,
fleeces, or pelts for ready-made clothing: only the gentry wore
tailor-made vestments. On the New England frontier, reaching the nearest sizable town would take weeks away from the

daily round of chores and days of travel. While there was virtually no cash and, because of British restrictions, no currency, for anything the Allens needed, they bartered or sold half the beef, half the Indian corn, most of the hides and pelts. They planted peas, turnips, and carrots. Apples began to dapple their one-acre orchard after about three years. In the meantime, the woods provided abundant wild berries, especially blackberries, for their children to help to harvest.

Many of Cornwall's first settlers remained absentee owners, putting an even heavier burden on residents: thirty-nine of the first forty male settlers had to take turns filling town offices. Life was precarious for the entire family of a frontier subsistence farmer. When Mary Allen's brother, Remember Baker, died at twenty-six, his only son, also named Remember, was passed from relative to relative until he was old enough to be apprenticed. A year older than Ethan, cousin Remember was tall, freckled, fearless, and profane. He was to become Ethan Allen's closest friend and, in many ways, his big brother.

As the Allens cleared the land and built a barn and a larger house, covering it with cedar shakes, they enhanced their stature in the new settlement and in the county. Moderator of Cornwall's first town meeting, the task reserved for a community's acknowledged leader, Joseph Allen also served as a selectman, tax collector, and chairman of the committee that divided up the lands. Over the next few years, he filled most of the growing town's important posts. As head of the pastoral search committee, he handpicked the Reverend Solomon Palmer, a recent Yale graduate, to be the town's new minister when his old friend the Reverend Collins wouldn't come along from Litchfield. Palmer had graduated from Yale just at the outbreak of the Great Awakening and served a parish at Huntington, Long Island, for half a dozen years.

Dexter's *Yale Graduates* says he "did not sympathize with the measures of the great revival," a fact that recommended him to Joseph
Allen. Palmer later described these difficult, dangerous early years
when his neighbors could barely afford to keep up paying his meager salary. "The people were scarcely able at first to raise provisions
for their own families," wrote Palmer. "So great was the expense,
fatigue and hardship that I endured for the first three years that
I would not suffer them again for the whole township."[1] So hard
was life at first that several of the town's founders died insolvent,
including the town clerk who had been the wealthiest man in
Cornwall that first year. As absentee proprietors broke up and sold
off their shares to settlers, Cornwall slowly became a model of a
New England village.[2]

ON THE MOUNTAINOUS Connecticut frontier, a boy like
Ethan Allen could expect at best an erratic and informal education. Once there were fifty families in a settlement, under the
Old Deluder Satan Law, first passed in Massachusetts in 1647
and later adopted by the other New England colonies, every town
was expected to build a common school where boys and girls
might learn to read, write, and do simple sums. Construction of
the schoolhouse often was not the first order of town business.
In New England at the time, the Puritan meetinghouse, as the
church was called, came first. Although his younger brothers and
sisters later received a rudimentary schooling, Ethan was born
too soon even for a primary school education. He learned, like
most children of his circle, to read and write from his parents.
Like most Puritan women, Mary Allen was expected to be literate so that she could copy down sermons, maintain, like Nathan
Cole, a spiritual diary, and inculcate in her crowd of children her
Puritan faith. Mary Allen taught her son Ethan to read the Bible

and memorize his catechism, the mainstay of Puritan education. His father had enlarged the shed into a barn where, when the fieldwork ended, he made and traded furniture. Inside the Allen house, Ethan later attested, it was always noisy. Amid a swirl of children, dogs, cats, and boys always fighting, his mother presided calmly. Mary Allen was pregnant every other year, a baby at her breast in between. She seemed always, always, to be cooking, baking, spinning, and darning. In the middle of a large room, between his appointed farm chores, Ethan, from an early age a voracious reader, sat blissfully poring over a book, stopping only long enough to argue with his brothers. He probably borrowed every book in Cornwall, especially from Pastor Palmer's extensive library, and extended his borrowing range to Woodbury (today's Roxbury), his mother's hometown twelve miles away, where her wealthy father, Remember Baker, lent grandson Ethan his books. Uncle Remember also introduced Ethan to the neighbors, including Benjamin Stiles, uncle of a future president of Yale, who encouraged the boy to read and to argue about history and politics.

Ethan learned that the elder Stiles served as the official surveyor of sprawling Litchfield County. Their talks no doubt introduced Ethan to the subject of frontier land. Stiles was impressed by the youth's eagerness to learn. Ethan took the books home and studied them, forming a lifelong habit of "commonplacing," copying passages from books into notebooks, a practice carried out by Thomas Jefferson and George Washington, among other country boys of the same period. Ethan remembered thirty years later,

In my youth I was much disposed to contemplation . . . I committed to manuscript such sentiments or arguments, as appeared most consonant to reason, lest through the debility of memory my improvement should have been less gradual. This method of scribbling I practiced for many years, from which I experienced great advantages in the progression of learning and knowledge . . . of grammar and language, as well as the art of reasoning, principally from a studious application to it, which after all I am sensible, lays me under disadvantages, particularly in matters of composition. However, to remedy this defect, I have substituted the most unwearied pains. . . .[3]

While all of the Allens had to know the Scriptures, Ethan particularly excelled in quoting the Bible and, almost as early, in arguing about the meaning of passages. His youngest brother, Ira, still remembered forty years later that, by the time Ethan was in his teens, "Ethan began early in life to dispute on religious matters."

From his father, Ethan learned to fish for trout in the raging Housatonic in the spring, when the melting snow sent water roaring past Cornwall, and to track deer in the nearby forest in the autumn, to spot the compressed leaves and pine needles where the deer slept and follow the trail of their droppings on the newly fallen snow. He became a crack shot, taught not to waste his father's precious gunpowder and lead. By the time he was sixteen, Ethan was unusually tall, over six feet, almost a head taller than many men around him. He grew muscular from the years of heavy farmwork, from swinging the clumsy ax, chopping down oaks and maples, reducing them to firewood. Taking the crop of grain twelve miles to the gristmill at Woodbury, Ethan had most of a day's wait. The miller's daughter, Mary Brownson, would cook Ethan a meal and sit and talk with him before he had to walk home. In a small, isolated wilderness settlement like Cornwall where he never went to school, Ethan found few opportunities to socialize with girls who were not his relatives, yet these trips to the gristmill let him also spend time with a woman. Mary was five years older than Ethan, but both ignored the difference in their ages. Ethan was physically impressive; Mary found him attractive. With his broad shoulders, Ethan could demonstrate his strength by hefting two sacks of corn at once, swinging them up to his shoulders before he flopped them onto the horse's pack frame. The young farm boy's legs had become hardened from digging in his heels to steady the ox-driven plow. His strength and fleet-footedness would later make him a legendary hunter and trapper. The rugged country around Cornwall offered a perfect training ground. On the winding trail up to Dark Entry Brook, Ethan could pass Colts Fort Cave, dug out under boulders on the slopes of 1,661-foot Mount Mohawk, where black bear hid and hibernated. In Black Spruce Bog, teeming with beaver and otter, he learned to bait and clear traps from his Mohawk neighbors.

Despite his outsized physique, Ethan could slip up silently on a herd of grazing deer silhouetted against the snow by moonlight. He would, Ira recalled, run after the deer until he "tired them down." He "turned" the fleeing herd "by often firing on them so as to kill them by night." Young Ethan's reputation for gliding swiftly on snowshoes and reloading and firing fast is all the more remarkable given the primitive weapons of the time. A musket's effective range was short, rarely one hundred yards. Ethan had to get in close, a risky maneuver amid flailing, sharp hooves. Not only could he help fill the family larder with fresh meat and fish and provide the buckskins for his mother to turn into shirts and leggings and the bearskins for blankets and rugs, but he also contributed cash, a rare commodity on the frontier, by hunting wolves and killing rattlesnakes and collecting the bounties the colony paid to rid the woods of them.[4]

. . .

ETHAN ALLEN MIGHT have spent his life as a Sunday-go-to-
meeting Congregationalist who didn't indulge in theological disputation had it not been for Litchfield County's venomous grand
inquisitor. With a zeal, Dr. Joseph Bellamy pursued and persecuted the friends of Joseph Allen. A leading New Light preacher
and disciple of Jonathan Edwards, Bellamy presided over the
sprawling western county's clergy as head of the Litchfield consociation of churches. This august clerical body approved the hiring
and firing of ministers, even though, under Connecticut's charter,
that was supposed to be the right of the individual congregation.
In effect, Bellamy set himself up as something of a Puritan bishop
in a church that, theoretically, opposed all hierarchy. In particular, Bellamy personally persecuted anyone who did not openly
and strongly espouse the born-again, hell's-fire-and-brimstone
revivalism of the Great Awakening. Bellamy had taken to having
his sermons printed and widely distributed. He made it a special
target of his crusade to purge Connecticut's frontier pulpits of any
moderates like the Reverend Palmer of Cornwall.

One Bellamy trumpet blast denounced the Reverend Palmer,
Joseph Allen, and other Congregationalists who refused to hew
to Bellamy's doctrinaire Puritanism. In particular, Bellamy contended that his readers had only two choices: either they were
Calvinists who believed that all men, women, and children and,
in a time of high infant mortality, even babies were predestined
to heaven or hell or they were deists, considered by Bellamy to
be atheists—dangerous unbelievers. According to orthodox Calvinistic doctrine, Joseph Allen had been born a saint not only
because of his birthright but because his father had been a devout
practitioner. But now Bellamy considered Joseph Allen damned,
a heretic for having questioned the doctrine of original sin. Calvinism held that Puritans shared the guilt of Adam and Eve, the

first parents, and must therefore serve as stand-ins for the original sinners. Allen refused to believe that a just God would unmercifully punish his human charges.

By the time Ethan turned thirteen, his father, like a growing number of skeptical New Englanders, had tired of the unquestioning doctrinaire Calvinism of their forefathers and was challenging this major premise of Puritan doctrine. Joseph Allen had long inveighed against the very idea of predestination. He refused to believe that, no matter what a person did, good or evil, he or she was already destined from birth for heaven or hell. In turning away from key Puritan doctrines, Joseph Allen in fact returned to his family's pre-Puritan Church of England roots. He rejected the basic premise of his family's seventeenth-century exodus from England. Most of all, he abhorred the doctrine that some people were born better than others. Years later, Ethan would write that his father had taught him what his Puritan neighbors refused to consider: "that if it was consistent with the perfections of God to save them, his salvation could not fail to have been uniformly extended to all others" who were equally deserving. God must be just. Justice demanded universal equality. A just God demanded that this include equal opportunity for salvation for all people. Joseph Allen passed this belief on to Ethan, and it would become the bedrock of his political as well as his religious philosophy.[5]

From an early age, then, Ethan Allen, in the eyes of orthodox New England Puritans, had become a heretic, too. To remain neutral on the sidelines of religious infighting in Connecticut had become impossible. Nevertheless, Joseph Allen not only openly declared himself an Anglican but also managed to convert his pastor, Solomon Palmer, to renounce his Puritanism from the Cornwall pulpit and openly embrace the Church of England.

Within a few weeks of Palmer's public change of denomination, Bellamy formally ousted him from the Cornwall pulpit he had filled for thirteen years. This dramatic turn of events soon enveloped young Ethan Allen in a lifelong maelstrom of religious controversy.

Shortly after Joseph Allen openly rejected Calvinism, he converted to Anglicanism a score of relatives and neighbors in addition to Palmer. On the Sunday morning when the Reverend Palmer announced that he, too, had rejected Puritanism, Ethan Allen was sitting in a front pew, his triumphant father beside him. Once before, the Allens had left behind a contentious Congregationalist town. By now, Joseph Allen, following family tradition, considered pursuing a new frontier by leaving Connecticut altogether.

ETHAN ALLEN WAS growing up in the most democratic colony in all of British North America—most democratic at least in part because it had become the most overpopulated. The colony's charter from King Charles I, the Fundamental Orders of 1638, gave voters the right to elect all their government officials. Retaining its original charter unaltered, Connecticut alone allowed the freeman to vote locally and directly for his governors. In most American colonies, governors were royal appointees. The property-owning qualifications for voting were more liberal in Connecticut than in Massachusetts and most other colonies. Except for Rhode Island, Connecticut was the only British colony with an assembly that could enact laws that the governor could not veto. It was one of only four colonies—along with Rhode Island, Delaware, and Maryland—not required by its charter to send its laws to England for royal confirmation or rejection.

While about half the men in Massachusetts met the franchise requirement, 70 percent in Connecticut could vote.

Connecticut's liberal charter allowed towns to decide the methods, the requirements, and the customs of their governance. In Cornwall, the entire community at the town meeting selected the minister; in Litchfield, only full church members made that decision. New Hampshire did not allow foreigners or indentured servants to vote; Connecticut did. New Hampshire had no residence qualifications for voting, thus enabling absentee landlords to dominate the electoral process; Connecticut required residency for voters. The property qualification for the right to vote ranged from New Hampshire's, where a minimum estate for voting purposes was £40 to Massachusetts' £50 and Rhode Island's vague "persons of competent estates." In Connecticut, the method of adjudicating disputes varied from town to town. Salisbury held one town meeting a year to decide all business; Woodbury tried to decide its differences in church and Litchfield in court.

Settlers crowded into Connecticut because, in addition to providing a more democratic political structure, it allowed them to own their land outright in fee simple. No annual quitrent had to be paid in gold or silver to the Crown after the initial purchase, as in many colonies. By 1750 Connecticut boasted numerous towns with populations over 4,000, but it possessed neither a first-class port nor a town with as many as 6,000 inhabitants. By the time Ethan Allen took over the family farm, Connecticut had a population of over 125,000, mostly farmers, second only to Virginia as the most populous colony. Its population had doubled in less than twenty-five years.

As Connecticut's land-hungry Yankees began to feel hemmed in, they had no room for expansion within the colony's borders.

But according to the colony's charter, granted by the king of England, its boundaries extended from Narragansett Bay west all the way to the Pacific Ocean long before anybody knew how far away that was. By the 1750s, Joseph Allen and other would-be investors began to look closely at the seventeenth-century charter, concluding that its validity still stood. Other American colonies, including Virginia, made the same claim, and several, such as Pennsylvania, acknowledged no western boundary at all.

As a result of this renewed assertion of Connecticut's charter rights, many Connecticut land speculators, including Joseph Allen, launched a movement to lay claim to the northeastern corner of what, in 1681, had become, also by royal charter, the province of Pennsylvania. In 1753, when Ethan Allen was fifteen and farming at his father's elbow, the Susquehannah Company of Pennsylvania was organized in Connecticut to colonize the Wyoming Valley in the northeastern corner of the Quaker colony. Two years later, the Connecticut Assembly endorsed the project. Joseph Allen became an original grantee, buying a proprietor's share.

THE POSSIBILITY OF moving to a new frontier, especially to the Pocono Mountains of Pennsylvania to the land his father had so recently purchased, disappeared just a few months later when, on July 9, 1755, some 3,000 British army regulars in brilliant red uniforms under the command of a parade ground British general, the lethargic Edward Braddock, slow-marched through dense forests toward a French fortress, Fort Duquesne, under construction at the site of present-day Pittsburgh. At Braddock's side as aide-de-camp rode George Washington, a twenty-three-year-old colonel of the Virginia First Regiment of Militia. Braddock expected the French to cower in their half-finished fortress until he arrived to besiege it with heavy artillery or, if they came out, to face off against in neat rows at musket range, European-style. But the French commander, Contrecoeur, dispatched his professional officers with Canadian militia and 650 Indians, ambushing the British on a narrow woodland trail in a ravine flanked by high, heavily forested hills. The scarlet British uniforms offered bright, easy targets to the French-led Indians, their bodies painted the colors of the woods, firing down from behind fallen trees. All the American officers and nine out of ten of their men were killed in a crossfire when the British mistook them for French. Some 450 Redcoats lay dead by the time the mortally wounded General Braddock, trying to retreat with the wounded, collapsed. The remnants of Braddock's army fled to Philadelphia, 350 miles to the east.

When word of the destruction of the largest British army ever sent to America flashed through frontier settlements, what impressed many colonists was that the British *could* be beaten. Most Americans had never imagined such an outcome, a possibility Ethan Allen would remember twenty years later. With the entire British American colonial frontier now defenseless, the French and their Indian allies became bolder, attacking isolated homesteads. Frontier cabins were too spread out, often a mile from the nearest neighbor. Settlers cut holes in their houses for gunports, but as the attacks continued, panic spread and thousands of frontier families fled to East Coast towns. By mid-October 1755, the Indians had burned more than forty settlements. Colonial governments could do little to stop them. From Massachusetts to Georgia, all along the mountainous backcountry, settlers who did not flee tried to hold out in makeshift forts, waiting for rescue by the British, who would have to come all the way from England and probably could not do anything to counter the French threat in less than another year. In the meantime, Indians once again held dominion over the forests of America, keeping up their attacks. It may have been at this moment that Indians, long considered by many colonists their compliant auxiliaries, in a sea change of feeling toward them, emerged as "savages" in American consciousness.

BY THE TIME Ethan Allen turned sixteen, his parents, clued in by his voracious reading, recognized his exceptional intellectual promise. While he would miss the boy's help with the ceaseless farmwork, Joseph Allen realized that Ethan needed a formal education. The elder Allen was himself disenchanted with the Puritan clergy, but he knew that Ethan from early childhood, nurtured by his pious mother, had exhibited a deep interest in the Bible and in religious disputation. To become an ordained minister and to prepare for the life of teaching that accompanied it, Ethan would need a college education. In Connecticut, that meant preparing for the stiff entrance examinations for Yale College. While more and more of colonial America's prosperous farmers were sending their sons off to prepare for careers in law, commerce, or medicine, the majority of Yale graduates became Congregational clergymen. A small but steadily growing number also were preparing themselves, since there was no bishop in America, to sail to England to be ordained as Anglican priests before returning to America to set up missions.

Of Yale's thirty-two graduates in 1757, the year in which Ethan could expect to matriculate, thirteen became clergy, seven merchants, six lawyers, three doctors, and two teachers; the others had no discernible occupation. Twice as many became clergy as the next most numerous groups, the doctors and the lawyers. The aspiring merchants generally came from wealthy mercantile families. Only one graduate in 1757 returned to the family farm. Nearly three to one, the divinity students outnumbered secular professions as the sons of the Great Awakening went off to college.

To pass the customary oral entrance examinations, Ethan would need at least one year in a private boarding school, such as Elizabethtown Academy in New Jersey, where Alexander Hamilton would study, or Boston Latin, where Benjamin Franklin had studied for only one year. While there were no such academies in western Connecticut, there were several respected dominies, clergymen who took small groups of boarding students into their homes and prepared them for college. Several founding fathers, including John Adams and Thomas Jefferson, prepared for college at such schools. The course of study rarely deviated. Students were supposed to be classically grounded along the model that produced and seasoned an English gentleman. Ethan would need to learn to write formally and be able to understand and exchange classical allusions in his speech and in his writing. He would have to read the Greek texts of Homer, Thucydides, Aristotle, Plato, and Pindar, be familiar with the Latin writings of Virgil, Livy, and Juvenal, the speeches and rhetorical techniques of Cicero, the difference between the authors of the Roman Republic and the Roman Empire, and acquaint himself with recent English writers, poets, and contemporary thinkers such as John Locke, James Watt, and Isaac Newton. He would have to be able to maintain accurate financial records and to know his legal rights. As if this were not daunting enough, he was expected to master anatomy, arithmetic, geography, and Euclid's geometry, all in the space of a single academic year.

The choice of a schoolmaster ranked as the paramount consideration, invariably a Yale graduate well known for preparing the student for Yale's regimen. A good letter of recommendation from the right teacher was critical. In Ethan Allen's case, the range of choice was narrowed by distance and, to some extent, money. Both of these factors could be addressed by sending Ethan no farther than the bags of corn he had often accompanied to the gristmill. He would be packed off to Salisbury, a larger and more sophisticated town, a dozen miles farther north of Cornwall along the Massachusetts border. Ethan's only formal teacher would be his distant cousin, a celebrated schoolmaster and popular New Light preacher, the Reverend Jonathan Lee, Yale class of 1742. Ethan's enrollment in the Reverend Lee's academy virtually assured his admission to Yale. Lee had been the student of Yale's president, the Reverend Thomas Clap, and had married Clap's stepdaughter, Elizabeth Metcalf.

The Allens had known the Reverend Lee's family for many years and were connected to it by marriage. Lee's ancestors had sailed to Massachusetts with the Allens and settled in Hartford with them. The Reverend Lee's father came from Coventry, where the Allens lived until widow Mercy Allen uprooted the family to Litchfield. Ethan's wealthier cousin Joseph Allen of Northhampton, Massachusetts, had married the town's midwife, Elizabeth, famous in New England for delivering no fewer than three thousand babies: their son, Thomas, was to become a famous preacher who, in turn, married the daughter of the Reverend Lee. Despite Lee's Great Awakening bent, Joseph Allen now chose to send his firstborn son to Lee's school to prepare him for the life of an educated clergyman. For Ethan to go to Salisbury to study under a popular New Light preacher was a step away from his father's Anglicanism and a wrenching decision for Joseph Allen, but with the Bellamy purge of moderate clergy in Litchfield County now complete, there was no other choice. Ethan Allen was sixteen when he rode with his father the ten

miles over to Salisbury to begin his studies with the Reverend
Lee in the autumn of 1754.

A rich farming center with nearly a thousand cattle grazing
in its pastures (ten times the number in Cornwall), Salisbury had
drawn its first settlers when a rich deposit of iron ore was discovered in Mount Carmel, which bordered the Wochogasticook
River. The picturesque 628-acre townsite, dotted with ponds
and surrounded by hills and lakes, was donated by Yale. Fittingly, First Church, the Congregational meetinghouse, stood
exactly in the middle of the town of fifteen hundred. Bushnell's
Tavern faced it squarely across the town green. Maple trees
shaded the main street. The white frame meetinghouse stood
two stories high, capped with a small, square tower and, inside a
cupola, the town bell. Records of the raising of the meetinghouse
show the consumption of sixteen gallons of rum and ample cakes
made from the wheat abounding around the town's margins.
From their Mohawk Indian neighbors, Salisbury's settlers had
learned to burn off the wheat fields every autumn to ensure future
crops. As the farmers scythed their wheat and their wives and
children bundled it, wolves and rattlesnakes still lurked in ravines
nearby. The Reverend Lee presided over every aspect of town life
as moderator of the selectboard and pastor of the church. Lee's
turreted house resembled a castle, its thick oak walls pierced with
portholes for defense against Indian raiders.

Ethan Allen must have felt right at home, boarding with
this patriarchal kinsman, the house echoing with the commotion of the Lees' five young children and as many students, all
of them tuition-, room-, and board-paying customers. The town's
nineteenth-century history describes Lee's "fine figure and pleasing manners." Attending the Reverend Lee's famous sermons at
least three times a week made up an important part of Ethan's
schooling. Here, he was exposed for the first time to the fire-and-

brimstone New Light evangelical style that was anathema to his father. In classroom and meetinghouse, Ethan learned a dynamic writing and speaking style. For nearly a full school year between the autumn of 1754 and spring of 1755, he crammed the classics, French, mathematics, moral philosophy, and geography. For the first time, in this sylvan mountain town, surrounded by lakes and hills, Ethan was cut off from the contentiousness and tedium that had plagued him at home. But news from home, terrible news, all too soon intruded. By the time Ethan received an urgent message from his mother to return home at once, his father was dead. After all the years of backbreaking toil trying to turn unyielding rocky hill country wilderness into a farm prosperous enough for his large household, after all the years of ceaseless religious strife, Joseph Allen, only forty-six years old, dropped dead on April 14, 1755.

Joseph Allen was buried in a pasture he had cleared behind the house that he had built. A family tradition survives that Ethan stood beside his father's grave and implored him to return and tell him whether there really was a life after death. No answer came but the cawing of crows and the roar of the river nearby. Finally, Ethan's younger brothers managed to pull him away. Inside the house where father and son had made furniture together, cleaned their guns together, gutted the wildfowl they had shot together, and disputed through long evenings about the Bible and the rights of the people to own land, Ethan had to face a cold new reality.[6]

Almost as soon as Ethan's formal education began, it was over. At seventeen, only months before he was to enroll at Yale, Ethan realized he would have to give up his schooling—along with any ambition he may have had to become a minister or a scholar. As the oldest son, with seven younger brothers and sisters as young as four-year-old Lucy, it would be all he could do to help his mother save the family farm, pay off his father's considerable debts, and hold the family together. That he would have to drop out of Dr. Lee's school and abandon his pursuit of a college education struck Ethan hard. But he was determined not to give up on his own education. Maybe, instead of a gentleman's ready store of classical tags, all the fashion at the time, he would learn to substitute adroit use of recognizable biblical references, especially from the Old Testament, whose heroes and their words he had already memorized. For the rest of his life, Ethan Allen would be able to muster a pertinent biblical allusion that amused his friends and confounded his enemies. He would pursue knowledge independently, a family tradition.

4.

"Any Furnace for
Making Steel"

❊

BY ASSUMING RESPONSIBILITY for his family's financial welfare, Ethan Allen not only cut short the time to mourn the abrupt
end of his formal education but also distracted himself from
grieving over his father's sudden death. As the oldest son, he was
now expected to help his mother raise her growing brood and to
maintain one of the more prosperous farms in northwestern Connecticut. Joseph Allen had invested considerably in land on the
Wyoming Valley frontier of northeastern Pennsylvania, but he had
also borrowed heavily to buy more land closer to home. Like generations before them, Ethan and his mother now faced a difficult
choice. They could either sell their established farm to clear their
debts or strike out for the newest frontier. When Ethan's grandmother Mercy Allen had been suddenly widowed and left with
her luckless husband's debts, she had chosen to resettle in the new
frontier town of Litchfield, but she hadn't had a mature son like
Ethan to help her make the decision and make sense of it.

Ethan had to take into account his mother. Mary Baker Allen's family was spread all over the Connecticut and Massachusetts hill country, her birthplace. Her cousins lived, at most, a day's ride away from Cornwall. To uproot her now and leave for the Pennsylvania wilderness would be another devastating wrench, so soon after her husband's death. As a widow, Mary also had something to say about the disposal of Joseph's land. Because Ethan was still a minor, under the English common law that governed colonial Connecticut, she became administrator of her husband's estate until Ethan turned twenty-one. Moreover, she had inherited the widow's traditional one-third portion of her husband's estate. At her death, her share would pass to Ethan, her firstborn son. As it turned out, Joseph had apportioned his estate in shares. As the oldest son, Ethan received a double share, including the house and barn. Each of the other children received one-twelfth. Ethan's immediate, outright inheritance amounted to fifty-two acres of hardwood forest in Cornwall and about forty acres in the Pocono Mountains of Pennsylvania if and when the Allens moved there or sold Joseph's Susquehannah Company share. Ethan could have harvested his timberland or sold off his land, but, with his mother's concord, he decided to keep all the Allen family land and children together and to continue farming in Cornwall with the help of his younger brothers and sisters. He set about helping his mother collect money owed his father and to apply it to paying off his father's £200 in debts.

As ANOTHER FULL-SCALE war between the French and English and their Indian allies loomed in the spring of 1756, frontier towns formed militia companies, elected officers, and constructed or reinforced stockades. Confronting the likelihood of a raid on the northwest Connecticut frontier, seventeen-year-old Ethan

Allen and his eighteen-year-old cousin, Remember Baker, joined the town militia and helped throw up a stockade in Cornwall, taking their turns standing guard duty as their neighbors harvested and threshed the crops. Ethan Allen eagerly learned the rituals of marching and drilling according to the manual of arms.

The Allens and their neighbors heard that Abenaki Indians, led by French officers, were raiding farther and farther from Fort St. Frederic, their base at Crown Point, on Lake Champlain. Unchallenged, the French were constructing an even larger fortress, Fort Carillon, at the lake's southern tip, the site of the future Fort Ticonderoga. In the spring of 1756, a New England army formed under the command of General John Winslow of Massachusetts. Once again, British recruiting officers strutted through Connecticut towns, their spit-and-polish formality making them appear, to the young frontiersman, more alien than the Indian. Yet Ethan and Remember jubilantly prepared to march off with Ethan's schoolmaster, the Reverend Lee, chaplain to the expedition against Crown Point. But the British American force moved too slowly, under orders from London to build a military road as it went. Having frittered away any strategic advantage they might have achieved, in the end, without having fired a shot, the New England troops returned to their homes in time for the harvest.

By the summer of the next year, 1757, nineteen-year-old Ethan Allen had grown thoroughly bored with life on the farm, hardly surprising given the rigor of his training to get into Yale. His only excitement came when, acting as his mother's attorney, he sued and obtained a judgment against a neighbor for money owed his father. In the self-sufficient town of Cornwall, little seemed to be affected by the war—until the French and their Indian auxiliaries suddenly left their Lake Champlain forts and, with reinforcements from Canada, moved south from Crown Point. Escorted by hundreds of canoes full of painted Algonquin warriors, the white-uniformed French regulars and buckskin-clad French Canadian *habitants* portaged around the waterfalls connecting Lake Champlain and Lake George and besieged the British at Fort William Henry, at the southern end of Lake George. His forces hopelessly outnumbered, the British commander surrendered. The French commander, Montcalm, who would die tragically two years later, promised the disarmed English safe-conduct to Fort Edward, at the northern end of the lake, but he could not control his Indian auxiliaries, who fell on the retreating British prisoners, killing and scalping scores of them. This time, Ethan and Remember enlisted in Captain Lyman's seventy-three-man company of Colonel Ebenezer Marsh's Litchfield County regiment in the New England army. By the time Ethan and his Connecticut comrades had marched west for a week, they learned that the British had been routed and the French had returned to their forts on Lake Champlain. There was nothing to do but turn around, march home again, and await reinforcements from England.

But during those two weeks, Ethan Allen ventured outside Connecticut for the first time. Marching north through the Taconic hills and the majestic hardwood forests of Berkshire County, Massachusetts, he crossed into the Valley of Vermont. He saw vast reaches of chestnut, walnut, oak, and maple covering steep, parallel crags, beckoning north toward Canada. At night, around the campfire, he heard the army's scouts describe uninhabited lands a hundred miles to the north with broad, flat, fertile intervales of floodplain-flanking deep rivers ideal for pastureland, and of innumerable beaver, bear, deer, and moose in a veritable hunter's paradise. Once the French were driven out, these lands would open up for hunting and trapping, virtually free for the taking for settlement by English colonists. Allen had often listened to his father talk about land speculation. Now, as the war dragged on, he thought more and more of speculating in, and one day moving to, a new and better frontier, much as his father had done. Yet, as long as lands on the Connecticut frontier might be attacked at any time, Allen had no choice but to do all he could to enhance the family farm. Paying off his father's debts, he began in his own right to buy up parcels of undeveloped land in and around Cornwall.

WHILE EMPIRES WARRED far from Cornwall, Cornwall fought at home—in church. Allen took up the cudgels where his father had left off after the Reverend Solomon Palmer had been stripped of his pulpit at the insistence of Dr. Bellamy. Allen joined eighteen other Cornwall churchgoers, including his mother, in breaking away from the Congregational Church and officially declaring themselves Anglicans. When the Reverend Palmer attempted to continue to preach, the Reverend Bellamy continued his personal purge: the consociation of Connecticut clergy excommunicated Palmer and sued him for breach of contract. When, in turn, Palmer sued for his back salary, he lost the suit. His expenses evidently paid at least in part by Allen and other born-again Anglican parishioners, Palmer sailed off to England to receive holy orders from the bishop of London. Sent back to Connecticut as a missionary for the Anglican Society for the Propagation of the Gospel in Foreign Parts, Palmer set up a mission in Litchfield, one of 130 Anglican churches established by the society between 1740 and 1775 in as many towns and villages in a growing threat to Puritan hegemony in the New England colonies. Dr. Bellamy, unremittingly hostile, pursued Palmer. Eventually, the animosity of Bellamy and Connecticut's Congregational clergy grew so intolerable that the Anglican missionary society removed Palmer from the Litchfield mission, offering him a more hospitable congregation in Perth Amboy, New Jersey, an Anglican stronghold. But even that royalist parish preferred a less controversial figure. Next, Palmer transferred to Rye, New York, where Anne Hutchinson and her children had been butchered by Indians a century before. Again the parishioners rejected Palmer. Given a small parish in New Haven, his pay too little to support his large family, he returned to Litchfield. Eking out a living as a missionary until his death, pleading for Ethan Allen and other former parishioners to restore to him glebe land once attached to his post as Cornwall's original pastor, he died in poverty, a victim of the intolerance of a relentless Puritan hierarchy in pre-revolutionary New England.[1]

Solomon Palmer's persecution in Connecticut infuriated Ethan Allen, moving him to break into print for the first time at age twenty-three in 1761. The principal coauthor of a pamphlet with his younger brother Heman and his cousin Elihu, Ethan penned a spirited defense of the Reverend Palmer, his views and his conduct in Cornwall. Though Ethan had failed to formalize his education at Yale, he did not lack verbal ability. For the first time in public, Ethan dissented from Cornwall's—and Connecticut's—orthodox religious majority. The Allens' break with the Congregationalists became a matter of official record when, in 1762, Ethan, his mother, brothers, and grandmother appeared on a town list naming the nineteen adult Cornwall residents who no longer had to pay the church tax for the use of the Congregationalist minister but instead would pay into a fund reserved for an Anglican mission, ironically a choice made possible by the Great Awakening. The Puritan elders of Cornwall agreed, at first, not to tax the Allens and Palmer's other followers to pay the salary of Palmer's replacement as the town's Puritan minister, but the town later repudiated the agreement, taxing the Allens and their faction a steep £64.15.3—nearly $10,000

in today's money. When the Allens sued to recover, the Puritans countersued the Reverend Palmer for breach of covenant.
The impoverished Palmer had to pay the congregation £15—
about $2,250 today—plus court costs. He no doubt had to bor-
row money from the Allens and other supporters. The Palmer
case demonstrated the persistent connection between the New
England clergy and the courts. Ethan's prominent public role
in defending Palmer would not be overlooked by Connecticut's
unforgiving Puritan clergy.

BY THIS TIME, Allen, who had needed seven years to pay off
his father's debts, was emerging as the conspicuous head of the
Allen clan. It had been important for him not only to support his
father's friend the Reverend Palmer but to help Cornwall build a
schoolhouse that his younger brothers and sisters could attend.
He allowed himself little time for socializing; when he did, it was
usually with people considerably older than his own twenty-four
years. It had remained impossible to think of leaving his widowed
mother and siblings so long as the threat of Indian attack hovered
over the backcountry. Fortunately, the French had not followed up
their victory at Lake George in 1757 and by the summer of 1758,
were on the defensive. Part of the largest army Britain had ever
dispatched to America, the British moved north the two hundred
miles from New York City up Lake George to the southern tip of
Lake Champlain with thirteen thousand Redcoats, Black Watch–
kilted Scottish Highlanders, green-uniformed colonial militia, and
their Mohawk Indian allies to attack the unfinished Fort Carillon. The entrenched French, outnumbered more than four to one,
slaughtered wave on wave of the British, who became ensnared on
the sharpened tree branches of abatis. Nearly three thousand of the
British force were killed or wounded by point-blank French fire

before the British officers abandoned their futile bayonet charges. Ethan's cousin Remember, among the Connecticut Yankees charging the French outerworks, was severely wounded.

But the British more than counterbalanced this debacle the next year. In the annus mirabilis of 1759, the British massively reinforced their American armies, subsidized their colonies to raise regiments, and, under a brilliant new first minster, William Pitt, Earl of Chatham, launched a coordinated three-pronged offensive. On Lake Champlain, they built a fleet of bateaux, sluggish thirty-three-foot long, deep-draft work vessels capable of hauling men and supplies and, taking advantage of the lake's strong current, struck north into the St. Lawrence Valley, capturing Montreal. As the outnumbered French retreated, they destroyed their forts at Ticonderoga and Crown Point and burned their settlements along the lake. At the same time, a second New York–based British army, reinforcing Fort Oswego, reclaimed the Mohawk River valley and, aided by Iroquois warriors, seized strategic Fort Niagara, cutting off French reinforcements and supplies from settlements in the Ohio and Mississippi valleys. A British fleet sailed up the St. Lawrence, besieged the walled city of Quebec, and enticed the French commander, Montcalm, out of his impregnable defenses into a final pitched battle on the Plains of Abraham. Before the day of September 18 was over, both the French and the British commanders, Montcalm and Wolfe, lay dead, and Quebec, the capital of all French America, capitulated, bringing to an end a century and a half of French expansion in the New World. Amid the celebrations, Ethan Allen could finally envision a future beyond the confines of Cornwall, Connecticut.

AT THIS JUNCTURE, Allen had to decide whether to continue farming in Cornwall or to sell off the family farm, or at least

his share in it, and migrate to a new frontier where his investment would go even further. Many of his Connecticut neighbors
had, like his father, bought proprietary shares in Pennsylvania's
Susquehannah Company before the war. The company, in turn,
had negotiated with the Iroquois Six Nations for the sale of the
Pocono Mountain region and the lush Wyoming Valley that
flanked the Susquehanna River between present-day Wilkes-
Barre and Scranton. The long war had stalled plans for the
company to begin its settlement, the mountainous region becoming particularly unsafe for whites in part because of a Delaware
Indian chief named Teedyuscung. Although he had converted to
Christianity and lived as a white for thirty years, when French-
led Indians followed up their victory over General Braddock in
western Pennsylvania in 1755, Teedyuscung had shed his Christian name—Brother Gideon—and clothes. Now, as the "King of
the Delawares," he defied his Iroquois overlords and, siding with
the French, led a Delaware war party into the Wyoming Valley. His band of one hundred warriors sought to avenge half a
century of indignities, land fraud, and humiliation at the hands
of white settlers. His father had been swindled by land traders
in New Jersey and by the sons of William Penn, who named the
Delaware Valley and their tribe after an English earl who had
cheated the natives systematically. Teedyuscung and his sons shot
or took captive whites working on isolated farms, torched their
farmhouses, stole their horses, and slaughtered their livestock.

In the summer of 1762, the war over, Teedyuscung, his warriors, their wives, and their children walked a hundred miles over
the Blue Mountains to sign the Treaty of Lancaster, which confirmed their right to the valley. Teedyuscung agreed to exchange
his prisoners for the services of fifty Philadelphia carpenters who
built the Delawares a village of ten solid log houses surrounded
with plowed gardens. At exactly this moment, 119 armed Con-

necticut shareholders of the Susquehannah Company asserted their claim to the valley. They harvested the Delawares' hay, built and armed three blockhouses, made huts for themselves, and planted grain. Iroquois chieftains en route home to western New York from the Lancaster treaty angrily warned the Connecticut settlers: the Six Nations would never permit the Susquehannah Company to have the Wyoming Valley. The Connecticut settlers agreed to leave but said they would be back the next spring with a thousand men and cannon. All that autumn, more Connecticut settlers, many of them friends of the Allens, made the trek to Pennsylvania. They built a sawmill near Teedyuscung's house and began to cut down trees to build houses. Someone stole Teedyuscung's horse; the settlers gave him a gift horse in return. He rode it to Philadelphia, where he received the provincial government's assurance of protection.

During the night of April 19, 1763, as Teedyuscung slept in his cabin, someone set it afire. Simultaneously, flames engulfed all twenty houses in the growing Delaware Indian settlement. Within minutes, the village of Wyoming burned to the ground. The survivors fled south to the settlements of the pacifist Moravians, who had converted them to Christianity. Teedyuscung died in the lodge his Pennsylvania brethren had built for him. Two weeks later, the first permanent settlers from Connecticut arrived, driving herds of cattle. Planting fields of corn and arming massive blockhouses along the Susquehanna River, they named the place Wilkes-Barre after two English defenders of Americans' rights. Six months later, under cover of Pontiac's War, his son, Captain Bull, led a Delaware war party more than three hundred miles from their new home in the Ohio Valley, and killed twenty-six Connecticut settlers in the Wyoming Valley. By the end of 1763, no white men and no Delawares remained alive amid the ruins of Teedyuscung's experiment in assimilation in the ill-fated Wyoming Valley.[2]

· · ·

WHEN WORD OF the debacle in northeastern Pennsylvania
reached Cornwall, Ethan Allen, fearing for their safety, decided
that his mother and his siblings should remain in Connecticut.
He would leave the farm intact for the rest of the family, especially since his younger brothers and sisters were attending Cornwall's new school. If he had ever planned to sell the farm, uproot
the family, and exercise his father's proprietary right in the Wyoming Valley, he now put aside the idea. As a boy, he had known
Mohawk Indians in the woods and mountains around Cornwall
and from them had acquired some of his mastery at hunting and
a smattering of their language. All his life, wherever he was, he
would shun the military campaigns organized from time to time
to drive away or extirpate Indian tribes; when he became a leading figure on the frontier during the American Revolution, he
refused to join militias from New York and Pennsylvania and the
Continental Army in an expedition that destroyed the Iroquois
Six Nations. In many ways, he emulated the Indians' respect for
nature and their disregard for living in a fixed place. On many
occasions, Indians offered to join his military expeditions, and,
more than once, what he had learned from them saved his life.
Allen found it unthinkable to kill Indians or to drive them off
their land.

By the time of Teedyuscung's murder, Allen had turned his
mind to another risky form of adventure—setting up a business.
All through the war years, as he retired his father's debts, he had
acquired and cleared more land and, through a series of trades,
accumulated rare hard cash. On October 31, 1761, just after he
published his first religious tract—and there seems to have been
no connection—Allen made his first investment. At age twenty-
four, the first record of his business acumen appears on the regis-

try of deeds of Cornwall. A neighbor Jesse Squier sold his Cream Hill farm, including fifty acres of cultivated land, a substantial house, a barn, and an established apple orchard, to Ethan and his cousin Elihu Allen. Ethan put up his half of the £100 price, Elihu the rest. Then Ethan turned over their farm to that cousin to manage. By financing the mortgage, Ethan furthered his claim to the position of head not just of his immediate family but also of the extensive Allen clan. He also gained a mortgage he could use as collateral for further investment.

AFTER HE RETURNED safely from his first brief foray out of Connecticut into military life two years after his father's death, Allen rode over to Salisbury to visit the Lees. Most of his old school chums had by now graduated and gone off to Yale. As a boarding student, he had sometimes indulged his passion to explore. He visited the town's first industry, a small iron forge founded by Thomas Lamb in 1732. That forge had initiated the iron business in western New England at a time when colonial Americans were beginning to rummage through the strip-cleared forests of the backcountry for mineral wealth as far south as Virginia, where George Washington's father was buying up iron-ore-bearing land. In Pennsylvania and New Jersey, investors were gathering the capital to open shallow-pit mines and make forges to process pig iron.

By the time Ethan matriculated in the Reverend Lee's school in the mid-1750s, Salisbury boasted a second and larger forge at the outlet of Lake Wononscopomuc. There Allen had first seen some of the abundant, high-grade ore unearthed in hills around the town and visited Salisbury's limestone pits and kilns. He now asked forge workers how to produce the soft pigs of iron needed for making wrought iron that blacksmiths then transformed into farm implements, tools, kitchen utensils, hinges, nails, wagon springs, and wheel rims. On this visit to Salisbury, Allen became convinced he could connect this burgeoning industry with a need created by another growth industry emerging in the Connecticut backcountry. By age twenty-four, he had already cultivated a penchant for long-term planning coupled with an ability to act decisively when he perceived an opportunity, a coupling of qualities that may explain why, when a new source of income suddenly cropped up on the New England frontier, one that could substantially increase the ability of frontier farmers to raise cash, he moved swiftly. It is hard to imagine the excitement of opening up a lucrative market for something as mundane as potash but, now that the end of the French and Indian War allowed commerce to move freely along New England's rivers, potash production boomed.

The opening up to English Americans of a vast new frontier created a power vacuum inhabited mainly by millions of acres of hardwood trees. As if overnight during the decade of the 1760s, the cash-rich new industry made it worthwhile to cut down the towering hardwood trees in these virgin forests to produce potash. Ash from the fireplace had always yielded soap and bleach for the family, but now ash became vital for England's new chemical industry, for mixing with saltpeter to produce gunpowder, for making bleach for dying textiles. The stirrings of the Industrial Revolution in England were also creating a conflict of interests in the expanded British Empire, making the mother country more dependent on the colonies for raw materials at a time when the colonists, freed at last from the threat of French and Indian attack, yearned for more economic independence. On the frontier, for a modest cash investment, a farmer could buy large tracts of undeveloped land. He could then cut down the hardwood trees— great oaks, hemlocks, and maples two or three feet in diameter—

for logs and boards to build his house and barn and his fences to keep in his hogs. Next, with beadle and frow, he cleaved the oak boards to make staves for barrels and casks. Overnight, land became not the end product but an intermediate currency on the way to quick profits.

First, the bark, especially of the oak tree, was stripped off and boiled down to produce tannin, vital in the leather tanning process. Then all the rest of a tall tree, all the limbs and branches and roots, once the waste product, were piled high and in winter burned to produce ashes. The ashes were then leached and poured into great iron pots. The residue of potash was reduced to rocklike chunks resembling quartz that were sold by the barrel and shipped down the Housatonic and the Connecticut, on their way to New York, Philadelphia, and Europe. Farmers like Ethan Allen stripped their hillside lots to produce enough cash from the sale of potash to buy more timberland, then clearcut that land to buy more land. The advent of the potash industry set off a postwar land rush in New England's and New York's once hardscrabble backcountry. Only the evergreen trees were spared, because their sap burned poorly, fouling the pots and yielding low-quality potash. Connecticut's land-hungry subsistence farmers began to look at the stands of wood not as on old enemy that could conceal marauding Indians but as a new friend that could mint money.

Exhibiting a business acumen his father had lacked, young Ethan Allen could see beyond the forests and the trees to the large quantities of iron cauldrons needed to render the potash. He decided to learn the craft of mining iron ore and manufacturing the huge cast-iron pots vital for the potash boom. He could not have made a shrewder business decision, given his limited capital and the inability of England to protect its own iron industry, despite royal writ and parliamentary law. By the early eighteenth century, the colonies' iron industry was growing so rapidly that English iron manufacturers became alarmed. Accordingly, in 1719, a bill passed Parliament that barred any colonist from fabricating ironware out of sows, pigs, or bars, the raw material from which blacksmiths produce hinges, bolts, hardware, even weapons. Nothing came of this early attempt at restricting American trade, save for the buildup of resentment against English stifling of colonial enterprise. Deep in the forests of America, iron mines were sunk and forges fired up, and illegal iron flooded the American market. Trying to compete with American ironworks, the British removed all duties on British iron being sent to the colonies. Nevertheless, by the 1720s, Americans were exporting their iron to London, ballasting English ships hauling American tobacco with American-produced iron sold at prices undercutting English iron. By 1733, New England boasted six foundries and nineteen forges; a quarter century later, there were fourteen foundries and forty-one forges in Massachusetts alone. In addition, Bay Colony ironmasters also operated four slitting mills, two plating mills, and one steel furnace not reported to authorities in London by Massachusetts' royal governor. He dutifully reported all of these illegal operations to the Board of Trade, which, until the mid-1760s, practiced an unofficial policy called "salutary neglect."[3]

Ethan Allen did not have to travel far to grasp the promise of the potash industry in a land rich in the raw material and the demand for the finished products. By the time he decided to become an ironmaster at age twenty-six, Americans had not only driven from their markets English axes to clear their potash-rich lands but were illegally manufacturing quantities of nails, kettles, scythes, even anchors. In Connecticut alone, there were eight ironworks and a steel furnace by the 1750s. All of this commerce ignored the fact that, in 1750, Parliament had passed the Iron Act, making it illegal to erect or operate "a mill or other engine for slitting or rolling of iron, or any plating forge to work with a tilt hammer, or any furnace for making steel." The fine was £200 for the ironmaster—or £500 for any royal official caught turning a blind eye. Connecticut Yankees like Ethan Allen totally ignored the law. By 1775, the American colonies were producing three times the amount of iron they produced in 1750. Young Allen had his first taste of the impotence of English law in America's forests, three thousand miles removed from the seat of government in London.

Ethan Allen at age thiry-seven.

PART TWO

—————————— ❖ ——————————

"GODS
OF THE
HILLS"

5.

"A Tumultuous and Offensive Manner"

IN THE SEVEN YEARS AFTER his father's premature death, Ethan Allen could not venture far from the family farm in Cornwall, Connecticut, not until the dreaded French and their Indian auxiliaries had been defeated. At twenty-four, he remained unmarried, tethered to his mother's burden and the family farm. By 1762, however, he was casting about for a new enterprise. A man of extraordinary intellect, he could not bear the idea of rusticating indefinitely on the farm, especially in backwater Cornwall. He had nursed the farm to a healthy self-sufficiency, expanding its acreage and improving house and barn to the point where he could turn their management over to his mother and younger brothers, the youngest of them now ten years old. Deciding to seek a new livelihood, Allen started out on his own and moved the ten miles over the Taconic Mountains to Salisbury, a more sophisticated town on the Massachusetts border, where he had so enjoyed his brief time as a student, and now found a job in the burgeoning iron industry.

As early as the mid-1730s, one of the first settlers of Salisbury had erected a small forge in the Lakeville section of town. The business sputtered along as the demand for its iron pigs and sows remained small. With settlement on the far western edge of Connecticut still sparse, the demand for manufactured farm implements remained minute, and the market was easily saturated even by such tiny furnaces. For much of each year, the furnace was out of blast. In western Connecticut, no ironmaster had yet been able to profit from his furnace alone. Few had enough cash to buy a steady supply of the wood or charcoal needed to feed the blast furnace. On average, a small forge such as Cornwall's consumed fifty acres of hardwood a year. The route to profit for the iron maker was, as in Cornwall, to be among the first settlers of a town, to prepare the way for coming farmers, and to reap a double profit from iron and the sale of the land already cleared to provide the fuel for the furnace. Cleared land brought a much higher price than forest; a forge could survive only so long as large stands of uncleared hardwoods were nearby.

Aware of the limitations of the Lakeville furnace operated by Leonard Owen and his brothers, Ethan Allen decided to put together a partnership and buy the forge in April of 1762. The purchase included only the forge and water rights. He moved quickly when an investor, John Hazeltine of Upbridge, came to town to visit Hazeltine's brother. Allen enthusiastically demonstrated his grasp of the iron business and persuaded the Hazeltines that there was an untapped potential for profit from casting the huge iron pots needed to boil down the prized potash into crystals. Impressed, John Hazeltine promised that, if Allen would provide his experience and manage the enterprise, the Hazeltine brothers would put up the money to buy the old forge and its water rights and build a modern blast furnace; Allen would also have to buy a one-eighth interest in an ore-rich hill just outside town and assure sufficient waterpower.

Allen knew that the Forbes brothers, who also owned one-eighth of the mountain, operated a forge in Canaan, five miles farther north. He went to them with his proposition and learned that they had put a value of £430 on their share of the mountain. Allen cut himself in on the deal. He persuaded the Forbes brothers to sell a half interest in their eighth to the Hazeltines and an eighth interest to him, and to retain three-eighths interest themselves. The Forbes brothers, in turn, had to provide enough ore for their own forge, for Allen and Hazeltine's in Salisbury, and for the forge of Thomas Day in nearby Norfolk. Everyone assumed the mountain would provide a limitless supply of iron ore for the indefinite future.

Allen borrowed some of the money from neighbors and covered his £54 share of the purhase price of the ore mountain by pledging a £50 mortgage he held with his cousin Elihu on their farm. For another £20, he was able to buy from the forge's original owners the water rights to the lake's outlet. There he intended to build a mill race and install a watershed. He also acquired the privilege of cutting and turning into charcoal two-thirds of a large tract of hardwood forest on nearby Tohconnick Mountain. Allen began construction of the giant cone, the first blast furnace in colonial Connecticut, in April of 1762 and completed it that spring.

RESOURCEFUL FROM LONG necessity, impulsive by nature, Ethan Allen had learned how to live on little cash. In April of 1762, as soon as the roads were passable, he saddled his favorite horse and began to make regular rides from Salisbury to Woodbury, some twelve miles to the south, to ease the loneliness of life as a bachelor, boarder, and wage earner. One way he had learned to live frugally and build up his family's stature was to stay single, although twenty-four was dead average for a man in New England to marry. His noisy Cornwall home already was too crowded for the addition of a bride, which invariably meant the start of another family. But the family-based culture of Puritan New England not only frowned on bachelors but also fined them and was especially harsh to them if they caused the slightest trouble. There was no inconspicuous place for an unmarried young man in Cornwall. Allen, outgoing, successful in business, was even more conspicuous in the dour, church-centered town, especially since he resisted attending New Light church services. His old family friend and erstwhile teacher, the Reverend Lee, pastor of the Salisbury church and town elder, was watching him. Lee found it inexcusable that Allen missed the Sunday meeting, its long sermons and bawled hymns. Between Sabbaths, Allen busied himself with mastering the iron business in all its elements. Learning what he would need to set up a forge of his own, he devoted long days to hard work, cracking his bullwhip over a team of plodding oxen towing a heavy cart of ore from a nearby mountain to one of the town's two iron forges.

ON SATURDAYS, AT the workweek's end, studiously avoiding Sunday church services, Ethan sloughed off the censorious atmosphere accorded a single man in his midtwenties and, risking the wrath of the Reverend Lee when he found Allen and his contribution to the church missing, slipped away to Woodbury to visit Mary Brownson. For nearly ten years now, since he had been an eager and unschooled boy of fifteen and she a woman of twenty-one, she had cooked for him, at first while her father, the region's prosperous miller, ground the Allens' grain. That millers literally prospered at the expense of the farmer—taking one-twelfth of all the grain they ground—made them rich in the eyes of their neighbors but often resented as well. It also had made the Woodbury miller selective in his daughter's choice of a spouse. No portrait, not even a vivid word picture of Mary Brownson survives. Just why she was still unmarried at the uncommonly advanced age of thirty may be explained by her having two older brothers, Israel and Abraham, rough, domineering ne'er-do-wells who expected her to wait on them as unpaid cook and maid. Only a confident and successful young man such as Ethan Allen could hope to penetrate the Brownsons' defenses.

Over the years since the death of Allen's father, no one had asked for Mary Brownson's hand in marriage while Allen had continued to visit her. Plain and pious, Mary had toiled ceaselessly for her brothers and father. Perhaps from his profound sense of injustice, Allen persisted from 1754 to 1762 to call on her. In Woodbury, Mary Brownson was "Ethan Allen's girl," a fact the entire community seemed to acknowledge. No evidence survives that he ever showed any interest in any other young woman in tiny Cornwall. He probably knew all of them too well or was related to them. While he still lived at home, it became his ritual to ride over to Woodbury, where everybody knew him and where he knew that Mary Brownson awaited him.

There was much to see when they strolled through Woodbury's lively streets, to Allen a mecca of New England culture and a cosmopolitan town after tiny Cornwall. They went to house-raisings, husking bees, and barn dances together; they rode on hay carts in summer, hunted rabbits in the fall—all the recreational events commonplace in predominantly rural America in the eighteenth century. They could ride out beside the romantic rapids of Roxbury Falls, where the Shepaug River leaps between tall cliffs, pause to reflect at Pulpit Rock, where the missionary John Eliot had first preached to the Pequod Indians before a Massachusetts army slaughtered them. Back in town, long leisurely visits with the prospect of dinners someone else had cooked beckoned them to the homes of Allen's favorite cousins, Seth Warner and Remember Baker, or to other members of his mother's large family.

If family legend is to be believed, Ethan and Mary spent nights together "bundling," sleeping together fully clothed. It was a custom from England that was long held to be widely practiced in New England, and, supposedly, Ethan and Mary were no exceptions, even though New Light clergy were railing against the custom as contributing to lewdness and disorder among youth. The historian Edmund Morgan has offered a more modern and cogent view. In an effort to gain control over their choice of a spouse and to encourage early marriage as an antidote to sex outside the marital state, a Puritan taboo,

> New England families . . . encouraged the young men courting their daughters to spend the whole night at it under their own roofs. After the old folks retired the couple slept together unattended. They were supposed to do no more than slumber, but did anyone really expect that a young man and young woman in bed together would simply whisper sweet nothings to each other before dozing off?

Marriages in New England at this time were commonly preceded by formal espousals, often public and sometimes lasting several months:

> Many people felt that espousals were a sufficiently binding commitment to justify intercourse and acted accordingly. In doing so they were not rejecting the substance of Puritan doctrine.

Morgan maintains that while sexual relations outside of marriage were still felonious,

> by the 1750s courts had lost interest in punishing pre-marital sex, despite a growing number of pregnant brides, amounting to 30 or 40 percent in some towns. . . . When young men went acourting now, they did not necessarily wait for permission from the girls' parents. Parents allowed their sons and daughters to frolic unchaperoned in late-night sleigh rides, corn huskings, and dancing parties.

However "shocking to outsiders," the practice of bundling thrived in part because it "had the advantage of giving parents some influence in their daughter's choice of a husband."[1]

The eighth of eleven children, Mary Brownson was described by one Ethan Allen biographer as "a delicate girl, deeply religious, humorless, and illiterate. She signed her name with a cross." But illiteracy in a frontier American village that had no common schools when she was of school age was not unusual. Even in larger towns or on great southern plantations, literacy among women in America varied widely at this time. Even though his sister Jane, a Puritan and lifelong resident of Boston, wrote quite well given the nature of their correspondence, Benjamin Franklin poked fun at the pitiful attempts at letter writing of his Philadelphia-born common-law wife, Deborah Read Franklin, the daughter of a prosperous bookseller and mayor of the Quaker city. In fact, while Franklin would not spend a farthing on educating Deborah, he admired the epistolary elegance of the women he knew in Paris. George Washington married the wealthiest widow in Virginia, but he rewrote even her shopping lists rather than let anyone see Martha's irregular spellings and poor grammar: the daughter of a county clerk, she had no formal education. Mary Brownson had not learned to write, but she must have learned to read, especially the Bible, a deep common interest she and young Ethan Allen had imbibed from their parents. On what could be stretched to be called their dates, young couples would discuss the Bible. Quotes from Scripture were their lingua franca, the language of frontier families; if they owned only one book, it was the family Bible.[2]

Some Allen biographers have suggested that it was her father's great tracts of land that attracted Ethan, that Mary would bring with her a considerable dowry of land, but there is no record of this. The only land she ever sold was a modest town lot some twenty years later, hardly an alluring inheritance. Her father owned considerable land and had the status of millowner, but there were eleven children, and she had older brothers. Mary's inheritance, if any, would be rather modest. From his many visits, Ethan had, quite simply, gotten to know Mary Brownson, who first mothered him, then became his big sister, then his girlfriend, and finally his wife. If, as one unsympathetic biographer put it, "Mary posed a rigid and unrelenting piety that hung like a pall over the Allen household," there is little suggestion of it in their blossoming courtship. But historians who have decided that "there was much to be scolded" in Ethan Allen have decided that Mary was "an intolerable scold."[3]

Very little historical evidence and no portrait remains of Mary Brownson Allen, but that has not deterred each generation of historians from embroidering it more, each time becoming less sympathetic, more condescending. On paper, at least, she became "dull, dreary, and far from pretty," as one biographer put it, "tailored by nature and training for a life of cheerless mediocrity." The person who could have shed some light, Ethan Allen, left no comment. In all the thousands of pages of his writings that survive, he never said a word about her. The only evidence, in fact, is that they were married for twenty-one years and had five children. And of all the brickbats hurled at Allen over the years, no one has suggested that he was ever unfaithful to her, or she to him.[4]

ERECTION OF THE first blast furnace in western Connecticut complete, Allen decided he could now afford to support a family. He seems not to have even considered, now that he had money, taking more time to date other women. It was, as far as we can determine, just the right time to get married, and Mary Brownson would do well enough. One day in June of 1762, about the time the first charge of iron poured out of the new blast furnace, Ethan rode once more to Woodbury and asked Mary to marry him. Not surprisingly, she accepted. There is no evidence that he ever asked her father for her hand, even though that was the custom. On June 23, they were married by the Reverend Daniel Brinsmade of Judea Parish in Woodbury. The ceremony cost Ethan four shillings, and the record shows no more than that. Then Ethan Allen, age twenty-four, hoisted Mary Brownson, thirty, up onto the pillion behind his saddle and rode with her through the romantic lake district of Litchfield County to their new home in Salisbury.

For the first year of their marriage, the newlyweds rented a small, clapboarded cottage in the heart of Salisbury, a frontier boomtown on the borders of Massachusetts, Connecticut, and New York. Their first home was small, probably only two rooms, with a cellar and the loft where brother Heman slept. The setting was picturesque, and the house possessed a charm its size belied, standing on a round little hill beside the mill brook. The newlyweds hauled water in a wooden bucket from a well in the side of the hill and crossed the brook on a plank that took them from house to furnace. Below the forge and the hill lay the village green, like so many in New England then and now, with its Congregational meetinghouse, a tavern, and a pillory. Lining the green were the unpainted frame houses of several prominent families, including Justice of the Peace John Hutchinson; the town doctor, Joshua Porter; Paul Hazeltine, brother of Ethan's business partner; John Knickerbocker, one of the original settlers and a Dutchman from New York; and the Tousley and Caldwell families. All of them were farmers who kept livestock, whatever else their professions became.

But picture postcards do not convey sound, and Salisbury, population 1,500, was growing rapidly. Ethan thrived on this noisy, bustling place, with scores of wagons and oxcarts, their drivers yelling and cracking their whips as they carried the raw materials to the furnace amid the roar of each blast and the hiss of the molten iron and the clang of the heavy metallic pigs and sows as they were manhandled and carted away. He was at work at the furnace all day, and Mary became accustomed to being alone for long stretches and probably liked it after the tense years in her brawling family's home in Woodbury. In many ways, her life was fairly typical of the new middling class of New Englanders straddling the old life of the farm and the new life of the small town. She always kept a kitchen garden. She had time to read her Bible, sew, and cook. She had money for whatever else they needed from Ethan's wages. When it was time to give birth to their first child, Ethan took her to Cornwall to stay with his mother during her confinement. Ignoring the persistent Puritan practice of adopting Old Testament names, they named their first child Loraine when she was born in April of 1763, ten months after they were married. Ethan was busy in Salisbury most of the time but came home to Cornwall for occasional visits.

· · ·

IN ITS FIRST three years, the iron furnace of Forbes and Allen proved profitable. Allen built dams, obtained additional water rights, and supervised construction of a toll road to bring the iron ore from mine to furnace, his efforts contributing to an iron-making business that employed upwards of fifty men. He hired and oversaw them and acted as the salaried timekeeper. The large egg-shaped stone and wood-framed furnace, ten feet in diameter and twenty-four feet high (a modern three-story building), consumed in a single charge three tons of crude iron ore reacting with 250 bushels of charcoal and half a ton of limestone flux to produce two tons of molten iron—and it would produce iron full blast right on through the American Revolution, when it was taken over by the state and produced heavy cannon for Henry Knox's artillery.

The success of twenty-six-year-old Ethan Allen, ironmaster—a title of great respect in colonial America—brought with it a kind of temptation he had never faced before. Within nine months of the business's inception, the partners were able to pay off Leonard Owen for the land, the water rights to the falls at the mouth of the pond, an ore bed, two coal houses, and two dwelling houses. As manager, Allen could have lived in one of these houses, but he had grander plans. When his first child was born, he decided that the new Allen family deserved a larger house. On a little hill opposite the furnace across the mill brook stood just such a house, a fine house situated on five hundred acres of land. It would provide pasturage for a large herd of cattle as well as a generous garden for Mary to grow vegetables. The steep £500 purchase price—more than the entire mine and forge had cost, did not deter the expansive ironmaster Allen. Cousin Elihu paid him the £50 he owed him for his farm, plus £10 interest, a 20 percent return for the use of his money for two years. Allen gave Eliphalet Buell a £50 cash down payment for the house and farm and mortgaged the Allen family farm in Cornwall to Buell for the remaining £450. One hitch in the exchange was that Allen did not own all of the family farm: his two-years-younger brother, Heman, owned some of the plowland. Ethan had to buy out Heman's land. So Ethan turned around and sold Heman a half interest in his share of the furnace for £300 and a half interest in the Buell house for £200. To pay Ethan, his brother Heman, who also had little cash, sold him the Cornwall plowland, then mortgaged his share of the Buell house to one Colonel Martin Hoffman and gave Ethan notes payable in "good neat cattle." The complicated transaction was typical of its time and place, involving only £50 in cash. But when the ink was dry, to buy his grand new house, Ethan had cut in half his interest in the furnace. Now, though, he would have time to spend at home because his hardworking, businesslike brother Heman came to work and helped him run the forge. In this new house, Ethan had leisure to study once again, to read, and to converse with the more interesting people of the town. Had it not been for his brief, newfound leisure for intellectual pursuits and his conspicuous success at business, Ethan Allen might not have run afoul of the clergy and magistrates of Salisbury, who still ruled town life.

WHEN ETHAN FIRST came to Salisbury, as a sixteen-year-old schoolboy, he was introduced to Dr. Thomas Young, a young, well-read physician who had recently moved to Salisbury and opened practice in the Oblong, a hilly section of land straddling the New York–Connecticut border. There, Ethan frequently visited Young, six years his senior, and Young's wife, Mary. The two men spent their evenings discussing theology, philosophy, and politics. Young, in his early twenties, was impressed by the sixteen-year-old's precocious knowledge and ability at biblical disputation. Young had studied a smattering of the works of Thomas Aquinas, Hobbes, and Machiavelli as well as the political poetry of Alexander Pope, the natural philosophy of John Locke, and the deist writings of Charles Blount. As a student at Yale, he had copied his favorite readings into notebooks in a practice called commonplacing, and he lent these to young Ethan along with pamphlets attacking New Light theology. While he could not offer him the books themselves, he watched in delight as Ethan pored over the notebooks. After hearing the New Light sermons of his schoolmaster, the Reverend Lee, several times a week, Ethan listened in wonder as Young skewered the works of Whitefield and Edwards, the Old Testament prophets and early Christian Fathers.

When Allen returned to Salisbury seven years later, they rekindled their friendship, spending long, happy evenings and weekends sipping rum and, by the firelight, reading to each other passages they especially liked, both delighting to find literate kinship in such a provincial backwater. Young, now in his early thirties, relished the role of the mentor. He loved an audience, and he never had a better student. For his part, Allen found not only the older brother he had lacked but also his most influential teacher, the man who, after his father, made the greatest impression on him, the man who possessed the Yale education he had been denied. Even while events would intervene, a lifelong friendship developed in those two years in Salisbury.

The story of Young's early life inspired Allen as much as his later life would pain him. Born the eldest of seven children of Scotch-Irish immigrants in a log house in New Windsor, on the Hudson River in New York, Young as a child with an exceptional memory could read any English book by age six, something he had in common with Allen. He was educated by his father at a local school but, beyond that, was entirely self-taught. He borrowed books from his neighbor and kinsman Colonel Charles Clinton (father of future New York Governor and Vice President George Clinton and great-uncle of Governor De Witt Clinton). He read some Latin and Greek and had a workable knowledge of Dutch and German and could read French, although he never learned to pronounce it. Interested in medicine, he studied botany, gaining a thorough knowledge of local plants and their uses. At seventeen, he became apprenticed to a local physician: there still was no medical school in America. Two years later, he began to practice in what is now Amenia, New York, a frontier town fifteen miles west of Cornwall and which he himself named. According to Young's brother, also a physician, he "acquired fame and a very extensive practice" after marrying the daughter of his landlord and moving with her to Salisbury. He then began to publish newspaper articles and pamphlets on medical topics.[5]

The degree of cultivation during Ethan Allen's evenings with Dr. Young eclipsed anything he had experienced in his frontier youth. At a time when fiddling at barn dances provided the only extra-ecclesiastical music in the New England backcountry, Young had learned to play classical violin, probably as a student at Yale. The concertinos of Corelli, the music of the minuet, were the current favorite at the subscription assembly balls of Philadelphia attended by Benjamin Franklin's son, William. At this time, George Washington hired a German music teacher for four-hour sessions of lessons and dancing at Mount Vernon for his stepchildren and his neighbors, confiding in a letter to Francis Hopkinson, a well-known composer in Philadelphia, "I can neither sing one of the songs or raise a single note on any instrument." Washington preferred the music of Josef Haydn and Johann Christian Bach, of Ignaz Pleyel and Johann Baptist Vanhal, as well as country fiddle music and the eerie sound of the armonica, a musical instrument made of glass goblets worked by a footpedal and perfected by his friend Benjamin Franklin. Whatever music emanated from the Salisbury soirees, it charmed Ethan Allen and his wife.[6]

From Dr. Young's storytelling, Allen was also imbibing a kind of iconoclastic humor that pricked pomposity. Young even poked fun at his own profession, quipping that doctors, "if they live near the sea, order the patient to take a ride in the country; if inland, to take the sea air."[7] Sometimes he even dared to mock the Bible, something he could risk in New England only with the most trusted of friends. Where, he asked Allen, did Eve get the thread to stitch together her fig leaves? And from whom, exactly, did the serpent learn to talk? Allen was getting his first exposure to rational inquiry.

Young also attempted to write poetry, his one publication a 608-line paean to Wolfe's victory over Montcalm at Quebec, its turgid couplets made worse by the profuse typographical errors committed by the nearest printer, in faraway New Haven, who, while inept, was the only printer in Puritan Connecticut unafraid to publish a deist's work. Already, by the time Allen renewed their friendship, Young had gained a reputation as a blasphemer. On August 8, 1756, at age twenty-four, Young had been hauled into court and accused of saying, "Jesus Christ was a knave and a fool." Young's punishment was to recant publicly to the court.[8]

Far from being shocked, Allen found himself drawn to Young's skeptical views on religion. Allen's and his father's clash with the intolerant Dr. Bellamy over the ouster of Solomon Palmer had predisposed him to begin to question orthodox Christian doctrine. Dr. Bellamy struck again in 1758 in an anonymous letter to a Boston newspaper circulating all over Connecticut, denouncing deism. After Allen's father's death, his erstwhile schoolmaster, the Reverend Lee, appointed himself Allen's spiritual watchdog. Lee was disturbed to hear that Allen was going around the town spreading deist views he was learning from

Dr. Young. When, after imbibing some rum in a local tavern, Allen ridiculed Calvinistic doctrine and said he did not believe in original sin, the Reverend Lee confronted him: without original sin, Lee argued, there would be no need for atonement, and thus no need for Christ, and thus no need for Christianity. Two decades later, Allen wrote that this altercation with Lee remained "uppermost" in his mind for several months. "After many painful searches and researches after the truth," he had resolved "at all events to abide [by] the decision" he had made to favor "rational argument [over] the premises" of Christianity and to reject "the whole—Original Sin, Imputation, Christ and Christianity."[9]

In writing about Ethan some thirty years later, his brother Ira stated flatly that, "after an Acquaintance with Doctor Thomas Young, a Deist my brother embrased the same centiments."[10] Ethan later published his own explanation:

In the circle of my acquaintance, (which has not been small,) I have generally been denominated a Deist, the reality of which I never disputed, being conscious I am no Christian, except mere infant baptism makes me one; and as to being a Deist, I know not, strictly speaking, whether I am one or not, for I have never read their writings. . . .[11]

Here, Ethan Allen was shading the truth: he had not read deist writings himself, but he had imbibed them from the commonplace books and long evenings of conversations over a two-year period in the parlor of his friend Dr. Thomas Young.

Ethan Allen's newly adopted set of beliefs, more a rational philosophy than a religion, acknowledged that God existed, that he was the remote Creator of the universe who did not intervene in the daily affairs of individual believers and did not saddle human beings with the burden of original sin, each person enjoying the freedom to choose or reject salvation. Allen's brand of deism also rejected the doctrine of the Holy Trinity and the divine incarnation of Jesus, who was a great moral teacher but not God. Deism's core beliefs, held by Isaac Newton and John Locke, would evolve eventually in the hands of the philosopher David Hume coming to conclude that miracles, which by definition went beyond the confines of rationality, lay at the core of Christianity. At the time Allen was espousing deism, its main tenets included worshipping the one transcendent God and demonstrating this worship by practicing morality, including dealing justly with others. Eventually, Allen would, like the Jewish philosopher Baruch Spinoza, believe that the Bible should be scrutinized in the light of reason. As if all of this were not shocking enough to Allen's New England neighbors, deists considered the Bible a holy book that was not divinely inspired or authored: to deists, the only word of God was the Creation. To New England Congregationalists, deism was just another word for atheism.

A quarter century before Ethan Allen was first exposed to deistic thought in Salisbury, in Philadelphia, Benjamin Franklin, who had printed the journals of George Whitefield, wrote to his close friend Thomas Hopkinson, the first president of the American Philosophical Society:

> I oppose my *Theist* to his *Atheist*, because I think they are diametrically opposite and no near of kin, as Mr. Whitefield seems to suppose where [in his journal] he tells us *Mr. B. was a Deist, I had almost said an Atheist.* That is *chalk*, I had almost said *charcoal.*[12]

In his famous *Autobiography*, Franklin would later write of his reaction when he had read Andrew Baxer's 1745 work, *Enquiry into the Nature of the Human Soul*:

Some books against Deism fell into my hands. They were said to be the substance of sermons preached at [Robert] Boyle's lectures [in London]. It happened that they wrought an effect on me quite contrary to what was intended of them, for the arguments of the Deists, which were quoted to be refuted, appeared to me much stronger than the refutations. In short, I soon became a thorough Deist.[13]

Other future founding fathers were similarly rebelling against the established religions in their native colonies, creating a profound historical movement that shifted theocratic control away from the leading clergymen and would, in time, influence these future leaders to write separation of church and state into the Constitution. George Washington became a deist with an unquestioning faith in Providence, his substitute for "God." His use of the word was not a rhetorical flourish but a mark of his reliance on a Grand Designer, as deists put it. Thomas Jefferson wrote in his own epitaph that, next to being the "Author of the Declaration of Independence," he was proudest of writing "the Virginia Statute of Religious Freedom" after a bitter fight that disestablished Anglicanism as the official taxpayer-supported religion in his commonwealth. As president, Jefferson was attacked from pulpit and Massachusetts statehouse by the Congregationalist clergy largely because he was an avowed deist. In his famous correspondence with former President John Adams, former President Jefferson decried Calvin in terms that Ethan Allen would have understood:

I can never join Calvin in addressing *his god*. He was indeed an Atheist, which I can never be; or rather his religion was Daemonism. If ever man worshipped a false god, he did. The being described in his 5 [theological] points is not the God whom you and I acknolege and adore, the Creator and benevolent governor of the world; but a daemon of malignant spirit. It would be more pardonable to believe in no god at all, than to blaspheme him by the atrocious attributes of Calvin.[14]

Franklin and Jefferson would learn firsthand as American revolutionary diplomats in France that deism was the very foundation of Enlightenment skepticism that led to the French Revolution. Among its leading practitioners were Voltaire, Diderot, and the *encyclopédistes*. "Deism proved influential in the United States from roughly 1725 through the first several decades of the nineteenth century," writes the historian David L. Holmes:

Emphasizing human inquiry, reason, and personal freedom, it catered to American principles of individuality. Paradoxically, the movement also failed in part because of these characteristics. Deism excluded the emotional and mysterious aspects of religion. It ignored the need of many humans for spiritual guidance, worship, and a community of faith.

Holmes views the appeal of deism for educated American colonists as "the idea of reason as a liberator from the shackles of repressive religion and tyrannical government." As a consequence, he finds, by the 1760s an alarmed clergy began to speak out against rational religion: when James Madison returned to Virginia from his studies at the College of New Jersey, later renamed Princeton, an opponent of deism warned the elder Madisons that their son's religious beliefs had clearly deviated in the direction of deism. The change in young Madison was due to "political associations with those of infidel principles" at that most orthodox of colonial colleges.[15]

In 1764, Ethan Allen and Thomas Young decided to challenge Calvinist orthodoxy openly. Together, by the firelight, the two young backwoods philosophers began to collaborate on a book of rational philosophy, Young serving up quotations from his eclectic readings, Allen drawing on his thorough knowledge of the Bible.

CONSISTENT WITH HIS character, Ethan Allen turned his philosophical ruminations into radical action. If indeed, as the two young deists believed, religious taboos were often mere superstition, then they should be challenged by rational scientific experiments. Every year, hundreds even thousands of American colonists died from a dread disease that it was illegal, in New England even considered sinful, to confront: Puritans deemed it a great sin to interfere with God's will by trying to prevent death. In the spring of 1764, smallpox scourged Salisbury and all of New England as it had periodically all of Allen's life. This time, Allen looked at the outbreak skeptically, through the prism of his new-found philosophy of questioning authority. A Connecticut statute forbade the use of smallpox serum without the express consent of the town's selectmen. Twenty-six-year-old Ethan Allen and his doctor, Thomas Young, decided to challenge this law.

After Congregational services on a Sunday morning, in front of the Salisbury meetinghouse, where Allen's kinsman the Reverend Lee presided as pastor, Dr. Young inoculated Ethan Allen before a horrified crowd. The experiment was all the more pro-vocative because of the personal relationship between Allen and the Reverend Lee. In a small New England town, all transactions were personal. Lee could only have taken Allen's intrepidity as a very public personal affront. He may have already known that his erstwhile pupil was determined to confront him. The prep-arations could hardly have remained secret in Salisbury. Under

Young's watchful eye, Allen had followed a special program of diet and purgings. Now, with virtually the whole town present for the obligatory Sunday service, Salisbury watched as Dr. Young passed a needle and a piece of thread that carried a small quantity of untreated pus from the suppurating sore of a patient with a mild case of smallpox through a scratch on Allen's arm. Their intent was to induce in Allen a milder case of the illness than he would have experienced if he had contracted the disease naturally. Both men knew they risked a stiff fine, but this was their first strong, overt act of rebellion against what they considered to be the irrational theocracy of Connecticut, and they were determined to test a law that struck them as irrational.

That spring, a major smallpox epidemic was ravaging colonial America. In most colonies, including Connecticut, smallpox inoculation was illegal. Allen and Young knew they were risking not only official sanction but mob action. For more than forty years, New England had been racked by controversy each time smallpox struck again. The Indians, who had no immunity to the disease, had already been decimated before the Pilgrims arrived, quite likely from contact with English fishermen who made annual visits to Cape Cod to dry and salt their catches and almost certainly because of the exploration and mapping of New England by Captain John Smith and his party from Jamestown Colony in Virginia, where colonists suffered from the disease after its introduction from England. As early as the arrival of the Pilgrims more than a century earlier, every year large numbers of smallpox deaths had stopped all travel and much farmwork. Every year in the eighteenth century, some 400,000 Europeans died of the highly contagious disease, which was spread by coughing and contact. Transmitted to the Americas on shipboard, the smallpox epidemics were most devastating during the sporadic imperial wars, spread in the colonies by soldiers and sailors. King

William's War in 1689 subjected maritime Boston, the largest town in British America at the time, to its worst outbreak in the seventeenth century, killing 1,200 in a population of 12,000.

Outbreaks of smallpox periodically rekindled the inoculation controversy that sometimes erupted into riots. Nobody remained neutral on the subject. Colony after colony had banned inoculation since that first long-ago epidemic. In 1720, smallpox again decimated Boston: of 12,000 citizens, more than 1,000 perished, a calamity from which Boston never fully recovered in the eighteenth century. Ships' captains began to boycott Boston, finding safer harbors—Portsmouth, Newport, Salem, and Newburyport—which siphoned off Boston's trade. Townspeople moved away, founding new towns, some joining new immigrants who bypassed Boston and moved out onto the frontier.

In that worst scourge of eighteenth-century Boston, the leading Congregationalist clergyman, Increase Mather, urged his neighbor Dr. Zabdiel Boylston to conduct an experiment. In addition to being the scion of New England's leading family of theologians, Mather at the time was one of only two Americans inducted into membership in the Royal Society of London. The English literary bluestocking Lady Mary Wortley Montagu had visited the Ottoman Empire two years earlier and written extensively to influential friends in England about the successful experiment she had witnessed. Mather, reading about the successful Turkish experiment in the Royal Society's *Transactions*, was impressed by the possibility of reducing mortality and suffering by inoculating healthy people with the smallpox contagion and thereby building up an immunity to the disease. Mather wielded enormous influence all over New England. From the pulpit and in print, Mather, joined by other clerical luminaries, supported the experimental inoculation of Bostonians. Mather urged Dr. Boylston to conduct the experiment. Boylston inoculated his own son, among others. Already divided by several political and religious fault lines, Boston split into two strident camps over inoculation.

To most Bostonians, the deliberate spreading of smallpox by inoculation seemed criminal stupidity when almost every house in town was flying the quarantine flag amid an endless procession of coffins to the graveyard. Not only were most Bostonians unlettered in the intricacies of science but they could see no benefit to allowing a doctor to slice open a vein and fill the incision with pus from a smallpox victim. Trying to avoid smallpox by natural means seemed preferable to agreeing voluntarily to contract the disease, even if in a mild form. But Dr. Boylston failed to prevent the further spread of the epidemic that summer, probably because he failed to isolate his patients while they were in the disease's incubation period, and smallpox actually spread by contact with his patients. Six of the inoculated patients died, a far-below-average number, but one victim who came close to succumbing was Boylston's own son. Mather and Boylston incurred the wrath of most of New England's Puritan clergy, who considered it a great sin to interfere with God's will by trying to prevent death.

The bitter controversy kept printers busy, the argument over inoculation confirming growing public opinion that the clergy where overstepping their proper clerical role. Benjamin Franklin's older brother, James, publisher of the *New England Courant*, lashed out at Mather and Boylston, inciting a superstitious public to riot. Ironically, a dozen years later, Benjamin Franklin's only legitimate son, Francis, would die at age four after Franklin refused to have him inoculated during an outbreak in Philadelphia. The controversy and the epidemic in Boston lasted a full year. Virtually the whole community blamed Mather. Public antagonism to the clergy became so great that someone lobbed a bomb through the window of Mather's study.

• • •

As ETHAN ALLEN confined himself in quarantine at home in Salisbury, the New England epidemic of 1764 was keeping cautious courting couples away from each other. John Adams and Abigail Quincy had planned to get married that spring, but the arrival of smallpox in Boston forced them to wait. The danger of accidentally infecting Abigail seemed so serious to John that he had himself illegally inoculated by his good friend Dr. Joseph Warren, and then quarantined himself under Warren's care away from Abigail and other patients. Because John and Abigail had to stay apart, their lifelong habit of corresponding blossomed. While she treasured John's letters, Abigail believed that anything that had been touched by someone infected with smallpox put her at risk: letters were themselves dangerous. Before she would read them, she held Adams's letters over smoke to decontaminate them.

Even Congregational clergy opposed to inoculation learned that they were not immune to what they considered a scourge by God for New England's errant ways. The fire-and-brimstone Great Awakening theologian Jonathan Edwards had inveighed against inoculation from his pulpit at Northampton's First Church. When the Reverend Aaron Burr Sr., president of the College of New Jersey, and his wife, the daughter of Edwards, died of smallpox, the trustees of the college offered Edwards its presidency, but, according to some historians, they made smallpox inoculation a condition of his employment. He reluctantly accepted the post and, convinced that he would have to submit to inoculation if he expected inoculation of his students, died within a month of smallpox, leaving his grandson, Aaron Burr Jr., future vice president of the United States, an orphan.

Obdurate superstition obviously was not the exclusive province of New England Puritans. In Virginia, two people died near coastal Yorktown after inoculated patients were released prematurely from quarantine. In 1768 and again in 1769, confrontations between pro- and anti-inoculation factions led to riots. Two doctors who carried out inoculations were indicted by the Norfolk County court. When one doctor attempted to inoculate his own family members at his plantation, a mob attacked his house and chased him and the inoculated patients three miles to the county pesthouse. The year after Allen's inoculation, Thomas Jefferson's favorite sister, Jane, died of smallpox at their Charlottesville, Virginia, home. Shortly after her death, the grieving Thomas, at twenty-three, journeyed alone in a one-horse buggy all the way to Philadelphia by a circuitous mountain route for an inoculation, because it was illegal to be inoculated in Virginia. Illegal immunizations had taken place in Virginia for twenty years, but Jefferson wanted a trained physician outside the colony to carry out his inoculation to keep smallpox from spreading closer to home. For many years after his sister's death from smallpox, Jefferson fought a battle in Virginia's courts without fee against the opponents of legalizing inoculation. (While American minister plenipotentiary in France in 1787, he arranged to have his slave Sally Hemings inoculated.) During the 1764 epidemic in New England, Samuel Adams took his children to the office of his friend Dr. Joseph Warren, who had just inoculated his cousin John Adams. Defying the taboo against inoculation was the first overt act of rebellion for these future founding fathers—Jefferson, the Adamses, and Ethan Allen—their iconoclastic act sparing them for later, more public revolutionary acts.

WHILE ETHAN ALLEN and Thomas Young put into public practice their deism in the Connecticut backcountry, the English Parliament was experimenting with imperial legislation. Find-

ing itself with a farflung empire, the British government under-
took a thorough review of American policies and taxes. After
the French surrender, the British in effect became the overlords
of all the Indians between the Appalachian Mountains and the
Mississippi River, now the western boundary of British territory.
By proclamation in 1763, the British forbade settlement west of
the Appalachians: what had been so hard-won by the British and
American colonial troops became a huge Indian reserve. Settlers already west of the mountains were ordered to leave, and
British troops were sent in to make sure any recalcitrant settlers
left. Someone would have to pay for the twenty thousand Redcoats in two hundred forts and stockades envisioned by Parliament. The British ministry expected the Americans to help. The
British national debt was enough to make any minister look for
new answers: as of January 5, 1763, according to the Exchequer,
funded debt stood at £122 million, a staggering sum that carried annual interest of £4.4 million. For the next three years, the
debt grew annually by £7 million because of the costs of maintaining the new empire. Financing the debt absorbed more and
more of ministers' time and turned their attention increasingly to
America, which, in British eyes, already possessed great riches. In
truth, this was more legend than reality.

Relatively little can be known about the exact scale of the
American economy in the years before the American Revolution,
because the fortunes of so many successful merchants were based
on smuggling. Every Connecticut and Rhode Island shipowner
who dealt with French, Spanish, or Dutch colonies in the Caribbean in the molasses trade, for example, was a smuggler, according to the records of the British Board of Trade and Plantations.
Nothing in customs duties was credited to the books of the Board
of Trade for the two maritime colonies in an account of all the
duties collected under the Molasses Act between 1733 and 1735,

even as of all the northern provinces they were the most dependent on the French sugar islands. Many of New England's most prominent citizens—the Hancocks of Boston, the Trumbulls of Connecticut, and the Browns of Rhode Island—built family fortunes by evading the welter of contradictory British trade laws metastasizing for over a century. In fact, smuggling had become an economic necessity on which depended the welfare not only of shipowners but of farmers and merchants and virtually everyone doing business in colonial America. British government ministers had understood for a century the wisdom of winking at trade laws, but, at exactly the time young Ethan Allen purchased his share in the Salisbury iron forge, the British began tinkering with the trade laws as one inept aristocratic minister after another tried to make sense of the administration of the new British Empire.

While the British triumph over the French ended a century and a half of commercial rivalry between the French and the English and should have brought a massive expansion of trade by English colonists, for many Americans, especially Ethan Allen and his Connecticut frontier neighbors, peace produced a long depression. The abrupt end of British wartime subsidies to colonial governments to pay their militias and the drying up of wartime contracts to feed, house, and transport British armies led to the collapse of colonial economies. Concommitantly, the British Currency Act of 1764 forbade the printing of colonial paper money just as the British were redoubling their efforts to tax American trade to pay for American defense. Thus, the new taxes had to be paid in silver or gold. Consequently, the first serious attempts to regulate American trade and enforce customs duties further shocked the markets in every American colony. In New Jersey, James Parker, erstwhile New York partner of Benjamin Franklin, shortly before issuing a wildly revolutionary blast at Parliament, coolly took the measure of the crisis in a letter to Attorney General Cortlandt Skinner:

> There is such a general scarcity of cash that nothing we
> have will command it and real estates of every kind are
> falling at least one-half in value. Debtors that were a year
> or two ago responsible for £1,000 can not now raise a
> fourth part of the sum. . . . There is an entire stop to all
> sales by the sheriffs for want of buyers, and men of the best
> estates amongst us can scarce raise money enough to defray
> the necessary expenses of their families. . . . Under the
> unsupportable distress we are now called upon for many
> thousands of pounds sterling to be paid by a stamp duty.

Even taxes long paid by the English at home, such as the tax stamp, triggered costly repercussions when Parliament tried to apply them in the colonies. In postwar America, unemployment was high and cash in extremely short supply. One sharp-eyed British visitor wrote home from Connecticut that this colony may have been the most strapped for cash, that he "would not give £800 sterling for the entire province." He had been "all over it"— including Litchfield County—and came away convinced that "they are all mortgaged to the full."[16]

As the postwar depression deepened, announcement of stamp levies set off a round of riots from Boston to Charleston. In Connecticut, antitax rallies and protest meetings in New Haven attracted lawyers and merchants. Jared Ingersoll, the colony's leading lawyer, warned a friend in the Treasury in London that Yankee merchants were unanimously opposed to the new taxes, that there was not a single merchant "with the most Distant intention to pay the Dutys." Ingersoll was ambivalent about the tax. While he protested it, he was, for financial reasons, eager to accept appointment as the colony's distributor of the stamped parchment. In Stratford, Connecticut, the Anglican lawyer William Samuel Johnson, a delegate to the colonial general assembly, gloomily wrote to the Yale professor Ezra Stiles, "From *this* time date the *Slavery* of the *Colonies*." The *Connecticut Gazette*, which Ethan Allen and Thomas Young eagerly read in Salisbury, asked its readers "whether Americans were going to allow themselves to be bondsmen." The *Gazette* ominously printed the names of all of the thirteen colonies' stamp commissioners in British America, branding them "mean, mercenary Hirelings, Parricides among yourselves, who for a little filthy Lucre would at any time betray every Right, Liberty and Privilege of their fellow subjects."[17]

As Royal Navy ships delivered strongboxes of the hated tax stamps to America's Atlantic coast ports all that summer of 1765, crowds brought pressure to bear on the royal establishment. On the evening of August 21, some 750 mounted Sons of Liberty burned Jared Ingersoll in effigy at Norwich Town and again the next day in New London. Officials in every colony and town now feared that mob violence would lead to anarchy. In the Connecticut River valley, away from the coastal towns where merchants, shipowners, and sailors were suffering from the postwar collapse in trade, there was little organized resistance, at first, to the new British taxes. In Salisbury, local civil, militia, and church authorities nervously kept tight control, quashing any flicker of dissent.

ETHAN ALLEN'S FIRST overt act of rebellion had been to defend in print a Puritan heretic, Solomon Palmer. Inoculation, his second and even more public act, took place in front of the Salisbury meetinghouse that symbolized the New England church-state. Carried out before a crowd that included all of Salisbury's leaders, that piece of defiance may have saved his life but did not go unpunished. For years, Allen had endured the Reverend Lee's unctuous ministrations in classroom, parlor, and pulpit. He considered Lee, this self-appointed family chaplain, overbearing and, in this case, just plain backward. When Lee, acting with another selectman, Peter Stoddard, threatened to arrest him, Allen lost his temper. According to Salisbury court records, Allen menaced the selectmen with his bullwhip. The charge of blasphemy entered on the town records alleged that Allen swore at them, a crime in theocratic Connecticut:

> By Jesus Christ, I wish I may be bound down in Hell with old Beelzebub a thousand years in the lowest pit in Hell and that every little insipid devil should come along by and ask the reason of Allen's lying there, if it should be said he made a promise . . . that he would have satisfaction of Lee and Stoddard and did not fulfill it.

In other words, Allen threatened two selectmen and demanded they give him "satisfaction," the unmistakable call to a duel. Lee and Stoddard ignored Allen's challenge and, instead of arresting him for violating the ban on inoculations, arrested him for breach of the peace. The charge was that he had blasphemed by referring to Jesus Christ, Beelzebub, and "every little insipid devil," all in one breath.

In New England since the time of Anne Hutchinson, court-room drama took the place of theater, and even a hearing on a misdemeanor charge filled the courtroom. When Ethan Allen's case came before the magistrates, Salisbury citizens packed the courtroom—the common room in Bushnell's Tavern on the green opposite the Congregational meetinghouse. That a young businessman was challenging the authority of the very symbols of the Salisbury oligarchy by denying the divinity of Christ undoubtedly piqued public interest. As he usually did, Allen acted as his own lawyer. He cleverly argued that he had "uttered the word 'By' at the same time turning his face and eyes upward, making a pause, and with a horsewhip wrote or marked on a rail of the fence and then said, 'This stands for Jesus Christ and add this and that together makes, 'By Jesus Christ.'"

He further argued that "he did not in an absolute sense wish he might be bound down in Hell with Beelzebub" but only if Lee and Stoddard prosecuted him under the law of inoculation, which they had not done. So, Allen contended, he had only implied the oath. It was only an oath on a condition, one that had not been fulfilled. Therefore, he had not breached the king's peace. Allen's casuistic logic brought howls of approval from the crowd and an acquittal from the town selectmen. He had won his case, but he would soon discover that he had lost the respect and patience of many of his neighbors in small-town Salisbury.[18]

ETHAN ALLEN'S NEXT legal altercation in Salisbury stemmed from a dispute over the differences between one town's and another's policy of dealing with the perennial New England problem of runaway pigs. Owners of large herds of the animals argued for their right to a free range even in town: pigs had the right to roam free. The Allens represented the majority point of view, however, consistently voting in town meetings that pigs must be kept properly pent up. Each town had an official hog reeve, often the local tavern keeper, who knew what to do with any unclaimed pork. It was his duty to round up strays to hold in a designated town pound until their owner ransomed them by paying him a fine. Soon after the smallpox inoculation controversy, eight pigs belonging to one of Salisbury's old-line families, the Tousleys, escaped their pen and got into Mary Allen's garden. Ethan and Heman apparently had complained to Samuel Tousley before, but to no avail. This time, the Allen brothers adroitly rounded up the vagrant pigs and confined them in the pigpen of a friend. Instead of simply going to the pen and rescuing his pigs, Tousley complained to Justice of the Peace John Hutchinson, his neighbor on the green, who brought an action against the Allens for failure to confine Tousley's pigs in the legally defined town pound.

The select board, including the Reverend Lee, summoned Allen to court again. Word of the popular Allen's latest legal skirmish flew through litigious Salisbury, packing the town tavern-turned-courthouse. Allen rose and insisted he had indeed provided a proper pound. When plaintiff Tousley insisted it wasn't, Allen's riposte that "one pigpen is as good as another" brought howls of laughter from the audience. But Justice Hutchinson didn't appreciate Allen's indecorous waggishness in such a serious matter. Insisting on upholding the point of law, Hutchinson ordered the Allens to pay damages of ten shillings to Tousley and assessed them five shillings in court costs, in all about a week's wages for a skilled artisan. Allen did not burnish his image among Salisbury's elite when he retaliated against Tousley by demanding immediate payment of a two-pound note owed him by Tousley's brother, John, and then, as was his right, hauled Tousley into court for refusing to pay up. Ethan Allen won this case, but at a cost.[19]

Apparently oblivious to the frost that was forming over his neighbors, Allen continued his public disputes at Bushnell's Tavern and at his forge. Meanwhile, his closest friend, Thomas Young, had by his outspoken deism made himself anathema to the New Light townsfolk. While Dr. Young was considered an excellent physician—his medical techniques would be adopted by the famous Dr. Benjamin Rush in Philadelphia, and Young would one day treat many members of the Continental Congress—there was another doctor in Salisbury with the "correct" theological views. Dr. Young's patients deserted him for the more conservative physician. In short, Salisbury turned against its two iconoclasts, ostracizing them—even though, by removing themselves from the town's church-centered social life, Ethan Allen and Thomas Young had already made themselves personae non gratae.

This did not deter Allen. Young had not only awakened his intellectual curiosity but enchanted him with a vision of the fortune that he could make in land speculation. Allen had already heard from some of Salisbury's leading citizens of a new El Dorado for land speculators about to open up far to the north. Like so many other Americans during this time, the end of the constant threat of French-instigated Indian attacks had led Young to speculate in lands west of the Allegheny Mountains that had opened up for sale and settlement. Allen had never met anyone who could daydream of landed wealth better than Thomas Young. In 1760, Young had invested in a real estate venture promoted by one John Henry Lydius, a shady land dealer who had been expelled from French Canada for violating the royal policy forbidding private land deals with the Indians. From his base at Fort Edward near Lake George, Lydius sold some two hundred square miles of surrounding lands in eastern New York and what is today southern Vermont, from Wood Creek to the Battenkill. Young was only one of numerous would-be landowners fleeced in Lydius's scheme. It was the same Lydius who had illegally negotiated with the Iroquois for Indian lands in the Wyoming Valley of Pennsylvania and had lured Connecticut investors, including Allen's father, to invest in the Susquehannah Company, even though officials had warned would-be pioneers not to depend on Lydius's Indian deeds, because they could not get clear title to the lands. Undeterred, Young regaled his acolyte Allen with dreams of landed wealth beyond the mountains, reawakening in him memories of stories he had heard at his father's knee and from the scouts leading the quick march to Fort William Henry. At the same time, Young blamed the shady land dealings on the royal government officials and owners of the great Hudson and Mohawk River tenant farms, "the great land-jobbers in New York," a pejorative term Allen was hearing for the first time.[20]

Drawing Allen into a tangle of intrigues over land claims that would eventually pull him northward into Vermont, Young rehearsed for him his arguments for a passionate defense of all landholders. By Young's fire in Salisbury, Allen was learning John Locke's *Second Treatise on Government* as paraphrased by Thomas Young in a pamphlet. Young had written that "liberty and property" were "the *Household Gods* of Englishmen," who have "called loudly for our *blood* and *treasure*":

> We, the common people, have freely lavish'd both; we are impoverish'd in war, and now want land to exercise the arts of peace upon, at such rates as we can promise ourselves some recompense to our labours. . . . All we ask, request, and implore, is that we may enjoy our undoubted rights, and not have them so cruelly rent out of our hands. . . .[21]

As Stamp Act protests ignited colonial America, Young was coining ringing revolutionary phrases that would echo through hundreds of speeches and pamphlets. "Our *blood* and *treasure*" invoked the century-long efforts of the American colonists to defeat England's enemy, the French. "Our undoubted rights" would become the watchwords in the Declaration of Independence a dozen years later. "We, the common people" in slightly altered form would become the opening phrase of the Constitution. For Ethan Allen, the stirring rhetoric of Thomas Young would become his new catechism.[22]

SOON AFTER YOUNG published his trumpet blast against New York's oligarchs, he suddenly moved away from Salisbury. His practice dwindling after the smallpox inoculation affair, he decided to return to his native Albany to establish a new practice. Allen would maintain a lifetime friendship with Young. Enthralled by the Stamp Act crisis in 1766, Young would uproot his family again, this time moving to Boston, where he continued on his erratic path to what one Philadelphian called "noisy fame." He served on Massachusetts' revolutionary Committee of Correspondence, the first extralegal step toward intercolonial organization. He was present, a sword in his hand, four years later at the Boston Massacre. He traveled widely, stirring up the spirit of revolt wherever he went, along with the resentment of less charismatic rebels. John Adams called Young "a Firebrand, an Incendiary, an eternal Fisher in Troubled Waters." He considered Young disreputable. "Boston will never be in peace while that fellow lives in it," he harrumphed. "He is a Scourge, a Pestilence, a Judgment." British forces occupying Boston at the time agreed. Two British officers nearly beat Dr. Young to death in a street fight after he delivered the oration commemorating the Boston Massacre on its first anniversary. Then Young was a principal organizer of the Boston Tea Party, where he refused to wear a disguise, making himself a marked man. And Ethan Allen, enchanted by his quixotic friend, followed his movements and, to a great extent, his example.[23]

· · ·

WHETHER IT WAS because of his growing unpopularity with Salisbury's theocracy over his religious views or his cocky public self-defense in court cases, Ethan Allen ran into financial trouble during the postwar depression of 1765. His legal squabbling with neighbors did not make it easier for him to borrow the capital he needed to feed the constant demands of the iron furnace. The drying up of markets for his expensive potash kettles only exacerbated his problems. If Salisbury was tired of Allen, he, too, was exhausted from trying to meet his debts, which, by the autumn of 1765, amounted to an astronomical £1,200.

All up and down the Allegheny frontier that year, as investors like Benjamin Franklin and the Whartons were forming corporations to fund silver- and copper-mining explorations, Allen learned of an opportunity to turn his iron holdings into silver and decided to sell his house and his interest in the iron forge and leave Salisbury. Always a speculator, he preferred the opportunity for great gain over a steady return on cautious investment. Allen was about to learn that so much of success or failure in business is a question of timing and, at this moment, his proved to be terrible. Selling his interest in the iron furnace, he bought a share in what was supposed to be a silver mine: it turned out to yield only lead. He bought mining rights in Woodbury, then hired the New York merchant Sampson Simpson to research other mines that were for sale, settling on a mine in Northampton, Massachusetts, once the home of his grandparents. Ethan and Heman sold their half of the Salisbury furnace for £500. Heman bought a general store with his share and decided to stay in Salisbury. Undoubtedly because the real estate market had collapsed in the postwar recession, Ethan took a beating on the sale of his handsome hilltop house for £272, little more than half what he had paid for it.

After the property settlement and the signing of deeds, Ethan, Heman, and George Caldwell, the purchaser of their

share in the furnace, adjourned to the nearby tavern for a celebra-
tory bowl of punch and the payment of the purchase price. At
this point, Caldwell refused to come up with all of the cash he
had promised Ethan. Technically, since the Allens had already
signed over the deeds to the forge, there was little they could do.
Ethan and Heman now lacked the cash they needed to buy their
shares in their new investment in Woodbury. By that evening,
when Ethan and Caldwell failed to find a peaceful solution, they
were summoned before Justice Hutchinson, charged with fighting. In the words of the official complaint, Ethan Allen

> did in a tumultuous and offensive manner with threaten-
> ing words and angry looks, strip himself even to his naked
> body and with force and arms without law or right, did
> assault and actually strike the person of George Caldwell
> of Salisbury in the presence and to the disturbance of many
> of His Majesty's good subjects.

Whether the townsfolk enjoyed the fisticuffs and the spectacle
of one of its leading citizens stripped to the waist and throwing
punches does not appear on the court record. The record does
show that Justice Hutchinson again fined Ethan Allen, this time
ten shillings.[24]

Immediately after his second conviction, Allen left Salisbury
and rode with a group of his friends down to Woodbury to make
final his plan to buy the lead mine with his new partners, his
brothers-in-law Abraham and Israel Brownson. The partners and
their friends were on their way north again to take possession of
the mine when they passed through Salisbury. In the street, they
encountered Allen's antagonist George Caldwell and a muscular
companion, Robert Branthwaite. They exchanged unpleasantries
and, according to this court complaint, Allen hit Branthwaite and

"soon after in a violent and angry manner stripped off his clothes to his naked body and with a club struck . . . Caldwell on the head."

According to the court record, Branthwaite grabbed the club. Allen hit him, evidently this time landing a solid punch, just as Luke Camp, the town constable, ran up and cited all three men for breach of peace. On the same day, before Allen and his friends could leave Salisbury, however, they again encountered Caldwell and his friends. Whatever Caldwell said to provoke him, according to the court record, Allen this time

> stripped off his clothes to his naked body and in a threatening manner with his fist lifted up, repeated these malicious words three times: "You lie you dog" and also did with a loud voice say that he would spill the blood of any that opposed him.[25]

No one tried to prevent Ethan Allen and his kinsmen from leaving Salisbury, where many of the townspeople were disgusted by his cockiness and apparently natural propensity to fight. But before he could leave town, the constable overtook him and served him with a subpoena to appear before Justice Hutchinson two weeks later. This fourth court action led to Ethan Allen's being "read out" of staid Salisbury. It was an intensely personal judgment. Allen's cousin and former mentor, the Reverend Lee, served on the selectboard that banished him from Salisbury, and the verdict fell heavily on Allen's entire family. Amid the turmoil, Mary, expecting her second child, was permitted to remain with Heman in Salisbury until her husband returned from moving their belongings to a new home in another town and colony. He reappeared in Salisbury in time to appeal this latest conviction to the Litchfield County court on October 28, 1765. Unanimously, the court rejected his appeal. The only concession was that Ethan was allowed to stay with Mary at Heman's until the baby was born. They named the baby Joseph, after his father and, as the beleaguered couple may have intended, after the father of Christ who had, according to their Bible, fled with his wife and infant child from oppression into a strange and foreign land. Then, as December snow packed hard on the road and the Connecticut River froze over, Ethan wrapped Mary and the babies in bear-skin robes for the frigid eighty-mile sleigh ride to Northampton, Massachusetts.[26]

6.

"The Greatest Hassurds
of His Life"

❋

LARGELY WON IN A GLORIOUS YEAR of victories over the French in 1759, the British Empire remained in its infancy as the Allens crossed the Connecticut River by calash in the harsh winter of 1767. England's foreign policy, clumsy and immature, depended on the whim of its ruling class of 125 aristocrats, all amateurs at governance. As if stuck in a revolving door, only 25 of them at any one time took active roles in governing an empire that now extended from the Mississippi River to the Indian Ocean, from the Arctic Circle to the equator. Gliding regally from hearing to hearing in Whitehall Palace half the year, they retreated to their country houses to hunt and feast the rest. The debt-ridden nation's most vigorous citizens made up an unacknowledged middle class, looked down upon by the nobility as mere "men of trade." As a result, one lordly bungler succeeded another in advising King George III on the delicate juggling act of balancing the recurrent crises that plague all nations. Far from familiar with

America's problems or even interested in them at this stage, England seemed permanently distracted by the irksome difficulties of the moment in other equally remote reaches: India, Gibraltar, Canada, the Caribbean. Its foreign service equally unprofessional, each British colony came under the nominal control of a semiretired military officer, courtier, cousin, or other kinsman of someone connected somehow with the court or the House of Lords.

In addition to salaries voted and paid by colonial legislatures, these royal governors received lucrative posts according to the standing at court of his patron. Under the English system of inheritance laws known as primogeniture and entail, only the oldest son could inherit the family estate. Consequently, many of the colonial officials had no other qualification than that they were younger siblings of an aristocrat. They could expect to make up for the accident of birth by collecting emoluments in specie for every marriage license, deed, charter, diploma, or land grant in their colony. In fact, many of this legion of royal placeholders came to America in anticipation of creating landed estates for themselves from Crown grants to vast tracts of land, eventually receiving a propriety right of, on average, 360 acres for every township they created with a mere flourish of the quill. Benning Wentworth, for example, longest serving of all colonial governors in the eighteenth century, luxuriated on the edge of a primeval white pine forest that had yielded him a fifty-two-room mansion in Portsmouth, New Hampshire. Sir William Tryon consoled himself for having to forgo the hunt in his native country by building a palatial Georgian manor house in New Bern with the proceeds of land sales and rents in the North Carolina backcountry. In the majestic turreted redbrick governor's palace at Williamsburg, Lord Botetourt languished through endless rounds of whist with the Tidewater oligarchy of Virginia. By appointing relatives and friends to paid posts on their governors' councils, the royal surrogates built long-lasting, lucrative fiefdoms in some colonies or, appealing to connections at court whenever a plush seat in a wealthier colony became vacant, acquired extensive holdings in several colonies. Thomas Pownall parlayed tenures in New Jersey and Massachusetts into a policymaking sinecure on the Board of Trade and Plantations in London.

With no police forces at their disposal and a thin red line of troops to patrol thousands of miles of borders and coastline, the royal officials in every colony were ill pressed to extend British authority from London. Understandably, when the HMS *Royal Charlotte* arrived in New York harbor in the autumn of 1765, bearing chests of stamps for distribution by the stamp commissioners of neighboring colonies, William Franklin, the illegitimate son of Benjamin Franklin and the last royal governor of New Jersey, refused to allow them to be landed, saying there was no safe place on the colony's entire coast. That colony's stamp commissioner had resigned before the law could take effect, forfeiting a £3,000 bond, when he was refused the rental of a house unless he could guarantee that it would not be pulled to pieces by a mob. To make sure he did not reconsider, the New Brunswick Sons of Liberty escorted him from Perth Amboy to Philadelphia, coercing him into taking an oath not to handle the stamps. With no collector for stamps and no armed place in New Jersey to protect them, Governor Franklin ordered the stamps transferred to the HMS *Sardoine*, anchored in the Arthur Kill off Perth Amboy. The ship's captain protested that he had to put his vessel into drydock for the winter and strip it of its guns. Franklin then appealed to the governor of New York for permission to store the stamp chest at Fort George on the Battery, but New York's governor replied that would be impossible because the fort was filled with troops and supplies: there simply was no room for a small strongbox! Finally, invoking his rank as the captain general and viceroy of New Jersey, Franklin persuaded the *Sardoine*'s captain to take the stamps wherever he planned to conceal his ship's stores for the winter.

During the summer of 1765, a secret organization known as the Sons of Liberty—a term coined by Colonel Barre in a speech against the Stamp Act in the House of Commons—sprang up in provincial towns to organize opposition to the act. Organized and often led, as was the case in New York City, by leading merchants and other men of wealth, the Sons today would probably be regarded by the ruling government as a terrorist organization. They were certainly not opposed to using violence to force Crown stamp agents to resign or to compel Loyalist merchants to cancel their orders for goods. At the same time, the Massachusetts General Assembly proposed an intercolonial meeting to seek repeal of the Stamp Act. In a circular letter dispatched to each colonial assembly, it suggested a congress in New York City that October. Delegates attended from nine of the thirteen colonies. Respectfully claiming all the rights and liberties of the king's subjects, the twenty-seven delegates to the Stamp Act Congress sent to the king, Commons, and Lords a series of fourteen resolutions. They insisted that taxation without consent, expressed personally or through representatives, violated these rights. They asserted that the colonists could not be represented in the House of Commons and, therefore, that no taxes could be constitutionally imposed on them except by their *own* legislatures.

Not waiting for, and probably not expecting, a response from London, New York City's leading citizens signed a nonimportation agreement. They imposed economic sanctions that banned the purchase of any English goods until Parliament repealed the Stamp Act as well as the trade restrictions imposed in 1764. Some 200 merchants in Philadelphia and 250 in Boston followed suit. All business in the American colonies effectively came to a halt on November 1, the day the act took effect. For Ethan Allen and businessmen in frontier towns, any intake of revenue from trade and from buying and selling land ceased. Before year's end, however, business resumed without the stamps, in open violation of the new law. In England, the decline in exports to America from £2.5 million in 1764 to £1.9 million in 1765 spoke louder than any colonial resolutions. English merchants organized to work for repeal, calling on thirty British towns to petition Parliament. The London petition cited the bankruptcies of several major exporters as a result of the diminished American markets.

Summoned to testify at the bar of the House of Commons, agents representing each American colony's legislature, principally Benjamin Franklin of Pennsylvania, emphasized the heavy expenditures voted by colonial assemblies during the French and Indian War. Pennsylvania had appropriated £500,000 and been compensated with only £60,000 from the Crown. There was not enough specie in the thirteen colonies to pay the stamp taxes for a single year. To enforce the tax with the use of troops would bring on a rebellion. Under personal pressure from the king, the bill to repeal the Stamp Act and to roll back duties on sugar and molasses passed the House of Commons by a 275–167 vote. News of the repeal reached New York City on April 26, 1766. Jubilant merchants, immediately abandoning nonimportation, restocked their stores. The New York Assembly commissioned an outsized equestrian statue to honor the king erected on Bowling Green. Amid the jubilation, few Americans noticed that, accompanying the repeal bill, Parliament passed a second bill asserting that it had full authority to make laws binding the colonies "in all cases whatsoever."[1]

BRANDED A HERETIC for his conversion to Anglicanism and a troublemaker after his banishment from Connecticut, Ethan Allen could hardly expect an unqualifiedly warm reception in the orthodox Congregational bastion of Northampton, Massachusetts, even if he and his family were welcomed in the comfortable home of his wealthiest relatives, Thomas and Betty Allen. One of the three emigrant Allen brothers had helped to found Northampton a century earlier, and now the Allens were among its most substantial landowners. But dissenters such as Ethan Allen were never tolerated in straitlaced Northampton. Again and again, religious controversies wracked the town. The earliest witchcraft trial in New England took place in Northampton. More recently, Northampton gave birth to the tumultuous Great Awakening. All through Ethan Allen's childhood, itinerant open-field evangelists disturbed the town's studied surface tranquility. Ethan would hear a great deal about the town's most famous divine, Jonathan Edwards. Ethan's cousin Thomas, the man who now welcomed the shivering Salisbury Allens, had been one of Edwards's staunchest supporters. Edwards had modified his theology somewhat from hell's fire and brimstone to a more moderate evangelical style. He preached a psychological Calvinism that focused on an understanding of the mind's operations, in part derived from his reading of the English philosopher John Locke. Edwards, in this respect following in the footsteps of the Mathers in Boston, incessantly berated his increasingly wealthy congregation, decrying the decadence of the "River Gods," as he termed them, in sermons that would have strongly appealed to Allen. Rejecting what he derisively called the "civilized" ways of New England, he feared that American culture and ideals were in danger of being "assimilated" by those of the corrupt mother country. He inveighed against parental laxity, from the pulpit denouncing the precocious sexual behavior of the sons and daughters of the town's grandees. One Sunday in 1744, he named several young men who had stolen a book on midwifery and, according to several young girls, were joking about its explicit descriptions and diagrams while they called the girls "nasty creatures." Edwards excoriated the boys from the pulpit, denouncing their wayward-ness, their "night frolics and lascivious behavior." Deciding to make an example of them, he read aloud their names from the pulpit, as well as the names of the girls who were witnesses.

That the community resented this public humiliation stunned Edwards. When one boy refused to "worship a wig" and said he cared not a "turd" or a "fart" for the church, Edwards preached even more vehemently about the town's "corruption." Mem-bers of the congregation grew outraged at Edwards and not at their children, and their attendance at Sabbath services fell off even as visitors from other churches filled the pews. After four years, when no new members sought admission to communion at First Church, one finally stepped forward, only to have Edwards refuse him. The Hampshire County consocation of Congrega-tional ministers voted to restrict his preaching, barring him from expressing his views from the pulpit and allowing him to speak only at a Thursday meeting. But Edwards refused to be silenced. As he became a world-famous theologian, and probably because of it, he was considered in Northampton nothing more than a com-mon scold. Finally, the majority of his congregation voted to fire him. For five years, Edwards was allowed to linger in the parson-age, the whole time writing the theological masterpieces that made him America's leading theologian. Finally, impoverished, Edwards became a missionary to the Stockbridge Indians, living among them for seven years in the wilderness. When his son-in-law, the Reverend Aaron Burr, founder of the College of New Jersey, died, Edwards accepted the call to become its president. Edwards's well-publicized dismissal from Northampton should have warned Allen to tiptoe into town. But caution was never his style.[2]

• • •

ETHAN AND MARY ALLEN and their children, four-year-old Loraine and the infant Joseph, found a warm welcome from Betty Allen, Thomas's wife, who would become Mary's midwife. In fact, it had been the theft of one of Betty's books on midwifery that led to Jonathan Edwards's firing. Ethan's kin warned him that it was unwise to incur the wrath of the River Gods, the score or so of influential families that had grown rich on fur trading with the Indians. That Thomas had urged Ethan to come to Northampton only a few years after publicly defending Edwards further increased the odds against Ethan's acceptance by Northampton's tight-knit society. Undoubtedly, Thomas and Betty Allen's enemies noticed Ethan's arrival. Ethan's notoriety for his confrontations with church and magistrate now spread from Connecticut to Massachusetts.

IF ETHAN COULD sidestep the religious fault lines in the town, he could hope to emerge from the darkest period of his life. From all outward appearances, he was joining the most prosperous branch of the Allen clan. Some of the town elders certainly remembered that Ethan's grandfather Samuel had inherited a fine farm in Northampton. As locals knew, when Ethan's grandmother Mercy Wright Allen had sold her Northampton land and moved to Litchfield, Connecticut, it was Ethan's great-uncle Joseph who had purchased the land and added it to his already prosperous estate. Now Joseph's son Thomas greeted Ethan and his family and spread the mantle of his wealth and social standing over them. Cousin Thomas now hoped to win Ethan over to his own born-again New Light views: his son Thomas had been ordained a New Light parson who married Elizabeth Lee, the daughter of Ethan's old schoolmaster (and more recent nemesis), the Reverend Lee of Salisbury. Thomas Allen must have known that it was his son's father-in-law who had driven Ethan and his family out of Connecticut. To escape the inevitably close-knit network of Puritan families, Ethan found, would be virtually impossible anywhere in New England. By the same token, the vaunted status of Ethan's family provided him with access to Northampton's closed, church-based society, which was indistinguishable from its commercial aristocracy.

Hired as the manager of his brother-in-law Israel Brownson's lead mine, Ethan Allen received Brownson's assurance that he would be paid a comfortable salary. Allen's new job was to supervise the miners and to procure and transport the iron ore, gunpowder, and steel needed for blasting and shoring up an excavation some fifty feet deep, then build pumps and a waterwheel to keep the ore pit drained. Allen also had to keep the records of materials and miners' hours. When his pay did not materialize, he found it necessary to rent out a room in his own rented house to one of the miners. Mary Allen decided to augment the family's meager cash by taking in boarders. Yet the Allens' penurious state did not keep Ethan from feeling he had to dress the part of a rising young gentleman. He always bought the best clothes he could find—or at least wore them. He quickly ran up a tab with a local merchant. This led to his first appearance in the Hampshire County court. Litigious New England now had more lawyers and judges than cash, and most disputes over money, even the pettiest amounts, wound up in court. This time, the litigant was the merchant Jonathan Warner, suing Ethan to collect £12 18s for purchases that included a fancy beaver hat, an accoutrement that was to become an Ethan Allen trademark. To his intense embarrassment, though, the lawsuit made it quite obvious to his new neighbors that the Connecticut transplant was still strapped for cash.

Allen had taken a risky plunge, investing in a lead mine in a quest for silver, only to find out that his plan was chimerical.

Silver and copper are often found side by side with lead, but not always. For nearly a century, speculators had gambled on finding mineral wealth in an ever-expanding pit outside Northampton. Once again, the mine proved to be a sinkhole, this time for the fortunes of two linked families, the Allens and the Brownsons. It hadn't taken long for Israel Brownson to fall behind in paying Allen's salary. While Israel and Abraham Brownson still lived on the income of the family gristmill in Woodbury, Connecticut, a seemingly safe distance away, they came from time to time to Northampton to visit their sister—or, more likely, their investment. After one such sojourn, Israel Brownson left a trunk behind. By the time he made a return visit the next spring, things had gone so badly at the mine that he still owed Allen his salary for a whole year. As if to give himself a token payment, Allen had opened the trunk and tried to sell some of Brownson's clothes to Mary's boarder. But the workman balked at the price. Nobody had any cash, not even for used clothing.

ON THE CHILL, moonless night of October 31, 1765, British soldiers with fixed bayonets manned the ramparts of Fort George on the Battery in New York City. The next day, the Stamp Act was to take effect. Warned of massive protests by the newly organized Sons of Liberty, General Gage, commander of all British forces in America, had given the order not to shoot. The soldiers' mission was to protect New York's seventy-seven-year-old acting royal governor, Cadwallader Colden, and a small wooden chest of the hated stamped paper. Colden found himself under siege inside Fort George. Shortly after midnight, the sentinels could see two columns of torches in the distance. The Sons, led by lawyers, ship captains, and master craftsmen, had split into two columns. One, mostly sailors, marched to the Commons, erected a gallows, and hoisted up an effigy of Colden, in one hand clutching stamped paper and a boot that symbolized the unpopular Earl of Bute (King George's favorite), in the other, a drum: Colden was a drummer boy in the rising of 1715. The second column broke into Colden's stables and dragged his carriage and two sleighs to Bowling Green. Tearing down its fence, they set afire the carriage and sleighs and threw in the effigies. Some two thousand cheering protesters paraded down Broadway to the fort, bombarding it with stones as they dared the Redcoats to open fire. A letter passed through the gate warned Colden that if he tried to enforce the act, "you'll die a Martyr to your own Villainy, and be Hang'd like Porteis, upon a Signpost, as a Momento to all wicked Governors, and that every Man, that assists you, Shall be, Surely, put to Death." Finally marching back uptown, the rioters torched a warehouse and ransacked the home of Major Thomas James, the fort's commander, destroying "Looking Glasses Mehogany Tables Silk Curtains a Libiry of Books all the China and furniture." That was their response to James's threat to "cram the Stamps down their Throats with the End of [his] Sword."[3]

A few days later, a new royal governor, Sir Henry Moore, arrived in New York from England, where he had received a baronetcy for suppressing a sustained slave insurrection in his native Jamaica, his last posting. Moore wanted to enforce the new tax but found his terrified executive council unanimously opposing him. Attempting conciliation, Moore refused to issue the stamps for most public business, ordering them affixed only to ship's documents and court records. Considering the fort as an irritant, he ordered it dismantled. His predecessor, Colden, wrote of his disgust at what he considered Moore's pusillanimity: "He has yielded everything in order to quiet the minds of the people and, notwithstanding of this, riots and mobs have continued frequent and are as much insulting on government as ever."[4]

By December, as the protests continued to make it uncomfortable outside his headquarters in New York City, General Thomas Gage sent a note to Sir Henry demanding that the New York Assembly provide funds for quartering and supplying his troops under the provisions of the Quartering Act, usually invoked only in wartime. From its chamber on Broadway, the assembly responded that the act imposed an undue burden on New York because Gage kept his headquarters there, and the assembly refused to comply. Throughout the spring and summer of 1766, tensions continued to mount. When the Sons of Liberty erected a Liberty Pole, British soldiers quickly cut it down. On August 10, the Sons of Liberty, led by the former privateer Isaac Sears, fought bayonet-wielding Redcoats in what became known as the Battle of Golden Hill. The most serious confrontation between the radicals and the British to date left Sears himself among the wounded.

When the assembly reconvened in December in its chambers in City Hall, it refused to vote any appropriation for Gage's forces. Moore could have dissolved it, but decided there was no point, since the same members would obviously be reelected to a new assembly. Responding to Moore's conciliation, the assembly finally agreed to provide Gage with a modest £3,000. Because of the weeks required to send and receive answers to transatlantic communications, Parliament, however, learning only that the assembly had refused Moore's initial request for funds, suspended New York's legislative powers because of its violation of the Quartering Act. It would be a full year, in May of 1768, before the Board of Trade learned of the assembly's retreat and restored New York's government.

One of Moore's assignments was to carry out London's commission to settle permanent boundaries for New York. He would succeed with its borders with Massachusetts and Quebec Province. Just which province controlled the territory between Lake

Champlain and the Connecticut River, present-day Vermont, stymied Moore. A year before Moore's arrival, King George III personally had presided over the nine members of his council at the Court of St. James in London as they issued an "order in council fixing the boundary between New York and New Hampshire." Acting on a report from the Board of Trade and Plantations "relative to the Disputes that have some years Subsisted" between the two colonies, the king-in-council voted unanimously to "hereby Order and Declare the Western Banks of the River Connecticut, from where it enters the Province of Massachusetts Bay, as far North as the forty fifth Degree of Northern Latitude, to be the Boundary Line between the said two Provinces of New Hampshire and New York."[5]

Before the king's proclamation could reach New York, Henry Schuyler, the sheriff of Albany County, had dispatched an express rider to Fort George to report,

> The New Hampshire people [have] turned Hans Jurry Creiger, an Inhabitant under the proprietors of Hoseck Patent, out of Possession of his Lands and Tenements; drove off his Cattle and took off with them a Parcel of Indian Corn, and for the Redemption of his Cattle compelled him to pay forty five Dollars. . . . The said New Hampshire People were the next Day to be at the Houses of Peter Voss, and Bastiane Deale . . . in like manner to dispossess [of farms] which they had peaceably enjoy'd under the Proprietors of said Hoseck Patent for upwards of thirty years past except only, when driven off by the Enemy Indians. . . .

A few days later, Sheriff Schuyler reported, he formed a posse of thirty armed men on horseback and pursued the New Hampshire raiders—who turned out to be a deputy sheriff, a justice of the peace, and two other "pretended owners of the Lands"—and dragged them off to the Albany jail, where he was holding them until he received instructions from the provincial government.[6]

Before Schuyler received an answer, Governor Benning Wentworth of New Hampshire wrote to protest that Schuyler had jailed the "Principal Inhabitants" of the town of Pownal, five miles north of the Massachusetts line. "It would be an act of cruelty to Punish Individuals for disputes between the two Governments," wrote Wentworth. The lands in question, he averred, were "within the undoubted jurisdiction of this province," New Hampshire. Neither governor had yet received the latest decree from London, but when it arrived, New York's governor, consulting his own councillors, ruled that the officials of Pownal had acted within their legal rights because they were "actually settled" under grants from New Hampshire before the May 22, 1764, order-in-council. Asserting New York jurisdiction, he ordered that no New Hampshire grantee be dispossessed, because it would be "ruinous to themselves and their Families."[7] In a dispute that escalated into a ten-year border war that ended only with Ethan Allen's leading the Green Mountain Boys, eighty-nine landowners in the region that had come to be called the New Hampshire Grants, in their attack on Fort Ticonderoga, in effect the moment of conception of a new state, to be called Vermont.

THE AMERICAN ECONOMY still staggered in the undertow of a long recession in January 1767, when a new administration came to power in London, the fourth in five years. Parliament, defying the ministry, cut taxes on its own landed estates, creating a £500,000 budgetary shortfall. The new chancellor of the Exchequer, Charles Townshend, decided to close the gap by imposing new American customs duties on glass, lead, paints, paper, and tea. The expected revenues would pay for the defense of the colonies but could also be used to "defray the charge of the administration of justice and the support of the civil government." To collect the new duties, in a companion bill Parliament affirmed the power of colonial supreme court justices to issue writs of assistance that allowed search and seizure of contraband goods in America, established admiralty courts to try smuggling cases, and set up an American Board of Commissioners of Customs reporting directly to the British Treasury.

In Boston, the town meeting responded to what it considered the latest onslaught on American privileges. Objecting that the new admiralty courts would deprive Americans of their ancient right to a trial by a local jury of their peers and convinced that, under the new law, American smugglers would be sent to England for trial, the Boston town meeting voted to reimpose sanctions on British imports, chiefly luxury goods. Nonimportation agreements followed in Providence and Newport. In New York City, a mass meeting appointed a committee to promote domestic industry. In western Massachusetts, the Townshend duties effectively killed one industry in particular: lead mining. The new law made the Brownsons' open pit mine in Northampton a worthless hole in the ground and left Ethan Allen without a job.

MONTHS WOULD PASS before the damage wrought by the Townshend duties penetrated the American interior. In seaport towns along the New England coast, however, where the smuggling of goods from French and Dutch colonies in the Caribbean thrived, the interposition of customs officials reporting to London combined with mounting pressure from impatient creditors in England to shatter the surface calm that had greeted repeal of the Stamp Act. Few Americans felt the British crackdown more directly than the New Haven merchant Benedict Arnold. According to an account he himself wrote and published in the *Connecticut Gazette*, when Arnold, who imported luxury goods to sell in his pharmacy, returned with a cargo of contraband, a disgruntled crewman, Peter Boles, who knew that the cargo in the hold of the *Fortune* was illegal, tried to blackmail him. Rebuffed, the crewman went to the New Haven customshouse to inform in return for the standard British offer of a percentage of the seized goods and prize money when Arnold's ship was sold at auction. Unfortunately, it was the Sabbath, and the staunchly Puritan customs collector had the day off. In small-town New Haven, a sailor going into the customshouse on the Sabbath was noticed.

When Arnold learned of the crewman's visit, he roared off to the tavern where he knew his crew gathered. When he told Boles's shipmates he was trying to inform on them, they found Boles in another tavern and "gave him a little chastisement"—beat him up—and warned him to leave town. Three days later, Boles returned and went to the house of a business rival of Arnold's. That night, Arnold and several crewmen found Boles and forced him to sign a document Arnold had prepared, swearing that he would "never hereafter make information, directly or indirectly, or cause the same to be done, against any person or persons whatever, for importing contraband or other goods into this colony." Boles further swore that he would leave New Haven and never return. But he did not leave.

Shortly before midnight, Arnold woke up to hear shouting in the street. A sailor had discovered Boles. As the town awoke, a large crowd hurried toward the gallows beside the courthouse. "I then made myself one of the party," Arnold wrote, "that took him to the whipping post." There they tied up Boles and, in the January cold, ripped off his shirt and bared his back. While Arnold and many other members of New Haven's Sons of Liberty looked on, one of the *Fortune*'s crewmen used a short piece of rope to lash Peter Boles "near forty times." Escorted out of town, probably astraddle a split rail, Boles never returned.[8]

In Ethan Allen's serene moments in Northampton, as usual, he passed the time reading and writing and arguing at a tavern near the Brownsons' mine. His cousin Thomas still hoped to reform Allen and win him over to New Light theology. He lent Allen printed versions of Jonathan Edwards's sermons. Ever an optimist, Ethan read them. He became intrigued by Edwards's fusion of rational scientific inquiry with old-fashioned Puritan orthodoxy, yet he was shocked by Edwards's gloomy, pessimistic spiritual landscape, his portrayal of the smug saints gleefully watching the hellfire torments of those they believed to be the damned, including infants unfortunate enough to have been born on the wrong side of the doctrine of predestination. Allen's reaction to reading Edwards's "damned, damned, damned" rhetoric was to go around Northampton mocking it. Disgusted with the pietistic grip of the clergy on their flocks, he tried deliberately to shock his touchy new neighbors.

In the summer of 1767, Allen's public use of profane language—and no record exists of just what he said—drew frequent visits to the lead mine by the Reverend Jonathan Judd, Northampton's incumbent Congregationalist divine. Judd chastised Allen in front of his men for profanity and telling rude jokes to his miners. When Allen refused to be silenced, the town's selectmen summoned him. It was all too much for the town's leaders to see one of the communion of Puritan saints sinking to the level of crude storytelling with the unsaintly mine workers. In a replay of his ouster from Salisbury, this time after only a single altercation, Allen was "read out" of Northampton by the select board. By refusing to adhere to Northampton's puritanical code of conduct, and by insisting on his right to speak freely to people on all social levels, he had made it easy for the Puritan magistrates of Northampton to persecute him, to banish him and, by extension, his wife and children. Mary Allen's feelings as she again packed up her two small children's belongings are not recorded.

The entire interlude in Northampton of little more than a year was a humiliating failure. There was no silver lining to the vast hole in the ground that Allen and his penniless miners had dug. Nobody wanted to buy the lead they had extracted, and *nobody* had any money. Mary's brothers never did pay Ethan his salary for that entire year and he wound up suing his brothers-in-law, but won nothing. The family quarrel became fairly ugly and quite public when, on Ethan and Mary's way out of town, the Brownsons countersued Ethan for the trunk full of old clothes and some borrowed furniture that Ethan had refused to relinquish until they paid him his back wages. Ethan Allen left Northampton—and Massachusetts. Under a law passed in 1750, he could remain only in Northampton, or any Massachusetts town, by "honest conversation." The code of 1750, enacted in the backlash of itinerant evangelical preaching during the Great Awakening, declared that "persons of ungoverned conversation" who "thrust themselves into the towns in this colony" could not be admitted to the town or remain in it. The law further stated that strangers could not abide in any town without the consent of the selectmen or the major part of the town. Anyone who was warned out of town was liable to a fine of ten shillings a week (a skilled artisan's entire pay) or a whipping of ten stripes if he did not leave. Allen and his family left Northampton and never returned.

• • •

NEARING HIS THIRTIETH BIRTHDAY, ostracized by towns in two colonies, by July of 1767 Allen was ready to hitch up the family oxcart and move again, this time, of necessity and to his intense embarrassment, back to Salisbury. With the help of young friends from the mine and the tavern, he loaded the family furniture and hoisted the heavy portmanteau of Mary's deadbeat brother, Israel, up onto the oxcart. Fond of invoking pregnant Old Testament references that Ethan recognized, Mary proclaimed that the chest belonged "to Israel and to Abraham." This was how she saw Ethan, like an Abraham of the Old Testament, always at the head of his clan in search of the promised land. With a snap of Ethan's bullwhip, for the second time in three generations, Allens were leaving Northampton to start over again. Returning to Salisbury pained Ethan, even if his kindly younger brother Heman offered to take them in. Heman had every reason to shake his head. In only three years, Ethan had shouldered his way to the front rank of Salisbury businessmen as manager, builder, and partner in the successful Forbes and Allen iron furnace. Mary Allen had presided over one of the best houses in town, where she had received Dr. Young, the Reverend Lee, and people of stature like Colonel Thomas Chittenden, the head of Litchfield County's militia, as well as Ethan's business partners and clients. The forge still blasted on and would remain a success for many years before being taken over by the new state of Connecticut to produce Revolutionary War cannon. Now, however, its hissing blasts seemed only to mock Ethan, who had no home of his own, no business, no job. Heman, always generous, gave them rent-free quarters above his thriving general store. He tried to persuade Ethan to come into the business as a full partner, but Ethan declined. He could not stand the prospect of his life as a storekeeper, especially in Salisbury, where so much had gone wrong. Besides, he had in mind other ways in which the Allen brothers could cooperate.

• • •

ALL THAT LATE summer and autumn of 1767, as Allen untangled his business and legal affairs, he turned his mind to the north, to the so-called New Hampshire Grants. Connecticut's frontier had vanished, its forests reduced to houses, barns, and potash. To the north, on the Grants, in the wake of the French withdrawal, hundreds of thousands of forest acres suddenly had opened to land speculators and settlers, the rich and the poor. More and more cash-strapped New Englanders like Ethan Allen, their debts piling up and their crops withering, thought of starting over again on New England's last backcountry frontier. There, Allen had heard, a farmer could purchase a few hundred acres of land cheaply from absentee speculators who were busy buying up and subdividing the wilderness. His favorite cousin, Remember Baker, had already moved north to the tiny settlement of Pownal, just north of the Massachusetts line, and become the only paid official in the new town, the town clerk. Relatives of other Salisbury folk whom Allen respected, including his neighbors, Colonel Chittenden's cousins, the Evartses, had moved a little farther up the Connecticut River to found Windsor (in southeastern Vermont), where they opened a tavern, traded furs, and harvested the tall trees around them. Mary Allen's deadbeat brothers had joined other Connecticut expatriates—defaulted on their debts, they were fleeing into the lawless north woods.

For Ethan Allen, the prospect of an ambitious new venture, no matter the risk, always drew him on, this time to the Green Mountains, to the eastern shore of Lake Champlain. That winter of 1767, remembering the legend told him by his grandmother, the financial advice of his father, and the daydreams of his best friend, Thomas Young, Allen decided to explore the new territory, to take several months to search out its best land. He arranged for Mary, the children, and his mother to stay with Heman while he went north alone. His plan was to trap for furs and hunt deer and, in the spring, bring back hides and pelts that his youngest brother, Ira, could cure in a tannery the family had purchased to prepare leather goods and furs for Heman to sell in his general store.

Even before the first snow carpeted the ground, Allen struck out with a party of pioneers, his snowshoes strapped over one shoulder, his musket over the other. Heading due north, he could see, from the peak of the 2,748-foot Dome, before him, the parallel ridges of the Valley of Vermont, their flanks clad in dark-limbed hardwoods crusted with snow. On snowshoes, he followed the Battenkill into the small settlement of Pownal, to the cabin of the hard-swearing, freckle-faced Remember Baker, the first of the Allen clan to move to the new northern frontier. Baker had lived in Pownal for four years, having arrived immediately after the French ceded the territory at the Treaty of Paris of 1763. Together, all day, every day for the next few weeks, Allen and Baker snowshoed into the woods to track moose and deer.

After learning his bearings, Allen preferred to hunt alone. Dressed in buckskin breeches, tunic, and fur hunting jacket, he used the skill at hunting he had acquired as a boy from his father and, since then, from the Mohawks. He followed the clues of freshly browsed branches at the animals' neck-craning height, the fresh oval depressions of deer resting in the snow, the trails of their feces, dark blemishes against brilliant white powder. Sometimes he came upon whole herds of deer grazing in the moonlight. The sight left him spellbound, but he would not hunt the deer until dawn. After the day's hunt, he feasted on Johnny Cake—cornbread he mixed with water he had melted from snow and then roasted on a hot rock—with salt pork and slabs of defrosted venison. He slept, head to the smoldering embers of the cook fire, wrapped in a bearskin, Indian style, if he was lucky in an abandoned beaver trapper's hut or under a crude lean-to of spruce boughs.

Allen was already acquiring a reputation as an expert woodsman, famous marksman, and prodigious hunter. His brother Ira remembered,

> One day in Poultney he Came a Crost a Company of dear Killed one which he Dressed. [He] hung up the Skin & meet then to Preserve that from the Ravens Hung his Hatt by it & went on. [H]e soon Killed an other Dear. [W]ith that [deer] he Left a Short Hunting Jaceout & soon Killed an other dear with that Left his Frock & went on & Killed an other with that Left his Breches Then he persu'd the Dear & Killed an other took the Skin about him & wen to his Camp—

Ira Allen, like most people in America's frontier, knew the risks of hunting alone in the winter woods. He recounted that "An other Time," later that fall, when Ethan was exhausted and after it had rained "in the after part of the day," Ethan did not have "a Dry thread about him," got bewildered and "Lay out all night." As "the weather Cleared off Extreamly Cold it was out of his Power to make any fire." Ethan's clothes began to freeze. He "Knew not what course to take." There was "An Extensive wilderness on one side."

Ethan, who often hunted with the Indians, had learned from his Indian friends what to do in this predicament to avoid becoming fatally lost. He marked out "a Path in a Circle." By walking in a circle, he could keep himself awake "by Going Round not Daring to Sit down Lest he Should fall a Sleep & Perrish." Ethan's ordeal that night, Ira "often heard him say was amongst the Greatest hassurds of his Life," requiring his "Greatest Exertions both of body & Mind to preserve life till day." Ethan traveled all day without eating, numb with cold and sleepy. When he "Repeatedly fell in the Snow," he sprang to his feet, a few minutes later falling again. Daylight revived him. After "Traveling a Short time," he "came fully to his senses." His clothes were frozen. Before noon, "he Reached a house where he Got some Refreshment."[9]

IN THE SPRING of 1768, Allen's first winter in the wilderness ended after the torrents of snowmelt subsided. His canoe sagging under bundles of pelts and furs, he paddled east along the Winooski River, followed streams and ponds through the four ridges of the Green Mountains, then glided down the Connecticut River. As he passed through Northampton in March of 1768, he encountered the merchant Jonathan Warner. Allen still owed him, and so did the Brownsons. Warner reminded Allen he still owed him for his beaver hat. Always able to bargain, Allen struck a deal with Warner, who released him from his debt and, in exchange, gave him his power of attorney to act as Warner's lawyer in Northampton so that Allen could collect the money the Brownsons owed Warner. So Allen was paying for his hat by suing his brothers-in-law, who hadn't paid Allen's wages. When he reached Salisbury, Allen went to court and attached Israel Brownson's farm in Woodbury for his back pay. He also sued Israel's younger brothers, Stephen and Elijah, for trespass. In the increasingly bitter family feud, Israel had sent his younger brothers to seize his trunk. Mary had driven off her brothers with an ax.

WHEN HE RETURNED to Connecticut, Ethan Allen enthralled his family and friends with his descriptions of the new promised land, its pristine beauty and rich natural resources. From the slowly rising eastern shore of Lake Champlain to the peaks of the Green Mountains, he recounted, he had traversed hardwood forests broken only by natural meadows and swamps cleared by beavers. Allen had rarely walked or snowshoed in the sun, his travels shaded by birch and chestnut, oak, elm and hickory, butternut and tall maple, hemlock, spruce and pine. Other travelers confirmed his descriptions. In his diary, the Reverend Timothy Dwight noted immense maple trees, some 120 feet tall. The future Vermont lay at the western edge of a vast white pine belt that extended five hundred miles from Nova Scotia to Lake Champlain and on southward into New Jersey and west as far as Minnesota. "These great trees measured six feet in diameter and frequently rose two hundred and fifty feet in the air," Dwight reported. "A gentleman told me that he had seen one which measured two hundred and sixty-four feet in height." A typical white pine, he added, had a "stem throughout a great part of its height which is usually exactly straight and elegantly tapering. . . . The [boughs] are finely formed and a beautiful green." Allen might have agreed with Dwight that the "sound of the wind in a grove of white pines" was like "the distant roar of the ocean."[10]

Allen became particularly enamored of a thirty-mile swath of forest flanking the Winooski River between present-day Burlington and Bolton. He found stands of lofty white pines blanketing this valley. Above him, in the breaks between the tall pines, he could see eagles soaring. In the woods, he hunted deer, moose, and bear. He startled ruffed grouse and wild turkey. The mountains sheltered lynx, black bear, packs of coyotes and wolves, and large and dangerous catamounts. Along the streams and around the ponds, Allen could trap muskrats, mink, otter, and beaver.

He hauled in, he wrote to his brother Ira, thirty-pound trout in Lester Lake. About April 25, before he headed south, he saw salmon weighing thirty to forty pounds leaping up over the falls of the Winooski on their suicidal spawning mission. As he paddled down the Connecticut River, he sliced through a splashing torrent of shad and salmon, the shad run so abundant that the fish sold two for a penny in Northampton.

Everywhere Ethan Allen went in his solitary exploration in this rich wilderness, he found tumbling hills interspersed with narrow valleys channeling fast rivers and roiling brooks. The mountains that he first saw as barriers stretching out in chains north to south he soon learned from his cousin Remember were cut by notches that made traveling easier from Lake Champlain to the interior valleys. The rivers, mostly narrow but fast, swelled, flooded, and overspilled their banks each spring, enriching the soil along wide riverbanks. Only the Winooski, rising in the east near the Connecticut and surging into Lake Champlain to the west, offered a challenge to such a skilled canoeist, especially where it crowded between the two highest mountains, Mount Mansfield and Camel's Hump. But the ascent between the lake and Montpelier in the mountains was a gradual five hundred feet. It would be possible to penetrate these mountains with oxcart and livestock.

WHILE AWAITING COLD weather for his second season of hunting and exploration, Allen passed his summer days and nights in brother Heman's house, joyfully writing. Years later, Heman's widow told Zadock Thompson, Vermont's first historian,

> that one summer when he was residing in her house he passed almost all the time in writing. She did not know what was the subject of his study, but on one occasion she called him to dinner, and he said he was very sorry she had called him so soon, for he had "got clear up into the upper regions."[11]

He also alternately sued creditors and defended himself in Hampshire County court. Yet Allen finally drew a line he would not cross in the legal tug-of-war. In June of 1768, when he returned to Northampton to procure sworn affidavits, he was impatient to settle the affair and get on with his plans. The two cases were scheduled for the November 1768 and January 1769 county court sessions. But, as the air chilled, Allen itched to head north and continue his explorations. He wrote instructions for Heman on how to handle the cases and hired a lawyer to argue them once they came up in court. Heman knew that Ethan was the more skilled negotiator, and he was relieved when his brother insisted that he not settle the lawyer's bill until he returned. If Heman won the suit against his brother-in-law, he was to wait to enforce judgment until Ethan returned in the spring. Ethan would not go so far as to put his brother-in-law into debtor's prison. "Take not his body," Ethan wrote Heman. The thought of confinement of any kind, especially in prison, repelled him. Before the case could come to court, Israel Brownson packed up his belongings, all but the offending trunk, and moved north to the New Hampshire Grants.[12]

For three winters, from 1767 through 1770, except for summers in Salisbury with Mary and the children (another daughter, Lucy Caroline, was born in 1768), Ethan Allen hunted, explored, and memorized the forests, rivers, mountains, and lake shorelines of the New Hampshire Grants. He worked out a set route, a rotation, with stopovers at the homes of friends and relatives who had already moved onto the Grants. First, Remember Baker's cabin in Pownal, then north to the Catamount Tavern in Bennington, then up the Mettowee River to Otter Creek and on to Lake Champlain, gliding on the current to Paul Moore's tavern in Shoreham, opposite Fort Ticonderoga, and then on to McIntosh's Tavern in New Haven. Following the shoreline to the Winooski River, portaging around its falls, he crossed the gradually sloping Green Mountains, following passes, streams, and ponds into the Connecticut Valley. To all appearances, he had lost his way in more senses than one, but, actually, he was waiting for the right moment to launch another business venture. With his brothers Heman and Ira and his cousin Remember Baker, Ethan Allen the hunter and fur trapper had been accumulating cash that they were eager to invest in the richest land Ethan Allen had ever coveted.

FOR MORE THAN a century and a half after the French explorer Samuel de Champlain, in 1609, had modestly named a lake after himself, the shores of 116-mile-long Lake Champlain, rimmed by receding ranges of Adirondack Mountains to the west and waves of Green Mountains to the east, had been a virtual no-Englishman's-land. For centuries the region was the hunting preserve first of the Abenakis and then of their mortal rivals, the Mohawks, members of the powerful Six Nations Iroquois confederacy. Rival Algonquins in Canada to the north entered at their peril. The Mohawks hunted, trapped, and fished from summer encampments around the lake, most of them returning after the fall hunt to their home villages in present-day New York. The lake region would become legendary for its beauty, abundant wildlife, and profusion of colorful trees.

The first white men to visit the mountainous region between Lake Champlain in the west and the Connecticut River in the east now called Vermont were the French explorer and founder of Quebec, Champlain, and two of his lieutenants. In June of 1609, Champlain, two aides, and sixty Algonquins paddled south along the Richelieu River, known then as the River of the Iroquois, and out onto the broad island-strewn lake that Champlain, as was his prerogative by European standards, would name after himself.

Later that same summer, Henry Hudson sailed the *Half Moon* up the river that took on his name to Albany, where instead of shooting an Iroquois delegation, he poured them Dutch gin and claimed the river, and its fur trade, for his masters in Amsterdam.

Back in his atelier in the basement of the Louvre in Paris a few years later, Champlain, who had mapped North America from Labrador to Mexico, wrote that there was "no place more beautiful that [he had] ever seen" than his lake. He noted that, even in midsummer, the tops of the Green Mountains were white-capped with snow. One of them, now called Camel's Hump, the French christened *Le Lion Couchant*, the sleeping lion.

At the future site of the fortress that Ethan Allen would one day attack, Champlain and his Algonquin war party on July 30, 1609, battled a Mohawk force three times their number. Sheltered behind a screen of warriors, his two marksmen concealed behind trees, Champlain loaded four one-ounce lead balls the size of grapes into his wheel lock *arquebuse à rouet*. Advancing toward two hundred Mohawks wearing wooden armor, Champlain stayed hidden behind his Algonquin allies until the Mohawks marched to within thirty yards. Then, as his allies parted into two columns, Champlain strode forward and, armored legs spread wide to steady his short-barreled, shoulder-fired weapon, fired once, killing three Mohawk chieftains with a single shot. As he reloaded, clouds of arrows flew from both sides. At the edge of the forest, two veteran arquebusiers he had hidden in the trees, kneeling side by side, fired into the Mohawks' flank. The Mohawks broke and ran as Champlain led a charge against them: "I pursued them and laid low still more of them."[13]

The victory by the three Frenchmen and three score Huron warriors that day touched the match to exactly a century and a half of sporadic warfare between the Iroquois and their European allies—first the Dutch, then the English—and the Huron nations and their newfound French partners. By 1660, the French were building forts and towns and planting settlements steadily southward along Lake Champlain's eastern shore. Until the out-numbered French destroyed their own forts and retreated to Canada in the last French and Indian War and finally surrendered to the British, the region that would one day become Vermont was too dangerous for even the hardiest of English colonists like Ethan Allen to explore safely.

During the four European imperial wars that spilled over onto the New England frontier, Algonquins, principally the St. Francis Abenakis, raided south along Lake Champlain from their home base in Quebec, racing east along the Winooski (a transliteration of their word for wild leek), then south along the Connecticut River to strike at English settlements in western Massachusetts and Litchfield County, Connecticut. As the commander of the Litchfield County militia, Colonel Thomas Chittenden, Allen's friend and neighbor in Salisbury, got his first glimpse of Vermont's lush river valleys as he pursued Abenaki warriors and hostages they had taken in a raid.

Camping one night at a bend of the Winooski River, Chittenden could see Mount Mansfield looming to his left and Camel's Hump to his right. He told neighbors when he got home of the stunning beauty and natural richness of the Winooski country. Like an Old Testament patriarch, he proclaimed that one day he would return with his clan and make this their home. "It was a paradise," he wrote. "If the time comes that I can get a title, this upland and intervale shall be mine. Here will I build my home and my sons shall be settled around me." Allen heard such tantalizing descriptions again and again from troops who, like Chittenden, had passed through during the war. After the defeated French ceded Canada, a land rush into the vacant wilderness was inevitable. Allen was among the first to exploit it.[14]

• • •

BUT TO BUY this land or settle on it would prove difficult, Allen
soon learned. For nearly fifteen years after the French left, it was
all but impossible to obtain a clear title. By the time Allen began
his winter treks into Vermont in 1767, only seven hundred settlers
lived on this newest American frontier. What neither he nor anyone else could at first fathom was the vast complications created
by avaricious British royal governors in the neighboring colonies.
The governors of New York and New Hampshire competed to
fill their purses with thousands of pounds sterling before turning
over title to the vacated lands to eager land speculators, often their
own relatives and friends, who then made handsome profits from
subdividing smaller parcels of forest to the inrushing settlers. The
two competing royal governors asserted each colony's jurisdiction
and their own lucrative right to issue charters for entire townships
of land in exchange for cash fees and their choice of shares of each
land grant, which they considered their prerequisites as Crown
officials.

The magnet that would one day draw Allen and eight thousand other pioneers to present-day Vermont in the decade before
the Revolution first attracted corrupt royal officials from England who envisioned making a fortune from selling not only the
land but the timber that covered the land. As Allen no doubt
learned, giant conifers, their lower branches at least a hundred
feet from the ground and their straight trunks as much as seven
feet in diameter, were highly prized for fashioning the masts
of sailing ships. It was a risky, wasteful business. Among the
larger trees, needed to make Royal Navy masts of thirty-four to
thirty-eight inches in diameter, forty-eight out of fifty proved to
be defective. Once the limbs and branches were chopped off by
crews of axmen, it took a straight road clear of all trees and rocks

and seventy or eighty pair of oxen yoked together to drag the felled trees over the frozen, snow-covered ground. Once the logs were put in motion down the steep riverbanks, they could not be stopped until they reached the river. Woodsmen with pikes prodded these "sticks," as they called the enormous trunks, down the Connecticut River.

The potential for fabulous wealth from these forests had been known in England for over a century, and the protection of the white pine forests for the exclusive use of the Royal Navy had a high priority. The English had long depended on the forests of Scandinavia and Russia for masts, an arrangement less desirable than a supply of ship's timbers from an English colony. As early as 1692, the English government appointed the first surveyor general of His Majesty's Woods to preserve the best white pines standing in unappropriated forests. His deputies marked the trees destined for the king's use by painting a broad white arrow on each trunk. Under parliamentary law, it was strictly forbidden, without a special license, to cut down any white pine with a diameter of two or more feet, twelve inches from its base. Working at cross-purposes, the government encouraged the harvesting of ship timber by paying a premium for its exportation to England. A mast thirty-four inches in diameter fetched £90 sterling, under a Royal Navy contract—little different from the £100 fine to the person who cut it, and any number more.

The fortune to be made from strip clearing provided the temptation for New Hampshire's royal governor, Benning Wentworth, to try to extend the borders of his province. To maintain the profitability of the governor's office, Wentworth attempted to shift New Hampshire's western border from the Connecticut River to Lake Champlain. He wanted to square off the colony by extending his territory all the way to the New York border and then shave off a twenty-mile-wide slice of New York to make it

line up north to south with the western boundary of Massachusetts. Wentworth had reason to believe this landgrab would pass
muster in London because his family had powerful connections.
The second royal governor in a family dynasty that controlled
New Hampshire from 1717 to the Revolution of 1775, the Wentworths made up the first American political dynasty.

The basis for their confident abuse of power lay in the fact
that, in an imperial aristocracy based on family connections, they
were related to Charles Watson-Wentworth, Marquis of Rockingham, twice prime minister of England, a fact that assured the
Wentworths a virtual free hand in America. From his fifty-two-
room mansion at Little Harbour near Portsmouth, New Hampshire, the portly, affable Benning Wentworth dealt lucrative
colonial offices to a brother-in-law (president of the governor's
council); another brother-in-law (chief justice of the supreme
court); his brother's brother-in-law (supreme court justice and
member of the governor's council); a son-in-law of a brother-
in-law (member of the governor's council); and a brother-in-law
(high sheriff). A family gathering was a meeting of the colonial
government; a government meeting was a family gathering. The
rewards for the Wentworth clan were fabulous. Benning Wentworth himself garnered seventy thousand acres of choice timberland as he cut up the future state of Vermont into townships and
charged a £20 fee for the charter of each township.

In one hour of one day, June 7, 1763, Governor Benning
Wentworth of New Hampshire, with a flourish of his quill
signed papers that granted charters to ten townships, each five
miles square, including half a dozen townships along a thirty-
mile stretch of the Winooski River from Lake Champlain. The
grants included present-day Burlington, Williston, and all their
scenic neighbors. The next day, he chartered eight more townships. Pocketing gold and silver coins and a choice 340- to 380-

acre corner of each township in exchange for each signature, Wentworth issued, in all, 140 charters between 1749 and 1764 to townships known for their majestic stands of white pines. The first township he chartered bore his name, Bennington.

A prosperous Portsmouth merchant, Wentworth became royal governor in 1741, two years into King George's War. As soon as that war ended, in 1749, Wentworth and his familial council were ready to assert New Hampshire's claim to all the lands west of the Connecticut River. Slowed down only by intermittent warfare, he began to issue charters in what quickly became known as the New Hampshire Grants. In the other New England colonies, only the legislatures had the right to sell off the land, and then only at auction. New Hampshire's charter, however, gave the royal governor the exclusive franchise.

Each chartered township included sixty-four proprietary "rights" of, on average, 360 acres each. Two "rights" were reserved for the royal governor, one as a glebe, or source of revenue, for the Church of England, one for the settled minister, one for a school, and one for the Anglican foreign missionary organization, the Society for the Propagation of the Gospel in Foreign Parts. The governor arranged the grants so that the four richest in a township formed a square with the corners of the best lands touching each other. Sold to speculators, the remaining shares were resold in 50- or 100-acre lots to poor farmers who migrated to the new township from England, Scotland, Massachusetts, and Connecticut, then drew lots for their land.

Bennington, the first permanent settlement, its charter sold in 1749, became a refuge for New Light revivalists escaping the tensions of the Great Awakening in Hardwick, Massachusetts. Samuel Robinson, a born-again deacon in Hardwick's church, had been captain of the town's militia company during the French and Indian War. Young Ethan Allen had marched with

Robinson on the ill-fated expedition to Fort William Henry. In 1761, the first three families, in all twenty-two settlers, headed north to clear the townsite of Bennington, planting corn and wheat before the main party of thirty families, led by Robinson, arrived in the fall.

At the same time, Allen's Salisbury neighbor John Evarts rode north to survey townsites along Otter Creek, which empties into Lake Champlain. With a partner, Evarts began to buy up proprietary rights from Governor Wentworth. Securing charters to three new townships, he named them Middlebury, New Haven, and Salisbury. These avid land speculators told Allen of their adventures and the profits he could have in the new land. By this time, his Salisbury neighbor Colonel Chittenden had decided to make good on his vow and speculate in Vermont land. One of Middlebury's original proprietors, he attended its first town meeting—at his brother-in-law's tavern in Salisbury. Chittenden bought proprietary shares for his eight-year-old son, Noah, and for his other sons. He was eager to aim his family toward the new land and away from cramped Connecticut: Salisbury's population had doubled in twenty years.

By the time New Hampshire's royal governor halted his wholesaling of township charters, in 1764, in fifteen years he had granted—and pocketed the requisite fees from—nearly three million acres in present-day Vermont—roughly one-third of the future state. Most of the grants lay in narrow bands in the Connecticut Valley from the Massachusetts line northward to Canada and along Lake Champlain in the west, the townships extending back three tiers from either flank. That left nearly two and one half million acres ungranted, mostly along the ranges of the Green Mountains and their foothills and the rivers and streams that flowed down from them. Most of the lands he granted would remain unsettled, except for the occasional squatter, for many

years. Every acre of the granted lands was sold subject to the
condition that each grant holder plant and cultivate at least five
acres out of every fifty acres in his grant within five years of its
granting and continue to "improve and settle the same by additional cultivation"—or forfeit the grant to the Crown, which
meant Wentworth could sell it again.[15]

AFTER YEARS OF lavish British subsidies to pay, feed, and clothe
their colonial armies during the French and Indian War, New
York merchants were flush with cash and eager to invest it in land
that they could sell or lease to settlers. They learned that, as soon
as the ink dried on the Treaty of Paris, Wentworth would issue
more land patents to the northern forests. Atop the list of a group
of Long Island merchants buying proprietary shares of a charter
Wentworth signed on June 7, 1763, was Colonel Samuel Willis,
a sometime militia officer who had at least seen some of southern Vermont during the war and then had gone back to Jericho,
Long Island, where he owned a general store, to drum up interest
among friends also seeking investments. Many of the Winooski
Valley's first proprietors were wealthy Quakers like Willis who
had been fined heavily for refusing on religious grounds to fight
in or support militia that fought in the wars against the French
and had risked confiscation of their properties. Instead, they paid
three shillings in gold for each day's drilling they missed. These
fines no doubt influenced their eagerness to lay the groundwork
for a sanctuary in the northern wilderness.

Under the charter agreement, the township took the name of
Willis. The proprietors convened for their first annual meeting
in Nathaniel Williams's general store in Huntington, on Long
Island's north shore. They elected as township clerk Dr. Samuel
Allen, no relation to Ethan, whose will reveals that he wore sil-

ver shoe buckles and gold sleeve buttons, displayed silver serving pieces on his dinner table, and had accumulated a fortune from treating the slaves of Long Island's wealthy Dutch landowners. It is hard to imagine him giving up his comfortable life on the island and transplanting himself into a wilderness 350 miles farther north. The proprietors selected Samuel Willis to find someone to "set up monuments the length of said township adjoining the [Winooski] river"—in other words, stake out their claim so that it could be surveyed and subdivided.

Of the sixty-five proprietors present or represented by proxy that summer day in 1763, nine also invested in other newly minted townships touching the Winooski River. Six of the investors, including Colonel Willis, bought rights in the new township of Burlington; a New York Quaker merchant, William Burling, purchased some forty thousand acres in the region. Among the other shareholders were Governor Wentworth, his relatives, and a few of his friends from Portsmouth who were speculating in the best trees to sell for masts for the king's ships.

THE RUSH OF postwar speculation touched off a twelve-year face-off between the acquisitive royal governors of New York and New Hampshire and a decade of violence among settlers caught between them. The speculative binge caught New York officials by surprise: for years, preoccupied by the struggle with the French on their Canadian border, they had paid little attention to the mountainous region, which was inhabited only in the summertime, and then only by Mohawk Indians. As long ago as November 17, 1749, New Hampshire Governor Wentworth had written to New York's royal governor, George Clinton, that he was considering issuing grants to unimproved lands between Lake Champlain and the Connecticut River. Not until April

1750 did Clinton advise Wentworth that it was his understanding that, according to the 1664 grant of a charter to the colony of New York by King Charles II to his brother, James, the Duke of York, the eastern boundary of New York Province was the Connecticut River, not the Hudson. For the next twenty-five years, the governors of both provinces claimed all of present-day Vermont, all the while issuing conflicting land grants and deeds.

While waiting to hear from New York's governor, Wentworth continued to grant charters to investors who would never see Vermont, thereby violating instructions from London that he should charter townships on the frontier only *after* families had arrived on the land, ready to build permanent, defensible settlements. There were to be no absentee landlords. By the outbreak of the French and Indian War in 1756, Wentworth had issued sixteen township grants west of the Connecticut River. After the war, he reopened his land-office business, issuing a staggering sixty-three township charters in 1761 alone, then nine more in 1762, thirty-seven in 1763, and two in 1764.

Wentworth paused his illegal activities in 1764 only because, under the new king, George III, the Board of Trade and Plantations in London became suspicious of Wentworth's tactics. By this time, too, Wentworth had, like every other royal governor, received a proclamation barring further settlement west of the Allegheny Mountains (including the Green Mountains) to avoid inflaming relations with the Indians. The Proclamation Line of 1763 not merely barred new settlers from crossing the mountains but ordered any whites already settled on the west side to remove themselves.

In a letter dated July 14, 1764, the Board of Trade demanded that Wentworth send London a list of all land grants and the names of all proprietors of each township. Wentworth could come up with the names of only the few grantees who had actually moved into the new townships. When he finally replied to London, of fifty-seven residents of Pownal, chartered four years earlier, Wentworth could list only three residents, including Ethan Allen's cousin Remember, who were actually the proprietors named in the grant. In Bennington, of eighty-one settlers, not one original proprietor on the 1749 charter resided there. In Arlington, only one of eighteen actual settlers was a proprietor. All the other grantees in the three towns were absentee speculators, a clear violation of Wentworth's royal instructions.

Worried that London would find his actions a "matter of surprise," Wentworth contended that his high-handed actions were good for the empire. He argued that there was no other instance "of such a rapid progress made in settling the wilderness lands in any of the King's dominions." But then, his tongue firmly planted in his check and his fingers crossed, Wentworth contended, "I never signed a charter before I had critically examined the list exhibited to me of the names and abilities of the grantees and . . . that fifty at least were able men brought up on farming business on whom I could rely to make immediate settlement." Nothing, obviously, could have been farther from the truth.[16]

Wentworth omitted one detail: by this time, he had enriched himself by 170,000-forested acres, nearly half, some 70,000 acres, in Vermont, in the disputed lands west of the Connecticut River. Between fifty and sixty grantees paid Wentworth, on average, forty English shillings in fees; he pocketed an estimated £2,740 for the 137 townships he chartered in Vermont before London declared a temporary moratorium in 1764. Only then did he begin to sell an acre of his ex officio proprietary lands. He had also arranged for his father-in-law, Theodore Atkinson, longtime secretary of New Hampshire colony and a member of its executive council, to receive grants of more than 300 acres in each of 51 townships, some 15,000 acres. And *Atkinson's* son, Governor

Wentworth's brother-in-law, obtained rights to proprietary shares in 16 townships, roughly 5,000 acres. In all, council members received shares of 340 township grants before New York began to contest them. Of this number, Wentworth's relatives and in-laws received grants in some 107 townships. Dealing themselves vast tracts of wilderness to attract landless immigrants, the British, with their connections at court in London and through their hereditary squirearchy, piecemeal, colony by colony, were fashioning a social hierarchy much like England's. By the late 1760s, when many of Ethan Allen's Connecticut neighbors were ready to load up their oxcarts and move north to the untracked Green Mountains, Connecticut had become uncomfortably overcrowded for farmers with large farm families who needed enough land to divide among their children to keep them from sliding back into poverty. In little more than thirty years, the population had shot up from 32,000 in 1732 to 150,000, making Connecticut the most densely populated American colony. It was common knowledge that Governor Wentworth was growing ever richer on the fees for granting lands he had never seen to speculating investors who, with rare exceptions like Allen, would also never see them, all in the name of a faraway King George III, who never came to North America. But the unvarnished venality of royal officials like Benning Wentworth and his self-aggrandizing confreres would soon create a new and revolutionary consciousness on the American frontier for a new generation denied its wealth.

7.

"No Better than Peddlers"

✳

ETHAN ALLEN WAS PREEMINENT among the second generation of shareholders in the newly chartered Vermont lands. By
May of 1770, after four winters of studying the terrain, Allen
made his first foray into Vermont land speculation. The year
before, he and his brothers had sold their remaining shares in
their birthplace, their parents' farm in Cornwall, Connecticut.
Ethan's mother, Mary, went to live with her married daughter,
Lydia, in Goshen, Connecticut. With specie in his purse, Allen
bought an entire proprietor's share, somewhere between 360 and
500 heavily forested acres in Poultney, at the foot of the Valley of
Vermont. There he built a house for his younger brother Heber,
who had lived with Ethan's family for the four years since his
expulsion from Northampton. Deciding to stake his future on
speculating in the new land, he bought an additional 500 acres
in New Haven along Lake Champlain straddling the only gap
through the mountains into the interior in Vermont's southwest.

Both became townsites. Ethan's first shrewd total investment for 1,000 acres of prime forest land was a mere £12—less than $1,000 in today's money.

But the flaw in Ethan Allen's grand plan to buy and sell land on the New Hampshire Grants was that he couldn't get, or give to a buyer, clear title to the land. As the clash between colonial governments worsened, Allen and many other American colonists weren't sure whether they ever could. The snag was that, in addition to New Hampshire's avaricious Wentworth dynasty, the royal governors of New York Province were also busy issuing grants to the forests and mountains between Lake Champlain and the Connecticut River, which they considered their colony's eastern boundary line. To colonial New Yorkers, present-day Vermont was nothing more than an extension of New York. Mimicking the behavior of the Crown in England, they considered Vermont their possession, its lands theirs to dispense. Their governors, based in the provincial capital of New York City, had, as soon as the French withdrew, carved up Vermont into four large counties, which they considered theirs to add to New York Province.

On December 28, 1763, Acting Governor Colden issued a proclamation declaring New York's right to the disputed lands, an edict intended to protect New York's claims and to evict the many families whom New Yorkers considered squatters. He warned all New Hampshire grant holders that "they could not derive a legal title under such grants." He then appointed sheriffs and justices of the peace for three counties. He named Charlotte County in the northwest for the queen of England, Gloucester in the northeast for a duke, and Cumberland in the southeast after the king's father. The southwest quadrant of the Grants he kept under the control of Albany County, New York. Then he began to grant vast tracts of land to veterans of the French and Indian War and to his cronies, his appointees to the province's courts and to the governor's executive council.[1]

Meanwhile, nervous New Hampshire grant holders were trying to break down their proprietary shares into 50- and 100-acre parcels, offering them to settlers for little or no cash down. These frontiersmen, who had been given deeds derived from New Hampshire, had already begun the backbreaking work of starting a new homestead in the wilderness. They girdled the great trees and then chopped them down for whatever timber they thought necessary to build their snug unpainted log houses, plowing an acre or two or three of land on which to grow wheat for their bread and corn to feed their livestock through the first winter. As more and more New Englanders arrived on the Grants, the Yorkers—a term that Vermonters sneered more than pronounced—reminded the Board of Trade in London of the 1664 charter.

Agreeing to turn the dispute over to the king's Privy Council for arbitration, the New York provincial government sent agents to a hearing in London. In the bluntest of terms, they lied. They outrageously testified that all the settlers already on the contested ground were amenable to being governed by New York and did not object to applying and paying a high fee for a second, or confirmatory, grant for the right to stay on land they thought they had already purchased. They also omitted the fact that, in a cash-strapped frontier economy, New Hampshire had granted the lands with a low annual quitrent to the Crown of nine pence per hundred acres, while New York was trying to resell the lands subject to a quitrent nearly four times that. When no one from New Hampshire arrived to testify in London, the Board of Trade ruled in July of 1764 that New York's territory, indeed, extended to the west bank of the Connecticut River. At first, the settlers on the Grants were not worried. They believed the ruling applied only to future grantees. Not so, New York officials declared, asserting

that all of the New Hampshire grants were null and void. Consequently, all New Hampshire grant holders were merely squatters
and would have to pay up, leave quietly, or be evicted. In Pownal,
Remember Baker, Allen's bellicose cousin, refused to accede to
New York's demands. A larger battle, one that would continue
for a decade until it became part of the Revolution, was brewing.

In the summer of 1765, James Duane, a prominent lawyer
in New York City who would one day become its mayor, accompanied the retired British army major Walter Rutherford on a
horseback tour of inspection of lands granted to them by New
York's governor in southwestern Vermont. The sprawling grant,
called Princetown by the New Yorkers, included part or all of
Arlington, Danby, Dorset, Bennington, Shaftsbury, and Manchester, all of which had already been granted to other people
by New Hampshire. By this time, there were seventy homes in
Bennington, Major Rutherford noted in his journal. The journey
beguiled the two New Yorkers, and their journals help to explain
why Duane would fight for his claim for the next quarter century. The thirty-two-year-old son of a well-to-do Anglo-Irish
immigrant, Duane had built, after studying law with one of New
York's leading attorneys, a practice as a collection and evictions
lawyer that would earn him a fortune.

That hardly begins, however, to describe his wealth or influence. First, he married Maria Livingston, daughter of the Hudson River manor lord Robert Livingston. Then, after Maria's
death, Duane continued his pursuit of matrimonial wealth, this
time marrying Gertrude Schuyler, daughter of Albany's land
baron Colonel Philip Schuyler. These unions secured for Duane
a place in the highest echelon of New York's landed aristocracy.
His two fathers-in-law employed hundreds of tenant farmers on
their vast Hudson Valley estates. Duane himself maintained a
fashionable house in the city, a home and office in Albany, and a

36,000-acre manor west of Schenectady where he managed 235 tenant farmers and engaged in potash making and milling. His 48,000-acre stake in the Princetown grant in Vermont eventually grew to 64,000 acres. An unflinching conservative, Duane was fond of saying such things as "Those who own the country ought to govern it."[2]

Duane had little respect for the intelligence or motives of such ordinary people as Ethan Allen's family and fellow immigrants to Vermont. Like Governor Colden, he saw the first Vermonters simply as squatters, not hardworking, albeit poor, pioneers. He worried about the consequences of mob rule, warning his father-in-law number one, Robert Livingston, of the dangers of aligning himself with tax protesters during the Stamp Act crisis at the same time Duane was decrying attempts by Parliament to tax Americans. He lamented the lack of an American peerage, ironic since his own roots were so humble. He detested republicanism. "God forbid that we should ever be so miserable as to sink into a republic," he exclaimed. Duane represented the fundamental clash between New England frontiersmen like Allen and New York landowners who admired and emulated English aristocrats. The Hudson River land barons considered labor as demeaning, leisure as ennobling, and slavery and its cousin, tenant farming, unquestioned adaptations to American soil.

In New England, colonists bought their land outright, "in fee simple." The New England colonies were more modern and more democratic than New York, encouraging home ownership by settlers who owned a permanent stake in the land. New Hampshire grantees had to occupy and build on the land (although many, at first, erected flimsy shacks called "possession houses" as placeholders). They posed a threat to the oligarchs of New York, who seemed not only in politics but in social status and even in fashion to mimic the grandees in London. Under the more feudal New

York model, major speculators like Duane bought vast tracts of land from the provincial governors and then leased small parcels to tenant farmers. Tenants could lose the improvements they had made to the land—houses and barns—if they missed a single rental payment—and then they could only lease it back as tenants for higher rents. Allen and his Vermont neighbors shuddered to think that, after all their labor and sacrifices, they could wind up as tenants of the likes of Duane, the Livingstons, or the Schuylers.

For both sides, the stakes were high. In their 1765 journals, Major Rutherford and Duane recorded their reactions to what Vermont looked like at the dawn of American protest against English rule. In Bennington, they found the Congregational meetinghouse built by Samuel Robinson and his born-again settlers "genteel," the land "extraordinary" on both sides of the Hoosick River. They saw gristmills and sawmills in operation. The land "continued good quite into Pownal, especially for grass, the timothy meadows quite the best I have ever seen," wrote Rutherford. Already, the forest was gone. In its place, meadow grass flourished to feed herds of fat cattle. If Bennington's settlers were polite and churchgoing, in Pownal, one of Allen's frequent stops to visit his cousin Remember, lived some fifty families whom Rutherford lumped as "a disorderly drunken rascally crew." In Arlington on the Battenkill visions of timber profits danced in the New Yorkers' heads. Rutherford noted "a white oak 3 *fathom* [18 feet] round and straight." The land here was "extremely rich." In the new town of Manchester, they found only "four families are come up [from Connecticut] but fourteen families were clearing land and beginning to build on it over the summer." A sixty-mile road ran along the Battenkill, around the mountains and through the forests to the old French fort at Crown Point on Lake Champlain, a trek that took ox-drawn wagons eighteen days. In Dorset, a handful of settlers feasted from "a fine pond of 100 acres," which was "full of perch and trout." The two New York tourists characterized much of what they had seen as "rich, fine land," although they noted that much of the countryside had been marred by burning to produce potash, in demand in nearby Albany. Rutherford and Duane rode back to Albany determined to make the forty families they found on their New York patents pay for confirmatory grants under New York land tenure law—or be evicted as squatters.[3]

In a barrage of letters to London, New York's Governor Colden described the danger of letting New Hampshire's claim outweigh New York's rights. The trouble was that the New Hampshire grantees were New Englanders whose governments were based on "republican principles, and those principles are zealously inculcated on the minds of their youth in opposition to the principles of the constitution of Great Britain." In fact, his characterization was correct. New Yorkers, on the other hand, followed the model of the more hierarchical English. Colden urged the Board of Trade not to extend further "the power and influence" of the republican New Englanders. Nearly ten years of confrontations between Yankees and Yorkers had begun. Settlers on the Grants panicked; sale of shares of land nearly stopped. Officials appointed by the two rival royal governments formed posses, tried to evict each other's alleged squatters, and arrested each other.[4]

IN 1765, WHEN the Bennington selectman Samuel Robinson discovered that three families of Dutch settlers had been farming land in Pownal under a New York grant for three decades, he obtained writs of ejectment from a New Hampshire–appointed magistrate. Robinson rode out with the sheriff and a pair of New England settlers who produced New Hampshire's deeds to the same land. They chased off the Dutch farmers and their families, confiscated their corn and their cattle, and sold the livestock back to them. Then, Colonel Harold Schuyler, the sheriff of Albany County, rode up with two New York justices of the peace and thirty armed men. Schuyler arrested Robinson and his sheriff and hauled them off to jail in Albany. Robinson was only released on bail fully two months later after New Hampshire Governor Wentworth objected to New York Governor Colden's "act of cruelty."[5]

Working desperately to preserve the property of all New Hampshire grant holders, Robinson asked Massachusetts' royal governor, Thomas Hutchinson, to mediate between his fellow royal governors. Robinson told Hutchinson that, if the British government did not validate New Hampshire titles, hundreds of New Englanders would be faced with ruin and would either have to abandon their lands or become impoverished tenant farmers, in either case wiping out years of investment and hard work. Hutchinson refused to intervene. A new royal governor of New York, Sir Henry Moore, was rewarded with the office after he brutally suppressed a slave revolt in the Caribbean. Robinson, as a delegate for Grants owners, journeyed to meet him in New York City. His timing couldn't have been worse. He arrived in New York as Stamp Act riots in the city alarmed royal officials.

At the same moment, an uprising broke out among tenant farmers on feudal Hudson River estates. Moore had been forewarned by the British secretary of state in London and authorized to use "the utmost exertion . . . and vigor necessary to suppress [the] outrage and violence" of "the lower and more ignorant of the people." When Robinson finally went before Governor Moore and his council, the governor asked him to make up a list of all the settlers who actually lived on the Grants. He pledged that New York would protect the farmers on twenty- and thirty-acre plots, but investors who had purchased proprietary shares or whole townships would have to pay heavy fees for confirmatory grants. Robinson went back to Bennington convinced that all future grants of land were to be quite large, reserved for wealthy New Yorkers or high-ranking former British army officers. In fact, he sensed that the whole mood of New England and New York was changing with inexorable force; a simpler, more orderly and predictable era could no longer be restored.[6]

Samuel Robinson's hunch was right. In England, in New York, and in Philadelphia, political and commercial leaders were forming private land companies and seeking enormous royal grants from the Board of Trade in London of all the land between the Alleghenies and the Mississippi River. In the largest single piece of inside real estate dealing in colonial American history, Benjamin Franklin, in London as agent to Parliament for five American colonies, and his illegitimate son, William, the royal governor of New Jersey, were assembling investors on both sides of the Atlantic.

In June of 1766, Ethan Allen read in the *Connecticut Courant* of Hartford that New York's provincial government had ordered that all holders of New Hampshire grants appear in person in New York City before the provincial council within the next three months to apply and pay for confirmatory grants or their land would be forfeited and regranted by New York. At emergency meetings all over New England, whether in the taverns of large towns or in isolated rural hamlets, investors like Allen and farmers like Robinson circulated petitions. They asked Robinson to go to London to petition the king himself to avert their financial ruin by confirming New Hampshire's land grants.

ETHAN ALLEN HAD just ridden into Bennington and dismounted at the Catamount Tavern when he learned that the

British government had relieved Benning Wentworth after twenty-six years as New Hampshire's governor, replacing him with his nephew John Wentworth. The younger Wentworth was also being given a second lucrative appointment as surveyor general of the king's woods in North America. By 1767, officials in London had learned that much of the magnificent stand of white pines in the Connecticut Valley was being wasted by timber thieves who were cutting down the tall straight trees reserved for masts for Royal Navy ships and the British officials decided to set up an office of inspection. It was clear that they would not countenance the thought that they would be denied their due.

By this time, the political wind in New York was also shifting. Samuel Robinson's mission to London had succeeded. A new and more liberal secretary of state, the pro-American Lord Shelburne, acceded to the Vermonters' argument that many of the grant holders were veterans of the colonial militias employed by the British in the French and Indian War. Shelburne, presiding over the Board of Trade and Plantations, issued an excoriation of New York's government. On April 11, 1767, the Board of Trade ruled that under no circumstances was New York to disturb any resident on the Grants who held a valid New Hampshire deed. The power to grant lands was intended to "accommodate not distress settlers," especially "the poor and industrious." The reform-minded Lord Shelburne personally chastised New York's governor for dispossessing poor New Hampshire grant holders and ordered him to stop all legal proceedings involving the Grants until officials in London had time for further study.[7]

Governor Moore, too weary from years of populist riots and confrontations with New York's oligarchs to object, obeyed his new instructions, refusing to grant any new lands or confirm any old grants. He referred all Vermont land dealings to his aged lieutenant governor, Cadwallader Colden—the very man who, as governor in 1764, had claimed all of Vermont for New York. Ignoring London's instructions, Colden argued that only Governor Moore had been ordered to stop New York's land dealings. He went on issuing new grants in Vermont and enforcing old ones, knowing full well that authorities in London were preoccupied by weightier matters. Colden also was well aware that James Duane had personally inspected the region, reporting back in detail the numbers, names, and locations of the holders of New Hampshire grants. He now proposed to use that information to evict the Vermont farmers by force.

Colden returned to power as acting governor at the sudden death of Governor Moore in 1769. By then, the temporary nature of the 1767 ruling from London made most investors hesitant to buy or sell the land. But others, principally Ethan Allen, saw this instability as an opportunity to buy up choice land cheaply from timorous investors. Sometime in 1769, he bought a farm in the small settlement of Sunderland in Bennington County. He did not move his family there immediately. From this base, as he hunted, he scouted out "rights," acquiring land with cash accumulated from the Allens' latest business venture. His wholesale hunting provided large quantities of deer hides to turn into buckskin leggings for his brother Heman to sell in his general store in Salisbury. The stolid Heman and the youngest Allen brother, Ira, rented an unoccupied fulling mill on the Housatonic River. Heman hired Irish leather dressers and tailors to tan and stretch the hides and fashion them into the leather pants. While Ethan shifted more of his efforts to buying up land, another brother, Levi, brought back hides from as far away as an Indian trading post he helped operate in Detroit. Levi went into partnership with Heman in the fulling mill, employing Ira as supervisor.

During a brief interlude of renewed prosperity in colonial America, the Allens sold off the remainder of their Cornwall homestead in September of 1769. Ethan could finally afford to leave Salisbury behind forever and buy a comfortable, one-and-a-half-story, gambrel-roofed cottage on the elm-shaded main street of Bennington between the First Congregational Church and the Catamount Tavern. There, he moved Mary and their four children; his mother, who had recently suffered a stroke and lost the use of her right arm, remained with Heman. Fifteen years Ethan's junior, Ira was eighteen when he took part of his £48 share and purchased his first rights of land in Poultney, near Ethan's first purchase, and in Hubbardton and Castleton. This modest investment gave him a swath of hilly, forested land some thirty miles north of Bennington—and a taste for land speculation that would one day make him, according to James B. Wilbur, his biographer, "one of the largest land-owners in New England and one of the wealthiest men in the United States in 1795."[8]

With the remainder of their inheritance, Ira, Heman, and Levi invested their proceeds in 350 hogs, a desirable commodity in Albany, seventy miles away. Ira, short and thin, bore the nickname Stub: his job was to bargain with farmers for corn to feed the hogs along the route of the hog drive. But first, with several hired hands, Heman and Ira drove the hogs through an early winter snowstorm some seventy miles to fatten them up free of charge on beechnuts lying thick along the banks of the Connecticut River. Then, in January of 1770, they drove 150 of the fattened hogs over eighty miles to Albany, where they sold them at a handsome profit. Risking losing their way as the swirling snow obliterated the blaze marks on trees that indicated the trail, the brothers drove the 200 remaining hogs to Ethan's farm in Sunderland. In spring, the 200 hogs once again fattened on beechnuts, the Allen brothers turned another hefty profit in Albany to reinvest in Vermont lands.

. . .

THERE WAS TO BE no respite in the escalating confrontation between New York and the inhabitants of the New Hampshire Grants. Indeed, New York Governor Colden, resuming his aggressive land policies, openly characterized New Englanders like Ethan Allen as "in appearance no better than peddlers" who were "hawking and selling [their] pretended rights to townships" for trifling considerations. Defying Colden, these "peddlers" had become more numerous after the Privy Council's 1764 ruling that the region might indeed come under New York jurisdiction. In fact, this trend had only served to bring in hundreds more New Englanders eager to settle their families and farm their new properties. The repeal of Chancellor of the Exchequer Townshend's unpopular British tax levies—except for a tax of a symbolic two pence in the pound for tea—coupled with the ascendance of the liberal Lord Shelburne had lulled many Americans into confidence that the king would benevolently protect the rights of actual settlers but not absentee speculators. But Colden, the royal official on the scene, had no such idea. He chose this volatile moment to send in New York land commissioners and surveying teams.[9]

In mid-October of 1769, Bennington settlers heard that a New York surveying team was on its way from Albany. On the nineteenth, James Breakenridge, an original settler of the region and a member of Bennington's select board, led hired hands into his cornfield in Shaftsbury to begin the fall harvest. A crowd of armed neighbors gathered on one side of the field as John Munro, who claimed a 4,000-acre New York patent in Shaftsbury and Arlington and had been commissioned by Governor Colden as a justice of the peace, pushed aside the rows of corn and warned Breakenridge against trying to keep the surveyors from entering his cornfield. If Breakenridge interfered, Munro would arrest him. Then he read Breakenridge and his neighbors the Riot Act, which forbade armed assemblage and enabled their arrest. When the New York surveyors entered the field, Breakenridge pleaded with his neighbors to leave. The armed men drew back slightly. When the New York party's leader asked why so many armed men still lingered nearby, Breakenridge, joined by another Bennington selectman, denied that he had anything to do with the growing crowd. His neighbors, he said, "Did Not understand Law." But, like him, they believed that the surveying party was infringing on land legally granted to him by New Hampshire and, furthermore, that "his Majesty had forbide them [New York authorities] from making any Grants on ours or hindering our Settlement." Finally, the surveying party, intimidated by so many silent, sullen, armed men, retreated to Albany.[10]

A few weeks later, Bennington settlers learned to their horror that Governor Colden had ordered writs of ejectment filed in the New York Supreme Court of Judicature in Albany. From eight townships where settlers faced being dispossessed, delegates raced to an emergency meeting at the Catamount Tavern. It proved to be the first step the settlers took toward organizing resistance to New York that soon developed into what Ethan's younger brother Ira described in his autobiography as "a state of war with the colony of New York, not in reality with the body of the people but with the governor, Council, court sychophants and land jobbers." In a hurried meeting, the anxious delegates voted unanimously to seek the help of New Hampshire Governor John Wentworth, who had succeeded his land-jobbing father. This first Vermont assembly of town delegates fired off two petitions to Wentworth, one containing the names of 470 settlers, the other the signatures of town representatives. Complaining that it was unjust for them to be placed under New York's jurisdiction and left to face ejectment suits, they pleaded with Wentworth to use his influence in London on their behalf.[11]

Before Wentworth could reply, on December 19, 1769, New York's governor issued a proclamation denouncing the Bennington settlers as "a Number of armed Men, tumultuously and riotously assembled," who had prevented New York surveyors from partitioning the Walloomsac patent. The proclamation cited Breakenridge and six other men as the principal "Actors in the said Riot" and ordered their arrest. Why they had any reason to be confident that Wentworth could or would defend them from New York's demands cannot be fathomed. They had recently learned that, even by sending a delegate to London, they could not expect any swift action. Samuel Robinson had died in London while waiting for the Board of Trade's decision on Vermont lands. There was no other leader in Bennington.[12]

Samuel's young son, Moses, meanwhile, joined in circulating another petition to dispatch directly to the king through New Hampshire, claiming that it spoke for eight hundred "owners and possessors" of legally granted land. Hundreds more of their fellow settlers had "expended the whole and others the greatest part of what they are worth in purchasing, clearing and cultivating these wilderness lands" and faced ejectment by "persons of wealth and influence" from New York. Unless the king came to their rescue, "numerous families" would be "utterly ruined and perish through want of bread" to "gratify those men of wealth and power who have coveted [their] possessions and sought [their] ruin." Of course, it would take months for all the petitions to reach New Hampshire's governor and then be forwarded to London, and then they would go to the bottom of a huge stack and probably not be read for many more months, if at all. But English colonists on the New England frontier still believed in their king.[13]

• • •

IN THE HALF DOZEN years since the Crown had declared further westward expansion beyond the Allegheny Mountains illegal
by the Proclamation of 1763, consortiums of American merchants
and British politicians had been jockeying to form companies
seeking enormous grants of land from the Crown: they would,
in turn, subdivide the wilderness in parcels of land they could
sell to the tide of new immigrants beginning to inundate coastal
colonies where all the arable soil had long since been sold. Benjamin Franklin had been defeated in his only bid for elective office
in Pennsylvania a decade earlier after he described the influx
of German farmers as "Palatine boors herding together." They
proved to be, Franklin learned too late, able to read their native
language in the Germantown, Pennsylvania, newspaper. In 1766,
with his illegitimate son William, the royal governor of New Jersey, and wealthy Philadelphia Quaker merchants who had grown
rich selling tomahawks and guns to the Indians, he had formed
the Illinois Company: its purpose, to establish a vast new province that would eventually become the states of Illinois, Indiana,
Wisconsin, Ohio, and Michigan! The scheme quickly embraced
officials in several colonies as well as senior British officials in the
Indian establishment, including Indian Superintendant Sir William Johnson. To ease its path to a royal charter, the Franklins
offered shares to key members of Parliament. Among the high-
ranking officials Governor Franklin approached, only one turned
him down: Sir Thomas Gage. It was his mission to protect the
Indians from English colonists to prevent friction that could precipitate another war; besides, he wanted to pull his troops off the
frontier to build up his forces in troublesome Boston. By the end
of 1768, Benjamin Franklin was still pacing impatiently outside
parliamentary offices and his son expectantly tearing open every

letter from London. Their scheme would languish among piles of proposals for subdividing the American continent for seven more years as British officials, uncertain how best to harness the growth and debt of a war-won worldwide empire, became increasingly distracted by the continuing chafing under the yoke of new laws and new taxes of the ungrateful American colonies.

IT WAS NOT UNTIL April of 1769, when Ethan Allen returned to Bennington at the end of his third winterlong hunt, that he learned that two New York grantees, Major John Small and the Reverend Michael Slaughter, had brought actions of ejectment in New York's Supreme Court of Judicature against four New Hampshire grant holders—Breakenridge, Samuel Rose, Isaiah Carpenter, and Josiah Fuller, all original settlers of Shaftsbury, a township near Bennington. The court acted on information gathered by Duane and Rutherford during their 1765 reconnaissance of the Grants. The court filing, the first of its kind, alarmed not only its targeted defendants but Allen and hundreds of other New Hampshire grant holders. Obviously, New York officials were intent on clearing the Grants, as they came to be called, of settlers and regranting the land to major land speculators and retired British officers.

Allen rushed back from Bennington to the home of Charles Burral in Sharon, Connecticut, where shareholders, largely prosperous farmers and merchants from all over the northwest of the colony, were gathering. They quickly learned that the man who obviously best knew the terrain and virtually everyone living on the disputed lands and who had emerged from the older, more timorous group as the most vigorous spokesman for openly opposing New York was none other than Allen. Allen asserted that this obviously would be the test case for the Grants. He impressed the group of investors with his insistence that New York's governors intended to clear the New Hampshire Grants of anyone who wouldn't pay for a second and high-priced confirmatory title from New York on land they thought they already owned, an action no one at the meeting favored, even if he was financially able.

It was impossible for Allen to fathom, much less to explain to the assemblage, the extraordinary level of defalcation of corrupt British imperial officials intent on subjugating while increasingly taxing their troublesome American subjects. Allen could not yet see or comprehend the tightening noose of British administration over its expanded American empire. As a revolving door of cabinet ministers imposed new measures until they were strongly resisted in America, Royal Navy ships moved closer to shore to reinforce a legion of customs agents and paid informers. Accused smugglers were hauled before Admiralty judges in special courts not responsive to English common law and could be transported for trial and punishment in England. Allen could not have imagined the full depth of New York's campaign to assert control over Vermont lands, but his analysis that day was astute and his words persuasive. He could not have known, even if he suspected it, that New York's governors had already secretly promised more than two million acres of the New Hampshire Grants to their political cronies, in addition to 300,000 acres in military grants to reduced French and Indian War officers. Among them, three New York governors, their greed rivaling the avaricious Wentworths of New Hampshire, had already pocketed £76,373 in fees, about $15 million today, five times Benning Wentworth's take. Moreover, some of the settled towns on the Grants east of the Green Mountains were buckling under pressure from New York: Guilford, Brattleboro, Cavendish, and Chester, all in the southeast near the Massachusetts border, had already paid high fees to New York to have their charters regranted and now would have to pay higher annual quitrents to the Crown. Allen explained that, if this trend continued, all settlers already on the Grants would end up as impoverished tenant farmers paying rent to wealthy absentee landlords in New York.

At a second packed meeting, the New Hampshire grantees appointed Burral treasurer and receiver general of all monies needed to combat the New York takeover. Each proprietor, and there were hundreds by now, paid Burral half a Spanish silver dollar because British law barred colonial currency for any business transaction; Americans had to use one of nine forms of foreign specie for all business transactions. At a third and still more clamorous meeting in Canaan, Connecticut, the shareholders unanimously chose Ethan Allen to travel to Albany and personally press their case for the New York Supreme Court. Emerging as the leader of the Grants, Allen, exuding self-confidence and zeal for the common cause, told the meetings that he was certain that, with the right help in England and enough financial backing, they, the proprietors in physical possession of the lands, could win in court (where he had considerable experience by now). Impressed, and less eager themselves to make the long journeys away from their homes and their businesses, the proprietors put their legal defense fund into Allen's hands and made him the spokesman for the Grants. Backed by their financial support and their trust in him, Allen immediately accepted the mission. He told the meeting he would first hurry to Portsmouth, New Hampshire, to obtain from Governor Wentworth an attested copy of the township charter of Shaftsbury, where the four defendants in the ejectment suit lived, along with any other legal documents he would need for the trial. He said he would then ride on to New Haven, retain Jared Ingersoll, the best trial lawyer in New England, and accompany him to court in Albany in time for its mid-June session.

. . .

ALLEN'S MAIDEN VOYAGE as a representative of the people
who owned and occupied the New Hampshire Grants took him
some three hundred miles on horseback from Salisbury, Connecticut, north to the Berkshires, then across all of Massachusetts
(following the route of the present-day Massachusetts Turnpike)
to Boston and then north along the Post Road to Portsmouth.
His journey epitomized the isolation and sense of disenfranchisement of the frontier backcountry in colonial America. Few
settlers had the time or money to absent themselves from their
farms or businesses to travel over treacherous mountain roads and
to stay in expensive and execrable taverns, the only inns, along
the way to press their legal business in colonial courts so far from
home. Already, Allen saw himself as a major speculator in Vermont's lands with a deep self-interest in the power struggle with
New York landowners. Yet, like so many of his countrymen, only
because he was being subsidized could he afford to plead the case
of his neighbors, first in New Hampshire's provincial capital on
the Piscataqua River two miles from the Atlantic Ocean, then,
hundreds of miles away, in Albany on the upper Hudson River,
simply to procure a handwritten copy of a township charter for the
royal governor's signature—for the prescribed fee in silver or gold.

Riding into Portsmouth, Allen found Governor John Wentworth conducting public affairs in regal fashion. This was Allen's
first glimpse at the power and opulence of the royal establishment in America and a personal representative of the king. Oddly
enough, the two men, frontiersman Ethan Allen and courtier
John Wentworth, so opposite in background, found themselves
surprisingly like-minded. Portsmouth, after Boston, was the
second-busiest seaport in New England, in part because of the
timber floated down the Piscataqua each spring, in part because

of its growing importance as a whaling port. Handsome frame houses lined the waterfront, supporting their signature widow's walks that testified to the long wait of families for news that the speculative life of a whaler would end in high profits and not distant death. Some 147 oceangoing ships of 200 to 300 tons came off the ways in Portsmouth's shipbuilding yards in the two years between 1769, when Allen saw the bustling port for the first time, and 1771.

But New Hampshire's forests not only provided timber for ships and lumber for the region's handsome frame houses but also yielded the makings of exquisite woodworking: desks, chests of drawers, and other furniture fashioned in Portsmouth's workshops by master craftsmen from England and then carried south in New Hampshire ships to the plantation houses of Virginia and South Carolina. Surrounded by more opulence than he had ever seen, Allen first observed how the wealthier class of Americans attempted to ape the expensive fashions and resplendent lifestyles of England's privileged classes. In Portsmouth, home to fewer than five thousand people, one visitor noted "more private carriages and liveried servants . . . in proportion to the inhabitants than in any other place in New England." A visiting Harvard student wrote in his journal, "Their manner of living here is very different from many other places [in America]. The gentlemen treat at their houses and seldom go to the taverns. Their treats are splendid [and] they drink excessively all sorts of wine and punch—their women come not into company, not even so much as at dinner."[14]

The self-assured young governor of the white pine province who greeted Allen clung to his uncle Benning's fifty-two-room riverfront mansion, one perk from twenty-five years of pocketing the perquisites of office. Allen curiously observed Wentworth's flamboyant style. Youthful and extroverted, energetic and approachable, all the things his uncle Benning had not been, John Wentworth possessed the common touch so rare in Crown officials in America. A Harvard classmate of John Adams, Wentworth staunchly advocated settling North America's interior. Acquiring a large estate at Wolfeboro in the center of the colony, he personally supervised the laying out of roads and lots. He roamed the frontier incessantly, greeting each new family of settlers. He took seriously his joint appointment as governor and as surveyor general of the king's woods in North America, catching timber rustlers in the act, prosecuting and fining them heavily. Wentworth was unusually open-minded for a royal official of the times. His crowning achievement was to recruit, in 1769, the Reverend Eleazar Wheelock to relocate his Congregationalist Indian school, Dartmouth College, from its birthplace in Lebanon, Connecticut, to a permanent home in Hanover on the Connecticut River. Two years later, Wentworth personally handed out Dartmouth's first diplomas.

For Ethan Allen and the frontier landowners he represented, Wentworth distinguished himself most when he refused, even under pressure from London, to disavow the rights of the Vermont settlers. When, in 1767, the king's Privy Council ordered the Green Mountain settlers to follow the laws of New York, Wentworth had boldly urged them "to regulate themselves according to their grants from New Hampshire," confident that his province's government would ultimately prevail. Allen came away from Portsmouth convinced that Wentworth would never repudiate Vermonters' grants. He was just as sure that Wentworth, with his formidable family connections in London, would succeed in defending the settlers' interests. Allen, in turn, convinced Wentworth that the Vermont landowners would no longer surrender their New Hampshire grants in the face of growing intimidation by New York. Allen was so confident of Wentworth's intentions that, before he left Portsmouth, he bought one Daniel Warner's proprietary right to 350 choice acres in the town of Poultney on the Grants for £4 (about $600 today) and, stopping off in Springfield, Massachusetts a few days later, bought Zenas Person's right in Castleton for £6 ($900). For less than a thousand dollars, Allen had grown from a small-time speculator in Vermont land to a major property owner, though with a sensibility different from those of the landholding class.

To REASSURE ALLEN and his constituents, Wentworth intimated his own interest in the Vermont land title controversy. Wentworth said he had written to one New Yorker who was asserting a claim to a New Hampshire grant that he was confident not only that the New Hampshire grants made by his uncle were valid but that New York's claims were "false, absurd and iniquitous." Many leading citizens of New Hampshire, Wentworth had written to William Bayard of New York, agreed: "Many gentlemen of respect and property here [Portsmouth] think themselves agrieved and seem determined . . . not to give up tamely."[15]

While there was nothing at risk from taking Allen into his confidence, Wentworth intimated he secretly backed a petition circulating among two hundred settlers in Windsor, Westminster, Rockingham, and Brattleboro that they preferred New Hampshire jurisdiction. New York authorities never did see the original of this petition and believed Allen sent it to Wentworth to forward to London. Unaware of Wentworth's deception, settlers in the Connecticut Valley who had bought New York's confirmatory grants fired off their own pro–New York petition. Their elegantly formal, engrossed petition obviously had been drawn up in New York City, probably paid for by Crean Brush, a major New York speculator in Vermont lands on the west bank of the Connecticut River.

Allen left Portsmouth sure that his relatives, friends, and other holders of New Hampshire grants would be protected by the governor and his patrons in London. Riding on to New Haven, where he persuaded Jared Ingersoll to defend Breakenridge and the others before the New York Supreme Court in Albany, Allen could not have retained a more capable lawyer in Connecticut, for Ingersoll had a reputation as one of the fairest and most powerful lawyers in the American colonies and had emerged as somewhat of a hero when he renounced his lucrative Crown appointment as the Stamp Act commissioner for the colony. As king's attorney for Connecticut and a member of the executive council of the assembly, he had grown wealthy representing New Hampshire's timber interests in contracts with the Royal Navy. He had also recently been appointed Admiralty judge for the Middle Atlantic colonies. Hardly in need of funds in June of 1770, when he met Allen, Ingersoll agreed to represent the New Hampshire share-holders as a protest against the Crown's increasingly aggressive policies. It would be many years before Allen learned, at the end of the Revolution, that both Wentworth and Ingersoll would one day leave America as Loyalist exiles.

Allen saw Jared Ingersoll as representing the opinions of intelligent and wealthy New Englanders. That Ingersoll took the case against other Crown officials proved to Allen that one of the leading judges in America believed the New Hampshire settlers' case was valid and just. Leaving New Haven the first week of June, they rode together to New York City and then took a fast sloop up the Hudson, past the towering Palisades, the step-roofed Dutch houses lining the waterfronts of Esopus and Poughkeepsie, alternating sail-luffing runs downwind with tedious tacking against the tidal current, finally arriving in Albany just in time for the convening of the supreme court.

8.

"Gods of the Hills"

❋

ETHAN ALLEN EMERGED as the primary active leader of the Green Mountain settlements because of a precedent-setting case against impecunious New England pioneers who, after years of cultivating the wilderness, suddenly faced eviction by New York. For more than six months, in which he attended emergency meetings and traveled through three colonies on horseback for hundreds of miles, Allen pushed on, first through snows, then over the flooded roads of New England's fifth season, mud season, and, finally, stifling summer heat, rushing to prepare for the legal defense of nine Bennington-area farmers facing immediate eviction and consequent poverty.

Allen carried certified copies of the charters of the New Hampshire townships granted by the late Governor Benning Wentworth and attested by his nephew Governor John Wentworth, along with copies of the titles to the individual farms. That Jared Ingersoll, Connecticut's most distinguished lawyer and recently appointed Admiralty judge, had agreed to take on the landmark case enormously reassured Allen and the proprietors of the New Hampshire grants. Allen was now certain that they could block the evictions and thwart New York's determined campaign to seize and resell some two million acres of Vermont land.

Colonial New York's highest court rotated on a circuit through the counties of the sprawling province. Its justices assembled for Albany County court days only for the last two days of June each year. Allen, Ingersoll, and Bennington's local counsel, Peter Silvester, met with their farmer clients, apprehensive and weary after the sixty-mile ride over the mountains from Bennington. After huddling briefly, they headed for the massive old three-story courthouse just as the bell in its cupola clanged the announcement that the supreme court would be in session in thirty minutes. They passed the gallows, the stocks, the whipping post and the outsized, outdoor iron cage—all of which seemed to Allen the visible symbols of English oppression. He and his companions joined the onrush of plaintiffs and defendants, lawyers, witnesses, and busybodies as they surged into the courtroom, quickly filling up its benches. The overflow crowd pressed up against the wooden bar that separated the justices from the scores of the accused, their lawyers, if they could afford them, and the plaintiffs trying to find swift justice from the full-wigged jurists filing into the packed chamber.

The justices could expect to decide within their two-day session cases involving treason, murder, theft, libel, trespass, and assault and battery, as well as cases specific to life in the American colonies. Among these were assessments of estates, arbitration, customs violations, indentures of servants, leases of tenant farmers, piracy, Sabbath-breaking, freedom of worship, salary disputes, and slavery—both Indian and African American—and disputed land patents such as the nine cases of ejectment carefully chosen to break the impasse over land grants between New York and New Hampshire. In at least some of these cases, especially the land grant cases that brought Allen to Albany, the supreme court justices undeniably had gross conflicts of interest.

Presiding over the court that day was Justice Robert L. Livingston, owner of the 166,000-acre Livingston Manor, which stretched for twenty miles along the eastern bank of the Hudson River and employed 285 families of first-generation immigrant Scottish tenant farmers. Livingston numbered among his cousins many of the wealthy and powerful land barons of the Hudson Valley, including the Schuylers, Van Rensselaers, and Van Cortlands, who, among them, held more than four million acres of prime farmland in New York and New Jersey that fed not only New York City but sent exports all over the Atlantic world. The youngest member of the panel of judges at twenty-four, Livingston stood to inherit even more land, including Clermont, a vast, tenanted Hudson Valley estate, the 500,000-acre Hardenburgh patent in the Catskills, and the extensive Beekman and Stevens landholdings, roughly 250,000 acres in Dutchess County. In acreage, he was a millionaire. Allen and his companions could hardly expect to find sympathy from him.

Also sitting in judgment that day was Chief Justice William Smith, an influential member of the colony's executive council and a member of the powerful Livingston coterie. Smith, a graduate of Yale and a cofounder of what became Princeton and Columbia Universities, was a second-generation land speculator who had inherited vast acreage overlapping the New York–New England borders, including partnership in a 30,000-acre tract in the Green Mountains. He could scarcely be counted on to be disinterested. The king's counsel who was prosecuting the case for the province that day was the very man who had carefully selected the nine farmers for ejectment. James Duane, whose wealth was discussed earlier, ranked as one of New York's leading speculators in Vermont land and a partner in the Princetowne patent that overlapped the land at issue in the first case, *Small v. Carpenter*. Duane was relying on personal observations and interviews he had conducted in 1765 during his tour of southwestern Vermont with Major Rutherford. After inheriting at age fourteen about 1,500 acres of land in Schenectady County from his father, Duane accumulated equal amounts from two brothers when they died and then purchased another 1,500 acres of the Mohawk Valley from a third brother, adding hundreds of acres in the region from other speculators. Duane had earned the nickname Swivel Eye for his shifty sidewise glances. He was, Allen and his compatriots knew, one of the most hated and feared lawyers in New York. In 1765, on a visit to Bennington with Major Rutherford, he had taken detailed notes on the area's real estate and tenants. By then, he had already begun to recruit tenant farmers from surrounding colonies for his projected township-sized tract, self-referentially named Duanesburg, in the Winooski Valley of Vermont. Spurred on by the Board of Trade's 1764 decision that the Vermont territory should come under the jurisdiction of New York, Duane had purchased 64,000 acres of the disputed lands, assuming that his purchase would be protected by fellow officials in New York and in London. He was already a leader in reorganizing the New Hampshire Grants into New York counties so that sheriffs, courts, and justices of the peace could be appointed to enforce his rights in these speculations. The backgrounds of the judges more than suggest that the judicial process in the colonies was essentially fixed, and that the landed classes had installed not merely their brethren but actual members of their class to create a judicial system that came to reflect more England than the United States that was to be.

Even more compromised, if possible, in the case was Attorney

General John Tabor Kempe, a notably successful British place-man. Kempe's father had arrived in America as a tallow chandler, but by age thirty-five, Kempe had risen to become the province's advocate general and, growing rich by inside trading of land patents, had by 1769 become the fourth-wealthiest man in New York. His lands were worth an estimated £65,650 (about $13 million today). The secret for amassing such a fortune in only fifteen years was Kempe's privileged access to timely information about government decisions on land acquisition. He had acquired 168,000 acres, some 134,000 acres of it for nominal considerations as well as 36,000 acres by marriage, something to which Duane, too, was not a stranger. Allen, on the other hand, had a wife who brought with her no dowry and could expect to inherit a share in her father's house and mill only if all her brothers died childless. Kempe was, as Allen knew by now, a partner with James Duane in the sprawling Princetowne patent, the grant that included the farms of at least two of the defendants.

Each of the New York jurists, Crown lawyers, and barristers was "well-versed in how to dress in a manner" expected from one in his station. The judges wore long, full-curled wigs and sumptuous robes. The prescribed "robes and bands" filing into court were part of a ritual calculated to "advance the dignity, authority, solemnity and decorum of the Court." The two king's counsels, James Duane and James Tabor Kempe, "appeared in bar gowns and bands" similar to those worn in London at Westminster.[1] Their finery had its impact on Allen. He himself was always fond of dressing well by frontier standards but, amid the splendor of the New York lawyers and judges around him, he instantly felt at a disadvantage.

To add to his discomfiture, the plaintiff in the case, Major John Small, a retired veteran of the Forty-second Regiment of Foot, appeared in his brilliant scarlet British officer's uniform.

New York's government had given Small 3,000 acres in Shaftsbury, the New Hampshire–granted township just northwest
of Bennington, some of it already being farmed by one of the
defendants, Isaiah Carpenter, who appeared in plain garb. Seeing Ingersoll at the side of Allen may have momentarily bolstered
Carpenter's confidence, but it did little to thwart the well-planned
prosecution by Major Small's lawyer, James Duane. Like all of
the other New York officials actively involved in the case, Duane
had another conflict of interest. It was Duane who, as lawyer
for a family of log rustlers, the Deans, had triggered the ejectment suits. After Surveyor of the King's Woods John Wentworth
caught the Deans rustling logs at Windsor the winter before,
Duane, their lawyer, had persuaded other New York officials to
refuse to prosecute them. He contended that the offending trees
were cut on the west side of the Connecticut River and therefore
had been felled in New York, where, he argued, Governor Wentworth of New Hampshire had no jurisdiction. As with many of
Duane's pleadings, it was a half-truth. Even if Windsor was in an
area that London had proclaimed in 1764 came under New York
jurisdiction, Wentworth had been acting as the surveyor general
of the king's woods in America, all of North America. To cut
down trees marked for Royal Navy ships was still a crime. That
settlers on the Vermont grants had attacked the New York sheriff's posse seizing the Deans had not eased the jurisdictional dispute between the two governments. As the Deans' lawyer, Duane
had prevailed, and the Deans were freed after paying Duane's
hefty legal fees.

ETHAN ALLEN PROBABLY should have known by this time
how grimly determined the landlord judges of New York had
become. At least he should have known why. For nearly twenty

years, chronic riots and disturbances had broken out on the ten-anted manors of the Hudson Valley. Rebellious tenants, encour-aged by the arrival of freeholding farmers on the neighboring New Hampshire Grants, were demanding more favorable leases and beginning to challenge the validity of the great manorial pat-ents. For nearly two decades, intermittent outbreaks of violence had threatened Presiding Judge Livingston's wealthy and power-ful family with financial loss, dishonor, and mob rule. By the late 1760s, the situation was so severe that the Lord of Livingston Manor dreaded losing the family estates.

Livingston's troubles had begun in 1751 when a band of New England settlers arrived at the easternmost corner of Livingston Manor. Backed by the General Court of Massachusetts, these settlers sought to establish Massachusetts' jurisdiction over a twenty-mile-wide swath of the borderlands between New York and Massachusetts. Some of Livingston's tenants welcomed the newcomers; they refused to pay their rents and, in fact, actually helped the New Englanders lay out their farms. In all, the new arrivals asserted claims to 26,000 acres of Livingston Manor for the Bay Colony. When Livingston had the Massachusetts leader arrested as a trespasser and ordered loyal tenants to pull down his house, the Massachusetts settlers, joined by Livingston's more rebellious tenants, marched to Livingston's iron forge, seized the workers, and cut down two thousand trees in a nearby forest. In turn, Livingston retaliated by ordering the fences and crops of the leading rioters destroyed. Finally, New York's royal gover-nor arrested several rebel leaders. It was as if an undeclared war was breaking out between the wealthy landlords and the landless farmworkers.

Four years later, the blood feud had hardly abated. As the French and Indian War distracted the colonial governments, riots flared anew on manors all along the Hudson in 1755 at the very time British armies were reeling after Braddock's defeat on the Monongahela. The Albany County sheriff, attempting to disperse rioters, was taken a prisoner to Sheffield, Massachusetts. Livingston and his kinsmen mobilized loyal tenants and captured and jailed the rebel leaders, killing one tenant as he fled. Once again, insurgents attacked Livingston's iron forge and seized his workers. Tenants next challenged Livingston's right to own his land. Buying up rival deeds from Stockbridge Indians in Massachusetts who claimed the land had been stolen from them, the tenants produced the Indian deeds in the Albany court. Livingston retaliated, commencing eviction proceedings. In a crisis portending both the resistance of the Green Mountain Boys and the civil war between Loyalists and Patriots in the Revolution, when legal remedies failed, Livingston armed his loyal tenants, who routed the Massachusetts settlers. Lieutenant Governor Colden, who always favored the landlord, called for the arrest of the Massachusetts intruders in 1762, and they finally withdrew from Livingston Manor.

Peace lasted but a few years. In 1765, in the wake of the Stamp Act riots in New York City, tenant protests broke out yet again on Hudson Valley manors. In what became known as the Great Rebellion of 1766, Parliament's repeal of the Stamp Act encouraged riots all along the Hudson River. Finally realizing they could never own the land they worked on, tenants demanded better leases. Governor Moore dispatched British regulars from New York City. In June of 1766, as Ethan Allen watched events from his iron forge just across the border in Salisbury, two hundred New York tenants, vowing to murder Livingston and tear down his manor house, battled armed Livingston loyalists until the royal governor again sent in Redcoats and captured the tenants' leaders. One of the British officers sent from New York City, the Swiss-born captain John Montresor, reported back to Governor Moore that hundreds of Livingston Manor tenants had stormed Livingston's mansion, demanding better conditions from the great landlord.

These memories remained fresh a few years later when Ethan Allen and his Green Mountain neighbors appeared before Judge Livingston, who, more than anyone in court that day, had reason to loathe quarrelsome intruders from New England. Nothing about him reassured the defendants as he looked down from the bench, declared the circuit court proceedings of June 1770 open, and called the first case: ejectment suits against Allen's neighbors.

As Allen, the Vermonters, and their lawyers came to the front of the packed courtroom and faced the supreme court, its provincial government had other options than evicting respectable farmers from the New Hampshire Grants. Probably the most honorable way would have been to validate all titles already granted by Benning Wentworth, royal governor of another British province. Of course, New York claimants probably would have construed this as capitulating to squatters and giving in to the threat of the mob. Furthermore, in the eyes of New York's royal establishment, to acknowledge any right of New Hampshire to grant the land in the first place would mean the forfeiture of some three million acres of the land and the loss of a fortune in fees that could be collected by New York's royal governor, attorney general, and assorted self-aggrandizing officials who expected to pocket a share of those fees. In several stints as acting governor, the accipitrine Cadwallader Colden had accumulated a fortune by demanding confirmatory grants for lands previously chartered by New Hampshire. But he would also have to collect fees from New Hampshire's governor, John Wentworth, as well as from his own uncle and from New York Supreme Court Justices Livingston and

Smith, who had purchased New Hampshire grants. Nonetheless, to obviate these embarrassing and expensive possibilities, a noble gesture from New York might have paid handsomely by winning the support of the New Hampshire landowners, especially those on the New York border. New York could have extended its jurisdiction over three million virtually uninhabited acres. An even more elegant solution—and there is evidence that Governor Colden and his council, which included Justice Smith, considered it—was simply to validate the titles of lands already settled by the time the Crown had issued the royal proclamation of 1767 with which the English secretary of state, Lord Dartmouth, had forbidden the late Governor Moore to disturb farmers already on the Grants. That would still leave millions of unoccupied acres for New York to grant. But then Acting Governor Colden insisted that the royal order applied only to the late Governor Moore, the person to whom it was mailed, and that therefore the Crown's order did not apply to successive governors. From New York's angle, such a gesture could have divided and probably silenced their opponents on the Grants. It would have distinguished hard-working resident farmers from nonresident absentee speculators who were already flouting the English government's requirement that they personally settle and develop the land. The absentee owners, such as the Connecticut speculators who were paying the Bennington farmers' legal fees that day in court, would have been powerless to resist New York's authority. Such a move could have obviated twenty more years of discord.

The third alternative was force. The settlers were still few and lived, for the most part, far apart. In 1765, only seven hundred settlers inhabited the ceded French territory; by 1770, probably no more than three times that number. Few could even afford enough gunpowder and lead to fight back. Settlers sometimes had to hunt for their food with bow and arrow. They could hardly have held out before a concerted sweep of a determined military force such as had driven Massachusetts squatters from Hudson Valley lands only a few years earlier. A thousand armed men with one or two cannon could have cleared the New Hampshire Grants for regranting to New Yorkers. Years of bitter rivalry could have been averted had New York's officials acted decisively and been driven by anything more farsighted than personal greed. In any of these three scenarios, there probably would have been no state of Vermont today—just four more beautiful, mountainous counties of New York.

THE TWIN ARCHITECTS of New York's eviction strategy were Attorney General John Tabor Kempe and the plaintiffs' attorney James Duane, both major stakeholders in the disputed lands. Duane, in addition to being the claimants' lawyer, as king's counsel, personally chose the test cases to be prosecuted. The first case called for trial was against James Breakenridge, whose farm lay along Bennington's western boundary, where Albany's surveyors and land commissioners had been faced down by armed neighbors. Breakenridge had the weakest case, his land having been included in a New York patent issued in 1739, fully a decade before Benning Wentworth sold the land to Samuel Robinson, who had passed it on to his son, Moses, who, in turn, had sold it to Breakenridge. Worse, the farm straddled the line twenty miles east of the Hudson River that Wentworth claimed as the western boundary of the New Hampshire Grants.

In this first case, New York could not possibly lose. New York Province's title to the land antedated New Hampshire's, even if it conflicted with Wentworth's Bennington grant. Duane would later declare that Jared Ingersoll had warned Breakenridge that he had no defense, but the farmer, carried aloft by his anger and determination, had insisted on coming to court and making no admission. This caught Duane off guard. Because Duane believed there was no need for documents in such an open-and-shut case and brought no formal proof of title with him, Breakenridge won a temporary victory. The plaintiff, Major Small, temporarily withdrew the suit of ejectment against Breakenridge, though later, at a jury trial, it went against him.

Ethan Allen and his lawyers and neighbors had little time for elation. With the Breakenridge case set aside temporarily, the first case to go to trial on June 28, 1770, was *Small v. Carpenter*. Here, plaintiff Small, suing Isaiah Carpenter of Shaftsbury, represented the favored and popular policy of New York to make substantial grants of land to former British officers, thus encouraging veterans of lower rank to buy land from him and settle on it. Major Small had received a military grant in October of 1765. As the trial opened, Duane produced Small's title. The major testified that his patent from New York provided that two hundred acres be reserved for each settler already on the land who could produce a New Hampshire title, on condition that he pay the usual New York annual quitrents of four shillings six pence per hundred acres. Major Small said he had offered this arrangement to Carpenter but that Carpenter had refused to comply with New York's terms.

Then Jared Ingersoll rose to defend Carpenter. He offered as proof of Carpenter's clear title the two documents that Ethan Allen had ridden to Portsmouth to procure personally from Governor John Wentworth, a certified copy of the New Hampshire charter for Shaftsbury Township and a copy of Governor Wentworth's instructions relating to land grants. The courtroom fell silent as Crown lawyers and New York judges paused to confer. At that moment, King's Counsel Duane objected. The court could not admit the New Hampshire title into evidence, he argued, because the disputed region had been within the boundaries of New York since its royal charter in 1664. Consequently, Duane asserted, all New Hampshire grants, issued at the earliest some eighty years later, were null and void and inadmissible. Taking a few more moments to pore over the 1664 charter, the supreme court justices ruled in favor of Duane's stricture. At the same time, at Duane's insistence, the justices refused to examine the documents that Ingersoll proffered. They ruled that, since no proper evidence had been offered to show that New Hampshire had ever included the land in dispute, Benning Wentworth never had any authority to grant it. Their verdict went in favor of Major Small. With the bang of a gavel that shocked the crowded courtroom, the court ordered Carpenter evicted.

Six more suits were still pending. Duane himself had acquired two thousand acres in 1765 from a military grant made to a British army chaplain, the Reverend Michael Slaughter. Now Slaughter was suing to evict the New Hampshire grantee Josiah Fuller, who had been farming the land when Duane inspected it during his 1765 tour. Duane, as a partner in the Princetowne patent, was also personally bringing suits of ejectment against four other settlers. Since Duane contended that his New York titles antedated the New Hampshire titles, Ingersoll decided that it was hopeless, that there was no point in his remaining in the Albany courtroom, because he would not be allowed to offer the New Hampshire documentation into evidence in any of these six cases. Gathering up his papers, Ingersoll declared the case "already prejudiced" and stalked from the courtroom with Allen.

In his 1779 book, *A Vindication of the Opposition of the Inhabitants of Vermont to the Government of New-York*, Allen still remembered the anger and humiliation he had felt as he left the Albany courtroom that day:

The plaintiffs appearing in great state and magnificence, . . . together with their junto of land thieves, made a brilliant appearance; but the defendants appearing in but ordinary fashion, having been greatly fatigued by hard labour wrought on the disputed premises, . . . made a very disproportionable figure at court. . . . In fine, interest, connection and grandeur . . . easily turned the scale against the honest defendants. . . .[2]

Ethan Allen left the courtroom acutely aware that the Bennington farmers' only legal remedy had been exhausted. Under New York law, a case could not be appealed to London unless the value of the disputed property exceeded £500, as if the verdict in London would have been any different. Cleverly, King's Counsel Duane had broken up the prosecution into nine separate suits, each falling below this limit, thus cutting off any chance for legal redress in a higher court in England.

IF THE NEW YORK Supreme Court justices acted out of self-interest, they were legally on firm ground. Despite the perception of the angry settlers on the Grants, Benning Wentworth had fleeced them. He'd had no right to sell the land in the first place. That the New England homesteaders had no legal recourse after subsequent New York jury trials upheld their evictions is another matter. Had the Vermonters been able to appeal to the king's Privy Council in London, it would doubtless have come out that King's Counsel Duane had deliberately colluded with Attorney General Kempe, who also stood to benefit from the evictions, by breaking up the eviction suits so that there could be no appeal. Many years would pass before the smoldering feud between territorial neighbors New York and Vermont could be settled. For the next two decades, Duane and Allen personally did more than anyone else to keep the quarrel alive.

For the time being, New York had been declared the legal

winner. Benning Wentworth had obviously enriched himself by illegally granting three million acres outside New Hampshire's jurisdiction. But in the tense summer of 1770, where did that leave the thousands of New England investors and farmers who had paid what little cash they had for the right to transplant their hard lives onto the New England backcountry frontier? That is what Allen wanted to know. What was he to tell the small-town merchants and farmers who had passed around their collective hat and financed the legal defense and his travels? Now they seemed to have no recourse except to pay the steep confirmatory fees and quitrents demanded by New York or forfeit their investments. And what about the hundreds of farm families with no cash to pay these fees and, after certain eviction, would have no money to buy land and start over yet again? All that Allen could muster that night was the hope, the threadbare possibility, that New Hampshire Governor John Wentworth had more influence at the royal court in London than did New York's self-interested officials.

Before Allen could apprise Bennington of the outcome of the hearing, a confrontation occurred that launched his reputation as the honest Green Mountain Boy refusing the blandishments of corrupt New York officials. The story was already a Vermont legend by the time the Harvard historian Jared Sparks in 1834 profiled Allen in his *Library of American Biography*: "It is recorded, that after Allen retired from the court at Albany, two or three gentlemen interested in the New York grants called upon him, one of whom was the King's attorney-general for the colony, and advised him to go home and persuade his friends of the Green Mountains to make the best terms they could with their new landlords, intimating that their cause was now desperate." Relying on Sparks, the biographer Henry W. DePuy, writing in 1855, added that Allen had "coolly" responded to the bribe offer. In 1858, the New York City journalist Benson J. Lossing, after interviewing descendants of the revolutionaries in New York and Vermont, in *Harper's New*

Monthly Magazine characterized the Albany hearing as "a solemn farce," adding, "Allen was exceedingly indignant, and it was with great difficulty that he could treat Attorney-General Kemp [*sic*] courteously when that officer called upon him the next morning. Kemp tried to flatter the sturdy pioneer, and then advised him to go home and persuade his Green Mountain friends to make the best terms they could with their new landlords. . . . The suggestion thoroughly aroused the sleeping lion of Allen's nature."[3] As brother Ira wrote in his 1798 *History of the State of Vermont*, Kempe explained that Allen would also be doing himself a favor because Duane and Kempe and their New York friends were prepared to give him a great tract of land within one of their New York patents in the Green Mountains as well as cash. In fact, they would give him the cash now as well as a good horse to carry him back to Bennington. He could keep the horse because he would need it to report the squatters' reaction back to them. The three men probably expected Allen to agree. They had studied him in court as much as he was measuring them. They saw him—handsome, virile, and unquestionably smart—as potentially one of their own, someone who might turn if they proffered enough lucre.

There is no record of what Allen was thinking, no impartial witness to what exactly they said to each other. In his journal, Duane recorded that he had "paid Ethan Allen for going among the people to quiet them." According to one version put forth by Allen, he wanted to keep Duane and Kempe off guard and guessing. Furthermore, he accepted the money and the horse because he had come by boat and had expended all the cash his backers had given him. At another time, he insisted he had protested that the offer was an outrage and had loudly declared his unwavering belief in the righteousness of Vermont's cause, only to be met by Attorney General Kempe's cool gaze and his rejoinder "We have might on our side, and you know that might often prevails against right." But in Allen's most famously repeated rendition, that morning in the tavern, he unambiguously retorted, "The gods of the valleys are not Gods of the hills." It was entirely in his character and experience to resort to a favorite rhetorical weapon, a line from the Old Testament, this time 1 Kings 20:28, sure that the two New York lawyers trying to bribe and buy him would not understand the implicit threat in the Bible passage. In this biblical analogy, New York had become Syria of old, underestimating the Vermonters. Allen's Bible-steeped generation, so more truly pious than the New Yorkers and in so many ways reflecting the honor and principles of any self-respecting leader, knew that a small number of Israelites had slaughtered one hundred thousand Syrians in a long and bloody battle. Allen may have had a good laugh later to remember that Kempe asked him what he meant. It was clear Kempe did not know the Book of Kings, even if he made his living interpreting the king's law books in his own favor. "If he would accompany him to Bennington," Allen said he had replied, "the phrase should be explained." Had Duane and Kempe taken Allen up on his offer, they would have seen that in the five years since Duane had last visited Vermont, a close-packed settlement of determined, armed, and experienced hunter-farmers like himself had spread over the valley. Instead, Duane and Kempe bought Allen a drink and pressed some money for the horse's feed and some travel money on him. Ethan Allen never disclosed how much it was. He certainly never gave it back.[4]

THE TOWN OF BENNINGTON, by the early 1770s, was divided into two poles: the Congregational meetinghouse to the south end of a broad street and, only a block away, Landlord Fay's tavern, more commonly known as the Catamount Tavern, because of a stuffed mountain lion atop a twenty-five-foot pillar that bared its teeth toward New York. Galloping into town from the eviction trial in Albany, Ethan Allen went before one hundred anxious townsmen who had crowded into the tavern to hear the news and decide what step to take next to protect their properties from the sheriff's posses now threatening to come and clear them off the disputed lands. The Reverend Jedediah Dewey, the town's Puritan minister, presided over the meeting in the tavern, the town's largest gathering place.

A head taller than most men, self-confident and persuasive, Allen at thirty-three appeared the obvious leader for the farmers who had lost patience with the timorous, passive petitioning of Bennington's town fathers. Even if he felt constrained to defer publicly to them, he argued that New York's officials might have once exercised legal jurisdiction over the Grants but now no longer did. Even if the 1764 order in council had brought the Grants under New York law, the 1767 order in council made it clear that, while New Hampshire could issue no new charters, neither could New York. It further decreed that New York was not to molest settlers already on the grants they had purchased from New Hampshire or from the original proprietors of the New Hampshire Grants. New York, Allen insisted, had to respect preexisting land titles and locally established political entities. New York had already defied the Crown's 1767 order by making illegal grants of already settled areas. Its officials were ignoring the Crown's intent and menacing settlers who had purchased their land legally and improved it in good faith. The arrogance of New York's landgrabbers would anger officials in London. As a consequence, Allen asserted, the king would decide to give New Hampshire final jurisdiction over the Grants. "He [the king]," he argued, "may cede the disputed lands back again to the province of New Hampshire or erect it into a new province." But not even the king could tamper with these property rights. Under English common law, only the owner could alienate his own property. The fight was over who owned the land. They had to be prepared to fight for the land they owned.[5]

Still smarting from the high-handed treatment he and the defense team of lawyers had received in the Albany courtroom, Allen told the stunned townspeople of Bennington what they were expecting to hear: that New York was hell-bent on evicting them. He told the crowd how the court had not even allowed him to enter into evidence the proof of the legitimacy of their cause, the documents he had procured at such effort and expense from New Hampshire. He told them everything, including the bribe offer by Duane and Kempe—Kempe, the attorney general of New York; Duane, the king's counsel—his honesty and rectitude no doubt gaining even more respect from the Vermonters. Allen pointed to the use of force to enforce writs of possession, to take away their homes and land. "Justice without mercy," his words dripped irony, had been the watchwords of a royal court without possibility of appeal, all carefully arranged by the king's swivel-eyed counsel. Allen, eager to act, confronted the lassitude of cowed older members of Bennington's establishment. To his surprise, the Reverend Dewey joined him in advocating resistance, his reaction contrasting sharply to the scorn the clergyman had shown Allen on earlier occasions. Forced evictions must be met by resistance in force. The townsmen of Bennington, some solemn, some cheering, voted to protect, especially, the farms of the town's evicted leaders, James Breakenridge and Josiah Fuller. To appease the timid, Allen agreed that they must continue their resistance only until they heard the Crown's final decision on the late Samuel Robinson's 1767 petition to confirm their New Hampshire grants. But there was no disguising the excitement that began to spread over the green hills of the Grants that day. Allen's scathing report produced the first organized resistance to New York's authority on the New Hampshire Grants. His speech triggered a new spirit of resistance, of confidence that the men of the Green Mountains could hold out against New York's tyranny while the New Hampshire governor they trusted prevailed in their appeals to London. Allen took the horse given him by Duane and Kempe back to them in Albany, where the two officials anxiously awaited his report of the town's reaction to his supposed blandishments. He told them only that "everything would soon be adjusted." Then he left. It would prove to be a seminal moment, a strong intimation of what lay ahead in just a few years.[6]

THE SETTLERS OF BENNINGTON did not have to wait long for an answer. On September 26, 1770, New York commissioners and surveyors again appeared in Breakenridge's cornfield, escorted by the Albany County sheriff and three hundred men. This time, a band of armed townsmen drove them off. But this confrontation merely made Breakenridge more apprehensive. The winners in the eviction suit had sent the surveying party to Bennington. Still believing the king would intervene to protect his grant, Breakenridge insisted on sending off yet another petition to London. He declared his dismay that the New York court had refused to consider "the least evidence we were able to produce in favor of our paid grants from New Hampshire." If the king did not act soon, many honest settlers would be cast off their farms "with our families into ye open wilderness." Off went the latest plea to Portsmouth for Governor Wentworth to forward to London. But Wentworth never sent it on to London: he yielded to his overriding impulse to make more money than he could foresee coming from the cash-strapped Vermonters.[7]

What Allen and his neighbors could not know was that the Grants settlers' and the absentee proprietors' last hope for help from political patronage or from any government institution or official had vanished. A year and a half before the Albany evictions trials and only a year before Allen visited him in Portsmouth, Governor John Wentworth had received a letter from a friend, Colonel William Bayard of New York, inquiring about buying a New Hampshire grant. Proving more venal than his father, Wentworth urged Bayard to make the speculation and asked him whether he could buy a 350-acre right in it. About the same time, making a tour of inspection as surveyor of the king's woods, Wentworth visited the new town of Windsor on the west bank of the Connecticut River. There he met major landowners in the area who held New Hampshire patents. One month later, a new town, Windsor, became incorporated after Wentworth granted the patent Bayard had requested. The New Hampshire governor not only sanctioned the first overt act against New York authority east of the Green Mountains but owned a piece of the patent. At the same time, the duplicitous Wentworth and his New Hampshire council began to bring pressure to bear on settlers in the lower Connecticut Valley to petition the Crown to transfer jurisdiction over the Grants from New York to New Hampshire. The petition, no doubt prepared in Portsmouth with Governor Wentworth's backing, circulated in several towns along the disputed west bank of the Connecticut River. New York officials never saw the original document, which contained the signatures of two hundred settlers. Off it went from Portsmouth to London. Wentworth successfully created the impression that the petition had been sent to him by the Grants settlers merely for his transmittal to the king.

Shortly after the Albany eviction trials in June of 1770, a major New York City land speculator, Crean Brush, who owned extensive New York–granted lands in the lower Connecticut Valley, circulated a counterpetition to the king in favor of continued

New York jurisdiction over the disputed Grants. The exquisitely printed petition, dated November 1, 1770, bore 425 signatures. Many may have been fraudulent. Brush sent the petition to the new governor of New York, John Murray, fourth Earl of Dunmore, knowing that he had powerful connections at the English court, at least as influential as Wentworth's. Murray was a nobleman descended from the Stuarts and one of sixteen Scottish peers in Parliament. In this latest spin of the revolving door of England's adolescent colonial establishment, Lord Dunmore would remain in New York only for eleven months before being packed off to become the royal governor of Virginia, a much more lucrative post. In that short time, Dunmore was extremely busy regranting some 403,000 acres in Vermont, including one patent for 48,000 acres in Rutland and Pittsford to King's Counsel James Duane and his partners. On his last day in office, Dunmore granted Duane 51,000 acres in the Middlebury area. In forwarding the pro–New York petition to Lord Hillsborough at the Board of Trade in London, Lord Dunmore in his covering letter accused "persons in power" in New Hampshire of fomenting all the unrest on the frontier.[8]

At about that time, Governor Wentworth suddenly lost interest in working behind the scenes to seek confirmation of the New Hampshire Grants directly from the Crown. That autumn of 1770, his uncle Benning Wentworth died. Childless, grossly obese, and infirm, Benning Wentworth had belatedly married his nubile young housekeeper, Martha Hilton. When the Wentworth family shunned the new Mrs. Wentworth, the old ex-governor changed his will. He cut off his favorite nephew, the young governor, his reputed heir, leaving his entire fortune, including his fifty-two-room mansion, to his young bride. Suddenly desperate for cash, the young and now much less wealthy Governor Wentworth won the assent of his council to revoke the

New Hampshire charters of all of the undeveloped land east of the Connecticut River that he had granted to himself so that he could regrant it and collect the customary fees. That reversal led Wentworth to worry about all the undeveloped lands, the 500-acres out of each of 178 townships, that his uncle had granted to himself in Vermont and that now would pass to his uncle's widow—and come under New York's jurisdiction.

On December 14, 1771, John Wentworth wrote to the latest New York governor, Sir William Tryon, who succeeded Lord Dunmore. In fact, legally all of Wentworth's uncle's self-granted but still unsettled, unoccupied lands were now only "reservations" that reverted to the Crown for the succeeding royal governor to grant anew. Apparently confused on this fine point of law, Wentworth now was supplicating Tryon for all "the lots in like circumstances that have fallen into" New York. They "are ungranted," he insisted. Here, he was abandoning any New Hampshire claim to his uncle's lands. "I should be happy in soliciting a grant thereof," Wentworth told the New York governor. If he received this huge grant, Wentworth said, he would "rejoice to cultivate and establish with the greatest attention" Tryon's "favor." In New York, land-rich royal officials had reason to rejoice, too. In this secret letter to New York's governor, New Hampshire Governor Wentworth made it clear that, if he received the grant from New York, he would no longer work behind the scenes at court to wrest the jurisdiction of the Grants away from New York.[9]

Other than personal gain, what may explain Wentworth's sudden about-face was a dramatic change in British colonial policy that brought the American colonies closer to open rebellion. By the end of 1769, only New Hampshire had escaped the material effects of a successful intercolonial resistance movement that had originated next door in Boston in response to implementation of the Townshend duties. Reviving nonimportation to force Par-

liament once again to yield, the Boston town meeting on October 28, 1767, drew up a list of English imports, mostly luxury
goods, that merchants would no longer purchase. Nonimportation agreements quickly followed in Providence and Newport. In
New York City, a mass meeting on December 29 created a committee to formulate a plan to promote the domestic economy and
local employment.

The strongest written elucidation of the protesters' basis for
opposing the new duties came from the wealthy Philadelphia
Quaker lawyer John Dickinson, writing *Letters from a Farmer
in Pennsylvania to the Inhabitants of the British Colonies* under a
pseudonym. First appearing as fourteen essays in the *Pennsylvania Chronicle*, the *Letters*, circulated widely all over the American
colonies and in England in pamphlet form, conceded Parliament's
authority to regulate trade but denied its right to tax in order to
raise revenue in America and declared the Townshend duties
unconstitutional.

Only a month after Dickinson's last essay broke into print in
Philadelphia, in Boston Samuel Adams drew up the first Massachusetts circular letter; approved by the colony's House of
Representatives, the letter informed the assemblies of the other
twelve colonies of the Massachusetts General Court's denunciation of the Townshend Acts as violating the principle of no
taxation without representation, pointing out that it was impossible for the colonies to be adequately represented in Parliament.
Adams further attacked the Crown's decision to put colonial governors' and judges' salaries on the civil list and thus make them
unresponsive to the colonial legislatures. Soliciting proposals for
continued coordinated colonial action, Adams's circular letter
drew the condemnation of Massachusetts royal governor, Francis
Bernard. In London, Lord Hillsborough, the secretary of state
for the colonies, denounced the circular letter and ordered royal

governors to dissolve their assemblies if necessary to prevent them from endorsing it. But he was too late: the assemblies of New Hampshire, New Jersey, and Connecticut praised Massachusetts' stand, and Virginia drafted its own circular letter, endorsing Massachusetts' initiative and advising other colonies to follow suit. When Governor Bernard ordered the Massachusetts House to rescind the letter, the representatives voted overwhelmingly, 92–17, to defy him. Bernard dissolved the legislature and called a new election. Under heavy attack by the Sons of Liberty, seven "rescinders" lost their seats.

The general obstruction of any new British measures by Bostonians led the detested customs commissioners to request an armed force to protect them. The Royal Navy dispatched the fifty-gun frigate *Romney* in May of 1768. Only weeks later, customs officials learned that a wharf official had been locked in the cabin of John Hancock's sloop *Liberty* while his crew whisked the cargo of Madeira wine ashore without paying duties. When customs officials ordered the sloop towed from her slip and anchored close to the *Romney*, a crowd attacked them on the wharf and demonstrated in front of their homes. Fleeing to Castle William in the harbor, the officials again appealed for more troops. By September 28, as British troopships sailed into Boston harbor, an impromptu provincial convention had urged the populace to arm. As the Sons of Liberty threatened armed resistance, two regiments of British infantry marched up Long Wharf and pitched their tents on the Commons, where they remained at the outbreak of the Revolution seven years later.

As nonimportation agreements proliferated in the coastal colonies, merchants from Boston to Savannah drew up lists of banned goods and, before royal governors could move quickly enough to dissolve them, colonial assemblies agreed not to deal with any merchant who refused to join the general boycott of

British goods. Imports from England dropped by one-third in 1769 as the movement spread, most strikingly in New York, by 85 percent, and in Philadelphia, by 45 percent. In January 1770, Townshend resigned; in March, Parliament repealed all of the duties except a two pence in the pound duty on tea. Lord North, the new head of government, pledged that his administration would impose no new taxes on the American colonies. Only New Hampshire's trade, consisting of an increasing demand for timber for Royal Navy ships' masts, had remained unaffected by the boycott movement, but Governor Wentworth would emerge from the crisis no longer a friend and protector of the rights of the ordinary colonist.

ONE YEAR LATER, in the summer of 1771, Governor Wentworth and his retainers rode through his own real estate development at Wolfeboro, in the New Hampshire pine forest, on his way to Hanover to preside over the first commencement of Dartmouth College. He stopped long enough to assure prominent settlers on the Grants that he was still working very zealously to have all the lands west of the river permanently attached to New Hampshire. It would be many more months before he informed the same settlers by letter of his change of heart. And he never did tell them that he had not forwarded their petitions to the king. He sent only the pro–New York petition to London. The last chance for a rescue from New York's jurisdiction and the evictions and seizures of farms that would surely follow had vanished. By this time, though, Ethan Allen was no longer surprised. He recognized the venal patterns of the New York oligarchy, and he anticipated their moves as he quickly advanced through the ranks of Vermonters who had decided to defend their farms by force of arms.

Instead of relief from London, what came to Bennington in the meantime was the news that, only a few weeks after he landed in New York City, Lord Dunmore, alarmed by reports that the Bennington settlers had chased off New York land commissioners, proclaimed that the surveyors had been terrorized by "a riotous and tumultuous Body of Men." Dunmore ordered the arrest of the four men identified as ringleaders. As tensions mounted all along the New York–Vermont frontier, the Albany court indicted twelve more Vermonters for rioting against the king's peace.[10]

Late in November 1770, Albany County Sheriff Henry Ten Eyck, his deputy, and New York–appointed Justice of the Peace Munro approached Bennington stealthily. Skirting the town and coming through the bare winter woods to the north, they encircled the home of one of the accused leaders, Silas Robinson, son of Bennington's founder, seized him, and bundled him off toward Albany. Alerted by Robinson's wife, Allen quickly rounded up forty armed men and, at their head, galloped after the New York posse. Late that night, they surrounded the farmhouse where Allen thought the New Yorkers and their prisoner were sleeping, only to learn from Munro that the prisoner and his escort had already left for Albany. Allen and his posse fired their weapons into the air and rode away. Shortly thereafter, they learned that Silas Robinson had been remanded to the Albany jail.

A few weeks later, a New York constable and his deputies galloped into Bennington. This time, they arrested Robinson's brother Moses. As the New Yorkers and their prisoner rode toward Albany, Allen gathered an even larger party of armed settlers. Their faces blackened, they surrounded the New York posse and, at gunpoint, rescued Robinson. Back in Albany, the constable reported that when he had warned Allen that he and his men were violating New York law, Allen shot back that "they damned the Laws of New York, and said they had better Laws of their own." Then, the constable reported, Allen and his followers chased him and his men all the way back to the New York boundary line.[11]

The tension rapidly escalated as the pace of face-offs quickened. Only a few days later, on the frigid morning of January 5, 1771, Sheriff Ten Eyck tried to serve writs of possession on Breakenridge and Fuller. The writs of ejectment, resulting from Duane's successful manipulation of the Albany court, meant that Ten Eyck now had the power to evict the Vermont farmers as squatters. But when Ten Eyck arrived at Breakenridge's farm, as he later reported in a sworn affidavit, he encountered a large number of armed men. Their leader was Ethan Allen, who warned the sheriff he was ready "to blow his brains out" if he proceeded. At Josiah Fuller's farm, the same scene played out again. Ten Eyck retreated, his warrants unserved. By that spring of 1771, guerrilla warfare seemed to predominate on the Vermont frontier. Bands of armed men were menacing the lives of any New York settlers still remaining on the Grants, threatening to tear down their fences, houses, and barns unless they left. At their head in these impromptu raids, the sheriff reported, was Allen himself, who had emerged as the undisputed leader of the Grants.[12]

9.

"The Law of Self Preservation"

Relations between American colonists and British colonial officials had been worsening for more than a decade. Unemployment was running high in the port towns, and poorly paid Redcoats garrisoning the town were competing for whatever cash-paying odd jobs they could find. Street fights between colonists and soldiers were becoming commonplace. Under a full moon on the icy night of March 5, 1770, unemployed sailors and young boys gathered on the waterfront near the customshouse. A young boy taunted an eighteen-year-old Redcoat on guard duty. The soldier struck the boy with his gun. The boy yelled out to some nearby Bostonians and pointed out the sentry: "There is the son of a bitch that knocked me down!" From the crowd came shouts of "Kill him, kill him, knock him down!" More Redcoats reinforced the sentry detail. A larger crowd, apparently led by a giant mulatto workman named Crispus Attucks, pelted the soldiers who retreated up the customshouse steps under a barrage of chunks of ice, hard-packed snowballs, oyster shells, and cudgels. The Redcoats loaded their muskets. The crowd drew closer, lashing out with cutlasses and clubs, screaming at the guards, "Come on, you rascals, you bloody-backs, you lobster scoundrels! Fire if you dare, God damn you! Fire and be damned! We know you dare not!" After a series of commands from their sergeant, the troops fired a volley at point-blank range. Attucks and two others dropped dead; six others were dragged away, leaving bloody trails in the snow. Nothing in colonial America would ever be the same after this, the Boston Massacre, and nothing would be the same again between English royal officials and Americans on the frontiers.[1]

In the spring of 1771, the stunned American colonies recoiled short of revolution in the aftermath of the Boston Massacre. The years of pent-up tensions that exploded in the killing of five rioters by beleaguered British sentries eased somewhat as seven British soldiers were tried for murder. The Patriot lawyers John Adams and Josiah Quincy agreed to take the case, their able defense leading to five acquittals and the branding on the foreheads of the two regulars found guilty of manslaughter. In a lull in the protracted colonial crisis, as soon as travel became possible, Ethan Allen rode from Salisbury, Connecticut, up to Sheffield, Massachusetts, signed a contract to buy a farm in present-day Sunderland, Vermont, and on May 30 moved his family onto the disputed Grants. In the sixteen years since his father, Joseph, had died, Ethan had never ceased to act as the paterfamilias, or, as Levi Allen later put it, his brother acted like "a dictator among the younger brethren." Levi had come back from fur trading northwest of Detroit to join Heman and Ira in the family's deerskin-curing business in Salisbury, freeing nineteen-year-old Ira to devote more and more time each year to survey land that

Ethan had explored by canoe and snowshoe over the past four years. As part of building up his own surveying business, Ira ran boundary lines for New Hampshire Grant proprietors far into the northern Champlain Valley. Ira had carried out Ethan's order to purchase several land rights in Poultney, barely inside the Grants and less than two miles from the New York boundary line. Then Ethan turned over the house he had bought in Massachusetts for brother Heber to live with his wife and infant son.[2]

Ethan's wife, Mary, had given birth to two more children, a son, Joseph, and a daughter, Lucy, during their years of living at close quarters with Heman and his wife above the general store in Salisbury. Now she was expecting their fourth child. Ethan had taken them to brother Zimri's farm in the Berkshire Hills in Sheffield. Ethan's mother had lived with his sister, Lydia, in Goshen, Connecticut, until Lydia had died in 1770. At the funeral, Ethan's mother, age sixty-two, no doubt grief-stricken over the loss of her beloved daughter, suffered a stroke that paralyzed her left side. Ethan took her back to Salisbury to live with Heman. It had been four years since Ethan's expulsion from Northampton. Each spring, he had returned to Salisbury, but now he was finally ready to provide a permanent home for his long-suffering wife as soon as their fourth child was born. Mary had more than one reason to rejoice when they headed for their new farm in the Valley of Vermont, not far from the hilltop in Poultney where Ethan had first looked out over the new land.

Many of the Allens' relatives and old Connecticut neighbors were already settled on the Grants. Mary's less fractious brothers, Timothy and Gideon, had moved to hilly Sunderland. Less than a day's ride away, Cousin Remember Baker had built up a prosperous surveying business in Pownal before moving north to the more cosmopolitan town of Arlington. The British govern-

ment had drawn the Proclamation Line of 1763 down the crest
of the Allegheny Mountains, banning all settlement to its west,
but many New Englanders like the Allens were openly flouting
the decree. Its principal effect was to force migration north from
overcrowded colonies farther south: between 1765 and 1775,
the population of the future Vermont increased tenfold, from
seven hundred to seven thousand, most of it west of the Green
Mountains proclamation line. The rapid population increase was
watched with mounting anxiety by the New York oligarchy.

Alternately orchestrating his family's various business endeav-
ors and organizing the growing resistance to New York "landgrabbers" and "monopolizers," as he now called them, Allen rode
through the hills and forest clearings, training and inspecting the
militia companies of twelve towns. All the while, he also looked
for choice parcels of land he could buy up at a bargain. His outspoken championing of the New England settlers on the Grants
promised to pay handsome dividends. His newfound prestige
contributed to the substantial profits he could expect to make
from his early investments in Vermont.

Returning from his first visit to Governor Wentworth in the
spring of 1770, he had stopped long enough to buy the "right"
to 350 acres of Castleton real estate from the bricklayer Zenas
Person for £6; he sold it a year later for £24, a 300 percent profit.
Allen did not overlook any opportunity, and it was apparent he
would make money without resorting to venality. Wisely, he
formed a lifelong partnership with his youngest brother, Ira. They
bought up thirty-two rights, nearly 12,000 acres, of hardwood
forest in Hubbardton near Castleton, for £60, about $12,000 or
a dollar an acre in today's money. Each brother then bought four
rights, some 1,356 acres of land, in Castleton. Often, they bought
land for a few shillings per hundred acres from erstwhile specu-

lators who had lost their nerve and given up in the face of New York intimidation.

For four winters since his banishment from Northampton, Ethan Allen had made himself the self-invited guest in the cabins of relatives and friends on the Vermont frontier. In addition to brothers and cousins, he annually visited Paul Moore's tavern in Shoreham, just across Lake Champlain from Fort Ticonderoga; and, farther north, in New Haven, he visited the McIntoshes. In between, he slept wherever he dropped after the day's hunt or trading session for furs and pelts with Mohawk Indians he had met and with whom he hunted and explored. For much of the past year since the attempts at evicting the farmers from the Grants had begun, he had rented a gambrel-roofed, one-and-a-half story house on Bennington's main street between the Catamount Tavern and the Congregational meetinghouse. This would be his home for most of the next two decades, and now it became the headquarters of the Green Mountains resistance movement.

As soon as Allen returned to Bennington in June of 1771, he learned that a New York surveyor was running lines in Pittsford, fifty-five miles to the northeast. Allen galloped off, his handpicked squad snowballing as he went, settlers eager to help him to overtake the intruding Yorkers, as they were called, in Clarendon. He loved disguises: dressing as Indians, faces blackened with soot, he and his militia found the Albany surveyor William Cockburn working with linesmen in the woods. Like James Duane, Allen did not shrink from strong-armed tactics if he thought them necessary. He rode up to Cockburn and told him that, if he wanted to return to Albany alive, he would cease.

When Cockburn appealed to neighbors for help, they warned him he would be murdered unless he stopped surveying and went home. As Cockburn later testified, Allen told Cockburn that, if he promised never to return, he would be allowed to leave. Cockburn and his crew fled.

As Allen and his victorious company rode back toward Bennington, a rider pelted up to them with the news that the sheriff of Albany with a posse of three hundred men had surrounded James Breakenridge's farm and was demanding that he surrender it. So many of the "Bennington mob," as Sheriff Ten Eyck described them in an affidavit, had turned out with their muskets, that he had decided to leave without even serving the writ of possession on Breakinridge. This fiasco by New York's authorities provided the first significant opportunity for Allen's outnumbered followers to assemble in force against a more numerous foe and stand their ground without any killings. Allen and his men simply rode up, muskets at the ready, and, after engaging their enemies in eyeball-to-eyeball intimidation, refused to disperse. One advantage they enjoyed was the oppressed sensibility of New York sheriffs' posses, almost invariably made up of Dutch farmers who detested their British overlords and who refused to fight or drive anyone off their land. At Breakenridge's farm, when Sheriff Ten Eyck ordered forty Dutchmen to advance, they refused to budge.

It was this raid that finally jolted many Vermonters off their fences. By now, it was increasingly difficult to remain neutral. Without doubt, there would be more surveyors, larger posses. Assuming New York authorities would persevere, emergency town meetings of eleven communities in southwestern Vermont voted to elect a standing committee of safety made up of each town's more prominent citizens to organize the resistance. Committees of safety then chose militia captains. By the time of a meeting late in 1771 in the Catamount Tavern, it was obvious that Ethan Allen had emerged as the natural leader of all the militias. The committees agreed to create the Green Mountain Boys and to constitute the paid post of colonel commandant. The committeemen, many of them veterans of the French and Indian War, unanimously elected Allen to the post and instructed him to organize and train militia units that were to be ready on a moment's notice to respond to incursions from New York anywhere west of the Green Mountains.

By autumn of 1771, the New York raids and Vermont reprisals were becoming more violent. Companies of Green Mountain militia were patrolling day and night along the New York–New Hampshire Grants borderlands. By way of warning reluctant New York patentees, they pulled down and burned fences and haystacks of reluctant Yorkers. When that tactic failed, after councils of war of the militia captains at the Catamount Tavern, sterner measures followed. In October, Colonel Commandant Ethan Allen and Captain Remember Baker led a handpicked company to the farm of a New Yorker settled in Rupert. When he refused to leave, this time, evidently for the first time, as a warning never to return, they burned down his cabin. Allen and his militia of roughshod Vermont settlers were, to be fair, exerting an eighteenth-century vigilanteeism that would repeat itself on the Far West frontier in the nineteenth century. Coupled with the tactics of intimidation used by ten thousand Sons of Liberty in the period before the Revolution, it raises an unsettling question: was America founded, at least in part, on terrorism?

As WORD OF his exploits rippled through the Vermont hills, Ethan Allen took on almost mythic proportions. He traveled the New Hampshire Grants with a band of chosen men, exhorting settlers to resist their unwanted New York overlords. Settlers and Yorkers alike spread stories of his prodigious physical prowess. He was a Paul Bunyan before Bunyan ever existed. He could seize a bushel bag full of salt in his teeth and throw it over his head, they said. He could grasp two Yorkers, one in each hand, lift them off the ground, hold them at arm's length, and slam them together until they begged for mercy, they said. Allen had tackled a New York sheriff and his posse of six burly deputies, they said, leaving them flat on the ground. He even rescued children lost in the wilderness when all hope for them had been abandoned. No stranger to hyperbole, Allen may have started some of the stories himself, ever conscious of his image as part of his influence. What is true is that, in a time when every settler knew the Bible, he was becoming a reverse Moses, driving the infidel out of the promised land. He was Moses the lawgiver, using Old Testament–like formulations as he cursed the oppressors of the virtuous frontier pioneers.

Early that autumn, word reached Allen at his Catamount Tavern headquarters that a Scottish veteran of the French and Indian War, Charles Hutcheson, had built a cabin and was clearing land at New Perth on a military grant he had received from New York for his wartime services. According to the deposition Hutcheson later swore before James Duane at Albany, Allen and a squad of Bennington militia surrounded his cabin and ordered them to tear it down. When the Scot asked the Vermonters to stop, Allen responded, "They would burn it, for that morning they had resolved to offer a burnt sacrifice to the gods of the world in burning the logs of that house."

Then, while Allen held his collar and Remember Baker brandished a club over his head, Hutcheson asserted, Allen harangued him: "Go your way now and complain to that damned scoundrel, your governor. God damn your governor, laws, King, Council and Assembly." According to Hutcheson, when he protested Allen's swearing, Allen retorted, "God damn your soul, are you going to preach to us?" At the conclusion of Hutcheson's testimony, he added, he heard that Allen "denies the being of a God and that there is any infernal spirit."[3]

WHILE ETHAN ALLEN was relocating his family to a farm in Sunderland, Vermont, North Carolina's royal governor, William Tryon, learned of his appointment in the spring of 1771 to become the fifth royal governor of New York in half a dozen years. Tryon accepted the most coveted colonial office in North America. Like most high-level British appointees in the lucrative colonial service, Tryon kept getting promotions because of his connections in London. Tryon's wife's cousin was Lord Hillsborough, the secretary of the Board of Trade and Plantations, which administered all of England's colonies. Tryon, a captain in the First Regiment of Foot Guards, had served thirteen years in the British army before being appointed lieutenant governor of North Carolina at the end of the French and Indian War. His unequivocal support of the hated Stamp Act brought business in the province to a halt even as he built a grand capital building in New Bern with an opulent redbrick Georgian palace with formal gardens for himself, modeling it after his estate in England. He raised the money for "Tryon's Palace" by streamlining techniques for collecting quitrents from farmers. In fact an officer without troops, he was actually helpless to quell the Stamp Act protests in the colony's port towns, but he effectively hinted at the use of force as soon as he could obtain a detachment of Redcoats.

No sooner was the Stamp Act repealed in 1766 than western North Carolinians revolted. Settlers charged that sheriffs and treasurers were ruthlessly wringing heavy taxes from hard-pressed

farmers, embezzling much of the money, and charging extortion-
ate fees. Calling themselves Regulators, settlers protested lack
of representation in the provincial assembly, a common problem
in colonies from New Hampshire to Georgia that straddled the
Allegheny Mountains. (In New Hampshire, fewer than one-third
of the towns were represented in the colony's assembly, most of
them east of the mountains.)

When the North Carolina Regulators demanded aboli-
tion of taxes and debts, Tryon declared it a rebellion, called out
the colony's militia, and led it into the backcountry twice, first
in 1768 and again in 1771. In April of 1768, 70 armed Regulators rode into Hillsborough, freed a horse that had been seized
by the authorities for back taxes, and fired into the house of the
Crown official Edmund Fanning. Fanning called out the militia
and arrested two Regulator leaders. When 700 Regulators surrounded the jail, Fanning released his prisoners. Tryon came to
the fall court session with some 1,400 troops to prevent further
disruptions. He faced down 3,700 Regulators, who dispersed.
They later came back to whip Fanning, tear down his fine house,
and run him out of town.

In January of 1771, the North Carolina Assembly, at Tryon's
urging, passed the "Bloody Act," making rioters guilty of treason.
That spring, Tryon again took the field and crushed resistance in
the Battle of the Alamance on May 16. Tryon ordered James Few,
the leader of the insurgents, hanged on the battlefield at about the
same time he was reading his new instructions to become New
York's governor. Twelve Regulators were subsequently convicted
of treason and six of them hanged.

Tryon soon proved to be the wrong man to be New York's
governor at the wrong time. A military governor with a paternal-
istic philosophy, he promptly set about establishing a New York

provincial militia in which only "gentlemen of the first families and distinctions" could receive officers' commissions. He used large land grants to himself and his supporters to augment his own fortune and to reinforce the social hierarchy that Ethan Allen had first seen during the Albany ejectment trials. When the Board of Trade upbraided Tryon for granting to himself and his cronies more than the officially acceptable one thousand acres, he argued that such grants promoted "the subordination which arises from a distinction in rank and fortune." It acted as a "counterpoise against a leveling and republican spirit" he found prevalent in several colonies, especially on the New Hampshire Grants. Tryon's reputation for retribution had preceded him to Vermont. While more timid leaders went on circulating petitions and sending them to London, Allen knew he could lose no more time organizing armed resistance.[4]

FORMING THE EXTRALEGAL MILITIA of the New Hampshire Grants was Allen's first act of open rebellion. No militia could be formed legally without the approval of the royal governor of a province. All officers had to receive written commissions from the royal governor, the king's personal representative. Yet boy and man, from fourteen to seventy, now flocked to join Allen's new militia. Looking on from New York City, Cadwallader Colden, again the acting governor of New York as he awaited Tryon's arrival, was incensed at Allen's raids. It was when, during an earlier incumbency, Colden had warned that he would send in Redcoats and drive the settlers back into the Green Mountains that the Grants militiamen had proudly given themselves the nickname Green Mountain Boys. Only Allen wore a distinctive uniform. The Boys, as they were instantly known, simply stuck a fir twig in their hats to identify themselves. In a dozen towns, then a score, the ranks of the nearest company of Boys swelled to scores, sometimes hundreds, whenever Allen and his squad of men rode through. And because of their vigilance, the farmers on the Grants now were able to harvest their hay and corn and sow their winter wheat without fear of predation by sheriffs' posses.

THIS MILITARY SHOW of arms came in direct defiance of the latest proclamation from New York. Because of the rout of the New York surveyor at Clarendon and the raid on Hutcheson's farm at New Perth, King's Counsel James Duane believed he had enough evidence to take up the case of Allen and the Green Mountain Boys with the new royal governor as soon as he arrived in New York City. Furious, Governor Tryon declared that Allen and eight of his lieutenants were to be officially outlawed, with rewards on their heads. Tryon ordered the arrest of Allen and his militia captains, including Remember Baker, Robert Cochran, and half a dozen others. Certain that his sheriffs would be reluctant to pursue them, Tryon placed a reward of £20 (about $3,000) on each leader of the Boys and ordered New York officials to report to him for severe punishment the name of every individual protester. Such a list would surely have helped him discover that some of the New Hampshire Grant settlers had been active in the tenant rebellions in Dutchess County, New York, in the 1760s. Many of the squatters on Livingston Manor who had been driven back into New England were now eagerly serving under a new leader, Ethan Allen.

As the year 1772 began, Allen conducted a defiant New Year's Day review of his troops in Bennington. Many of the companies were led by his kinsmen, including his cousin Remember Baker of Arlington, his cousin Seth Warner of Bennington, and his cousin Ebenezer Allen of Poultney. Someone had somehow scrounged a rusty old French cannon from an abandoned fort on the Hoosick River. Reviewing his Boys, Colonel Allen wore his new, dark-green provincial militia uniform with gold buttons and epaulets, his sword and brace of pistols, and his by now legendary beaver tricorn hat. The forest green he chose provided an appropriate contrast to the scarlet favored by New York. After the military review on the Bennington common ended, an Albany man named Benjamin Buck stopped by the Catamount Tavern, where he found Allen and his friends reading Governor Tryon's proclamation. Somebody asked Buck what he thought the outcome of the land dispute would be. Buck replied, "My opinion is that the York government will hold all the lands."

Apparently recognizing the man, Allen came up behind him and hit him three times. "You are a Damn Bastard of old Munro's," he said, alluding to the New York justice of the peace. "We shall make a hell of His House and burn him in it, and every son of a bitch that will take his part." Echoing the line that Allen had first heard at Albany after the eviction trial, Buck insisted, "If it should be the right of New Hampshire, might would overcome right."

"How can you be such a damn fool?" Allen asked. "Have we not always overcome them, here and one hundred miles to the northward? If they shall ever come again, we shall drive them two hundred miles and send them to Hell." At that, one of Allen's captains loudly read the governor's name on the proclamation. As if addressing the absent official, Allen boomed, "So your name is Tryon, tri on and be Damn."[5]

SO DEEPLY ENSCONCED was Allen now in the Vermont backcountry that he gave less and less attention to his native Connecticut. He sold the rest of his interests in Connecticut, including some 177 acres in Cornwall, all that was left of his paternal inheritance. With the £23 (about $4,600 in today's currency) in hard money he realized, he galloped back to the Grants to pay off lands he had under deposit in Hubbardton and Castleton. Then, at his cousin's house at Poultney, he huddled with his trusted lieutenants, his cousin Remember and Robert Cochran. Far from being shaken by the reward on their heads, the threesome decided to make up a wanted poster of their own:

£25 Reward.—Whereas James Duane and John Kempe, of New York, have by their menaces and threats greatly disturbed the public peace and repose of the honest peasants of Bennington and the settlements to the northward, which are now and ever have been in the peace of God and the King, and are patriotic and liege subjects of Geo. the 3rd. Any person that will apprehend these common disturbers, viz: James Duane and John Kempe, and bring them to Landlord Fay's at Bennington [the Catamount Tavern] shall have £15 reward for James Duane and £10 reward for John Kempe, paid by

ETHAN ALLEN

REMEMBER BAKER

ROBERT COCHRAN

Dated Poultney

Feb. 5, 1772

Offering lower rewards than the £20 price for each of their captures, Allen and his lieutenants were mocking the New York officials as worth less than a Vermonter. Allen was also lampooning the idea of a reward by suggesting that royal officials had to be kidnapped and dragged to a barroom in the woods for justice to be rendered. Taking the poster off to be printed in Hartford, he spread copies all over the Grants. He was already used to the trip: more and more, he was appealing to a largely literate Congregational constituency through their favorite print medium, the *Courant*, which was widely read and respected on the Grants as well as all over Connecticut.[6]

IN MARCH OF 1772, as Allen prepared to leave for Connecticut, he sent Remember Baker to his new home in Arlington and Robert Cochran back to Bennington to watch for trouble. It came soon enough. When New York Justice Munro heard from a pro–New York neighbor of Baker's that he had come home, Munro decided he would collect the £20 reward for Baker's arrest himself. Rounding up fifteen other Scottish veterans living on New York grants, Munro's posse surrounded Baker's house at night, broke down the front door with an ax, and captured Baker in his bed. Fighting back, both Remember and his wife, Desire, were wounded as they were dragged out of their bed. Munro chopped off Remember's thumb with his ax. He left Desire lying naked and injured on the floor as he dragged Baker off in a sleigh toward Albany. Only slightly hurt, Desire rushed to the cabin of a neighbor who, in turn, roused one of the local Boys. In minutes, a company of the Boys was riding after the sleigh. They overtook it after a thirty-mile chase through the snow. As soon as Munro's men saw the Boys approaching, they fled, leaving Munro and his deputy to be captured and a semiconscious Baker to be taken home in the sleigh. When Allen learned of the attack, he wrote it up as "this wicked, inhuman, most barbarous, infamous, cruel, villainous and thieving act." He sent his account off to Hartford to be printed in the *Courant*, where he now launched a one-man newspaper campaign against New York's "massacring G—— Tryon" and his council, those "mercenary, intriguing, monopoliz- ing men, an infamous fraternity of diabolical plotters."[7]

AT A TIME when colonists throughout British America were riveted to the latest weekly installments in the pamphlet wars over British policies between radicals and loyalists, Allen devoted much of the spring and summer of 1772 to winning a wide readership on the Grants, at the same time gaining a following throughout Connecticut. In strong, dramatic prose, he penned five essays and paid to have them published in the *Courant*. He asked his readers basic questions that touched on landownership and the extent of royal authority and could have been construed by British officials as seditious:

> When New York, by the handle of jurisdiction, aims at the property of the inhabitants, and that flagrantly, can they expect obedience? Can the New York scribblers, by the art of printing, alter wrong into right? Or make any person of good sense believe that a great number of hard labor- ing peasants, going through the fatigues of settlement, and cultivation of a howling wilderness, are a community of riotous, disorderly, licentious, treasonable persons?

Allen summed up before the jury of his readers with an emo- tional appeal to his fellow New Englanders. He had become the voice of the oppressed "women sobbing and lamenting, children crying and men pierced to the heart with sorrow and indignation at the approaching tyranny of New York." His *Courant* essays, signed "Land of Truth and Reason" and "Friend of Liberty and

Prosperity," were immensely popular, providing underpinning for the extralegal actions of the Green Mountain Boys with political argument and justification. The instant popularity of Allen's forceful, if bombastic, prose prompted him to begin writing his first book-length work of political propaganda, the 201-page *A Brief Narrative of the Proceedings of the Government of New-York Relative to Their Obtaining the Jurisdiction of That Large District of Land to the Westward from Connecticut River.*

Neither brief nor a narrative, Allen's tome introduced a sophisticated new argument while refuting New York's claim to the Grants in detail. Since the disputed lands had not been settled after King Charles II granted them to the Duke of York in 1664, Allen maintained, they reverted to the Crown. Thus, the Crown's representative, New Hampshire's royal governor Benning Wentworth, had every right to grant the land west of the Connecticut River all the way to the New York border, twenty miles east of the Hudson River. This was made manifest when the Crown asked New Hampshire to take over maintaining and garrisoning the only fort between the Connecticut and the Hudson rivers, Fort Dummer at present-day Brattleboro, to defend the region. If New Hampshire had the responsibility of defending these lands, it also had the right to grant them to a protective mantle of settlers who bought and occupied them in good faith. "Common people are not capable of judging upon a higher principle," he wrote. They should not be punished for trusting the authority or the legality of the royal governor of New Hampshire to sell those lands.

No one had ever put the case for leaving the settlers unmolested on the New Hampshire Grants more clearly. But, for the first time, Allen was going beyond jurisdictional arguments. He was demonstrating publicly and in print his resentment of selfserving gentlemen of money and power who were using their influence to take advantage of the powerlessness of the common people. Hardworking farmers on the Grants, he averred, should not be exploited by greedy aristocrats who controlled the laws and courts. The settlers had no choice but to resist:

> The inhabitants being thus drove to the extremity of either quitting their possessions or resisting the sheriff and his posse. In this state of desparacy they put on fortitude and . . . defended their possessions; and the sheriff with his posse returned to their own land without any bloodshed. . . .

The struggle on the Grants pitted a large number of ordinary "families settled upon the land" against "that crafty, defying and monopolizing government" of New York. In letters to the editor of the *Courant* between late March and early July of 1772 and, in a pamphlet too long to be considered anything but a book, Allen unabashedly projected himself into the front rank of resistance to British imperial policy in New England—without firing a single shot.[8]

IN EARLY MARCH OF 1772, Allen still found time to compose a long and careful letter to a New York justice of the peace, Colonel Philip Skene. He sent it to Skene's palatial manor, Skenesboro, at present-day Whitehall, the head of navigation of Lake Champlain. A Scots major in the British army during the French and Indian War, Skene had received a direct Crown grant of thirty thousand acres. His indentured servants had built Skene a stone mansion, sawmills, docks, and stores that supplied the five hundred New York settlers living in the region. Skene cruised the lake in an armed schooner, the *George*, delivering lumber and ironwork all the way to Quebecois settlements on the Richelieu River. Skene and his family lived in baronial splendor. He had

asked New York to designate Skenesboro the seat of newly created Charlotte County, with Skene as its justice of the peace. The
county's leading citizens dined at his table. Ethan Allen, obviously a rising leader, had also dined there frequently.

To both men, it was clearly Skene's duty to arrest anyone who
was declared an outlaw by New York, but Skene liked Allen and,
under the code of honor of the time, found it difficult to arrest
a guest. Late in 1771, he sent him a note by way of his cousin
Ebenezer: Allen must leave the Grants and "repair to Connecticut" or Skene would have to arrest him. From Salisbury, where he
had gone to sell his holdings, Allen fired back a letter to Skene:

> I Now Inform You that I Cannot flee to Connecticut. I have
> a Spirit above that. I shall stay in Your Neighbourhood I
> hope Till I Remove to the Kingdom of heaven. Your Gener-
> ous & sotiable treatment to me when at Your house Prompts
> me to write to You Tho Your Station in Life is Honourable
> and Commands Submition from Those of an inferior rank
> Yet it is your Personal Merit that Demands esteam.

Allen was tipping his hat here, not doffing it: he was self-
assured and no flatterer. To answer Skene at all was bold. Allen
was making it plain that he was writing not for himself but as
head of the settlers. Calling Skene "the Most Consummate politician" yet one who "acts from Generous and brave principles," he
"Infer'd [Skene] would Not be an Adversary to the Setlers." Allen
had never had "Ground to Distrust Your friendship Either to me
or them." Writing as an equal, he was refusing deference:

> I Do Not esteam You Merely Because You are Col Skane
> but Because You act the Honourable part. [A] man is
> Either famous or Infamous in Proportion as Either Brave

or Mean are the principles of his Conduct. [B]y this Rule
Undoubtedly You Will pass Sentence on my Past and
future Conduct. [I]f by this Rule I shall be Denominated
Disorderly and Riotous I Desire You would be my adversary but if Otherways my friend s[r], the law of Self preservation Urges me to Defend my Property.

In his most courageous exposition to date, Allen, by risking to
appear arrogant, actually was strengthening his friendship with
Skene, who could see that Allen was maturing into a man of stature,
a leader of his people. Allen ended on a confidently jocose note:

You have heard many accounts of my Conduct Called by
the Name of Riatous Disorderly &ce and it is probable
before Next Campaign is out You may hear more Such Sort
of News. I am Informed Governour Tryon has Advertised
me and some Others and Offered Considerable Reward to
have us Delivered at New York But a Late account from
there Informs me that by virtue of a Late Law in [that]
Province they are Not Allowed to hang any man before
they have ketched him.[9]

AS SOON AS the snows had abated and the road was dry enough,
Allen opened the 1772 campaign with a beating and a bet. He
rode from Bennington to Arlington, gunning for Benjamin Spencer, a New Yorker who lived in Clarendon. Spencer later wrote
to James Duane in Albany that Allen had ridden into Arlington
with "twelve or fifteen of the most blackguard fellows he can get
double armed in order to protect him." Soon after Allen's arrival
in Arlington, as New York Justice of the Peace Munro reported in

another affidavit to Duane, "the rascally Yankees spoiled my best hat and sword coat with their pumpkin sticks." While they were thrashing him, they were also swearing: "It is shameful to hear the sentiments of the wicked ones amongst them. They even go so far as to deny a Divine Being and will not suffer a Bible in their houses. Whatever can be expected from such men but to serve the Devil." More alarming to New York authorities was Munro's afterthought: "They have great many friends in the County of Albany and particularly in the City of Albany, which encourages them in their wickedness."[10]

The accuracy of Munro's intelligence became evident a few weeks later when, in April of 1772, Allen accepted a wager with his lieutenants at the Catamount. Someone dared Allen to leave a copy of his poster advertising rewards for the capture of Duane and Kempe in a well-known Albany tavern. Forthwith, Allen rode the sixty miles from Bennington to Albany, hitched his horse in front of Benedict's Tavern, strode into the taproom, and ordered a bowl of punch. The patron instantly recognized him as a crowd gathered around Allen, who downed the punch, handed the poster to Benedict, bade him farewell, and galloped away unscathed. But there were New York sympathizers present who coveted New York's reward money, and Allen narrowly escaped capture soon afterward. While he and a friend, Eli Robards, visited a tavern in Bridport on the Vermont shore, a squad of Redcoats from nearby Fort Amherst, tipped off by an informant, burst into the tavern to search for him. But first they ordered dinner. Apparently, they had no idea what Ethan Allen looked like. After the meal, Allen, an expert at mixing punch, offered the soldiers a bowl, then regaled them with stories. Toasting the king and queen, among others, he helped them forget their mission. Once they were deeply into their cups, the landlord's daughter, who was enamored of Allen, helped him and Robards out a back window and handed them their muskets and pistols. They rode through the forest, avoiding the shore road, until they reached the safety of the house of a friend, Paul Moore, in Shoreham—opposite Fort Ticonderoga.

THE GAME WAS obviously becoming more dangerous. Not everyone on the Grants was amused by Allen's escapades. Some settlers and speculators had decided that, sooner or later, mighty New York with its Redcoats and sheriffs' posses was bound to prevail. Tryon, the latest royal governor, was offering a half-price sale on the fees for confirmatory grants. The owners of some fifty-six townships, predominantly on the east side of the Green Mountains in the lower Connecticut River valley, sought confirmation of their grants under Tryon's half-fee plan. At the same time, Tryon, in direct defiance of the king's Privy Council order of 1767 order to await further study by the Crown, began making major New York grants that overlapped existing New Hampshire grants. Of the six grants he made, one was to himself. He pocketed the customary fees from patentees of the other five.

GOVERNOR TRYON DANGLED an olive branch in front of the town fathers of Bennington. In March of 1772, he invited them, with the express exclusion of Ethan Allen and the other outlawed officers of the Green Mountain Boys, to come to New York City to present their case personally to him and his council. Some Grants settlers in and around Bennington had become jittery. They welcomed Tryon's overture, especially since rumors were flying that Tryon was on his way up the Hudson with a regiment of Redcoats. Many of the Bennington settlers were refugees from confrontations they had lost to a New York governor and Redcoats during the Hudson Valley land riots half a dozen years earlier. As tensions mounted, the Grants committees of safety met at the Catamount Tavern with Allen and his captains. There were evident signs of growing friction between town elders on the committees and Allen over his aggressive tactics. Some of the white-haired committeemen wanted to send a flag of truce to Tyron. Allen accused them of timidity in the face of force. He insisted that Tryon would respect only a show of strength. Allen finally prevailed. The majority of committeemen pledged to go on supporting the Green Mountain Boys, but several of the Bennington elders did not want to be connected with any military preparations. They walked out.

Expecting an attack, Allen and his captains brought two cannon, a mortar, and ammunition they had found in an abandoned fort from Williamstown, Massachusetts, and reorganized their companies to defend Bennington. Worried, the town leader James Breakenridge rode to Portsmouth, New Hampshire, to implore Governor Wentworth to resolve the crisis short of violence, to intervene with the king to confirm their titles and return the Grants to New Hampshire jurisdiction. Like Breakenridge, Bennington's conservatives could not know that Wentworth had already abandoned them in return for favors from Tryon. But support for the Grants settlers now came from a new quarter. The Reverend Eleazar Wheelock, founder and president of Dartmouth College, had embraced the settlers' cause when he moved his Indian mission school to the new town of Dresden (today's Hanover) on the east bank of the Connecticut River. When Wheelock heard that Governor Wentworth, instead of appealing to London on behalf of the settlers, now was telling them to appeal directly without his help or his influence at court, he dispatched a letter to Wentworth demanding an explanation. Wentworth sent him a copy of his obsequious letter to Tryon in which he criticized the settlers for being "so indolent and backward in their own affairs, so covetous in money matters, & so unconnected with one another." He told Wheelock in this private letter that he "saw no prospect of success." The Grants jurisdiction would remain with New York. But he still contended that, in "propriety," the settlers already farming the Grants should remain unmolested.[11]

At a June 1772 meeting at the Catamount Tavern, as Allen urged preparations for defense, Bennington's conservative committeemen decided on a two-pronged strategy. They would accept Tryon's invitation to travel to New York City and make their case before him; at the same time, they would send two emissaries to London to appeal directly to the king. On June 19, Stephen Fay and his son, Jonas, left Bennington in a rainstorm for the backcountry ride to the Hudson to sail down to New York City on the sloop *Albany*. Emblematically, the sloop ran aground three miles south of Albany. As the Fays waited to sail on, they visited Sheriff Ten Eyck, who had led the 1770 raid on Breakenridge's Bennington farm. After a six-day passage marked by thunderstorms, they reached New York City and, on the morning of June 26, visited Governor Tryon at his country house. They presented him with papers that included a long letter signed by Allen and three of his outlawed captains, Seth Warner, Remember Baker, and Robert Cochran. Tryon and his councillors must have writhed as they had to sit and listen while Stephen Fay read aloud Allen's letter to them.

Allen went far beyond a perfunctory recitation of the Grants dispute. He enlarged on his *Connecticut Courant* essays, stressing his growing belief that the increasingly violent struggle on the Grants was part of a wider clash between a small group of wealthy landowners and a much larger community of industrious farmers and their families. It was a struggle between hardworking yeomen and socially and politically prominent aristocrats. This "certain number of designing men" used political connections to secure patents from New York's governors for lands on the Grants that were already settled and then, without any labor, used the courts to dispossess settlers "who had already spent their meager savings" in bringing their farms out of a wilderness state into one of fruitful fields, gardens, and orchards. Such evictions as he had seen in court in Albany a year before would lead to "universal slavery, poverty and horror." New York's officials were shattering the social compact, which promised protection in exchange for the allegiance between the people and their rulers that was the essence of civilization.

Here, Allen was enunciating John Locke's social contract theory, much as Jefferson would in the Declaration of Independence some four years later. In a simplified version of seventeenth-century philosopher Locke's *Second Treatise on Government*, Allen argued that no individual or group of men could be "supposed to be under any particular compact or Law, except it pre-supposeth that Law will protect such person or community of persons in his or their properties." Otherwise, the citizen "would, by Law, be bound to be accessary to his own ruin and destruction, which is inconsistent with the Law of self-preservation."

Shifting from Locke to the French philosopher Jean-Jacques Rousseau, Allen argued that this law was "natural as well as eternal" and could "never be abrogated by the Law of men." On the Grants, "law has been rather used as a tool rather (than a rule of equity) to cheat us out of the country, we have made vastly valuable by labour and expence of our fortunes." Accusing some of the men now listening to his words of being "a set of artful, wicked men seeking our ruin to enrich themselves," Allen charged that

"under colour of punishing rioters," and posing as zealous uphold-
ers of "loyalty and veneration for good government," the New
York landlords were out to "rob the inhabitants of their country."
Concluding with a burst of Rousseauian rhetoric, he demanded,

> Can any man, in the exercise of reason, make himself
> believe that a number of Attorneys and other gentlemen,
> with all their tackle of ornaments, and compliments, and
> French finesse, together with their boasted legality of
> law, . . . have just right to the lands, labours and fortunes of
> the *New-Hampshire* settlers?[12]

Even as the Fays were sailing to New York City, Allen
unleashed another editorial salvo in the *Connecticut Courant*. His
writings were now being read aloud in taverns and homes all
over the Grants. He sharply contrasted settlers with the "wicked,
inhuman, most barbarous, infamous, cruel, villainous and thiev-
ish agents of New York." He detailed Justice Munro's capture of
Remember Baker in his bed in March, describing in lurid detail
how the Yorkers had smashed down the Bakers' door and hacked
off Remember's thumb while "ruffians" were busy "mauling, beating and bruising his children." By overtaking the New Yorkers
who had strapped Baker to a sled, Allen and the Boys were being
"loyal and faithful subjects to the Crown of Great Britain, whose
banner they mean evermore to live and die under."[13]

But when the Fays returned from New York City, Allen's
impassioned inveighing seemed pointless. At a July 15 mass
meeting in Bennington's Congregational meetinghouse, the Fays
reported that Governor Tryon had sworn he had never seen a
copy of their petition to the king, had never intended to raise an
armed force against them, and had no desire to dispossess anyone
from his farm. The Fays read aloud a report from Tryon's council

detailing New York's claim to the Grants and expressing "great tenderness to a deluded people who are in danger of forfeiting the favor of the Crown by resisting the authority of the laws." The council, the Fays said, had recommended that Tryon cease prosecutions for eviction until the king made a final decision. Meanwhile, settlers could quietly possess their farms. To Allen's dismay, the Bennington settlers voted unanimously to accept Tryon's terms. In celebration of what appeared to be a peaceful victory, Seth Warner and his Bennington militia, who had sided with the town's more conservative elders in recent months, fired salutes with their muskets and their twin cannon. Everyone drank toast after toast to the king, to Tryon, to the New York council, to "universal peace and plenty, liberty and property." The long crisis appeared to be over.[14]

PEACE LASTED LESS than a month. While the Fays were negotiating with Governor Tryon and his council in New York, Allen discovered that Tryon's promises did not match his actions. He learned that Tryon's rumored attack, which had the effect of cooling Bennington's enthusiasm for armed resistance, was merely a deployment of Redcoats up the Hudson on their way to reinforce the British fort in Detroit. The delegates to the Bennington meeting of July 15 had scarcely decided to call a convention of ten towns, this time at Manchester, when Ethan heard that New York's surveyor, William Cockburn, chased out of Clarendon a year earlier, was back on the Grants, this time running lines along the Winooski River. Captains Baker and Warner rode north at once at the head of a company of the Boys. Along the way, they discovered that a settlement of New Yorkers had taken root along Otter Creek for the second time in a year. Presenting a New York patent, Colonel John Reid's Scots armed

tenants had driven off New Hampshire settlers already farming
the land. This time, when Remember Baker arrived, one of the
New York tenants asked him by what authority he acted. Baker
said the Scots "lived out of the bounds of the law." Brandishing his musket, he added, "This is the law," and then held up
the hand without a thumb. "This was his [Munro's] law." After
allowing the tenants to carry off their belongings, the Boys set
fire to the cabins, pulled down the gristmill, broke the millstones,
and threw the pieces into Otter Creek, then trampled the corn
with their horses' hoofs. Then they hurried north in time to capture the surveyor Cockburn. As they prepared to punish him,
they learned of the truce with Tryon and released him. Governor
Tryon was not so forgiving. On August 11, he fired off a letter
to Bennington accusing the town's leaders of being "disingenu-
ous and dishonorable." He ordered them to reinstall Reid and the
Scots tenants or face the "fatal consequence that must follow so
manifest a breach of public confidence."[15]

At a second Manchester convention, on August 27, at Allen's
urging, the delegates approved a letter pointing out to New York
officials that the incidents had taken place before word of the
Grants had reached them but insisting that New York's latest
encroachments were "a manifest infringement on [their] property," like so many that had been "all along a bone of contention."
This was a stronger stance than the Bennington convention had
risked, but Allen still saw it as straddling when the delegates from
ten towns to the Manchester convention pledged to protect their
property without "insult[ing] government authority." The convention then voted to send two delegates to London to lobby for
confirmation of their grants.

This latest attempt at moderation fell apart on September 29,
less than a month later, when Remember Baker and Ira Allen, at
the head of a surveying team of the Boys, found Benjamin Ste-

vens, New York's deputy surveyor of lands, with a team of his fifteen armed men violating the agreement by again trying to run survey lines near Waterbury on the Winooski River. Ira's version of what next transpired differed from the affidavit James Duane prepared for Stevens. According to Ira Allen,

> There being a truce . . . we thought it would not be politic to inflict corporial punishment on Stevens. He and his men were dismissed, on pain of death never to come within the district of the New Hampshire Grants again.

According to Duane's document, Ethan Allen was part of the punitive party: Duane had never heard of any other Allen. He quoted the surveyor's description of "the gang," depicting Remember Baker as "a tall slim fellow with a sandy complection." On October 21, Duane took the affidavit before Governor Tryon and his council. Duane averred that Baker, Allen, and five other persons had held Stevens and two assistants, who were "without any provocation stript by them of their property and Effects, insulted and threatened and [one assistant] thrown into the Fire, Bound and Burned and otherwise beat and abused in a Cruel manner." Governor Tryon immediately issued a warrant for the arrest of Allen and Baker and offered a £100 reward for their capture.[16]

AS THE BORDER WARFARE resumed and intensified in the summer of 1773, Ethan Allen led one hunderd Green Mountain Boys to New Haven Falls, five miles north of the Middlebury Falls, and erected what Ira Allen described as a "block fort"—a blockhouse—to discourage Scottish settlers from New York from penetrating one of the few known passes into the central valleys of the Grants. Then, "for personal safety," he continued,

Capt. Baker and I thought proper to erect a block fort
near the falls of the Onion [Winooski] river, twenty by
thirty two feet, every stick of timber was at least eight
inches thick. In the second story, were 32 port holes
for small arms. The roof was so constructed, in case of
fire, we could throw it off—the second story jutted four
inches over the other, so that we could fire down, or
throw water to put out fire; and the fort was built over
a boiling spring for certainty of water. We made double doors, blocks, for the windows, and every part proof
against small arms.[17]

THE SEESAWING LAND WAR would go on forever unless
someone came up with a more constructive solution. Ethan
Allen thought he had one. The Crown could create a new province between New York and New Hampshire. This was not
a far-fetched possibility. At Whitehall Place in London, the
Board of Trade and Plantations was pondering half a dozen
such schemes for creating new provinces out of the spoils of the
French and Indian War. At the southern end of Lake Champlain, Colonel Skene was urging the creation of Skenesboro as
the seat of a new county. It was Allen who proposed to Skene
that he enlarge the scope of his undertaking, go to London
and petition for the creation of a new province based at British forts at Ticonderoga and Crown Point. On their way back
from the Manchester convention, Allen and Jehiel Hawley of
Arlington, who had been chosen at the meeting to go to London with James Breakenridge to present the settlers' latest petition, stopped off at Amos Bird's house in Castleton. The three
men all knew Skene well. He had asked them to help circulate

his own petition to make his manor the county seat of the new county of Charlotte, named after the queen.

From Bird's house, Allen wrote Skene to tell him he was reluctant to help New York create the new county on the Grants because it would conflict with the settlers' petition for annexation to New Hampshire. Skene liked Allen's idea to create a new province. As a result, Allen, Bird, and Skene met at Skene's manor to draw up their proposal. The province of Ticonderoga and Crown Point was to encompass all of New York north of the Mohawk River on both sides of Lake Champlain, including the New Hampshire Grants. Three years later, the Crown approved Allen's scheme, but the bureaucratic wheels in London had turned too slowly. Skene was on the high seas with his commission as royal governor of the new province when the American Revolution broke out. A storm diverted his ship. Instead of landing in New York, Skene landed in Philadelphia during the Second Continental Congress. He was promptly jailed.

WHILE COLONEL COMMANDANT Ethan Allen stayed close to his headquarters at the Catamount Tavern in Bennington, his youngest brother, Ira, roamed the west side of the Green Mountains with their cousin Remember. A skilled surveyor, Baker taught Ira all he had ever learned about the craft in only one week. Yet his transit and compass and chains gave Ira the tools he needed to pursue something like a pyramiding scheme of acquiring large tracts of land with little or no money.

Small, wiry, and wily, Ira Allen had sold his share of his father's Cornwall, Connecticut, farm when he was only nineteen. With the cash, he went to the New Hampshire Grants, just weeks after the Albany ejectment trials and the first meeting of the Green Mountain Boys. While he astutely sensed the jitteriness of absentee speculators and settlers alike, he was still a minor. He was ignoring the advice of his businesslike brother Heman when he purchased his first proprietor's rights in over one thousand acres in hilly Poultney, where Ethan and Remember already owned rights to considerable land. In the course of the next year, Ira made shoestring purchases, borrowing and making small deposits as he wheeled and dealt. He put deposits on more than 10,000 acres of Hubbardton land owned by Isaac Searl of Williamstown, Massachusetts. Ira's silent partner in the deal was probably Remember. The purchase price was only £64, about $10,000 today. Then Ira purchased four more rights, another 1,400 acres, in Castleton. After buying these lands, Ira and Remember decided to go north and survey the Winooski River valley. They had heard so much about it from Ethan and from Salisbury neighbors who had pursued French and Indian hostage takers nearly ten years earlier. Heman warned his younger brother not to take too much of a speculative plunge into the river valley, worried that Ira was operating on rather shaky credit. Ignoring him, Ira bought fifty-two more proprietary rights on credit and tied up another six rights in the region.

But Ira needed cash. To keep his land schemes solvent, he persuaded his brother to form the Onion River Land Company, organized by Ethan and including Heman, Levi, Zimri, and Ira Allen and Remember Baker as partners. The partners would, at one time or another, own fully 200,000 acres of the land between the Green Mountains and Lake Champlain. While the family members that led, first, the revolt against New York jurisdiction and then against the British in the opening weeks of the American Revolution were actually cash poor, they were rich in nerve, operating on badly strained credit and amassing land, on paper at least, by clever tactics and, on one occasion, by outright trickery.

Along with Remember, Ira made a contract to survey the township of Mansfield, in present-day Lamoille County, which, at the time, included little more than the steep slopes of 4,400-foot Mount Mansfield. In the autumn of 1772, against the brilliant gold backdrop of the sugar maples on the mountain slopes, the two cousins set to work dragging their chains up and down the steep slopes. Ira by this time owned about one-third of Mansfield Township, but their surveying revealed there was not enough arable soil on his tract to make one good farm. With Remember's jokes about his prowess at choosing farmland ringing in Ira's ears, the cousins explored south along the mountain range through Waterbury, Middlesex, and Moretown, where Ira had bought other land. By December of 1772, they returned to Poultney to find Ethan, and, as winter set in, Ethan and Ira set out on a hunting trip, tracking deer through the fresh snows. Even then, Ira was keeping a sharp eye out for vacant land near Tinmouth at the headwaters of the Poultney River. He now decided to sell his land around Hubbardton in the south to concentrate his efforts in the north. Returning to Heman's store in Salisbury, Connecticut, he drew up the survey notes and map of Mansfield Township and went on to Sharon, Connecticut, where most of the Mansfield proprietors lived. He shaded the truth of the township's land values by misnaming the varieties of trees growing there. Disguising the poor quality of the soil for farming, he was leaving the impression that there were valuable forests that would yield profitable timber and potash. He later wrote that he sought and found slow-witted investors, persuading them he wanted to buy more Mansfield land from them. Then, when his rights were talked up around Sharon, he agreed to sell back the twenty rights he had acquired and was eager to dump—in addition to £90 (about $17,000) for the surveying work he had done.

Ira Allen, before turning twenty-one, owned outright or had

placed deposit on thirty-six rights, nearly 13,000 acres, including about 1,000 acres of mountainous land in Bolton, Moretown, Duxbury, and Middlesex townships that he wanted to unload so that he could buy more fertile lands along Lake Champlain. He had tied up this hill country land from one Samuel Averill of New Milford, Connecticut, paying with a promissory note for £150 (about $30,000). To carry out this maneuver, he paid a call on relatives of Averill's, who lived near Milford. Averill learned from his sons that young Allen was in town and summoned him to tell him about the Winooski Valley lands. Ira had been busy talking up the rocky mountain lands. Averill said he would tear up the £150 debt if Ira would reconvey the mountainous lands to him. Ira refused because he wanted to make a profit, he said.

In his first advertisement in the *Connecticut Courant*, Ethan called the family venture "Ethan Allen and Company." They had to move quickly now. Ethan, Heman, and Ira, with the proceeds of their collective business ventures, Heman's collateral and Ethan's clout as colonel commandant of the Green Mountain Boys giving them strong credit, rode nearly two hundred miles and back again to White Plains, New York. The Onion River Land Company had acquired the entire thirty-mile-long Winooski Valley as well as other prime Lake Champlain front lands in present-day Shelburne and Colchester. Did the Allens know that their nemesis in New York, Attorney James Duane, also claimed much of this same land, including a township Duane called Deerfield (present-day Williston), about 35,000 acres lying on a river called Onion River?

To cross over into New York with rewards on their heads, Ethan, Ira, and Remember traveled disguised as British officers, armed with pistols and swords, supposedly on their way from

Canada to New York City to sail home to London. To people they passed on the road south, Ira later wrote, they made "no small parade." Heman, for whom it was safe to travel in New York, went separately as if to buy goods for his store, as he often did: he was well known and trusted in the region. At an inn in White Plains, Heman contacted Samuel Burling, the Quaker merchant whose group had bought the rights to the lands at the mouth of the Winooski from Benning Wentworth a decade earlier, and asked now to set up a meeting. Meanwhile, Ethan, his brother, and cousin took rooms in the tavern. At their meeting, Burling sold the Allens 45,000 acres along with shares several of his Quaker friends were happy to unload. After three days, Ethan and the two "officers" were ready to leave, but Heman could only persuade the tavern owner to let him approach the would-be officers by buying them a "liberal" bowl of punch. Revealing their identities as they left, they hurried back to Connecticut while a peddler rode pell-mell to New York, hoping to get a reward for them.

After dashing to the safety of Connecticut, on their way home to Salisbury, they rode north until they were opposite Quaker Hill, then galloped into New York again to visit an old family friend, the Quaker preacher Benjamin Ferris. Surprised that the Allens were packing pistols, Ferris asked, "What doth thee do with these things?" "Nothing amongst our friends," Ethan answered, explaining that they had formed the Green Mountain Boys to protect their property, their neighbors, and themselves from the New York authorities. Entertaining the Allens with a splendid dinner, Ferris hired Ira to locate and survey rights he owned near the Winooski River. He sold one of the parcels of land to Ethan and paid Ira seven of his fourteen rights in Shelburne for his surveying services. When word of the Allens' bold intrusion reached Albany, as Ira later reported,[18] James Duane dutifully made out one more affidavit but discouraged the sheriff from pursuing the Vermonters:

> James Duain Esqr. observed that we were daring fellows, and no doubt well mounted, & had given this alarm to raise a party to pursue us, and had gone directly out of the colony in hopes of being pursued, to laugh at our pursuers, & that it was in vain to pursue Green Mountain Boys on their guard.

Flushed with the success of their mission, Ethan, Heman, and Remember rode back to Salisbury to begin selling their company's most valuable land. But Ira, still determined to dispose of his hardscrabble Mount Mansfield acreage, rode on to New Milford for another crack at Samuel Averill. He found only Mrs. Averill at home. He told her he was planning to build a road along the Winooski River and he expected Averill to "bear his share of the expense." Pretending to be exhausted from his travels, he accepted her offer to show him to a bedroom before Averill came home. The room shared a thin unplastered wall with the Averills, and he could hear Mrs. Averill tell her husband about the expensive road-building project. The next morning, he brought up the road again over breakfast, offering to settle if Averill would tear up the £150 note and deed him ten rights to Middlesex he owned. Ethan would later boast that this was "the very town I chose—thus by two contracts I got ten rights of land [about 3,500 acres] without paying one shilling for a wide, fertile swath along the Winooski River, all his own."[19]

The Middlesex lands eventually turned Ira a handsome profit, selling for £500 (about $100,000 today), but not until the Revolution was over and he could produce a clear title. While Ira was bamboozling Averill, his partners in the new land company were busily selling the choicest section of the Winooski Valley to several of the leading investors of Salisbury. Once again a respectable citizen in the town where he had had his first business success as an iron foundry owner and then been so unceremoniously expelled eight years earlier, Ethan must have relished one particular transaction there. To Colonel Thomas Chittenden, head of the Litchfield County militia, and to his second-in-command, Major Jonathan Spafford, and Abijah Pratt, the Onion River Land Company sold 1,236 acres along the Winooski River, at present-day Williston, "for the sum of £500 current money of the Province of New York." (Connecticut would not have its own currency until the 1770s.) One-half of the land was to be prime intervale land; the rest, wooded upland. Later, Chittenden bought another 2,000 acres. He already owned some 350 acres across the river in Jericho. Chittenden had made good his vow of a decade ago to someday acquire his "paradise." The upland, the intervale, with the magnificent view of Camel's Hump, was now at last his. "Here I will build my home and my sons shall be settled around me," he had sworn. Chittenden and his friends bonded themselves to start clearing the land within a year and to hire three men to work, except in winter, until the land was cleared. Within a year, with his wife and ten children, he would leave Connecticut and trek to the Winooski Valley, home ever since to his descendants in the county that now bears his name. That name and his purchase then gave Ethan Allen and his land company a new kind of credit and respectability, as well as a quick return on their best investment ever.[20]

AFTER SELLING THE Chittenden group such a large share of his land company's choice acreage, Ethan Allen was in an expansive mood. He hurried south to Hartford to his printer's shop, something of a second home by now, to place his first real estate ad. Calling his enterprise "Ethan Allen and Company," he declared that the tract contained 45,000 acres. The Winooski was a bountiful river, "with a diversity of sorts of excellent fish particularly the salmon," Allen wrote, in his best real estate prose. The river was bordered by wide, lush littoral intervales of deep soil with "little or no timber" to clear, except a "scattering [of] buttonwood, elm, and butternut trees. The land rises from the intervale, in graceful oval hills, and spreads into swailes of choice mowing ground." This was, Allen believed, the finest farmland he had ever seen, and he knew how to appeal to farmers, even if in Lockean terms:

> There is no tract of land of so great quantity between New York and the government of Canada, that in a state of nature can justly be denominated equally good. . . . A number of men are already gone to cut a road to the prem- ises from Otter Creek which is about twenty miles, and a settlement will forthwith be carried into execution. The land will be sold at a moderate price.[21]

In this ad, Ethan directed potential buyers to contact himself (listed first) or Ira or Zimri or cousin Remember "on the premises" or Heman or Levi at their store in Salisbury. Ethan, Ira, Zimri, and Remember, Ira wrote in his autobiography, had hurried north to build a blockhouse at the falls of Winooski, the highest water- fall in New England. Then they canoed south again:

> We took some provisions in our packs, and returned to Middlebury falls, and proceeded to mark a road to Onion river. This road was soon after cut out so as to make a bri-

dle road. . . . My brother Heman and others visited Onion
river by the way of that road in 1773.

In many places the "road," the first road of any kind on either
shore of Lake Champlain before the Revolution, was only four
or five feet wide with blaze marks hacked on trees flanking its
seventy-mile length and just wide enough for an ox pulling a
sledge or a sleigh to pass through. The Chittendens and their
Salisbury neighbors followed the road one year later in the
summer of 1774. Ira Allen viewed this project as one of his signal
accomplishements: "Thus in a short time, I led a people through
a wilderness of 70 miles about the same distance that took Moses
40 years to conduct the children of Israel." The Allens saw this
accomplishment in biblical terms. Ira, who never seemed to like to
use the first-person plural personal pronoun "we," took full credit
in his autobiography, often downplaying Ethan's contributions.
But self-absorbed Ethan didn't seem to notice: as patriarch, he
was proud to offer, as surety for titles to his promised land, "The
Great Seal of the Province of New Hampshire."[22]

WITH THE WESTERN frontier officially closed off by the British
government and Redcoats patrolling between some two hundred
stockades to keep settlers from encroaching on Indian lands, the
population was being forced farther and faster northward. Almost
immediately, New Englanders began pouring north toward the
new settlement. The Chittendens with their ten children came
north in the summer of 1774, following a familiar pattern. To
perfect their claims, the men came first to cut down trees, make
a rude cabin, called a "possession house," then dam a stream for a
pond. One or two hired men spent the winter planting and har-

vesting winter wheat for the livestock. The next spring, the entire
family migrated north, all their belongings pulled by the invaluable team of oxen. Women and children rode the family horses.
The men walked, shouldering their muskets, guiding the oxen
with light flicks from their bullwhips.

As THE BORDER war with New York intensified in the summer of 1773, to prevent settlements under New York jurisdiction from taking root, the Allens went beyond the bounds of
any lawful authority and carried out attacks on anyone between
the mountains and the lake who accepted the authority of New
York Province. By now, New York had organized the region into
a new county, Charlotte, and appointed royal officeholders for it.
Ethan Allen's first target was a newly appointed New York justice of the peace, Benjamin Spencer, who lived in modern-day
Clarendon, its name under the New Hampshire grant. Holding
New York deeds, its residents insisted on calling their town by its
New York–patented name of Durham. The settlement was governed by New York–commissioned officials—a judge, two justices, a coroner, and an Anabaptist minister. Allen finally could
no longer tolerate such a "hornet's nest" of New Yorkers, as he put
it. On Saturday night, November 20, at about eleven o'clock—a
month before the Boston Tea Party—he attacked the village with
a large contingent of the Boys. In much the same scenario as the
New York raid on Remember Baker's bedroom, Allen, resorting
to bald violence, ordered the front door of Judge Benjamin Spencer's house shattered with a single blow of an ax. Allen and Baker
burst into the room where Spencer, his wife, and, according to
their affidavits, "some others of his family were sleeping." Allen,
armed with a musket, cutlass, and pistols, ordered Spencer to get
up, telling him

that he had been a damned old offender and the Township of Durham a Hornets Nest in their way and they were now determined to put an End to it by making them concede to take and hold their Lands under New Hampshire and submit to the Rules of their Mobb, or by destroying their property and making them quit the Country.

According to Spencer, when he took his time getting dressed, hoping to stall until help could arrive, Allen hit him over the head with his gun. Other Boys were pointing their guns through the windows as Spencer got to his feet and dressed, his wife screaming and holding their children in the bed. They took Spencer away on horseback and held him in a house two miles away, guarded by four Boys. When the minister, the Reverend Benjamin Hough, came to visit Spencer the next morning, he asked Allen to explain the raid. Allen told him in biblical terms that "the day of Judgment was come when every man should be Judged according to his works." He had warned the townspeople often enough. He was driving out the Yorker officials, and, if they ever returned, the Boys would "Lay all Durham in Ashes and leave every person in it a Corpse."

On Monday morning, November 22, Allen gave Judge Spencer his choice of courtrooms. He chose his own doorstep. For such trials, which were becoming more frequent, Allen had devised a ritual that mocked judicial decorum. He had the Boys erect the "judgment seat," something like an elevated portable bench that they carried on a horse. Sometimes a tree stump had to make do. Allen then mounted the bench, and three of his captains took their seats on chairs they brought from Spencer's house. Allen announced that the proprietors of the New Hampshire Grants had delegated himself and Captains Baker, Warner, and Cochran, the other judges, to inspect the Grants and discourage any intruders. He declared that Spencer's crimes were applying for a New York deed, accepting a New York judgeship, issuing warrants against New Hampshire settlers, and trying to influence others to accept New York's authority. Allen and Baker decided the punishment: Spencer's house was a public nuisance and had to be burned. When Spencer pleaded that his family would be ruined, Allen feigned pity and decreed that only the roof should be taken off and would be put back on if Spencer declared it was under New Hampshire's authority and would buy a New Hampshire deed to his property. Spencer agreed amid "great Shouting of Joy and much noise and Tumult."

Before he left, according to Spencer's affidavit, Allen "damned the Government, said they valued not the Government nor even the Kingdom; That force was force in whatever Hands, & that they had force and power sufficient to protect themselves against either."

After he rode away with his militia, Allen saw to it that the Durhamites were charged fair prices by the New Hampshire proprietors—and he didn't try to sell them back their land. Treading a blurred line between self-aggrandizing land speculator and latter-day Robin Hood, Allen was maintaining the mantle of dispenser of justice before the Green Mountain Boys, even as he asserted uncontested power in the borderlands region and, in landownership at least, grew wealthy. After leaving Clarendon, he wrote an open letter, assuring his protection to the townsmen. Then he rode off to Salisbury to buy up, at bargain prices, land offered by absentee New York Quakers. It is an open question whether his paramilitary power wasn't translating into intimidation that made potential sellers of these Vermont lands more liberal in the prices they were willing to accept for their properties.

In his absence, Allen's surrogates continued their punitive evictions, next targeting Jacob Marsh, a newly appointed justice of the peace of Charlotte County. Facing similar charges before a "judgment seat" occupied, in place of Allen, by Captain Remember Baker, the New York justice was released after Baker sentenced him to a severe flogging on his bare body with "twigs of the forest," a sentence he would commute if Marsh promised to give up his New York commission. When Marsh returned home, he found the roof torn off his house and his farm ransacked. Marsh no longer attempted to act as a New York justice. The only justice being dispensed on the Grants by late 1773 was the version practiced by Ethan Allen and the Green Mountain Boys.

BEFORE ALLEN COULD return to his farm in Sunderland that winter, a provocative raid shattered the deceptive calm that had set in in the port town of Boston. On the evening of December 16, 1773, some three thousand Bostonians watched as a well-organized contingent of the Sons of Liberty disguised as Mohawk Indians boarded three British merchant ships laden with East India Company tea and threw 342 lacquered chests valued at £10,000 overboard. Samuel Adams, the brewer and leader of the Sons had organized the "Indians"; among other leaders was Allen's old friend Dr. Thomas Young, who refused to wear a disguise. The British Parliament promptly responded by closing the port with a naval and land blockade and, when a dispatch ship brought the news to London, by firing Massachusetts' parliamentary agent, Benjamin Franklin, the deputy postmaster general for America, convicting him of opening the mails of royal officials. Such mutinous actions by American radicals only toughened the English ministry's resolve and hastened imperial measures calculated to bring not only the coastal towns but the rebellious frontier to heel.

• • •

JOINING IN THE crackdown on American radicals, the New York Assembly on March 9, 1774, passed what the Grants settlers called the "Bloody Acts." Proclaiming that a riotous state prevailed on the Grants, the acts were the direct result of the attack on the Durham settlement by Allen and the Boys in September of 1773. The New York royal government was responding to

> the Petition of Benjamin Hough, in behalf of himself and many of his Majesty's Subjects inhabiting the County of Charlotte, and the North Eastern District of the County of Albany, complaining of many Acts of Outrage, Cruelty and Oppression, committed against their Persons and properties by the Bennington Mob, and the Dangers and Injuries to which they are daily exposed, and imploring that this House will take them under its protection. . . . That at present prevails . . . a dangerous and destructive Spirit of Riot and Licentiousness, subversive to all order and good Government, and that it is become an intollerable Grievance. . . .

The assembly resolution also alleged that the "Bennington Mob" had "seized, insulted, and terrified several Magistrates and other Civil Officers so that they dare not execute their respective Functions." They had

> rescued Prisoners for Debt; assumed for themselves Military Commands, and Judicial Powers; burned and demolished the Houses and property and beat and abused the persons of many of his Majesty's subjects, expelled them from their possessions, and put a period to the Administration of Justice. . . .

The chair of the legislative committee gathering evidence for the assembly and principal author of the punitive act was Crean Brush, an Anglo-Irish immigrant lawyer who, as a minor Crown official, had acquired patents to 20,000 acres of New York land grants in and around the town of Westminster in the Connecticut River valley, lands originally granted by Governor Wentworth of New Hampshire. Brush had moved to the region in eastern Vermont claimed by New York as Cumberland County and, in addition to being appointed registrar of New York deeds and clerk of the county court, was elected from Westminster to the New York Provincial Assembly. He continued to acquire land on the Grants, eventually claiming title to 60,000 acres in the Connecticut Valley. In Albany, he vigorously contested New Hampshire's jurisdiction over Vermont lands.

In the wake of the Boston Tea Party and Ethan Allen's ever more violent attacks on New York settlers, in February of 1774 George Clinton, chair of the legislative committee studying the upheaval on the Grants, appointed Crean Brush to write the committee's recommendations. Clinton would become the longtime post-Revolution governor of New York and then the fourth vice president of the United States, under Thomas Jefferson. It was Brush, a major recipient of New York land grants on the Connecticut River shore of Vermont, who authored what became known in Vermont as the Bloody Acts. The acts outlawed the leaders of the Green Mountain Boys by name—Ethan Allen, Seth Warner, Remember Baker, and Robert Cochran—as well as four Bennington town leaders—Peleg Sunderland, Silvanus Brown, John Smith, and James Breakenridge. Now, if any of the eight men accused of leading "the Bennington mob" left the protection of their own extralegal militia, they faced arrest and condign punishment. Any further "riots or disturbance" would be indictable as capital offenses. If, for the offenses already charged to them, Allen and the other seven outlaws did not surrender within seventy days from the March 9 passage of the act, they would be adjudged guilty without a trial and "to suffer death."[23]

On the assembly's advice, Governor Tryon raised the rewards for Allen and Baker to £100 and £50 for each of the others. If they were captured, Allen, his subordinate officers in the Green Mountain Boys, and Bennington's town leaders were now deemed, by extension, by the entire British government, outlaws and rebels. If they could be captured anywhere that New York claimed jurisdiction—all the lands from Lake Erie east to the Connecticut River, from the northern boundaries of Pennsylvania and Massachusetts to the Canadian border—Ethan Allen and the outlawed leaders of present-day Vermont could be arrested and returned to Albany and then shipped to England for summary execution. In England, where there were some one hundred capital offenses at the time, upwards of one thousand felons were executed each year. Outlaws from the American frontier could expect little mercy from Governor Tryon, who had hanged the leaders of the Regulators movement in the North Carolina backcountry and who, at any time, could lead British troops onto the Grants and make arrests. Ironically, now, more than ever, the Grants depended on the protection of Allen and the Green Mountain Boys.

INSTEAD OF FLEEING to the relative safety of Connecticut, as Colonel Skene had advised, Allen, evidently burning the midnight candle at his room in the Catamount Tavern where he could respond rapidly to a New York raid, coolly set to work compiling his answer to Crean Brush. In a letter dated May 19, he accused Brush of "hatred and Malice Toward the N. Hampshire Settlers" and "particularly Towards me." Noting that Brush was one of "a

Number of Learned Attorneys and Gentlemen (by Birth) Interested in the Lands" on which the settlers dwelt, Ethan accused Brush of deluding any "Honestly Disposed" members of the New York Assembly by "Beguileing them Into a false Opinion that Those People You Call the Bennington Mob are Notorious Rioters. . . . You Know better. . . . They Onely Contend for their Property and . . . they have No Design Against the Government any further than to Protect the Same."

Allen claimed that Brush was one of "the Land Schemers" who used the acts to lay "a Trap for the Lives" of the settlers and called him and his legislative coauthors

> busie understrappers to a Number of more Overgrown Villains which Can murther by Law without remorse. But I Have to Inform that the Green Mountain Boys will Not Tamely resign their necks to the Halter to be Hanged by Your Curst Fraternity of Land Jockeys who Would Better Adorn a halter than would we, therefore as You regard Your Own Lives be Carefull Not to Invade ours for what Measure you meat, it Shall be Measured to You Again.

In a sarcastic postscript to "Mr. Brush sir," Allen threatened Brush with a very personal retribution:

> As a Testimony of Gratitude for the many unmerited Kindnesses, and services, you have Done us [in] the last Sessions at New York &c &c we Intend Shortly visiting your Abode, Where we hope to have the Honour of Presenting you with the beech seal [a flogging with a long, thick beech switch]—which we Beg your kind Acceptance of as a mark of the high Esteem we have of your Person. . . .[24]

. . .

SETTING ASIDE HIS beech switch and sharpening his quill, Allen wrote his second book. He would not allow the New York legislature to utter its official condemnation of the leaders of the Grants movement unchallenged. Spelling out the settlers' case in 224 pages, he penned *Brief Narrative of the Proceedings of the Government of New-York.* Not only did he thoroughly detail the history of the decade-long struggle, but he boldly included the New York act outlawing him, naming the names of its instigators and pointing out their conflicts of interest dating back to the 1770 ejectment hearing before the New York Supreme Court of Judicature. Then he rode off to Hartford to see it through the press. He had accumulated enough money now to pay the printer even though he had no reason to doubt that he would be reimbursed by the New Hampshire grant holders at their next annual meeting. *Brief Narrative* went beyond the legal case for landownership to build on conversations he had had a decade earlier with Dr. Thomas Young and his own years of readings, conversations, and experience to make a frontal attack on entrenched privilege in a hierarchical society where the rich and powerful exploited "the poor and needy."

Then, once again translating rhetoric into action, Allen led the Boys on a retaliatory raid against the informant who had provided the details of the Durham raid that had triggered the Bloody Acts. As if in response to the harsh New York reaction to his four-year campaign of resistance, he seized, on January 26, 1775, Benjamin Hough, the Anabaptist minister who had stubbornly remained in Clarendon after his public humiliation in the September 1773 raid. This time, treatment of a New York grant holder was proportionately harsher than ever before. In a ritualized "judgment seat" trial, Allen as presiding judge, Seth Warner, and five other officers of the Boys served as the jury. With a severity that rivaled the brutality of British officers of the time, they sentenced the Reverend Hough to a flogging of two hundred lashes of the stiff beech switch, then banished him from the Grants under threat of five hundred lashes—enough to kill most men. Four Boys tied Hough, pulled off his shirt, and took turns administering the two hundred hickory lashes. In five years of enforcing control over the Grants, Hough's harsh punishment represented the most extreme case. But now, Allen and his followers believed, they were engaged in open warfare. Condemned to death if they were captured, they were no longer satisfied with their usual resort to humiliation and intimidation. Hough was an informer and was being treated as such.

A more typical punishment befell Dr. Samuel Adams of Arlington. He insisted on exhorting his neighbors to accept New York's terms. Allen and the Boys promptly captured him, "tried" him, and sentenced him to be tied to a chair and hoisted up to dangle beneath the stuffed catamount that served as the Bennington tavern's signpost, where he remained the butt of taunts for several hours. While demonstrating that they would tolerate no support for New York's authority on the New Hampshire Grants, Allen and his Boys had so far never killed anyone.[25]

By November 15, 1774, long after the seventy-day deadline for surrender had passed, Allen was busily sending copies of his *Brief Narrative* to influential figures in surrounding colonies. One copy went to Theodore Atkinson, brother-in-law of Governor Benning Wentworth and chief justice of New Hampshire's supreme court. Allen styled Atkinson the "father" of New Hampshire's "right of extension," under which right Atkinson owned considerable acreage on the Grants, including the town of Grafton. Allen revealed that he had paid for printing the pamphlet and, if he had failed to cast considerable new light on the border controversy, he would *"Drop into myself, and be a fool."* Here he paraphrased his favorite poet, Alexander Pope, who wrote in his *Essay on Man*, "Go, teach Eternal Wisdom how to rule / then drop into thyself, and be a fool." He struck a stronger note in writing to Oliver Wolcott of Litchfield. A future signer of the Declaration of Independence, Wolcott owned no land on the Grants but was one of the prime movers of the Susquehannah Company's settlement in the Wyoming Valley of Pennsylvania. Allen had already consulted with Wolcott on the Grants crisis; they had been introduced by Colonel Chittenden, Allen's former Salisbury neighbor and largest single customer of the Onion River Land Company.

For the first time, Allen confided that he and other leaders on the Grants were considering "the Expediency and Polocy of [forming] a Covenant Compact"—instituting an independent government. They were quietly talking about drawing up resolutions "Calculated with a View to be Adopted [as] a political System for the Conduct of Those Settlers." Wolcott was sympathetic, and Allen shrewdly calculated that he would be. Even to speak, much less put anything into writing, about a plan to create a new state beyond the bounds of recognized British jurisdiction would certainly have been construed by Britain as an act of treason. Allen knew that Wolcott was active in the growing resistance to British colonial policies. He offered Wolcott a quid pro quo: "Provided the Controversy between Great Britain and the Colonies Should Terminate in a War the Regiment of Green Mountain Boys Will I Dare Ingage to Assist their American Brethren in the Capacity of Rangers."[26]

What Allen was not revealing in these letters to New Hampshire and Connecticut may already have become known in neighboring New York. Two months earlier, on January 31, delegates from towns on the Grants had gathered at Manchester and taken a step toward declaring their independence from either New Hampshire or New York and creating a separate government. Responding to the "twelve acts of outlawry passed by the legislature of New York against those settlers," they signed a covenant, formed a compact, and drew up resolutions for their future conduct. Word of this meeting undoubtedly had gotten back to Governor Tryon of New York, who promptly requested troop reinforcements from Governor-General Sir Guy Carleton in Quebec for an expedition he planned to launch in May 1775 to suppress the spreading rebellion on the Grants.

EAST OF THE Green Mountains, in settlements normally beyond the reach of Ethan Allen and the Green Mountain Boys, many townships originally granted charters by New Hampshire had acceded to New York's demands. Settlers had paid a second and much higher set of fees to confirm their grants, and they now owed higher annual quitrents. Since they had accepted the authority of New York's courts, many of these farmers, strapped for cash and with nothing to barter, fell behind in their rents and were unable to pay other debts when three years of drought left them destitute. This natural disaster, however, proved beneficial to Allen and his adherents. By March of 1775, New York–appointed judges were carrying out foreclosures and evictions. Farmers petitioned the courts to postpone foreclosures for debt until they could gather their fall harvests. Chief Judge Thomas Chandler agreed to the delay and limited the spring term to a murder trial. But a rumor nonetheless spread that other, more hard-line New York judges were coming and that they would insist on hearing the foreclosures cases and would refuse to postpone them.

Only one month before the battles Lexington and Concord, in what may be taken as a harbinger of the American Revolution, in the southeast corner of Vermont, an angry crowd of settlers descended on Westminster and tried to seize the Cumberland County courthouse. Sheriff William Paterson, representing New York, swore in a posse and led it to the courthouse. There the posse and the protesters shouted insults at each other until the sheriff, persuading only a few settlers to leave the building, withdrew to a nearby tavern. Pouring one tankard of rum after another, the sheriff and his posse waited there until midnight and then stormed the courthouse. Twice the protesters repulsed them. When the court clerk Samuel Gale menaced the mob with a pistol, firing broke out on both sides. The posse mortally wounded two rioters and wounded several more, then jailed ten others.

The judges tried to convene the court the next day, but an even larger crowd freed the prisoners and forced the judges to adjourn the court session. As New Hampshire and Massachusetts militia poured into the town, they rounded up Sheriff Paterson and his posse and bundled them off to jail in Northampton, Massachusetts. A company of the Green Mountain Boys dispatched by Ethan Allen arrived from Bennington across the mountains in time to join the erstwhile rioters, now heroes on the Grants, for the funeral of William French, one of the rioters, on March 15. Allen called the affair the Westminster Massacre, reminding Vermonters of the first bloodletting of the revolutionary era in Boston five years earlier. The Revolutionary War and the movement for independence from British colonial government, and therefore from the British Empire, had already begun in the events on the Vermont frontier. Those events of March 1775 have been glossed over as history has memorialized the bloody days of the next month. As John Adams would say a year later at the time of the signing of the Declaration of Independence, the Revolution was already complete. It had taken place in the mind and hearts of the people on the frontier as much as in the coastal town of Boston.

· · ·

ETHAN ALLEN'S EFFECTIVE mix of propaganda and intimidation had kept New York sheriffs and royal governors at bay for
nearly five years. During that time, he built up the loyalty of thousands of settlers. By some estimates, the population of the Grants
had ballooned from scarcely 800 in 1764 to nearly 8,800 a decade
later. Allen acquired legendary status when he helped find two
little girls who had been given up for lost in wolf-infested woods
and when he gave generously of the land he bought for himself to
poor members of the Green Mountain Boys. He became Colonel Commandant Ethan Allen, but he also was becoming rich,
at least on paper, with a strong vested interest in protecting the
independence of Green Mountain settlers and landowners.

On March 15, 1775, only five weeks before Lexington and
Concord, Ethan Allen rode north with Heman, Ira, Levi, Zimri,
and cousin Remember from Salisbury to Sheffield for the second
annual directors' meeting of the Onion River Land Company. Up
until then, the company had operated in an extremely informal
manner, each partner buying and selling land when opportunities appeared. They bought an estimated 77,622 acres and sold
16,793 acres, leaving available some 60,829 acres, all in towns
bordering Lake Champlain. Ethan accumulated enough money
to pay Ebenezer Watson of Hartford nearly £550 for printing his
Brief Narrative and for pamphlets he had edited out of his letters
to the *Courant*. Even though his skill as a propagandist is rarely
mentioned in history, his writing was ready-made propaganda
that won over many reluctant Grants settlers from allegiance
to New York. He unabashedly peddled his prose door-to-door.
If Ethan Allen couldn't sell you land when he stopped by your
house for a few pounds sterling down payment, he sold you his
political philosophy for a shilling. The board voted to reimburse

Allen his printing costs: he was, after all, promoting the cause of all the company's shareholders. At Sheffield, where the partners now met annually to accommodate investors in land from western Massachusetts and Connecticut, Allen also collected funds he had advanced to Levi and Ira and to the company, enough to settle a sizable tab at Landlord Dewey's Catamount Tavern for the company's business. He charged the company for having a clerk transcribe a pamphlet, for keeping a horse at Captain Fay's house in Bennington for "public causes," and for petty cash spent in the "General Cause." But Allen, no longer strapped, didn't take cash. The company totted up his expenses and agreed to pay him in his choice of lands. Before adjourning, as with all such meetings, the directors planned ahead. They set the date for another gathering one year later. It never happened.

10.

"In the Name of
the Great Jehovah"

❈

IN THE SERE SPRINGTIME OF 1775, every rider who swung
down from his mount and clambered into Catamount Tavern in
Bennington brought news of fresh alarms, where British troops
were quick marching into small towns all along the Massachusetts
coast to seize stores of gunpowder and weapons. General Gage,
the British commander in Boston, would later quite accurately
blame the system of postriders who crisscrossed New England
and saddle stitched it to neighboring colonies for the mounting
resistance to new British policies. Radical leaders in Massachusetts, Connecticut, and to the south kept abreast of the latest
British maneuvers and were able to coordinate their responses
within days of each British provocation. Systematically stripped
of their munitions, devoid of artillery, radical leaders on the coast
knew that only in the Green Mountains could they hope to muster a large, trained force when they decided to attack the heavily
armed Lake Champlain forts on short notice.

With British posts thinly garrisoned, the militia Ethan
Allen had so assiduously recruited and trained for four years now
became, by default, the second-largest military force in North
America, second only to the Redcoat garrison of Boston. It was
common knowledge that, in all New York, there were only 150
Redcoats. After receiving a written warning about the unrest in
the backcountry two months earlier from Gage, New York's royal
governor, Sir William Tryon, had appealed to Quebec's royal governor, Sir Guy Carleton, for reinforcements. In fact, Carleton had
few men to spare. In January, he had written to Lord Dartmouth,
secretary of state for the Northern Department, that there were
"not six hundred rank and file fit for duty upon the whole extent
of this great [St. Lawrence] river, not an armed vessel . . . the
ancient provincial forces enervated and broke to pieces." When he
wrote back to Governor Tryon, he downplayed the threat from
the Green Mountains: Tryon should not be worried about "a few
lawless vagabonds."[1]

As ETHAN ALLEN, acting on orders from the Connecticut
Committee of Correspondence, dispatched couriers north and
east through the Green Mountain settlements to raise the Boys,
as described earlier, Benedict Arnold, unaware of Connecticut's
strategy, quick marched his red-coated militia company to Cambridge. There he talked the Massachusetts Provincial Congress
into letting him lead the attack on the Lake Champlain forts.
The leaders of the congress listened enthusiastically to Arnold's
report of the forts' strategic importance, their armaments and
vulnerability, and they commissioned him a Massachusetts colonel, providing him with ten packhorses, two hundred pounds
of gunpowder, and a like amount of lead. Arnold and his per-

sonal orderly and string of swaybacked packhorses picked their way west, reaching Williamstown in northwestern Massachusetts after a 110-mile, three-day trek through a heavy spring downpour that had turned the road into a quagmire. His countenance the color of his uniform, Arnold learned that Allen, who would actually lead the invasion, was acting on the intelligence that Arnold himself had provided Colonel Parsons two weeks earlier.

The furious Arnold's decision to assert overall command of the northern expedition nearly wrecked the expedition when he rashly fired off an order to the New York Committee of Safety demanding New York revolutionaries' support. He was "now on the march for the reduction of Fort Ticonderoga." It was a reckless step. If Arnold's message had been intercepted by the British or a New Yorker loyal to the royal government, it could have ruined the surprise attack on Ticonderoga and led to the death or capture of Allen and many of his Boys, an event that would not have displeased many of New York's officials.[2]

As town committees hurried preparations, more and more of the Boys, armed with pistols, swords, and knives, clambered into Catamount Tavern. Those who had arms, stacked their muskets around the walls, awaiting orders. The news of the carnage outside Boston sobered and excited Allen and his comrades. All the years of raids, reprisals, and confrontations with New York sheriffs and settlers were now subsumed into a greater cause, which, as it must have occurred to Allen, would benefit the settlers and landowners of the Grants, including his family. Any chance for political reverie, however, was cut short as he rode north to Castleton to prepare the imminent attack on Fort Ticonderoga.

• • •

WHEN A SCARLET-UNIFORMED Colonel Benedict Arnold pushed open the front door of the Catamount Tavern, Boys who had been cursing the Redcoats now thought they were seeing one and dived for their guns. A score of weapons, hammers cocked, pointed at Arnold before he could identify himself. Presenting his written commission to Captain Mott, Arnold brusquely recited his orders to take command. The score of Boys left behind by Allen began to hoot and mimic Arnold and jump up on the tables. When the catcalls subsided, Captain Mott coolly explained to Arnold that the leadership of the Grants had convened a week ago. They had constituted a council of war and had allowed the Boys to elect their own officers, according to New England tradition, a tradition that Arnold did not share. Ethan Allen had been unanimously reelected colonel commandant of the Boys, the post, Mott explained, that he had held for four years since he had organized the Vermont militia. If Arnold hurried, he might overtake Allen at Castleton, fifty miles to the north, and offer his services.

THE LAUNCHING POINT for the main attack on Fort Ticonderoga was to be a promontory at Hand's Cove, on the Vermont shore, directly opposite the fort. All day on May 9 and into the night, only 230 of the Boys had arrived in Shoreham. Allen had reason to be nervous. He knew that it was planting season in Vermont, an especially important one after three years of very little rain. Rumors of British marches brought by couriers from the east further dissuaded some of the Boys from leaving their farms and the defense of their families for very long. The sight of Arnold riding up to the Shoreham schoolhouse only complicated Allen's plans. It was here that Arnold met Allen for the first time. Captain Mott later reported to the Hartford Committee of Safety that Arnold had "insisted that he had a right to command them and all their officers, which bred such a mutiny among the soldiers which had nearly frustrated our whole design."[3]

After the brief altercation over command mentioned earlier, Allen tried to ease the tension by proposing that he lead his Boys and the sixteen Connecticut militiamen forwarded to him by the Hartford committee and that Arnold, exercising his Massachusetts commission, lead any Massachusetts troops. At dusk on May 9, Allen, with Arnold at his side, led the Green Mountain Boys and their new comrades from Connecticut and Massachusetts silently toward the lake, their movements shielded by dense spruce trees as they waited for the boats within a mile of Fort Ticonderoga's sentries. Most of the officers were members of the extended Allen clan: Heman, Levi, Zimri, and Ira were joined by cousins Ebenezer Allen, Seth Warner, and Remember Baker. Among the lieutenants was a future congressman, Matthew Lyon, who later became the only congressman to be elected from three states and, continuing the Vermont tradition of insurrection, the only congressman to be imprisoned in 1798 under the Alien and Sedition Act. Lyon had brought men all the way from the Onion River Land Company's fort at the mouth of the Winooski River.

By sunset, three hundred men waited soundlessly, anxiously, but six hours later, at one-thirty the morning of the tenth, as the wind whipped the lake into whitecaps, still there were no boats. A fierce storm had lashed the lake half the night, nearly wrecking the expedition. There was barely enough time left now to ferry a fraction of the men across to the New York shore before daylight. What Allen would not learn for several more days was that, according to an affidavit later sworn by Major Skene, some of the Boys raiding the manor had been distracted by a cellar stocked with choice liquors. Even if they had remained sober, the raiders couldn't have found Skene's schooner, because it was docked more than one hundred miles farther up the lake at the British fort at St. John. Captain Asa Douglass's detachment, sent north toward Crown Point, could locate only a single, thirty-three-foot lug-sailed scow with a terrified young black slave at its tiller. Douglass had told the youth they would pay him to take them hunting. The lumbering workboat finally tacked into Hand's Cove at three o'clock the morning of May 10. Already the sky to the east was turning gray against the black silhouettes of trees and hills. A few minutes later, a second small boat appeared.

Even as the scow bumped the Vermont shore, Allen and Arnold made their first joint decision. They had to attack with as many chosen men as they could get across the lake in the next hour. As it set out on its first crossing, the scow wallowed in the choppy water under the weight of so many men, nearly sinking into the darkened lake. A sudden storm now kicked up white-caps, sending water sloshing over the gunwales. The lugsail was useless. In the high wind, it could capsize the unwieldy, over-loaded boat. Squall-whipped water drenched the novice oars-men, blinding them. At that time of year, the water temperature rarely reached more than forty-five degrees Fahrenheit. It took a nerve-racking ninety minutes for the small boat to cross one mile of heaving water. After a second crossing, only eighty-three drenched, shivering men had been deposited on the New York shore a quarter mile east of Fort Ticonderoga. The sleepless little army picked its way up the slope just north of a jutting piece of shoreline known as Willow Point.

AT FOUR O'CLOCK in the morning of May 10, Allen gave the signal of three owl hoots. With only a third of their men and none of their supplies having made it across the lake, Allen and Arnold led the way along the path up from the shore toward the main gate. The ghostly line of frontiersmen hugged the crumbling granite south wall of the main star-shaped fortress until they reached a breach where, after years of neglect, the stones had parted. Despite intelligence to the contrary from the spies, the French and Indian War veteran officers Noah Phelps and Ezra Hickok, whom Allen had sent into the fort, he now found the main gates closed. Had a Loyalist neighbor suspicious of all the men and activity on the Vermont shore warned the British? Cut out of the main gate was a wicket gate, a narrow, low door with a sentry box just inside. The solitary Redcoat sentry on duty had dozed off.

Both Allen, on the right, the traditional position of honor, and Arnold, on the left, would later claim that they had rushed the guard simultaneously, but eyewitnesses said the smaller, faster Arnold was first to squeeze through the narrow gate. The startled guard aimed his musket and pulled the trigger, but it had been a damp night and the gun misfired, the hammer snapping harmlessly in the pan. The terrified soldier threw down his gun and ran, yelling, toward the barracks. A second sentry appeared. This time, Allen reached him first. The Redcoat fired, but the shot went high. Then he lunged at Allen with his bayonet. Sidestepping, Allen swung at the soldier's head with his heavy cutlass. The blow, enough to behead a man, struck a wooden comb in the Englishman's carefully coiffed and powdered hair, sending him sprawling. Allen later wrote that he had deliberately spared the man's life by deflecting the sword's arc: "My first thought was to kill him with my sword but; in an instant, [I] altered the design and fury of the blow to a slight cut on the side of the head."[4]

Allen demanded that the stunned guard get up and lead him to the commandant's quarters. Despite reconnaissance, none of his men knew the fort's exact layout. Arnold, meanwhile, had run toward the main barracks. Finding the garrison's muskets neatly stacked out on the parade ground, he raced ahead of his men upstairs to wake the Redcoats at gunpoint. With half a dozen of the Green Mountain Boys, Allen prodded the wounded sentry before him, crossing the parade ground to the west wall and hurried up a stone stairway toward what obviously was the officer's quarters, yelling, "No quarter! No quarter!" In his room, Lieutenant Feltham, the young artillerist posted to Ticonderoga little more than a week earlier, jumped up and ran in his underwear to the door of Captain Delaplace, the commandant. The subaltern banged on the door and, as he later reported to General Gage, waited, his trousers in his hand, "to receive orders." Delaplace didn't answer. Feltham ran back to his room, pulled on his red coat and, still naked from the waist down, ran toward the din on the stairs, clutching his trousers, hoping that his few visible symbols of authority would help him rally the garrison.

As more of the Boys surged upstairs, yelling at him, Feltham fled. He later reported, "With great difficulty, I got into Delaplace's room." The commandant was coolly dressing, putting on his sword. Feltham opened a side door and started toward Allen, who was running up the stairs. Trying to stall him, Feltham loudly asked "by what authority [had] they entered His Majesty's fort." Brandishing his cutlass, Allen bellowed, "In the name of the great Jehovah and the Continental Congress!"—or that is what Allen later wrote he said. According to Lieutenant Feltham's official account, however, Allen invoked neither the deity nor congress. Instead, Allen said, "Come out of there, you old rat." One of Allen's own men insisted that Allen bellowed at Captain Delaplace a more characteristic "Come out of there, you goddam old rat."[5]

Pivoting toward Lieutenant Feltham, Allen waved his sword

over the terrified subaltern. Several of the Boys had leveled their flintlocks at him. Allen warned Feltham "that if there was a single gun fired, neither man, woman or child would be left alive in this fort." (There were approximately forty women and children, the soldiers' families.) Finally, Captain Delaplace, in full dress uniform, came out and asked Allen what terms he would give. Allen replied that he would have Delaplace's immediate surrender or instant death from his right fist, the "beetle of immortality," likening his hand to a wood splitter's hammer. Delaplace instantly surrendered his sword, his pistols, and Fort Ticonderoga.[6]

Pendennis Castle in Cornwall, England.

PART THREE

"NO DAMNED ARNOLD"

11.

"Thou Bold Blasphemer"

❋

WITH ONLY EIGHTY-THREE MEN, Ethan Allen had taken the mightiest fortress in colonial America, complete with all its vital artillery and munitions, without firing a shot or suffering a single casualty. In the first American offensive of the Revolutionary War, Allen had won America's first victory and made himself its first war hero. As more of the Green Mountain Boys streamed into the fort, Allen ordered the captured garrison confined to their barracks at gunpoint. According to Lieutenant Feltham's official report to General Howe, about four hundred Green Mountain Boys "came now to join in the plunder."[1]

They soon discovered a cellar under the officers' quarters housing ninety gallons of rum, Captain Delaplace's private stock. Some of the Boys, who were normally not given to rowdiness but who'd had little to eat in several days, quickly got drunk. Allen sympathized with them: after years of intimidation and threats of dispossession and even execution by New York's royal officials, he thought it perfectly understandable for them to celebrate the stunning achievement of capturing the king's fort. Allen wrote a few days later to the treasurer of Connecticut to reimburse Captain Delaplace, by then a prisoner on his way there, for the rum, which Allen said had been "Greatly wanted for the Refreshment of the Fatigued Soldiery."[2]

But Arnold, who had arrived on the frontier only the day before, was intent on his mission and his commission. He tried to get the Boys to help him strip the fort of its cannon and gunpowder and get them moving toward Boston. When a few of the Boys began to loot the barracks, Arnold recited military law to them. His interference infuriated Allen, who felt Arnold was abrogating their agreement about a joint command. After two inebriated Boys somewhat unsteadily fired at Arnold and missed him and another leaned the barrel of a musket against his chest and cocked it, Allen did not discipline his men but instead stripped Arnold of his command, confined him to quarters, and placed a guard at the door. By this time, Allen had organized and controlled his militia for four years. Arnold, a merchant ship's captain, had no prior combat experience but he did not hesitate to judge Allen's. To the Massachusetts Provincial Congress, he denounced Allen: "Colonel Allen is a proper man to head his own wild people, but entirely unacquainted with military service. . . ."[3]

Benedict Arnold and Ethan Allen had much in common but possessed decidedly opposing styles. Both were Connecticut patricians by birth; the families of both were among the founding generation of New Englanders. Arnold was Benedict V, descended from one of the original settlers of Rhode Island who had served as that colony's longest-tenured governor. Arnold had a natural abhorrence of alcohol: his father had squandered the family's wealth and twice been jailed for public drunkenness. Yet he would not be averse to serving his crews rum in the absence of food as they went into battle on Lake Champlain. Allen's grandfather had gambled away the family fortune in bad real estate speculations, but his grandmother, born wealthy, had earned it back. Arnold's and Allen's forebears were visible saints, among the Puritan elect. Allen was a fourth-generation town founder. Both men, like so many of the founding fathers, were orphans who had struggled to achieve position and wealth. Both were competitive and unaccustomed to sharing power or praise, exceedingly aware of their images. And, like so many of their revolutionary generation, they were more a team of rivals than part of a band of brothers.

WHILE ARNOLD SCRATCHED out angry salvos, Allen was also busy writing. His version of events not only assured his place in history but also helped his friends and harmed Arnold. In a popular memoir, Allen ultimately published his own account of taking the great fortress without firing a shot or killing anyone. It was a "gray morning," he wrote. "The sun seemed to rise that morning with a superior luster." His men were "conquerors who tossed about the flowing bowl." At first, he did not mention Arnold in his dispatches—"I took the fortress at Ticonderoga by storm." The day after the attack, Allen sent off reports to Connecticut, to the Continental Congress, to Albany. In Ticonderoga's commandant's quarters, its new occupant was busy writing some of the most euphoric sentences of his life. To the governor of Connecticut, Allen wrote, "I make You a Present of a Major a Captain and Two lieuts in the regular Establishment of George the Third. I hope they may serve as ransoms for some of our Friends of Boston. . . ."

In this letter, Allen for the first time laid out his next bold objective. At Skenesborough, the Boys had seized the newly built armed schooner *Betsey.*

I Expect in Ten days Time to have it rigged, man'd and arm'd with 6 or 8 Pieces of Canon which with the Boats in our Possession I Purpose to make an Attack on the arm'd Sloop George the Third which is Now Cruising on Lake Champlain and about Twice as bigg as the Schooner. . . . The Enterprise has been approbated by the Officers and Soldiary of the Green Mountain Boys. Nor do I hesitate as to the Success. I Expect Lives must be Lost in the attack as the Comander of George's Sloop is a man of courage.

Moreover, Allen was certain there would be a British counterattack from Montreal. "Governor Carleton will Exert himself to oppose us & Command the Lake." With perspicacity, Allen signed himself "at Present Commander of Ticondaroga." Along with the prisoners, he sent back an accountant, the clerk of the Connecticut war committee who had been sent on the expedition to keep track of the Connecticut money that he had spent that could later be charged to the Continental Congress.[4]

Allen wrote with particular relish to the committee of safety in Albany, where he had so long been the subject of warrants and rewards and where he was still considered an outlaw who could be executed if he were arrested by some of the same people he was now notifying of his coup:

May 11, 1775

Ticonderoga

Gentlemen

I Have the Inexpressible Satisfaction to Acquaint you that at Day break of the Eleventh [sic] Instant (Pursuant to my Directions from Sundry Leading Gentlemen in the Colonies

of Massachusetts Bay and Connecticut) I Took the Fortress
of Ticonderoga with About one Hundred and thirty Green
Mountain Boys. . . . Col. Arnold Entered the fortress with me
Side by Side. The Guard were So Surprised that Contrary our
Expectation Did Not fire on us but fled with Precippitancy.
We Immediately Entered the fortress and Took the Garrisson
Prisoners without Bloodshead or any Opposition. . . . You know
Governor Carlton of Canada will Exert himself to retake it . . .
Your Country is Nearer than any Other Part of the Colonies . . .
I Expect Immediate [aid] from You Both in men and Provi-
sions. . . . Pray Be Quick to our relief and Send us five hundred
men Immediately. Fail Not. . . .

Ethan Allen Commander of Ticondaroga[5]

One day after taking Ticonderoga, Allen, continuing his
heavy reliance on his own trusted clan, dispatched his cousin
Captain Seth Warner with forty Boys to seize Crown Point.
From this strategic vantage point, ships could be seen approaching from the north for a dozen miles. Lightly garrisoned by a
sergeant and nine enlisted men accompanied by ten women and
children, Fort Amherst fell without resistance. Only a few cannon
were visible at first, but in all one hundred and eleven had been
abandoned by the retreating French. Back at Ticonderoga, Allen
was excitedly cataloging an inventory of artillery from the two
forts that he could send off toward Boston. He sent to congress
a detailed list of seventy-eight serviceable cannon and large siege
mortars and three howitzers plus a number of swivel guns, 18,000
pounds of musket balls, and 30,000 flints. The fieldpieces, ranging from three-pounders to forty-two-pounders, were an unbe-
lievable treasure of state-of-the-art weaponry that would enable
the Americans to fight the British on more even terms.

At their next council of war, Allen and Arnold, expediently reconciled, agreed that they had to protect this trove by taking Fort St. John on the Richelieu River five miles inside Quebec Province, to deprive the British of an advanced base for a counterattack. Arnold and fifty of his Massachusetts men fitted out Colonel Skene's captured schooner with swivel guns, renamed it *Liberty*, and set sail north toward Canada. Allen and a contingent of the Boys followed them in slow bateaux, the sail- and oar-powered workboats of the lake. Arnold arrived first and took the fort's thirteen-man garrison by surprise. He was already sailing back toward Ticonderoga at the helm of the captured British sloop of war, which he renamed *Enterprise*, when he saw Allen's men struggling toward him down the Richelieu River. "[Arnold] saluted me," Allen later wrote,

> with a discharge of cannon, which I returned with a volley of small arms. This being repeated three times, I went on board the sloop with my party, where several loyal Congress healths were drunk. We were now masters of the lake, and the garrisons depending thereon.

As Arnold headed back toward his new base at Crown Point, Allen and one hundred Boys rowed on into Canada. While they had agreed on it initially, as was his own custom to varnish and manipulate the truth, Arnold later depicted Allen's incursion onto Canadian soil as "a wild, impractical, expansive scheme" carried out by "one hundred mad fellows." What Arnold probably didn't know, because Allen never told him, was that Allen was carrying out the second phase of his secret orders from the revolutionary leaders of Connecticut and Massachusetts.[6]

• • •

ETHAN ALLEN'S FIRST, brief foray into Canada ended unceremoniously on May 19. He camped across the river from the captured fort at St. John, while he sent a Major Brown on to Montreal to request the support already proferred by English merchants to the Boston Committee of Correspondence. Allen wrote to James Morrison, a wealthy wheat exporter who was chairman of the secret Montreal Committee of Correspondence. Morrison had met with Brown, earlier in the spring. Brown assured Massachusetts Patriot leaders that Morrison was one of many Montrealers transplanted from New England at the end of the French and Indian War who were willing to support Boston's cause. In February, little more than two months before the British attack on Lexington, the Massachusetts Provincial Congress directed the Boston Committee of Correspondence to send a mission to Canada. Lawyer Brown carried a letter from Samuel Adams to the Canadians, inviting them to set up their own committees of correspondence. Marking the first step toward concerted revolutionary activities, these committees infuriated British officials but put leaders of all the colonies in constant contact, making it possible for them to act in concert. In early April, Adams sent Brown back to Montreal, this time to invite the English Canadians to send a delegation to the Continental Congress.

When Brown reached Montreal on April 9, only ten days before Lexington and Concord, he read Adams's letter and made a motion that Montreal send two delegates to Philadelphia to represent the three thousand transplanted New England settlers and traders now living in Quebec Province. But, if they joined the radical cause, some Montreal merchants asked, would they have to join Congress's embargo on trade with England? Yes, Brown answered. The motion failed. At least one of the merchants believed that Massachusetts would invade Canada "if a man of us should dare to take up arms against the Bostonians."

The merchants could agree only to set up a secret committee of correspondence, with John Walker, the province's wealthiest merchant, as chairman.[7]

FROM HIS BIVOUAC on the Richelieu River opposite Fort St. John, Ethan Allen wrote on May 18, 1775, to the merchants of Montreal.

> I Expect the English Merchants as well as all Virtuous Disposed Gentlemen will be in the Interest of the Colonies. The Advance Guard of the Army is Now at Saint John and Desire Immediately to have a Personal intercourse with You. Your Immediate Assistance as to Provision Ammunision and Spiritous Liquors is wanted and fourthwith Expected . . . . I am Impow'd by the Colonies to Purchaise the Same . . . . My directions from the Colonies is not to Contend with or any way Injure or Molest the Canadians or Indians. . . .

Allen's message never made it to Montreal, for the British had intercepted his courier, Joseph Bendon, a member of the Montreal committee.[8]

Allen awoke abruptly the next morning to "a Canonading of Grape Shot." He found "the Musick was both Terrible and Delightfull." He had been taken by surprise by a large force of Redcoats. To Noah Lee, the officer he had left in command at Skenesboro, Allen wrote on May 21, "None of our Party was Killed," despite a bayonet charge by the Redcoats. The Boys stood their ground and returned fire that "Broke their [Redcoats'] ranks but we Know Not as we Killed any of them." At a hasty council of war, Allen, Seth Warner, and the other officers decided to retreat ten miles to the Ile aux Noix, on the Canadian border, and fortify it. Allen intended to draw all the troops he could from other positions to this advanced base. Captain Lee was to leave only five or six men at Skenesborough and rush the rest of his company to reinforce Allen. But most of the Green Mountain Boys had already gone home to do their spring planting. Lee couldn't spare anyone. Ignoring Allen's request, Lee wrote back, holding out for a promotion. In his reply, Ethan assured him, "Undoubtedly we Shall all be rewarded According to our Merit in this or the Coming world."[9]

WITHOUT REINFORCEMENTS, ALLEN again had to move his base camp back down Lake Champlain to Crown Point. He decided to open negotiations with the Indians. Since his boyhood on the frontier, he had hunted, fished, and feasted with Mohawk Indians in Connecticut and in the Vermont wilderness. He had gained much of his prowess as a famous hunter from the Indians. One hint of his affinity for the Indians is that they never molested any of the neighboring settlements on the Grants; another, that Allen had decided against transplanting his family to the Wyoming Valley of Pennsylvania, still claimed by the Six Nations Iroquois, after the death of his father, an original proprietor of the region, and the murder of Teedyuscung by settlers from Connecticut. Immediately after the capture of Ticonderoga, local Caughnawaga Mohawks paid a friendly call and offered to serve with him, but said their Iroquois confederacy overlords forbade them to get involved. He learned from a band of Stockbridge Indians from western Massachusetts, also visiting him at Ticonderoga, that members of their tribe had joined Massachusetts militia companies and marched to join the siege of Boston. In a letter to the Connecticut Assembly, Allen described their leader, Captain

Abraham Nimham, as "a friendly Stockbridge Indian" who had
volunteered to carry a letter to Indians in Canada as "our Imbas-
sador of Peace to our Good Brother Indians" of four tribes in
Quebec province. To the Caughnawagas, Allen wrote,

> I hope as Indians are Good and Honest men You will Not
> fight for King George Against Your Friends in America
> as they have Done You No wrong and Desire to Live with
> You as Brothers. I was Always a Friend to Indians and
> have Hunted with them many Times and Know how to
> Shoot and Ambush Like Indians and am a Great Hunter.

Allen offered to give the Indians money, blankets, tomahawks,
knives, and paint if the Indians would come to join him. "I want
Your Warriors to Join with me and my Warriors Like Brothers and
Ambush the Regulars." He offered "to Go with You Into the woods
to Scout and my men and Your men will sleep Together and Eat and
Drink Together and fight Regulars." Even if the Canadian Indians
remained neutral, "still we will be Friends and Brothers and You
may Come and Hunt in our Woods and Come with your Canoes in
the Lake and Let us have Veneson at our forts on the Lake and have
Rum, Bread and what you want and be Like Brothers."[10]

Sending a copy of this letter to the Connecticut Assembly at
Hartford, Allen reported that his embassy to the Caughnawaga
Mohawks was being led by Captain Nimham, the son of a chief
of the Wappinger band at Stockbridge and also included Winthrop Hoit, who had been a prisoner of the Mohawks and spoke
their language, and two Mohicans from Stockbridge. When
Allen's four Caughnawaga emissaries were intercepted at Fort St.
John, they were instantly arrested by British regulars, hauled off
to Montreal, and sentenced to death by hanging. Only the angry
intervention of Mohawk chiefs had obtained their release. Nim-

ham was able to go on to deliver Allen's message to the Caughnawaga Mohawks.

AT THE END OF May 1775, Ethan Allen received his first direct
communication from the Continental Congress in Philadelphia.
The message shocked him, since it challenged his view of himself
as an independent fighter and colonial leader who had to answer
to no one. Congress expressed approval of his capture of the British forts and their trove of invaluable cannon but ordered him
to "remove the Artillery to the South End of Lake George and
there to make a Stand." Allen argued that such a maneuver "must
ruin the Frontier Settlements." Didn't Congress know that "Several Thousand families who are Seated on that Tract of Country
Called the New Hampshire Grants" in settlements extending a
hundred miles north of this arbitrary defensive position would be
exposed to British retribution?

He wondered whether any member of Congress owned a
map, his question already reflecting a growing divide between
him and what he was coming to consider the upstart leaders in
Philadelphia. The southern tip of Lake Champlain was almost
as far south as the position Congress was advocating. Seizing the
lake forts "at the Special request and Solicitation" of the governments of Massachusetts and Connecticut, "Those Very Inhabitants" have "Insensed Governor Carleton." To dig up and haul
the guns away and abandon control of Lake Champlain and its
forts would give the British advance bases and leave the country
neglected and exposed. Only two days earlier, Allen, Arnold, and
their officers had held a council of war on board the captured
British sloop and decided to advance with all their captured vessels to Point au Fer, six miles south of the Canadian border where
the New York shore juts out into the lake, allowing control of the

deepwater passage of ships. There, Allen and Arnold had agreed, they could successfully defend the frontier settlements and their eight thousand inhabitants.

For the first time, Allen contended that, if only Congress would send him an army of two or three thousand troops, he could take Montreal. He would have

> Little to fear from the Canadians or Indians and would Easily make a Conquest of that Place and Set up the Standard of American Liberty in the Extensive province of Quebec whose limit was Enlarged [by the Quebec Act] purely to Subvert the Liberties of America. Strikeing Such a blow would Intimidate the Torie party in Canada . . . . They are a Set of Gentlemen that will Not be Converted by reason but are Easily wrought upon by fear.

The only way to stop Carleton and the British ministry's scheme to remake America, Allen told Congress, was to project an American army into Canada.[11]

THE NEWS THAT Ethan Allen and the Green Mountain Boys, with Massachusetts Colonel Benedict Arnold at his side, had captured British fortresses in New York and seized their cannon jolted the Continental Congress, which had been far from ready to authorize such an overt act of war. It had not yet even established a military committee of any sort, offensive or defensive. Congress still was mulling what to do about the British attack on Lexington and Concord and the ferocious response of Massachusetts' militias. A divided Congress was still reeling from this news when it received Allen's letter announcing the captures of Ticonderoga and Crown Point. Allen's bold attack horrified many conservative members of Congress. Until now, Congress had pre-served the appearance of acting only on the defensive. Seizing Crown forts and taking prisoners complicated Congress's task and reflected the growing chasm between the wise men in Pennsylvania and impetuous fighters like Ethan Allen in Vermont.

On May 18, Major Brown reached Philadelphia, and the secretary of Congress read aloud Allen's report of the capture of the Lake Champlain forts. Behind the closed doors of the Pennsylvania State House, Brown briefed Congress on conditions in the north. On May 26, on the same day that it sent another conciliatory petition to the king, Congress passed a resolution to put the American colonies "into a state of defense." On June 1, the delegates voted against authorizing or supporting any "expedition or incursion" into Canada. As fifteen thousand New Englanders, many of them combat veterans of the French and Indian War, massed along the siege lines outside Boston, Congress passed a resolution to take a tentative first step toward approving a continental military. The Virginia delegate George Washington, brevetted a brigadier in the last war against the French, was named chairman of a committee to study the disposition of the New York forts.

Congress remained visibly divided. It would be exactly another year before members were ready to debate independence. It was as if two committees, one aggressive and militaristic, the other diplomatically inclined and accommodating, had written the congressional resolution and spliced together the document ordering that, after seizing the lake forts to protect themselves, Ethan Allen and his neighbors were now to dig up and haul the heavy guns, not to Boston, but to the south end of Lake George. Then, "if necessary," they were to apply to New Hampshire, Massachusetts, and Connecticut for forces to "establish a strong post" there. But the first thing Congress wanted Allen to do was to take "an exact inventory" of "all such cannon and stores" so that they could be "safely returned when the restoration of former harmony between Great Britain and these colonies, so ardently wished for" rendered their return "prudent and consistent with the overruling law of self-preservation."[12]

Slapping Allen's wrist, Congress insisted he not seize any more of the king's forts, and New York, it resolved, should not disturb the Redcoats in any other forts so long as they proved peaceable and did not attempt to erect any new fortifications. According to the careful wording of the document, New York, overwhelmingly Loyalist at the time, was *not* on the list of colonies that Allen could ask for troops. Yet New York was to get all the cannon from Ticonderoga and Crown Point along with the British sloop of war, Colonel Skene's schooner, and the five bateaux taken at St. John. There it was, a prime piece of back-bending political compromise couched in lawyer's language. When he read the document, Allen had little doubt that it was the handiwork of one particularly conservative New York lawyer, Congressman James Duane, the principal New York claimant to Vermont lands, the man who four years earlier had tried to bribe Allen to betray his neighbors in exchange for a large New York land grant and a good horse. Indeed, as a New York delegate to the Continental Congress, Duane was taking a vigorous part in the proceedings in Philadelphia, especially in any discussion of what was to be done in the north country. It was difficut to see how Allen could have thought anything else when he read Congress's orders to pull back and abandon Vermont's settlements to British reprisals.

WHEREVER BENEDICT ARNOLD ventured in the summer of 1775, Ethan Allen, uneasy with their forced alliance, tried to be somewhere else. Arnold had fashioned himself "Commodore of the Lake" and made his headquarters aboard the captured British sloop of war. He named it *Enterprise* and usually kept it moored at Crown Point. Allen designated himself "Commander of the Forts" and made Ticonderoga his base. He found out that Arnold had spread the word that Allen had failed to hold St. John after he, Arnold, had captured it along with half a dozen vessels. Arnold gloated to Dr. James Warren, president of the Massachusetts Provincial Congress, that Allen and one hundred Boys had been "obliged" by two hundred regulars with six artillery pieces "to make a precipitate retreat with a loss of three of their men." Arnold added that Allen and the Boys "have returned without provision and much fatigued" while he, Arnold, had fitted out the captured vessels with cannon and swivel guns.

There were only two things that Allen and Arnold agreed on. One was that something was terribly amiss in Albany. Between them, the two commanders had only 150 pounds of gunpowder to share among their troops and ship's guns, and their repeated appeals for ammunition and supplies were being ignored by Albany. The other: that it was insane to abandon the forts and retreat to Lake George. Arnold wrote to Congress, this time calling himself "colonel and commander of Ticonderoga"—an active misrepresentation—that there were five hundred families around Lake Champlain north of Ticonderoga "who will be left at the mercy of the King's troops and Indians." They had joined the army and "cannot now remain neutral." Together, Arnold told Congress, he and Allen had decided to advance to Point au Fer with their armed boats to "make a stand," hastening to add that they would only "act on the defensive."[13]

One of the leading citizens of the Lake Champlain region, William Gilliland of Willsboro, New York, could not refrain from writing to Congress to support his friend Allen:

There are now in these parts a very considerable number
of men under the command of Mr. *Ethan Allen*, as brave
as *Hercules*, and as good marksmen as can be found in
America, who might prove immediately serviceable to the
common cause, were they regularly embodied, and commanded by officers of their own choice. . . . [E]xcellent
wood rangers and particularly acquainted in the wilderness
of Lake *Champlain*, [they] would, in all likelihood be more
serviceable in these parts than treble their number of others . . . especially if left under the direction of their present
enterprising and heroick commander, *Mr. Allen.*[14]

While Arnold sailed north on June 10 on an inspection
cruise, Allen called a council of war, technically the prerogative
only of a commander in chief. Eighteen officers were present at
the meeting: Ethan and Ira Allen, Seth Warner and Remember Baker, Major Samuel Elmore of Connecticut, Captain James
Noble (the man Arnold had left in command at the Point), and
a dozen of Arnold's company commanders, lieutenants, and
commissaries. Ethan asked Elmore to preside over the meeting.
Outlining a plan of attack on the British entrenching the Ile aux
Noix and completely ignoring, as increasingly was his wont, the
instructions of the Continental Congress to pull back, Allen convinced the other officers that they should attack now and, at the
same time, send a delegation to explain their decision to the Continental Congress. The assembled officers voted to send Allen,
Baker, and Warner as a delegation to Philadelphia. In the resolution Allen himself had written to carry to Congress, the council
advised Congress that some three hundred Redcoats had landed
at Fort St. John and were building boats to invade Lake Champlain and retake the forts. Allen, the resolution added, needed
Congress's approval to raise five hundred men, but "as they are

poor," they would have to be put on the regular Continental army establishment. Even Allen must have blushed as the council voted unanimously to endorse his actions during the Lake Champlain campaign: "Colonel Allen has behaved, in this affair, very singularly remarkable for his courage, and [we] must, in duty, recommend him to you and the whole Continent."[15]

Benedict Arnold arrived toward the end of the meeting and evidently didn't interrupt it, but he was, predictably, fuming. Arnold later maintained that Allen and his second-in-command, Major Easton, had gone on record at the meeting as "in possession" of the forts. In Arnold's view, once again, as before the attack on Fort Ticonderoga, they had trumped up a council of war to write their own orders and then had sent off its proceedings to the Continental Congress. Arnold summarized his reaction to the episode in the regimental memorandum book:

Colonel Allen, Col. Easton and Major Elmore had called a council of their officers and others not belonging to my regiment. I sent for Major Elmore, who excused himself. On which I wrote the council I could not, consistent with my duty, suffer any illegal councils, meetings, etc., as they tended to raise a mutiny. That I was at present the only legal commanding officer and should not suffer my commands to be disputed, but would willingly give up the command whenever anyone appeared with proper authority to take it.

To avoid the risk of Allen's retaliating by ordering him seized, Arnold waited until nightfall and then rowed out to the *Enterprise*. Allen, too, was eager to get away from Crown Point before any more public display of the rift between them, but he waited until the next morning before climbing into a bateau with his officers. When he "attempted passing the sloop without showing their pass"—a pass signed by Arnold—the officer on duty on the *Enterprise* ordered Allen to come about and return to shore until he showed the proper pass. Arnold was insisting on his orders. Returning to the fort, he summoned Major Elmore for "private discourse." Elmore explained that he had been sent by Connecticut with reinforcements. At this point, Major Easton brushed past the guard on the door and stalked into Arnold's office. There is no record what Easton said, but, whatever it was, Arnold's building frustration toward Allen boiled into a full-blown rage. Arnold wrote in the regimental memorandum book, "I took the liberty of breaking his head." Losing his temper, resorting to brute force, Arnold drew his sword and cracked Easton over the head with the flat of the blade, demanding that the erstwhile innkeeper, whom he considered a coward, fight a duel with him: "On refusing to draw like a gentleman, he having a hanger (sword) by his side and cases of loaded pistols in his pockets, I kicked him very heartily and ordered him from the Point."[16] Arnold remained unrepentant about this serious breach of decorum and military discipline by striking an officer in the presence of subordinates. To make matters worse, not only had he lost control in front of several officers, but any plan he had to return to the Canadian frontier was dashed when the Albany Committee of Safety decided at exactly this moment to pull back its men to Ticonderoga at the same time that Allen and his officers sailed away from Crown Point. It appeared there was a connection between Arnold's treatment of Easton and the withdrawal of the New York troops. In fact, the Albany committee was only carrying out the orders of the Continental Congress and was pulling back all of its men to Ticonderoga on their way to Fort George. The coincidence merely deepened the rift between Arnold and Allen. Neither man knew that they both were about to be superseded with the arrival of massive reinforcements from Connecticut under a new commanding officer.

EVER SO SLOWLY, supplies and reinforcements came trickling toward Ticonderoga from the provincial congresses of New York and New England. Assured by the Continental Congress that the cannon were to be sent south, the New York Provincial Congress, meeting in New York City, sent one hundred barrels of pork, two hundred barrels of flour, and twenty barrels of rum to Albany to forward to the lake garrisons. But it would take Allen's personal visit to the Continental Congress, six weeks after the capture of Ticonderoga, to break the logjam in Philadelphia. As they sailed down the Hudson River, Allen and his cousin Seth Warner heard for the first time of a terrible battle outside Boston that now made it virtually impossible to talk of peace and reconciliation with the mother country.

For nearly a month since Lexington and Concord, both the British inside Boston and the Americans surrounding them had been building up their strength. By mid-June, the Americans had about 15,000 men. On June 15, the Massachusetts Provincial Congress was informed that the British commander, Thomas Gage, whose American wife probably again leaked the information, intended to occupy Dorchester Heights and decided to move immediately to fortify the high ground overlooking Boston. On the night of June 16, some 900 young farmers marched on the double to Breed's Hill on the Charlestown peninsula. From its 75-foot-high summit, shells could be lobbed down on British warships in the harbor and on Boston itself. Marking out a small redoubt roughly 45 yards square, they began digging at midnight and ran the east wall, a breastwork, 100 yards down the hill to an impassable swamp. Expecting that the British would try to outflank them, they deployed 200 Connecticut marksmen behind a rail fence with a stone base 100 yards to the rear and downhill from the mud fort atop Breed's Hill. Between the Mystic River beach and the fence lay fresh-cut hay. Soon they were reinforced by four companies of New Hampshire frontiersmen, who threw up a stone breastwork across the beach to the water's edge. All night, 800 rugged farmers, including 7 freed African Americans, were busy digging a square hole 5 feet deep, piling the excavated dirt into a 6-foot-high wall behind it that baked hard in the searing noonday sun. They laid wooden platforms along the insides of the redoubt to stand on when firing, but they forgot to pierce the front parapet for their two small cannon. Two shots at point-blank range did the job.

At dawn, British forward observers were startled to find that the entire hill had been fortified overnight. General Gage called a hasty council of war. There was to be an immediate attack before the rebels could entrench the other hills and cut off the British from the mainland. The general officers decided on a quick and classic flanking attack up the Mystic River to Morton's Point. As Bostonians hurried into their houses, crowded into windows, and scurried onto rooftops for a better view, British men-of-war maneuvered closer to shore, anchored, and disgorged their barges ashore as their cannon began sending shells crashing into the hillside in front of the redoubt. By noon, British grenadiers marched through the streets and down to the bank of the Charles River to wait for the landing craft to ferry them across. American snipers with long rifles posted in the deserted houses of Charlestown began peppering them, most of their shots falling short. British ships lowered their guns and shelled the town, setting it ablaze.

By the time the landing boats waited for the tide and inched up onto the beach, the sun blazed high and hot. The regulars wore their only uniforms, wool, and carried 125 pounds of weapons and gear, three days' rations of boiled beef and bread and cooking implements on their backs. Their orders were to roll over the peninsula and march the four miles to the American camp at Cambridge and beyond, if necessary, to break up the rebellion before it could spread any further. From the start, things went badly for the British. Their field artillery mired down in the muddy fields. The advance light infantry, trotting up the beach on the right, stumbled into the reinforced rail fence and a withering fire. A bayonet charge proved impossible: the rebels were firing in rotation with no pause for reloading that would have allowed time to rush them. Row on row of Redcoats—most of them shot in the groin so they would never fight again—pitched into the fresh-mown hay as they tried to clamber across the fence. Ninety-six lay dead on the beach.

While the flanking effort failed, Howe had at the same time unleashed 600 men up the steep rough hillside over fallen trees, tangles of blackberry and blueberry through tall grass toward the strangely silent earthworks. Behind the breastwork, a fifty-seven-year-old veteran thanked God for sparing him to fight this day. Colonel Israel Putnam of Connecticut, cutlass in hand, lectured his sharpshooters: "Men, you are all good marksmen. Don't one of you fire until you see the whites of their eyes." At one hundred yards, the Redcoats fired a volley, too high, too far away. At fifty yards, they fired again. Again, too high. Up they trudged, bayonets glimmering, until the Americans could make out the brass matchboxes on their coats. At fifteen yards, the earthworks erupted. Three long, scarlet rows of England's best troops crumpled, pitching into the grass, thrashing and screaming.

Only the best American marksmen had fired, sighting in on the crossed white sashes of the Redcoats where they intersected at the belly. Behind the earthworks, young boys rammed home rusty nails and double-charged buckshot and bits of glass and lead balls and cloth wadding and handed them up to the sharpshooters on the parapet. By now, British artillery was pounding holes in the crude fort, sending shells through the useless little sally port, and killing defenders with solid-iron shells that skittered along the ground, shearing off arms, legs, and heads. Suddenly, the little fort turned into an open grave. As carefully as the sharpshooters had conserved their precious powder, untrained artillerymen had wasted it. They opened the last two cannonballs and divided the gunpowder among the marksmen.

Sensing victory, the British regrouped, charged through the ragged fire, surrounded the ramparts, and stormed over them. There was no way out. No escape route remained for the last 150 men trapped inside the fort. The British fired down into the mass of stumbling, running, yelling, rebellious Americans. Dr. Joseph Warren, the handsome young president of the Massachusetts Congress and the father of four small children, was shot in the head as he fled. One hundred and forty Americans died; 301 were wounded, of whom 30 were taken prisoner. Proportionately, it was the costliest victory in all British military history: 1,054 killed and wounded out of 2,000 combatants. Yet both sides were to claim a Pyrrhic victory. While ardent Patriots were sure that, given enough gunpowder, time, and men and the support of the rest of the colonies, they would be the match of the best soldiers in the world, at first, Patriot morale plummeted. Then, as news of British losses came from Boston, it skyrocketed. Inside blockaded Boston, even as they slaughtered their horses to get fresh meat and carts of moaning wounded rumbled over the rough rutted streets, the British command declared that they had fallen short of totally crushing the rebellion only because they lacked adequate manpower. General Howe demanded 30,000 fresh troops from London.[17]

• • •

ON JUNE 23, 1775, after a nearly two-week journey, Ethan Allen and Seth Warner, stopping off only briefly in New York City to draw £30 of travel money from the New York Provincial Congress, arrived in Philadelphia, the largest town in British America and the most populous place Allen had ever seen. He was accustomed to New England's backcountry frontier settlements, where, often, the nearest house was a mile away. In Philadelphia, nearly twenty-five thousand people, three times as many people as in all of the New Hampshire Grants, lived in a two-square-mile area and ships with goods from as far away as the Mediterranean crowded the waterfront and towered over the elegant four- and five-story brick mansions of Society Hill.

Arriving on a market day, the Green Mountain delegation had to thread through a cavalcade of Conestoga farm wagons and herds of sheep and pigs. In the cool early morning air, clouds of steam rose from the flanks of great black draft horses as they strained to pull wagons crammed with cargoes of the produce, cheeses, baked goods, and cured hams of Pennsylvania German farmers. The canvas covers of the wagons fluttered as women and children inside jounced down Second Street Pike, the first cobbled street in America. Allen and his cousins passed the massive white spire of redbrick Christ Church before they crossed High Street, its long covered stone sheds coming to life for market day. As they approached the ornate Pennsylvania State House, the largest building in colonial America, they passed a long line of carriages, scores of them. No other town in America could rival the more than four score equipages in the town, or the snarled traffic they helped to produce. And everywhere, they saw militia drilling.

Just before Allen's arrival, John Adams wrote his wife, Abigail, that he had seen

a very wonderfull Phenomenon in this City—a field Day,
on which three Battalions of Soldiers were reviewed, making full two thousand Men. Battalion Men, Light Infantry, Grenadiers, Rifle Men, Light Horse, Artillery Men,
with a fine train, all in their Uniforms, going thro the
manual Exercise and the Maneuvres, with remarkable
Dexterity. . . . All this has been accomplished in this City
since the 19th of April [the date of the outbreak of fighting
at Lexington and Concord]. So sudden a formation of an
Army never took Place any where.[18]

Later that day, Ethan Allen and Seth Warner strode into the
State House to present the Continental Congress with a declaration of principles signed at Crown Point by thirty-two soldiers
and citizens of the Lake Champlain region and a request that
Allen be allowed to brief the entire Congress on conditions on
the Lake Champlain frontier. For him, it was an exhilarating and
humbling moment. He was known as the hero of Ticonderoga,
the sole hero of the Revolution so far. In the eyes of conservative
Americans, a majority in New York and New Jersey when Allen
and his cousins had just passed through, the ragtag New England
army besieging Boston had been thoroughly routed in the bloody
Battle of Bunker Hill.

Two days before the battle in Boston, the Continental Congress had appointed George Washington commander in chief of
its newly minted Continental army, in part a gesture to include
Virginia and the South in the until then entirely New England
war. As Allen and his cousin rode into Philadelphia on June 23,
Washington, with a small staff and an escort of Philadelphia's
shakoed First City Troop, rattled north over cobbled Second
Street Pike and up the Boston Post Road to take command of
New England's forces. The news of what was being called the

Ethan Allen demands the surrender of Fort Ticonderoga.

Aerial view of Fort Ticonderoga.

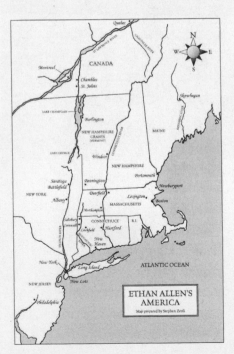

Ethan Allen's America.

Ethan Allen at
age thirty-seven.

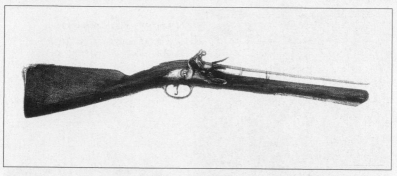

The blunderbuss Ethan Allen lent to Benedict Arnold.

Benedict Arnold in his only portrait from life, by Pierre
Eugene du Simitiere.

George Whitefield preaching.
(NATIONAL PORTRAIT GALLERY,
SMITHSONIAN INSTITUTION / ART
RESOURCE, NY)

The Reverend Jonathan Edwards.

Royal Governor Benning Wentworth of
New Hampshire. (NEW HAMPSHIRE ARCHIVES)

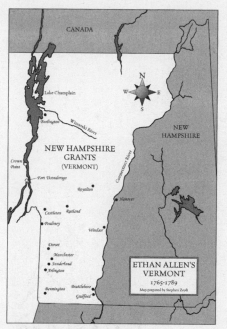

Ethan Allen's Vermont.

The Catamount Tavern in Bennington, Vermont. (COURTESY IMAGES OF THE PAST)

Governor Thomas Chittenden of Vermont.
(COURTESY UNIVERSITY OF VERMONT SPECIAL COLLECTIONS)

George Clinton.

Ira Allen, Ethan Allen's
youngest brother, founder of
the University of Vermont.

Statue of Seth Warner, cousin of Ethan Allen, Bennington, Vermont.

Montreal in 1762. (PUBLIC ARCHIVES OF CANADA)

Pendennis Castle in Cornwall, England.

Phillip Schuyler.

Guy Carleton.

Governor General Frederick Haldimand.

(COURTESY ETHAN ALLEN HOMESTEAD TRUST)

Ethan Allen at age forty after
captivity; portrait by John Barr,
from family descriptions.
(COURTESY ETHAN ALLEN
HOMESTEAD FOUNDATION)

Frances Montresor Buchanan Allen.
(COURTESY FORT TICONDEROGA MUSEUM)

Ethan Allen before General Prescott, by Howard Pyle, from *Century Magazine*, July 1902.

Daniel Shays and Job Shattuck, leaders of the 1786 Massachusetts rebellion.

Bennington, Vermont, in 1792, by Ralph Earl.

Ethan Allen's residence in Bennington.

Ethan Allen's homestead in Burlington, Vermont, during restoration.

Ethan Allen statue atop forty-foot column in Green Mountain Cemetery, Burlington, Vermont, by Peter Stephenson, dedicated in 1873. (COURTESY ETHAN ALLEN HOMESTEAD FOUNDATION)

REASON
THE ONLY
ORACLE OF MAN,
OR A
Compenduous System
OF
Natural RELIGION.

Alternately ADORNED with Confutations of a variety of DOCTRINES incompatible to it; Deduced from the most exalted Ideas which we are able to form of the

DIVINE and HUMAN
CHARACTERS,
AND FROM THE
Universe in General.

By Ethan Allen, *Esq*;

BENNINGTON:
STATE OF VERMONT;
Printed by HASWELL & RUSSELL.
M,DCC,LXXXIV.

Title page of *Reason, the Only Oracle of Man*, by Ethan Allen.

Thomas Jefferson (left) and James Madison (center) visit Bennington in 1791;
Catamount Tavern, Ethan Allen's headquarters, appears in the rear.
Oil painting by Leroy Williams. (COURTESY BENNINGTON MUSEUM)

Timber Raft on Lake Champlain, by John Warner Barber.
(COURTESY UNIVERSITY OF VERMONT SPECIAL COLLECTIONS)

Ethan Allen statue at State Capitol in Montpelier, Vermont.

Battle of Bunker Hill reached Washington on the road. Congress had also appointed three major generals, including the Hudson River land baron Philip Schuyler, who was given command of the northern department, chiefly made up of New York and any territories where the American army became engaged to the north. Schuyler, a slave owner who employed hundreds of tenant farmers to farm his immense holdings in the Mohawk Valley and along the upper Hudson River, had served in the provincial assembly as the representative of Albany County through Allen's struggle with New York claimants to the New Hampshire Grants. Many of the other New York claimants were his relatives or in-laws. As he hurried north, Washington stopped on June 25 in New York City to confer with Schuyler.

SPEAKING IN HIS SLOW, confident, distinctive voice, Allen told Congress that, amid all its military preparations and political organizing, he could not get food, ammunition, uniforms, or pay for his men. Unless Congress moved quickly, they could expect massive retaliation from the British. Governor Carleton was raising Loyalist militia, had reinforced St. John, and was building assault craft and escort vessels to come down Lake Champlain and retake the forts. Congress had to authorize an invasion of Quebec Province and seize Montreal and Quebec before the British could send massive reinforcements from England.

Many of the congressional delegates seated in high-backed Windsor chairs at the green baize-covered tables in the provincial assembly room were impressed by this tall, self-assured Colonel Allen they had heard so much about. As Allen outlined the critical state of affairs around Lake Champlain and argued for an immediate advance into Canada, all the New England Patriots who had ordered the Champlain campaign were in his audience.

John Hancock and John Adams sat at the Massachusetts table. A bifocaled sixty-nine-year-old Benjamin Franklin, returned from a decade of frustrating diplomacy in England only a month earlier, sat at Pennsylvania's table, his gouty foot propped on a special stool of his invention. Patrick Henry and Thomas Jefferson, Peyton Randolph and Richard Henry Lee of Virginia sat coolly in their silks while the New Englanders in their heavy broadcloth suffered in Philadelphia's sultry humidity.

Not everyone, however, was thrilled to see so much adulation paid to Ethan Allen. At New York's table with James Duane, the king's counsel at the 1770 Grants ejectment trials, sat another Hudson River land baron, Philip Livingston and his brother Robert, whom Allen had last seen scowling down at him from the bench of the Supreme Court of Judicature of the Province of New York. To all of them, including Allen, it was a paradoxical moment. Allen ironically was still was under sentence of death as an outlaw in New York. The nascent country needed to coalesce men of all socioeconomic classes, and this convocation, with Allen in attendance, underscored that as poignantly as anything.

Duane and many other wealthy conservatives in Congress, including a majority of the New York delegates, still favored continued attempts at reconciliation over an expanded war into Canada that would have to be launched from their province, which would thus be the first target of a destructive retaliation. Making no secret of his scorn for the man he had once tried to bribe to join forces with him in dispossessing settlers on the Grants if they would not pay a second time for their land and agree to higher annual rents, Duane for four years had drafted—and doctored— accusatory affidavits detailing Allen's activities that he submitted as evidence in the New York Assembly hearings in 1774, leading to the outlawing of Allen and seven Grants leaders. One year earlier, Duane had written caustically of "Mr. Allen," calling him "fickle and enterprising." Allen, he wrote, "was joined by men of rash and violent tempers" who had "vainly conceived of themselves as invincible." Later that year, Duane, still a British official paid by the Crown, served as a delegate to the First Continental Congress. He voted in favor of a plan of union proposed by Joseph Galloway, the conservative Speaker of the Pennsylvania Assembly and supported by the royal governor of New Jersey, William Franklin. The plan, which was based on a plan formulated by Governor Franklin's father in an imperial crisis twenty years earlier, anticipated the British Commonwealth of Nations by 150 years. Under the Galloway-Franklin plan of union, which rested heavily on British acquiescence in the scheme, each colony would continue to govern its own affairs, but there would be a central administration of the American colonies that would consist of a president-general appointed by the king and holding veto power over the acts of a grand council, whose members were to be chosen for three-year terms by the assemblies of each colony. The governor and council would constitute an "inferior and distinct branch of the British legislature." When the proposal came to a vote, it failed to pass and had to be tabled. Before it could be brought up again, the Sons of Liberty sent Galloway a box containing a torn life insurance policy and a noose. Galloway, who became the Loyalist police superintendant of Philadelphia during its British wartime occupation and later fled to England, resigned from Congress, and the proposal was never mentioned in Congress again.[19]

Despite their misgivings, the New York delegates went on record in the *Journal of Congress* as taking part in the unanimous vote that was one of the greatest triumphs of Ethan Allen's life. Congress instructed General Philip Schuyler to "procure a list of the men employed in taking and garrisoning Crown Point and Ticonderoga." He was to see that each man was to be given the same pay as officers and privates in the Continental army. Particularly pleasing to Allen was Congress's recommendation that the convention of New York, "consulting with General Schuyler, employ those called the Green Mountain Boys under such officers as the said Green Mountain Boys choose." Entering the congressional chamber an outlaw to New York's royal officials, a traitor who had seized the king's forts, Allen emerged the first Continental army lieutenant colonel of the Green Mountain Regiment. As a fringe benefit of his commissioning as an officer in the Continental service, he became, in American eyes at least, subject to military law and immune to prosecution and execution by the New York royal government. In the eyes of the Continental Congress, at least, Allen no longer had a price on his head.[20]

Later that day, President of the Congress John Hancock, the wealthy and urbane Boston radical leader who had so recently been a prime target of the British attack on Lexington and Concord, sent for Allen, whose boldness and charisma he admired. Allen was to carry a letter immediately to the New York Provincial Congress:

Gentlemen, By order of the Congress I enclose you certain Resolves, passed yesterday, respecting those who were concerned in taking and garrisoning *Crown Point* and *Ticonderoga*. As the Congress are of opinion that the employing the *Green Mountain Boys* in the *American* Army would be advantageous to the common cause, as well on account of their situation as of the disposition and alertness, they are desirous you should embody them among the Troops you shall raise. As it is represented to the Congress that they will not serve under any officers but such as they themselves choose, you are desired to consult with General *Schuyler* in whom the Congress are informed those people place a great confidence, about the field officers to be set over them.[21]

Certain that this meant that he had won the command of the new Green Mountain Regiment of the Continental army, Allen hurried off toward New York City, his cousin Seth at his side, only pausing long enough to say goodbye to his oldest friend and some wonderful new friends he had met in his short stay in Philadelphia.

BEFORE THE CONTINENTAL CONGRESS and in the taverns of Philadelphia after hours, Ethan Allen enjoyed one of the most satisfying interludes in his tempestuous life. As soon as he arrived in the city, he learned that Dr. Thomas Young, his old friend and mentor from Salisbury, was now, not surprisingly, at the center of Philadelphia's most radical revolutionary circle. The group around Young was by then known as the Independents and included Thomas Paine, whom Allen would quickly come to influence. Paine had arrived from England only six months earlier with letters of recommendation from Benjamin Franklin. He immediately launched in the city's newspapers—under the pseudonym "Humanus"—epistolary assaults on the mother country he had just left behind. Raised as a corset maker, twice fired as a customs collector, and twice married and twice widowed, Paine went to work on Franklin's newly founded *Pennsylvania Magazine* and wrote its opening essay. He edited the other contributors, including the Reverend John Witherspoon, president of the College of New Jersey, and the lawyer-poet Francis Hopkinson. Paine's blunt, direct, prosecutorial writing style instantly became popular, making the journal the best-read magazine ever attempted in colonial America. Paine delighted its rebellious readers with attacks on King George III, calling him "the Honorable plunderer of this country" and "the Right Honorable murderer of mankind." Dr. Young's and Tom Paine's radical literary circle soon expanded to embrace Dr. Benjamin Rush and, when he returned triumphantly from England, Franklin himself.[22]

News of the fighting at Lexington and Concord, followed immediately by Ethan Allen's electrifying conquest of Fort Ticonderoga, thrilled the editor Paine, who was quickly becoming more American than many Americans. When Allen arrived in town, Paine's June edition was being pulled from the press. Allen and Dr. Young applauded Paine's descriptions of "ministerial corruption" and "the tempest" around them. The loquacious Dr. Young regaled Allen with his account of the dozen-odd years since they had last toasted each other over tankards of hot-buttered rum. Young had moved away from Salisbury after his smallpox inoculation of Allen had led to his expulsion from the town and the collapse of Young's medical practice. He settled in Albany and aided the Hudson Valley rent strikers. When Stamp Act protests swept America, Young organized resistance in Albany and became one of the founders of the Sons of Liberty, traveling to the first intercolonial conference of the Sons in Annapolis, Maryland, and the Stamp Act Congress in New York City. As he rose through the ranks of radicals, his medical practice began to fall off.

Moving to Boston, the epicenter of the gathering storm in 1766, he found new patients to support his sickly wife and six children. He discovered a tumultuous seaport where, as his brother put it, "American patriots were in full operation." In the larger theater of Boston, the radicalized Young flourished. Among his patients and fellow Patriots was Samuel Adams. The two became political intimates. At Adams's behest, the Boston town meeting of 1772 placed Young on two key committees. From then on, he was at the heart of the colonial protest movement. With a sword in hand at the Boston Massacre, he prevented more bloodshed after five Patriots were slain, then eulogized them at the first annual Boston Massacre Day. When merchants marched through Boston streets to protest British customs levies, they paraded "with Dr. Young at their head with three flags flying, drums beating and a French horn." His early ties to Allen would prove pivotal in Allen's own ascent in the politicial hierarchy of rebelling leaders.

In October 1772, while Allen and the Boys were driving New York surveyors off the Grants, Adams organized the first committee of correspondence to link radicals in all the colonial legislatures. Adams appointed Young one of the original twenty-one members of this historic committee. John Adams, in fact, praised Young as "an unwearied assertor of the rights of his countrymen." An organizer of the Boston Tea Party who refused to wear a disguise, Young had made himself a marked man. Soon afterward, when the British retaliated by closing the port, Young was the first to speak openly of resorting to arms against "our oppressors." Shortly after he wrote this to John Adams at the First Continental Congress, two British officers attacked Young on the street. The officers, aware that their commanding general was watching Young, beat him savagely and left him for dead. Young was carried home "all bloody," he wrote, from a saber slash that glanced off his temple and struck his shoulder.[23]

Pursued by the British and fearing for his life, Young escaped to Newport, Rhode Island, on September 13 and then, still stalked by the British, dressed as a sailor and escaped by ship to Philadelphia only weeks before the Second Continental Congress learned of Allen's bold attack on Fort Ticonderoga. As soon as he arrived, he wrote to Sam Adams, who was sequestered with the

First Continental Congress. Adams found time to write a long letter to Young on October 17. He had apparently put off writing because he was disappointed that Young had fled Boston:

> *My dear sir,*
>
> *... I regretted your Removal from Boston when you first informd me of it, but I trust it will be for the publick Advantage. Wherever you may be I am sure you will improve your ten Talents for the public Good. I pray God to direct and reward you.... I am with due regard to Mrs. Young, affectionately yours*
>
> *Saml Adams*[24]

Administering medication to members of Congress, Young brought his family to Philadelphia and, introduced by Sam Adams, plunged into its most radical political circle, lending his pen to revolutionary petitions and papers, befriending Paine and the prominent physician Benjamin Rush. Joining the revolutionary medical service as surgeon to a rifle company, he also worked late at night with Paine, Timothy Matlock, and Sam Adams, plotting to overthrow Pennsylvania's conservative, Quaker-dominated government. Eventually, according to Dr. Rush, Young worked with Paine and Franklin in drafting the radical Pennsylvania constitution, the model for the Vermont constitution. He would also suggest the name Vermont for the new state. The week that Allen appeared before Congress, Young published a medical treatise on bilious fever in the *Pennsylvania Packet*. For Allen, reuniting with his old mentor Young, visiting Young's family, and making friends in the Revolution's most radical circle was a milestone in his evolution into a revolutionary philosopher. Before he left the capital, Allen renewed his vow to one day complete, with Young, the work of deistic philosophy they had begun so long ago but left only one-third finished.

BEFORE ALLEN COULD return to Ticonderoga, as he later learned from Benedict Arnold, the emissary Allen had sent to the Caughnawaga Indians in Quebec brought back word that the Mohawk chiefs were determined *not* to assist the king's troops. But, at the same time, they had also ordered that any Indian who took up arms against the English would be punished by death. Five Caughnawaga chiefs, their wives, and children had accompanied Winthrop Hoyt to Crown Point with the message. Offsetting this discouraging news was intelligence received from Allen's scouts in Canada that Governor-General Carleton had been able to raise only a force of twenty French Canadian noblesse and then only by promising them offices and honors. Disgusted with the English merchants of Montreal, Carleton declared martial law and threatened to burn the town if they would not help to defend it. He also learned en route that the Congress had directed that, since New York refused to send troops to garrison the lake forts, Connecticut was to send in a thousand reinforcements under a new commanding officer. This would resolve the dispute over command between Allen and Arnold. Both would be replaced by the commander of the Connecticut relief force.

The sanguinary battle at Bunker Hill had finally persuaded wavering congressmen that the British intended to crush the rebellion. The news awaiting Allen at Ticonderoga was that, the very day of his arrival at Ticonderoga, Arnold, under investigation by auditors for the Massachusetts Provincial Congress, had resigned his Massachusetts commission after being superseded by Connecticut troops and investigated for padding his expense account—an action not surprising, given Arnold's lavish tastes—

by auditors from the Massachusetts Provincial Congress. On his way back to his home in New Haven, Arnold stopped off long enough to visit the baronial Hudson River mansion of General Philip Schuyler in Albany. Schuyler had just learned from the Continental Congress that he was to prepare for an invasion of Canada, he reported to Arnold. Schuyler was shocked to learn that Allen's years of frontier resistance were now being crowned by the Continental Congress with command of a Continental regiment. He urged Arnold to write a report criticizing Allen's command:

> When I left Crown Point, there were at that post near three hundred men, without employ, having received no orders to fortify; at Ticonderoga about six hundred in the same state; at Fort George, upwards of three hundred men; some few building batteaus, and on scouting parties. Very little provision at any of the places. . . . Great want of discipline and regularity among the troops. On the other hand, the enemy at St. John's indefatiguable in fortifying, and collecting timber (supposed) for building a vessel.[25]

Shortly afterward, Schuyler sent a courier with a letter to Daniel Fay, one of Bennington's town leaders. It was important, Schuyler stressed, that the leaders of the New Hampshire Grants choose their own officers and, by implication, not Allen. The message was not lost on Fay, who knew that other members of committees of safety had long feared reprisals from the Hudson River oligarchs, their neighbors, and especially wished to please Schuyler, whose command now included the Grants as well as New York.

· · ·

His time to tarry in Philadelphia drawing to a close, Allen rode north to New York City, carrying the Continental Congress's resolution making him a Continental army colonel in charge of the newly constituted Green Mountain Regiment to the provincial congress. As Allen headed north, the roads and ferries across New Jersey were thronged with Loyalists leaving the city and going to their country houses to avoid the upheaval on crowded Manhattan Island. The shocking news of the fighting in Massachusetts had produced a dramatic and sudden transformation in the city of New York. Even as the British had prepared to march on Lexington and Concord, the city's Sons of Liberty had begun a systematic purge of Loyalists sympathetic to England. In April 1775, more than 22,000 residents crowded Manhattan's one square mile. Only 5,000 residents remained one year later, many of them freed blacks.

The ominous scent of war, like the acrid smoke of an out-of-control, approaching fire, pervaded the entire city. All over Manhattan, volunteer militia companies were drilling. At King's College, twenty-year-old Alexander Hamilton transformed his literary discussion club into a militia company. Drilling every morning in the churchyard of St. George's Chapel in short green coats, they wore leather caps with the inscription "Freedom or Death" on the front and a cockade on the side. The time for drilling was brief. Rallying at the Liberty Pole in City Hall Park, the Sons of Liberty marched downtown to the East River docks and forced their way aboard two British munitions ships. Raiding City Hall arsenal, in the spirit of their comrades in New England, they carried off six hundred muskets plus bayonets and cartridge boxes. A week later, a crowd of five thousand, many of them laborers—virtually everyone in the city who had not fled—jammed City Hall Park as local committees crossed the line from resistance to revolution, forming a new provincial congress to control the colony. It, in turn, put the city under the control of a revolutionary committee of one hundred. Isaac Sears, a former privateersman, led 360 Sons of Liberty as they, echoing a new tradition begun by Ethan Allen, seized the keys to the customs house and declared the port of New York closed. The Sons of Liberty, a coalition of sailors and shopkeepers, took over the town watch, patrolling the streets at night.

New York's deposed royal officials felt powerless to do anything but grumble. Attorney General William Smith Jr. confided to his diary,

> It is impossible fully to describe the agitated State of the Town. . . . At all corners, People inquisitive for News. Tales of all kinds invented believed, denied, discredited. . . . The Taverns filled with Publicans at Night. Little Business done in the Day. . . . The Merchants are amazed and yet so humbled as only to sigh or complain in whispers. They now dread Sears's Train of armed Men.

Another Loyalist called it a "total revolution." New York City was being ruled by "a parcel of the meanest people, Children & Negroes."[26]

WHETHER ALLEN SHOULD be allowed to present the resolution of the Continental Congress to the New York Congress provoked a sharp debate. Allen and Seth Warner wrote on July 4 to Eliphalet Dyer and Silas Deane, both members of Connecticut's congressional delegation in Philadelphia. When Allen asked to address the New York Congress, meeting behind heavily guarded doors in City Hall at the foot of Broadway, he was forced to wait several days during a heated debate. Finally, it was Isaac Sears, leader of the Sons of Liberty, who insisted, as Allen reported, that Allen be allowed to speak:

> We have been Detain'd in this City Longer than would have been Necessary had Not former Prejudices Interfered. We were Nevertheless this Day allowed to appear before the Congress and Defend our Characters against sundry Aspersions. . . . Having Acquitted our selves in the Opinion of by far the Majority of Members [we] were Honourably Treated and the Requisition of the honble Continental Congress was Comply'd with. . . . Next morning we shall Proceed to raise the men. . . .[27]

New York's congress included many members who had a serious conflict of interest in the day's proceedings as major speculators in New York grants in Vermont. Although his appointment as a Continental officer had won him immunity from arrest and prosecution, no longer leaving a price on his head, several delegates to the New York Congress loathed Allen and considered it presumptuous of him to ask to speak to them.

When the provincial congress voted, a majority of 18–9 favored admitting him. The delegates from Albany, Richmond, and New York counties, where there was the heaviest speculation in Vermont lands, dissented. As the Continental Congress had recommended to New York (that's all it could ever do, recommend), the divided New York Congress passed a resolution creating the Green Mountain Regiment, authorizing the election of officers by enlisted men. The provincial congress authorized commissions for two field officers and half a dozen captains and lieutenants, assuming that Allen would be the regimental commander.

On his way back to Ticonderoga, with Captain Seth Warner, his cousin and subordinate, Allen stopped over in Bennington.

When they strolled into the Catamount Tavern on July 26, Allen received startling news. The New York Congress's resolution provided for the election of two field-grade officers, one as lieutenant colonel, the other as a major. It did not stipulate just who they would be. In Allen's absence, a convention of the committees of safety of twenty-nine towns east and west of the Green Mountains had met at Cephas Kent's tavern in Dorset and elected officers for the new regiment. This flew in the face of Allen's appeal to the Continental Congress and the resolution it had passed and forwarded to General Schuyler that the soldiers, as was the custom in New England, choose their own leaders.

In fact, the New York land baron Philip Schuyler, now in command of the northern department of the incipient Continental army, had been working behind the scenes to block Ethan Allen from taking command of the new Green Mountain Regiment. Hardly neutral on the subject of Allen and the Boys, Schuyler would write bluntly to the Continental Congress on July 21, denouncing the raid on the Loyalist Colonel Philip Skene's manor as part of the attack on Fort Ticonderoga two months earlier. Labeling Allen and his men "a set of people calling themselves a Committee of War," Schuyler told Hancock that the Green Mountain detachment, commissioned by Connecticut, had taken Skene's forge and farm under the pretense of public service but actually "to embezzle everything." Schuyler gave orders to restore Skene's property so "that no disgrace may be brought on our cause by such lawless proceedings."[28]

Schuyler failed to mention that, a little more than a week earlier, on July 12, he had written to Daniel Fay, one of the town fathers of Bennington,

Who the people are that are designated by the appellation of Green Mountain Boys, I am at a loss particularly to determine. Perhaps such of the inhabitants of this colony [New York] as reside on what are commonly called the New Hampshire Grants are intended. In this doubt I find myself under the necessity of applying to you for information, which I entreat, and make no doubt but you will give me with all that candor which, as a friend to your country, is your indispensable duty to do.

Schuyler then urged Fay to take whatever steps were necessary "as that the Green Mountain Boys, whoever they may be," might immediately elect their officers, "and fill the regiment without delay." He went on to tell Fay that Governor Trumbull of Connecticut and President Warren of the Massachusetts Congress had urged him to advance the Green Mountain Boys to Canada and to "invest Montreal." But, Schuyler added, he refused to do this without orders.[29]

Schuyler also received an urgent correspondence from William Marsh, a grandee of Bennington's equally conservative neighbor, Manchester, that some independent-minded town leaders might revolt against the faraway Continental Congress's dictates. Marsh wrote to Schuyler on July 16 that he had heard of the new regiment authorized by the Continental Congress and that the Grants towns were to select their own officers: "I hope you will consider before you grant either warrants or commissions, for I am bold to say that neither the settlers nor the committees in the towns in the New Hampshire Grants have not been consulted on this important matter."[30] A former Green Mountain Boy, Marsh had attended the January 31 convention of committees of safety and, alienated by what he considered disloyalty to the king, thrown in his lot with New York, representing Charlotte County in the New York Provincial Congress, and doubtless voted against Ethan Allen.

When the leaders of Vermont's southern towns convened again on July 26, in Kent's tavern in Dorset, a majority were older, wealthier, and more conservative than the men Allen had led for so many years. Nathan Clark of Bennington chaired the meeting of delegates from twenty-nine towns. Many were alarmed by Allen's confrontational tactics. Still not aware of the broader implications of the Revolution, they were worried that he would bring down the wrath of the British and their Indian allies on their settlements. Some committeemen, especially Clark, were outspoken born-again Great Awakening Christians who remained appalled at Allen's youthful attacks on Puritan leaders, were horrified by his conversion to Anglicanism, and were scandalized to learn that he had been read out of towns in Massachusetts and Connecticut for his irreverent clashes with the clergy and magistrates. Ignoring the wishes of the Continental and New York congresses, the village elders rebelled. By a landslide 41–5 vote taken by secret ballot, the convention elected the devout Congregationalist Seth Warner, not Ethan Allen, as colonel in command of the Green Mountain Regiment. In all, the convention elected twenty-three officers. In addition to Warner, four other Allen cousins received commissions. Heman, who had left his store in Salisbury to bring the orders from Hartford that triggered Ethan's capture of Ticonderoga, retained his captaincy. Ethan's youngest brother, Ira, and his cousins Ebenezer Allen and Remember Baker were commissioned lieutenants. But Ethan Allen was not even elected a lieutenant.

To Allen, this was an entirely unexpected blow. An overnight folk hero whose exploits were appearing in newspapers the length of America and in Europe, he had been rejected by the very neighbors whose lands he had so long protected. For nearly five years, he had organized, trained, and led the Green Mountain Boys as they shielded these same farmers first from New York's courts' seizures and then from invasion by the British. Allen's rejection came only six days after his gracious and conciliatory letter to the New York Assembly, praising "the union that hath lately taken place between the [New York] Government and those its former discontented subjects, [by] making a united resistance against [British] ministerial vengeance and slavery." His brusque and confrontational tactics had finally caught up with him.[31]

To Allen, at this humiliating moment, it seemed more a betrayal by the people who had lived so close to him that he had never suspected their feelings toward him. More, it felt to him like a mortal wound, far more injurious than anything the British could have delivered. As a clerk was reading his conciliatory letter to the provincial congress in New York City, the man who had kept the New York "landgrabbers" at bay for five years was reeling from the overwhelming nature of his rejection by his own Vermont neighbors. To Governor Jonathan Trumbull of Connecticut, Allen wrote,

> Notwithstanding my zeal and success in my Country's cause, the old farmers on the *New-Hampshire Grants*, who do not incline to go to war, have met in a Committee meeting, and in their nomination of officers for the Regiment . . . have wholly omitted me. . . . I find myself in favour with the officers of the Army and the young *Green Mountain Boys*. How the old men came to reject me, I cannot conceive, inasmuch as I saved them from the encroachments of *New-York*.[32]

In fact, Allen realized that many of the older, wealthier, and more conservative landowners had never liked him. They considered him a reckless troublemaker whose guerrilla tactics surely would one day bring retribution from the royal govern-

ment. Some Vermonters just found him arrogant, but his premature attempt to take and hold the reinforced fort at St. John
also called his military judgment into question. Many of the
gray-haired town elders far preferred the cautious style of Allen's
more conservative cousin, Seth Warner, who long had held the
commission of captain in charge of Bennington's militia. Warner, whose family had moved to Bennington from Mary Baker
Allen's hometown of Roxbury, Connecticut, in 1763, was considered a member of one of the more established Bennington families, Ethan a newcomer and interloper. Warner, like his cousin
over six feet tall but modest and unassuming, could scarcely have
offered a more striking contrast to Allen. When Allen and Warner presented themselves to Schuyler at Ticonderoga, Schuyler
told him that the congressional resolutions left the choice of all
officers to the people. He did not tell them he had instigated the
shift from the Green Mountain Boys' electing their officers to
authorizing their election by far more conservative village elders,
thus asserting his authority over the New Hampshire Grants and
virtually nullifying the settlers' years of resistance to New York
authority.

After their meeting with Schuyler, Allen expressed his outrage, but Warner, now in command, would not back down. After
a violent quarrel, the two parted. But it was clear to both men
that an important shift had taken place in the frontier settlements. At Vermont's seminal political convention at Dorset, delegates decided almost unanimously that they wanted their troops
under a commanding officer who would collaborate with them,
a planner even if he was a plodder, not an opportunist like Allen
who, far worse, took the Lord's name in vain when he was with
his bumptious men. Ethan's brothers Ira and Heman and cousins
Remember Baker and Ebenezer Allen decided against resigning
their commissions; Ethan decided to serve as a volunteer. Ira,

writing in his memoirs of the growing rift between Ethan and Warner, told of Schuyler's fear

> that the contest between Allen and Warner would result in few enlistments, but neither Ethan Allen nor his brothers took any action to that end. Far from taking offense and sulking in their tents in a fit of Achillean anger, all rallied to the common cause. . . . Had Warner been of similar temper, he would have insisted on Allen's appointment.

Instead of an independent Vermont regiment serving under the Continental Congress, after all the years of border strife the Green Mountain Boys dissolved into what Ira Allen denominated "Warner's regiment," serving under Schuyler and "enrolled under the Province of New York," still a royal, and largely royalist, province of the British Empire. "Not without difficulty were men led to enlist under Warner's leadership, nor were those who did so all that could be desired in number or quality."[33]

NOT LONG AFTER the attack on Fort Ticonderoga, the citizens of Bennington gathered at First Church, a few hundred feet from the Catamount Inn, to hear the Reverend Jedediah Dewey, brother of the owner of another tavern that stood opposite the Green Mountain Boys' headquarters, lead a thanksgiving and prayer service. The oldest meetinghouse in Vermont, the church was packed, with Allen and his officers and many of the men who had stormed the fort in its pews. The Reverend Dewey went on at great length, praising the Almighty and giving credit to God for the victory. After he heard Parson Dewey connect divine providence with the triumph for the third time, Allen could stand it no longer and stood up.

"Don't forget, Parson, that I was there," he called out.

Parson Dewey pointed his finger ominously at Ethan. "Sit down, thou bold blasphemer!"

Less than three months after his greatest achievement, while technically he still held the rank of lieutenant colonel in the Continental army, Ethan Allen was out.[34]

12.

"I Had No Chance to Fly"

❄

DESPITE HIS REPUDIATION by many of Vermont's elders,
Ethan Allen audaciously marched into General Schuyler's headquarters at Fort Ticonderoga—so recently his—and offered to
serve on Schuyler's staff. Schuyler's cold rebuff came after he had
authorized his paymaster, and kinsman, Colonel James Livingston, to advance Allen £200 New York currency, a year's pay as a
Continental colonel. But, Schuyler informed Allen, he was afraid
he would have to decline Allen's proffered services. Allen took
the money and left. He galloped off to Sheffield, Massachusetts,
where he gave the money to his wife, Mary, who, with their four
children, was living on one of the farms his younger brother
Zimri managed for Ethan. Then he rode back to Ticonderoga
to make Schuyler another offer. He would serve in any capacity,
with or without a commission, with or without pay.

A patrician, Schuyler had never liked the brash Allen and was
prepared to go to considerable lengths to keep him beyond arm's

length. By urging Daniel Fay and, through him, the town elders of the Grants to hold a convention and to elect the officers of the Green Mountain Regiment, he was, ironically, echoing the express wishes of *his* commanding officer, George Washington. A veteran of the strictly hierarchical British army, Washington was horrified at the New England custom of soldiers electing their superiors, of common soldiers choosing their sergeants, the sergeants electing the lieutenants and captains, and on up through the chain of command.

At this very moment, at his headquarters in Cambridge, Massachusetts, Washington was dismantling this democratically conceived system and insisting on complete subordination in command. Washington was shocked to find officers shaving enlisted men. He insisted on precise discipline and forbade cursing, swearing, and drunkenness, which would hardly have endeared him to Allen's men. He required punctual attendance at daily worship, neatness among enlisted men and officers. He imposed severe sanctions for infractions, especially for theft and straying from camp. Each day, the men were formed up to witness floggings of wrongdoers, from a commonplace thirty-nine lashes up to five hundred. Soon, the guardhouse was filled with malefactors as Washington fumed about the exceedingly dirty and nasty New Englanders he was supposed to pit against the spit-and-polish British regulars. He blamed the "unaccountable kind of stupidity" he found among the soldiers on the "leveling spirit," the "principles of democracy which so universally prevail." There can be little doubt he would not have approved of the conduct of the Green Mountain Boys.

Now, when Schuyler once again refused Allen's offer, other members of Schuyler's staff spoke up for him. Finally, Schuyler acquiesced, but he would later claim "only after a solemn promise, made me in the presence of several officers, that he would demean himself properly." With orders to act as a scout, Colonel Ethan Allen headed north with the American army about to invade Canada.[1]

PHILIP SCHUYLER'S ORDERS from Congress were to mount a full-scale invasion of Quebec Province up the Richelieu River, take the British forts at St. Jean-sur-Richelieu and Chambly, then seize Montreal and Quebec and any other strongpoints necessary to impede the invasion of New York by Carleton's forces. The American invasion of Canada—the main campaign of the first year of the Revolution—began on September 6, 1775, when Schuyler's army tiptoed across the Quebec border. Nearly four months had slipped away since the capture of Ticonderoga and Crown Point, more than three months since Allen's and Arnold's first sorties into Canada. The main attack, under the command of the chronically ailing Schuyler, began amid high winds and heavy rains on Lake Champlain that further delayed the invasion. The American invasion fleet consisted of the armed schooner *Liberty*, the sloop of war *Enterprise,* and three plodding gondolas.

It was September by the time the American army disembarked on Canadian soil to wait for General Schuyler, who had been bedridden in the commandant's quarters for more than a month with a flare-up of gout. A frigid wind, a foretelling of a dire winter, was coming off the lake by the day Schuyler sailed north with artillerymen and cannon in big bateaux to lead the second wave, followed by five hundred Connecticut militia and three hundred New York militia. Before shoving off, Schuyler had dispatched Colonel Allen with Major Brown to Montreal on an intelligence-gathering mission. Allen hurried back with a report that Quebec's Governor Carleton had heavily reinforced St. Jean, was building invasion craft, and was planning a counterattack with the support of the Caughnawaga Mohawk Indians.

At the same time, Allen also learned ominous news. By August of 1775, an all-out Indian war had erupted just north of the border. A French Canadian militia captain, François de Loumier, had been reconnoitering with five Mohawk scouts, when he spied an empty bateau hitched to a clump of alders near the mouth of the Richelieu. As the Mohawks were towing it away with their war canoe, a party of buckskinned Green Mountain Boys hollered at them that it was their boat. When Captain de Loumier refused to heed their warning, Remember Baker, the leader of the patrol, opened fire on the Indians from behind a tree. The Indians returned fire until the Green Mountain Boys stopped firing, then fled north. De Loumier came back the next day with a larger force of Mohawks. In the underbrush, they found the lifeless body of Remember Baker, Allen's cousin. He had been shot through the head. In his pockets they found letters proving he had been corresponding with a leading Montreal merchant and with the Caughnawaga chief, Captain Ninmans. The Indians beheaded Baker. Dangling his severed head, they carried his corpse to St. Jean, where they paraded around the town with it until a British officer bought Baker's corpse and had it, in more civilized British tradition, buried inside the fort.

The news that his cousin, his boyhood companion, his closest friend, his business partner, and the man who had hunted and surveyed with him for more than twenty years had been killed, and killed so brutally, devastated Ethan Allen. Only a month earlier, they had traveled triumphantly together to Philadelphia and appeared before the Continental Congress. Allen's grief turned into fury when he learned that Philip Schuyler had reacted by writing to George Washington that he believed Baker's skirmish with the Indians was to blame for the lack of Indian support for the Canadian invasion: "The Canadians and Indians [would] be friendly to us, unless the Imprudence of a Capt. Baker who without my Leave went upon a Scout and Contrary to the most pointed & Express orders" had fired on Indians.[2]

Schuyler didn't send condolences to Allen or to Baker's family. Instead Schuyler, who owned large and vulnerable estates in the Mohawk River Valley, promptly sent off an apology to the Six Nations Iroquois of western New York, overlords of the Mohawks, for the incident, once again stalling the northern invasion, his action indicating that he regarded Allen as more potent an enemy than the Mohawks. Schuyler took the time to ride back to Albany and, as if playing both sides, convened an Indian conference ordered by the Continental Congress and met with Six Nations leaders in the old Dutch church. There, seven hundred tribesmen received gifts of lace-trimmed hats, ruffled shirts, and blankets decorated with prized wampum. Schuyler and his staff and the Indian commissioners sent by Congress, including Oliver Wolcott, sat cross-legged with the Indian chiefs in the churchyard and promised to "keep the hatchet buried deep." For Ethan Allen, however, it was too late for peace pipes. The hatchet had been buried in the neck of his closest friend in the world, the first casualty of the Canadian war. Grief mingled with his rage and prompted him to make a rash and ultimately fateful decision.[3]

THE FIRST FULL MOON in September, near the northerly Canadian border, deposited a frost on the pumpkin, and it sent a chill through Allen that it was almost autumn and Schuyler had not set foot onto Canadian soil. Fall foliage began to mask the treacherous winter weather slipping up on the boats and tents of his immobilized army. With Schuyler sidelined by illness, Richard Montgomery, his in-law and second-in-command, a former

British officer married into the Livingston family of Hudson River land and mine owners, took over command of the invasion of Canada. Learning from Allen that the British at St. Jean were building a fleet, Montgomery within six days sent north fifty boats full of troops from Ticonderoga. As the flotilla of New England farm boys and idled New York City shipyard workers glided over the invisible line into British-held Canada, Allen first learned that Mohawk Indians had carried Remember Baker's head on a pole until a British officer bought it and respectfully buried it. Months later, when Fort St. John fell to the Americans after a long siege, Baker's remains were dug up and shipped back to Arlington, Vermont, his home for many years. It was Allen who had to break the tragic news to Remember's widow, Desire, and son, Ozzie, at the Winooski trading post of the Onion River Land Company. He could not believe that the man who had survived hand-to-hand combat in the French and Indian War, who had taught him how to shoot and track game in the woods, and then had protected him during his brash attack at Ticonderoga, was gone.

As if to make sense of, as much as to avenge, his best friend's death, Allen chose five men from the new American base at Ile aux Noix, fifteen miles south of St. Jean, and plunged into the forest where Baker had been slain on a reconnaissance mission. "I had no commission from Congress, yet [General Montgomery] engaged me, that I should be considered as an officer the same as though I had a commission." Allen was told, he later wrote, to "command certain detachments of the army. This I considered as an honorable offer." His mission: "to go in company with Major Brown, and certain interpreters, through the woods into Canada" and spread the word among French-Canadian *habitants* and Indians that a vast American army was coming and invite them to join the side that was sure to win the fight against British tyranny.[4]

Possessing a smattering of French and far more gestures, Allen brought to bear the courage, confidence, and enthusiasm of a missionary as he went from village to farm to Indian town. "Colonel *Allen* has been very serviceable in bringing in the *Canadians* and *Indians*," reported one of Montgomery's officers to Governor Trumbull.[5] The officer added, "The *Indians* of all the tribes, and the *Canadians* who join us, have all learned *English* enough to say Liberty and *Bostonian*, and all call themselves *Yankees*. The *Indians* boast much of it, and will smite on their breasts, saying, 'me *Yankee*.'"[6]

"Having through much danger negociated this business, I returned to the isle Auix Noix in the fore part of September," Allen later wrote—just as Schuyler turned over command to Montgomery. Allen found Montgomery installing cannon Allen had taken at Ticonderoga—including a thirteen-inch mortar nicknamed "the Old Sow"—in siege lines. Allen pitched in. "I assisted in laying a line of circumvallation round the fortress." Offering advice to the veteran British officer and declaring himself ready to lead a charge against the British stronghold, Allen was eager to do exactly what had made his Vermont neighbors choose a less flamboyant officer. Most of all, he yearned to be in at the kill at St. John, where his best friend lay buried. Tactfully, Montgomery instead suggested that what would be far more valuable to him right now would be to continue his part-spying, part-recruiting missions. "I was ordered . . . to let [the Indians and the French *habitants*] know that the design of the army was only against the English garrisons, and not the country, their liberties, or their religion," Allen later wrote, but was also ordered "to observe the disposition, designs, and movements" of *habitants* and Indians. "This reconnoitre I took with reluctance, . . . but my esteem for [General Montgomery's] person, and opinion of him as a politician and brave officer, induced me to proceed."

Dressed in the buckskin vest and toque of the French Canadians, Allen led an eighty-man detachment made up of Sergeant Jeremy Duggan, a French-speaking Montreal barber, eight Connecticut militia, two interpreters, and seventy French Canadian volunteers. They left St. John on Sunday, September 17, and headed north along the forested east bank of the Richelieu River. Allen "passed through all the parishes on the river Sorel" to its mouth, where it flows into the broad St. Lawrence, "preaching politics," as he put it. Following the river "through the parishes" to Longueil, opposite Montreal, he "so far met with good success as an itinerant," a reference to the open-field evangelists of the Great Awakening.[7]

By his third day out, Allen wrote back to Montgomery from St. Tours. He had some 250 *habitants* under arms and had retained a French Canadian commissary to supply bread, beef, pork, and rum—promising he would pay as he went:

> As I march, they gather fast. . . . You may rely on it that I shall join you in about three days, with five hundred or more Canadian volunteers. I could raise one or two thousand in a weeks time. . . . I swear by the Lord I can raise three times the number of our Army in Canada. . . .

He sweetened the message by sending along with the courier six hogsheads of rum he had purchased.[8]

On the morning of September 24, 1775, he set out with his "guard of about eighty men, from Longale, to go to Lapraier," intending to return to General Montgomery's forces at St. Jean. But he "had not advanced two miles" before he met with Major Brown, who asked him to halt. Brown said he wanted to communicate "something of importance" to Allen and his confidants.

The two New Englanders went into a house just outside the village of La Prairie, and Allen "took a private room" with him and several of Allen's associates. There, Brown urged Allen to return to Longueil and "procure some canoes, so as to cross the river St. Lawrence a little north of Montreal." Brown would cross the river "a little south of the town, with near two hundred men." He said he already had enough boats, probably the wooden dugouts used by Indians in the area. In his memoirs, Ira Allen maintained that Seth Warner was to join Allen and Major Brown with some five hundred Vermonters. Brown declared, Allen remembered, "that we would make ourselves masters of Montreal."[9]

It would be three years before Ethan Allen could consign to writing the details of the day's events and his travels before and afterward, but there is no reason to doubt the general thrust of the narrative that he eventually set down. Too many men were still alive and had come to power who knew the circumstances of Allen's seemingly impromptu decision to attack Montreal. He could not stand to wait any longer to carry out the mission entrusted to him by Connecticut's revolutionary leaders fully five months earlier. Having spent months urging action, he was forced to stand by idly, only to watch the short northern summer slipping away. And now the American army at Fort St. John was digging in for the slowest kind of attack. A classic siege would allow the British ample time to reinforce Canada from England and move troops south from Quebec to buttress Montreal. Both Brown and Allen believed that, with Fort St. John surrounded, a show of force at the gates of Montreal would throw its 9,000 inhabitants into panic. Because both had met with great success recruiting French Canadian *habitants*, no lovers of the English, they had every reason to expect more to join their ranks as Allen and Brown prepared for the attack. Furthermore, bilingual barber Jeremy Duggan seems to have swayed Allen by his insistent assertions about what he had learned inside Montreal. Duggan reported that the leading English merchant, John Walker, chairman of the Montreal Committee of Correspondence, would readily join Allen at the head of at least 500 armed English merchants and their followers. Both Schuyler and Montgomery believed, quite accurately, that Carleton had only 600 Redcoats in all Canada, some 200 downriver at Quebec City and another 300 tied down in St. Jean. By contrast, Allen and Brown may well have believed, especially considering the number of French Canadians who had been flocking to their standard, that they would have 800, 900, maybe even 1,000 men at their disposal—and Allen could remember taking Fort Ticonderoga with one-tenth that number! Allen could not have known that Chief Joseph Brant, leader of the Mohawks, had arrived with 220 warriors and about 130 Loyalists from the Mohawk Valley to reinforce Montreal.

In an impromptu council of war, the "plan was readily approved by me and those in council," Allen later wrote. Both Allen and Brown sent messages to General Montgomery, but neither waited for answers. Both officers knew that it was the express wish of the New England revolutionary leadership that Quebec Province be taken quickly before the British had time to reinforce and launch a massive counterinvasion from the North. Allen seemed satisfied that his orders no longer came from Schuyler, who had resigned his command, but from Montgomery, who had entrusted him to raise a detached force for the main American army. That was enough for Allen, and it might have been for any field commander, who customarily has broad discretion to react expeditiously and take advantage of favorable battlefield conditions. Besides, Allen relished any risk, and here was an opportunity for glory, one that might also repair his damaged reputation among his neighbors and his loyal followers among the Green Mountain Boys. Allen hastily retraced his steps to Longueil, "collected a few canoes, and added about thirty English Americans to [his] party."[10]

Could Allen have reasonably expected Walker and the transplanted New England merchants of Montreal to take such a bold step as joining his revolutionary force? Carleton at first had thought so and considered abandoning the city and concentrating on the defense of the far more strategic and defensible Quebec. But he decided, instead, to call for help from landless veterans of the French and Indian War and offered a recruitment bounty of one hundred acres of land per volunteer, plus fifty acres for each family member, and the waiving of quitrents for twenty years. And he threatened the Montreal merchants that he would burn the city if they would not help to defend it. Then he moved quickly to wipe out any organized resistance, striking first at the leading member of the Montreal Committee of Correspondence. Walker had led a spirited opposition to Carleton's Quebec Act and for months had corresponded with members of the Continental Congress. On May 1, the Quebec Act took effect. Hundreds of Montrealers milled around the tarred and garlic-bedecked bust of George III in the Place d'Armes. A French Canadian official appointed by Carleton loudly declared, "Que le roi est maitre"— "The king is master." Walker challenged him:

> I deny that the King is my master. I respect him as my lawful Sovereign and King, and am ready to pay due obedience to his lawful commands; but I cannot acknowledge him for my master while I live by my own industry. When I receive pay from him, I will acknowledge him for my master.

Later in May, as British officers and French noblesse repeatedly denounced him and threatened him with arrest, Walker retired to the countryside, to his manor house and potash works at L'Assumption. Governor Carleton was able to intercept packets of letters sent to Walker by American patriots and their Canadian sympathizers. Finally, Carleton, with great secrecy, sent out an officer and thirty Redcoats with orders to take Walker dead or alive. They surrounded his house at daybreak and demanded he surrender. Instead, one eyewitness reported, Walker opened fire, defending his house

> a long while with great courage, and wounded the [British] officer, and a soldier or two. At last, finding they could not get at him, they set fire to the house, and then he, with Mrs. Walker, were obliged to make their escape from the flames, out a garret window, naked; and thus he fell into the soldiers' hands, who then . . . fell upon him and beat him unmercifully.[11]

AT BEST, ALLEN and Brown's plan of attacking Montreal was, without Walker and the support of his adherents, sketchy, a little short of suicidal. According to their battle plan, when Brown crossed the St. Lawrence at the southern end of the island and was in position at its southern tip, his men were to give three "huzzahs," a salute that Allen's forces would return, and they would together attack the town. Too many flaws riddled the plan, at least as it is recoverable, to explain why neither of them considered how far apart that would place them, making it impossible for them to hear each other. Brown obviously couldn't round up enough dugouts to get his supposed two-hundred-man force across the wider river, if he ever tried. The kindest interpretation is that he lost his nerve and left Allen and his small contingent stranded and unsupported. If Allen ever found out Brown's intentions, he left no record that he did.

Crossing the half-mile-wide St. Lawrence that night, Allen ferried over his meager command, including eighty impoverished French Canadian *habitants* hired at fifteen pence a day and promised a share of the plunder of Montreal. The rest of his force was made up of Connecticut troops who had volunteered for this hazardous reconnaissance in force, men from nine Connecticut towns, including Salisbury, where Allen had become legendary. The problems turned out to be the same as those at Ticonderoga—not enough boats, a shuttling of canoes three times across the wide river—but the results were quite opposite and, ultimately, catastrophic. It was dawn before Allen could even find his agreed-upon position and listen for Brown's huzzahs.

But Walker's adherents failed to come. Two hours of sunlight passed. Still no huzzahs, no Brown. And still no legion of English Canadian merchants and their auxiliaries. Allen couldn't retreat and regroup in daylight with only a few canoes. Desperate, he halted his column and took up a defensive position about two miles from the town walls. He dispatched scouts to La Prairie to look for Brown and to Walker's manor at L'Assumption. Allen later wrote of that morning,

> My whole party, of this time, consisted of about one hundred ten men, near eighty of whom were Canadians. . . . Soon after day break, I set a guard between me and the town, with special orders, to let no person whatever pass or repass . . . and another guard in the other end of the road. . . . [In] the mean time I reconnoitered the best ground to make a defence expecting [Major] Brown's party was landed on the other side of the town. . . . I had no chance to fly.

If he tried to escape back across the river, only one-third of his men could recross at a time. The other two-thirds would be captured. His honor would not permit such a recourse: "This I could not reconcile to my feelings as a man, much less as an officer: I therefore concluded to maintain the ground, if possible, and all to fare alike." Passing up the opportunity to flee with his fellow Yankees, Allen busied himself arresting "sundry persons who came to [his] guards" as spies, "as they proved to be." One escaped and "exposed the weakness of [his] party." Expecting a cannonade, the Montrealers panicked. Carleton was on the point of ordering all British official personnel and records put aboard the armed schooner *Gaspee* and fleeing. But no cannonade came, no attack. Between two and three in the afternoon of September 25, 1775, 30 Redcoats, 130 Royal Highland Emigrants, and 30 Mohawk Indians led by Walter Butler surged out of the Montreal city gates to attack Allen's little army. Allen's later account makes it clear he thought the odds against him were even more lopsided than they actually were: "I encouraged my soldiery to bravely defend themselves, that we should soon have help, and that we should be able to keep the ground. . . . The enemy consisted of not more than forty regular troops, together with a mixed multitude . . . in all . . . 500."

Outnumbered and outgeneraled by any measure, Allen seemed helpless as Butler's Iroquois and Allen Maclean's Loyalist rangers slowly, methodically enveloped his position, centered on a barn and surrounding swampy meadows. It seemed to Allen that the enemy was attacking from all directions, "from woodpiles, ditches, buildings." He remembered, "At a considerable distance . . . I returned the fire." Gunfire continued

for some time on both sides. . . . It is rare that so much ammunition was expended and so little execution done

by it. . . . Such of my party as stood their ground behaved
with great fortitude, much exceeding that of the enemy,
but were not the best of marksmen and, I am apprehensive,
were all killed or taken.

Allen later reported, "The action continued an hour and
three-quarters, by the watch, and I know not to this day how
many of my men were killed." He was hoping to keep the Montrealers at bay until dark so that he could make his escape, but
"near half the body of the enemy began to flank round to [his]
right." He decided to detach Sergeant Duggan to post fifty
French Canadians to his left in a ditch. Instead of advancing,
Duggan escaped with his men as fast as he could. Another few
score French Canadians followed his lead.

From 130 men, Allen was down to 35, 7 of them, including
his brother-in-law Isaac Brownson, wounded. "The enemy kept
closing round me," he recalled. "Almost entirely surrounded,"
he ordered a retreat but found that "the enemy, who were of the
country, and their Indians, could run as fast as [his] men." He
retreated "near a mile," but the Indians kept working around
behind him. "I expected in a very short time, to try the world of
spirits." Anticipating no mercy, Allen "determined to sell [his] life
as dear" as he could, he wrote. "One of the enemy's officers boldly
pressing in on [our] rear, discharged his fusee at me; the ball
whistled near me, as did many others that day." Allen "returned
the salute" and "missed him." The running fight "had put us both
out of breath." Allen wasn't frightened, he averred, but "with [his]
tongue in a harsh manner" told the officer that, since the British

numbers were so far superior to mine, I would surrender,
provided I could be treated with honor, and be assured of
good quarter [mercy] for myself and the men. . . . [The

British officer in charge] answered I should; another officer coming up directly after[ward], confirmed the treaty;
upon which I agreed to surrender with my party.

Allen later learned that the commanding officer of the British
force, a Major Carden of the Twenty-sixth Regiment of Foot, had
been killed by one of his long-range shots.

Half a minute after he surrendered his sword, one of the
Mohawks,

part of whose head was shaved, being almost naked and
painted, with feathers [in] the hair of the other side . . .
came running up to me with an incredible swiftness; he
seemed to advance with more than mortal speed . . . less
than twelve feet of me, he presented his firelock. . . .

Allen dodged around behind the British officer who held Allen's
sword, but the Indian "flew round with great fury, trying to
single me out to shoot me without killing the officer." Then
another Indian attacked. Nearby, William Stewart, one of the
Green Mountain Boys who had helped the Allens survey much
of Vermont and had charged into Fort Ticonderoga with him,
surrendered, only to be struck in the head by an Indian's tomahawk
before a British solder, less vengeful than his Indian allies, could
rescue him. As warriors encircled Allen, a one-eyed Canadian
and an Irishman drove away the Indians at bayonet point. "The
escaping from so awful a death, made even imprisonment happy,"
he wrote. "My conquerors on the field had treated me with great
civility and politeness." Ethan Allen would not again feel that
way about his captors for a very long time.[12]

13.

"Ye Shall Grace a Halter"

✳

WHEN ETHAN ALLEN surrendered after prematurely attacking Montreal in September of 1775, he could not have known
that his captors considered his status as a prisoner unequivocal.
With a commission from the Continental Congress, he thought
of himself as an officer of the Continental army. As such, had
he been more restrained himself, he may have assumed he was
entitled to the milder treatment normally accorded to an officer
and a gentleman under the rules of war in the eighteenth century.
That meant he could expect to be held on his parole of honor in
something like house arrest. Under this code, his captors would
afford him the right to travel in the daytime within a radius of
twelve miles until he could be exchanged for a British prisoner
of equal rank, in his case a lieutenant colonel. But even though
this vestige of the code of chivalry of the Middle Ages was still
observed in wars between two sovereign nations, those rules of

war, in the minds of British government officials and military officers, did not apply in a rebellion such as this.

Allen could not have known that, three weeks before his capture, King George III, on his throne at Westminster on August 23, 1775, read his Proclamation of Rebellion, declaring his American colonies to be in open rebellion. Any American in any way suspected of involvement in the American Rebellion, as the English termed it from that moment, was to be considered a rebel in arms against the king, guilty of the felony of treason, for which the penalty was a certain and excruciating death.

When Ethan was seven years old, the leaders of the Jacobite Rising of 1745 were hanged, drawn, and quartered—hanged until they were half-dead, then lowered from the gallows and disemboweled, then hanged until they were dead, only to be beheaded and quartered. After this gruesome spectacle before a jeering, roaring crowd, the rebels' severed heads were placed in cages at the Aldgate, the main entrance to London, as a lesson to passersby. For the past thirty years, as Americans who had traveled to London knew, ravens had nested in their skulls.

British officers in America, if they did not yet know that the king had read his proclamation to Parliament, acted as if Allen's sentence of death had not even been open to question. His captors surely knew that the notorious leader of the Green Mountain Boys had been declared an outlaw by the British colonial government of New York, had a reward on his head, and as a result, if captured, faced summary execution. No trial was necessary. In British eyes, General Richard Prescott, in command at Montreal, would have been entirely justified in hanging Allen and his fellow prisoners on the battlefield, just as Sir William Tryon had put to death the leaders of the North Carolina Regulators after the Battle of the Alamance only four years earlier. For Allen to take one royal fortress had been galling enough to the British, but then to try to capture the second-largest fortified town in Canada—he could expect no leniency. The only reason for Prescott and his superior officer, Governor-General Sir Guy Carleton, to send Allen and his followers to England for trial and execution was to present him as a trophy of their capture of the great rebel of Ticonderoga and to provide an example of what awaited other rebels. Only a miraculous rescue or escape could now spare Allen's life.

FROM THE TIME George Washington assumed command of the Continental army, he made the humane treatment of prisoners a linchpin of his policies. To protect prisoners taken at Bunker Hill and in skirmishes around Boston, he wrote to Gage, protesting the harsh treatment meted out to captive Americans. Washington complained that American officers had been "thrown indiscriminately into a common jail appropriate for felons," regardless of their rank or physical condition. He would retaliate against British prisoners, Washington warned Gage:

> My Duty now makes it necessary to apprize you, that for the future I shall regulate my Conduct towards those Gentlemen who are or may be in our Possession, exactly by the Rule which you shall observe, towards those of ours, now in your Custody. If Severity & Hardship mark the Line of your Conduct, (painful as it may be to me) your Prisoners will feel its Effects.[1]

Washington well knew British prisoner-of-war policies as they had been applied only a dozen years earlier in the French and Indian War, when he had risen to brigadier, a general in the British army.

Washington warned that, if Gage treated American prisoners as common criminals instead of prisoners of war, he would follow the ancient Roman legal principal of *lex talionis*, the law of the claw—revenge. Understanding Washington's meaning, Gage tried to cast their dealings in a more personal mold: if he, an English gentleman, spared his captives, it would be from his own virtuous motives, not as a matter of law or custom. Responding to the first American attempt at prisoner-of-war negotiation, Gage wrote Washington that Britons were "ever preeminent in Mercy" and had, in this case, "overlooked the Criminal in the Captive":

> Upon these principles your Prisoners, whose Lives by the Laws of the Land are destined to the Cord [hanging], have hitherto been treated with care and kindness . . . indiscriminately it is true, for I Acknowledge no Rank that is not derived from the King.[2]

Washington also advised the British commander that the Americans were determined to achieve recognition as belligerents, not as criminals, and were therefore entitled to the benefits of the laws and customs of eighteenth-century warfare. Gage studiously responded to "George Washington, Esq.," refusing to recognize Washington's rank: he would dignify only a rank conferred by the king. A long minuet began, and Washington all too soon had to reiterate his threat of reprisal after Allen's capture at Montreal.

WHEN THE PRISONER Ethan Allen was taken, at bayonet point, inside the walls of Montreal and prodded up to the headquarters of General Richard Prescott, the British still did not know whom they had captured. The British commander asked his name, and, as Allen later recounted, this is what happened:

> He then asked me, whether I was that Col. Allen, who took Ticonderoga, I told him I was the very man; then he shook his cane over my head, calling me many hard names, among which he frequently used the word rebel, and put himself in a great rage. I told him he would do well not to cane me, for I was not accustomed to it, and shook my fist at him, telling him that that was the beetle of mortality for him, if he offered to strike; upon which Capt. M'Cloud of the British, pulled him [Prescott] by the skirt, and whispered to him, as he afterwards told me . . . that it was inconsistent with his honor to strike a prisoner. . . . The General stood a minute, when he made the following reply: "I will not execute you now, but ye shall grace a halter at Tyburn, God damn ye." . . . Gen. Prescott then ordered one of his officers to take me on board the Gaspee schooner of war and confine me, hands and feet, in irons. . . .[3]

Prescott made it very plain that he regarded Allen and his compatriots as common felons. Until the *Gaspee* could be prepared to hold such a large number of prisoners, Prescott ordered them manacled and shackled in a small house under heavy guard. Even then, Allen seems not to have understood his new and degraded status. He demanded paper, pen, and ink to complain to General Prescott:

> *Honourable Sir:*
>
> *In the wheel of transitory events, I find myself prisoner, and in irons: probably your Honour has certain reasons, to me incon-*

ceivable, though I challenge an instance of this sort of economy of the Americans, during the late war, towards any officers of the Crown.

On my part, I have to assure your Honour, that when I had the command, and took Captain Delaplace and Lieutenant Felton, with the garrison at Ticonderoga, I treated them with every mark of friendship and generosity, the evidence of which is notorious, even in Canada. I have only to add, that I expect an honourable and humane treatment, as an officer of my rank and merit should have. . . .[4]

Allen received no answer from Prescott, nor did Governor Carleton respond when he wrote him a similar note. For the next three weeks, Allen and his thirty-four men remained crammed, under heavy guard, in a small stone house at the southeast corner of Montreal Island along the town's busy waterfront.

IN ONE AFTERNOON in mid-October, as American artillery pounded away at Fort St. John only twenty miles to the east, Ethan Allen's known world collapsed into the dark, foul, rat-infested, and contaminated bilges of an armed ship. He didn't have time to wonder what had happened to all of his men. Manacled in pairs, they had been dispersed among the ships moored off Montreal. Now they were rowed out to the twelve-gun schooner of war *Gaspee*, where they joined Allen belowdecks in the anchor cable tier. From that day on, they were all "treated with the greatest severity, nay as criminals." Years later, when Allen had recovered enough to set down the remembered details of that day, he was nonchalant about the handcuffs—"a common size and form"—"but my leg irons (I should imagine) would weigh thirty pounds." His leg irons were held down by a forty-pound iron bar:

The irons were so close upon my ancles, that I could not lie down in any other manner than on my back. I was put into the lowest and most wretched part of the vessel, where I got the favour of a chest to sit on; the same answered for my bed at night. . . . [I procured] some little blocks from the guard (who day and night, with fixed bayonets, watched over me) to lay under each end of the long bar of my leg irons, to prevent my ancles from galling, while I sat on the chest, or lay back. . . . [M]ost of the time, day and night, I sat on it.[5]

When Allen appealed to the ship's captain to loosen his chains so that he could lie on his side, the captain said "that his express orders were to treat me with such severity, which was disagreeable to his own feelings; nor did he ever insult me." Ignoring orders, another officer each day had a cabin boy distribute "victuals from his [the captain's] own table" and "a good drink of grog."[6]

In the infernal gloom of his cold, damp, swaying, reeking cage, Allen was barely able to see all the other prisoners who had been packed in and enchained, but he soon learned they included John Walker, the wealthy fur trader and chairman of the Montreal Committee of Correspondence, and another pro-American merchant from St. Jean, William Hazen. For three more weeks, as the unseasonably mild October weather gave way to the biting chill of November dampness, the *Gaspee* rocked in the river as sailors, officers, and Englishmen loyal to their king came to gawk at Allen and insult the great rebel. He had become a chained tourist attraction who could be counted on "to throw out plenty of extravagant language." One day, in a fit of frustration, he "twisted off the ten penny-weight iron nail that went through the mortise of the bar of [his] handcuff"—with his front teeth, no less. For the rest of his life, Allen would relish any opportunity to grin and bare his chipped front tooth and recount the

story. "I heard one [guard] say, damn him, can he eat iron? After
that, a small padlock was fixed to the hand-cuff. . . ."[7]

ON NOVEMBER 11, 1775, Allen and his fellow prisoners were
abruptly hurried off the *Gaspee* and rowed over to a larger man-of-
war, the sixteen-gun sloop of war *Adamant*, a fast ship that served
as the dispatch vessel between Canada and England. Each day
the gunfire had grown louder, tantalizingly closer to Montreal.
By this time, the American invasion of Canada had been bogged
down for nearly two months as a glowingly optimistic summer
turned into a saturnine autumn of diminishing possibilities for
the quick offensive that not only Ethan Allen but George Washington and the Continental Congress had believed would bring
Canada into the continental union. With a more than twenty-to-
one numerical superiority over the six hundred British soldiers in
Canada, the American army's plan to have Major General Philip
Schuyler strike north from Lake Champlain and take Montreal
and Quebec seemed only to lack two ingredients: a decisive leader
and soldiers with any experience at war.

Early in September, after returning from the futile Indian
conference at Albany, Schuyler wrote to Washington that he no
longer had "a trace of doubt on [his] mind as to the propriety
of going into Canada." His second-in-command, Richard Montgomery, was a tall, slender, and amiable Irish-born veteran of
sixteen years as a British officer. Passed over for promotion to
major after distinguishing himself during six years of fighting in
the Champlain Valley and Canadian campaigns of the French
and Indian War, Montgomery was thoroughly familiar with the
terrain. In late summer, he decided to launch the invasion without waiting for the phlegmatic Schuyler to return, his decision
triggered by intelligence provided him by Ethan Allen. Allen

had reported that Carleton evidently considered the small fort, a collection of brick barracks and outbuildings only twenty miles southwest of Montreal, too strategically important to abandon. Carleton ordered two strong new redoubts constructed and sent in two hundred Redcoats and three hundred Iroquois to blunt the American attack.[8]

Buoyed by a glorious sunset over the Adirondacks on August 28, Montgomery had led his flotilla out onto Lake Champlain, only to run into a tropical storm that scattered the vessels and blew gale-force winds all the next day. It took nine days to regroup and cover the twenty miles to Ile aux Noix, a swampy, malarial, low-lying island in the Richelieu River. There Schuyler, leading five hundred raw recruits from New York City, joined Montgomery and reassumed the command. By now, the Americans outnumbered the beleaguered British garrison more than four-to-one.

Washington would later criticize Schuyler for slowing down at this critical moment and digging into a defensive position instead of leaving Lake Champlain fortified, bypassing Fort St. John, and hurrying on to Montreal before mild weather could turn into the bitter Canadian winter that would frustrate any attempt to take Canada. But Schuyler ignored Washington, reasoning that he must build defenses on the island to block British ships from getting out onto the lake.

On Schuyler's first attempt to storm Fort St. John, some one hundred Indians and Loyalists outflanked the Americans and killed sixteen of them in a skirmish in dense underbrush. Schuyler decided not to pursue the British force. In his tent, where the forty-four-year-old hypochondriac spent most of his days complaining of one malady or another—Schuyler received a visit from a mysterious messenger who convinced him that Fort St. John was too strongly defended for the Americans to capture. Another week passed before Schuyler ordered a night attack. As his five hundred New Yorkers plunged into heavy woods in an attempt to invest St. John from the north, they collided in the dark with part of Montgomery's force. The skittish New Yorkers, who had never been in combat, thought they were being ambushed by Indians, and most of them stampeded back to their boats. Rallying some of them, Montgomery ordered them forward. A few rounds of British artillery fire shook the trees over them, triggering another panic. The British, firing from a small house, repulsed two more assaults by the remaining fifty New Yorkers. Colonel Rudolph Ritzema, their regimental commander, called off the attack at three in the morning and withdrew his men to the beachhead. The next day, as his men panicked again at a rumor that two British ships were approaching with landing craft and were going to open fire any minute, General Montgomery declared his troops "a set of pusillanimous wretches."[9]

Another ten days passed as more reinforcements poured in on both sides. From the Grants came Seth Warner with 170 Green Mountain Boys; from New Hampshire came 100 rangers and the Independent Company of Volunteers, including Dartmouth College students. Finally, despondent and claiming new illnesses, this time a fever and rheumatism, Schuyler resigned his command and turned it over to Montgomery, who immediately ordered all 1,400 effectives—600 men on Ile aux Noix were claiming to be too sick—to advance and begin to dig siege lines around the British fort. It took Montgomery two more weeks to bring two batteries of artillery from Crown Point and Ticonderoga within eight hundred yards of the British works, close enough for a British cannonball to rip through his greatcoat, spin him around, and fling him, unhurt, over the breastworks. For the next month, as Allen and his men sat in chains aboard the *Gaspee*, able to hear more and more often the exchange of cannon fire, Montgomery's siege trenches inched ever closer to the British fort, now held by

725 experienced fighters. His supplies and ammunition dwindling, several infantry attacks repulsed with casualties, Montgomery seemed stalemated—until he hit on a stratagem.

Ten miles farther north, at the rapids of the Richelieu River, stood a small fort at Chambly. Carleton had considered it too unimportant to reinforce. On the night of October 18, two American bateaux armed with nine-pounders slipped past the guns at St. John, and a mixed force of 300 Canadian militia and Major Brown's company of 50 New England militia surrounded Chambly's thin-walled fort. A few nine-pound balls fired from the bateaux persuaded the British garrison—88 men, 30 women, and 51 children—to surrender. At last, Montgomery had the supplies he needed: at Chambly, he garnered three vital cannon, six tons of gunpowder, 6,500 musket cartridges, 125 stands of muskets, and, equally important, 80 barrels of flour, 134 barrels of salt pork, and a large quantity of rice and peas.

Thoroughly alarmed, Carleton attempted to relieve Fort St. John in late October. By now the temperature was dipping below freezing at night. Carleton pulled together a force of nearly 1,000 men, including 150 regulars, 80 Caughnawaga Indians, and drafted French Canadian *habitants*. Just south of Montreal, a large force of Green Mountain Boys and New York Continental artillerymen had set up their guns on both banks of the Sorel River. Intercepting Carleton's force, the Green Mountain troops routed the untrained French Canadians while their artillery raked Carleton's vessels with heavy fire, forcing him to turn back. Two days later, Montgomery completed his last battery of newly captured British guns to fire on Fort St. John at point-blank range, subjecting the British garrison to accurate and constant barrages. The British, hopelessly cut off from reinforcement and down to their last three days' rations, surrendered on November 2. In all, Montgomery had by then taken nearly 900 prisoners.

As the Canadian winter set in, two months after the summer Patriots had drifted leisurely down Lake Champlain into Canada, Montgomery negotiated lenient terms for his prisoners. He had somehow heard of Ethan Allen's unusually harsh treatment. The humane Montgomery tried to inject some civility into the treatment of prisoners and sent Captain John André off to find suitable quarters where the captured officers could live on parole far from the front lines. After visiting Schuyler at his mansion in Albany, André rode on, stopping to visit Loyalists in Philadelphia before riding west to Lancaster, Pennsylvania, where he made the arrangements for his fellow prisoners. The rest of Montgomery's prisoners were allowed to retain their personal possessions, including their winter uniforms, which provoked a short-lived mutiny among shivering New York troops. But Montgomery was determined to carry out no reprisals. Instead, no doubt with the hope of exchanging some of them to free Allen and the prisoners taken at Montreal, he set out to attack Montreal only three days after St. John surrendered. Days of cold rain and nights of snow now turned the road into a knee-deep quagmire that made the twenty-mile march to the St. Lawrence a nine-day ordeal.

Carleton's garrison had been reduced to 130 regulars to hold Montreal by the time the first of Montgomery's Americans paddled across the St. Lawrence on November 11. As Montgomery's men closed in, Carleton and his Redcoats attempted to flee to Quebec, filling seven whaleboats with supplies and crowding onto three armed vessels, including the *Gaspee.* They got only as far as the mouth of the Sorel, where they were enfiladed by the same shore batteries that had ruined Carleton's relief expedition to St. John. Unwilling to run the gauntlet of American fire, Carleton surrendered most of the ships, men, and supplies, including General Prescott. Disguised in the clothes of a French Canadian peasant, the governor-general of Canada slipped through the captured vessels in a rowboat, clambered ashore, and escaped to Quebec. He made sure, however, that Ethan Allen did not escape.

On the day he fled, Carleton gave strict orders that Allen and his men, all except the two wounded prisoners, Allen's brother-in-law Israel Brownson and William Stewart, were to be transferred to the *Adamant* and taken to England. Allen must have seen the American forces approaching as his guards whisked him at bayonet point from vessel to vessel. Aboard the sloop of war, he and his thirty-two comrades were forced into a lightless wooden pen specially constructed to house them deep belowdecks, their only furniture a pair of buckets; once again, they were manacled. Above them, they could hear wealthy New York Loyalists joking at their expense as they escaped with a rich cargo of furs toward exile in England. If he had known it at the time, Allen might have found some small satisfaction that General Prescott, now himself a prisoner, would be fitted with manacles and leg irons on the special orders of the Continental Congress in retaliation for his treatment of Allen.

ON THE DUSTY GRAY Sunday morning of September 3, 1775, the 16,000-man American army besieging Boston formed up for an inspection all along the line of fortifications investing the British. The newly commissioned Continental army colonel Benedict Arnold, riding a big chestnut horse and resplendent in the brilliant red uniform he had himself designed, accompanied Commander in Chief George Washington and his staff as Arnold took his pick of the entire army for an invasion of Canada. "Volunteers step one step in advance." Down the line, nearly one-third of Washington's army, soldiers bored with camp life and his increasingly harsh discipline, stepped forward. By noon, Arnold had five times the volunteers he needed. He and his adjutants asked two questions: "Are you an active woodsman? Are you well acquainted with bateaux?" A liars' contest ensued, all too many men willing to shade the truth to escape the tedium and summer heat. By nightfall, Arnold had his handpicked regiment of 1,080 men.[10]

Sending a courier ahead to Gardiner, Maine, Washington commissioned the shipwright Reuben Colburn to build two hundred lightweight bateaux. From the surveyor Samuel Goodrich, he ordered maps for his battalion commanders. Neither Washington nor Arnold knew that both Colburn and Goodrich were Loyalists. To make the maps, Arnold relied on a travel diary by the Swiss-born captain of engineers John Montresor, who had accompanied the British march down the Kennebec from Quebec Province in 1761, at the end of the French and Indian War. As was the custom of the time, the British officer made two sets of maps, one accurate, the other bogus to throw off any enemy attempting to use it. Arnold had the wrong one.

Arnold's march to Quebec hit snags from the outset. It took two precious weeks to process his orders. In the lead as Arnold's regiment of rangers stepped off were Virginia riflemen led by Daniel Morgan, quickly covering the fifty miles to Newburyport, where eleven fishing boats were waiting to transport them to Maine. Before they sailed, Arnold's officers visited the basement crypt of the First Congregational Church, where the Great Awakener George Whitefield lay buried. There, each officer snipped off a small piece of Whitefield's white collar as a relic and fastened it to his hat brim.

Arnold waited for heavy fog to burn off, then threaded his makeshift fleet at night through the British naval blockade toward Maine. To his horror, he soon learned that a summerlong drought had all but dried up the Kennebec, leaving exposed rocks and shoals. Instead of sailing upriver, his force would have to march along the riverbank, its supplies in overloaded canoes dodging half-submerged rocks. At Colburn's shipyard, Arnold received another shock—a meadow full of neat rows of 220 bateaux, small flatboats that could be rowed or poled—badly built from heavy, wet, green planks that would shrink and crack over their even heavier oak frames. He'd ordered boats twenty-five feet long; many were only eighteen feet. These hastily built, undersized, overweight boats would have to be carried through 350 miles of rough water and portages on a route that would turn out to be 200 miles longer than his map indicated. Three more days evaporated while the boats were caulked and twenty replacements built.

It was September 27—two days after Allen's surrender at Montreal—before Arnold finally shoved off. At every rapid, every portage, it became more apparent how ill suited these boats were. It took four men to carry each empty bateau as it dug hard into their weary shoulders while they slithered uphill over thickly wooded dirt paths and around high waterfalls. At Skowhegan, the soldiers bullied the boats up a three-mile slope while teams of men marched alongside, bent under the weight of barrels and bearskin-wrapped bundles of provisions, covering only half the distance they needed to travel each day. One man wrote that they could have been mistaken "for amphibious animals, as they were a great part of the time underwater." The men slept on the ground in wet uniforms, their clothing "frozen a pane of glass thick." When Arnold ordered the boats ashore, he emptied out the bales and barrels and sorted through waterlogged supplies. The planks had leaked and the barrels filled with water, rinsing and rotting the salted meat and cod, turning flour and peas into a moldy paste. Repairing the boats cost another eight days. By then, the food shortage was so acute that one unit of men stole supplies from another.[11]

At four in the morning on October 18, the day that the British surrendered at Chambly, Arnold's detachment awakened to the roar of a wall of water rushing through the river basin, stirred up by a West Indian hurricane. The river had risen twelve feet overnight, strewing the army's remaining food and gear over twelve miles. By then, supplies were so low that some men were eating their candles. Seven more boatloads of food, guns, gunpowder, and clothing were lost. Leaving "Camp Disaster," Arnold called a council of war to decide whether to go ahead. Almost all of his officers voted to continue, but downriver, in the rear, his second-in-command, Lieutenant Colonel Roger Enos, in charge of the bulk of the remaining supplies, called his own council of war, which voted to turn back to Massachusetts with 350 men, most of the remaining provisions, and all the medical supplies. His desertion stunned Arnold. That night, his men, wrote Captain Henry Dearborn, "made a general prayer" that Enos and his deserters "might die by the way."[12]

Arnold proceeded to order his officers to abandon the remaining bateaux and conserve the men's strength while he went on ahead to find food in the French settlements on the Chaudière River, his starving army's rations now down to half a cup of flour a day, an ounce of pork, and broth made from bark. With two Penobscot Abenaki Indian guides and fifteen of his own men, Arnold paddled on toward Canada. Behind him, men took raw hides intended to make shoes, chopped them up, singed off the hair, boiled them, and wrung the juice into their canteens.

The morning of October 29, the army descended into an ocean of swamp under an enticing layer of moss, stumbling into frigid water and ice. Men tripped into mire holes up to their armpits. Day after day, what was left of Arnold's proud little army struggled, sometimes naked, with their clothes wrapped around their rifles over their heads through the freezing waters of lakes not on their maps. When they finally crossed into Canada, exhausted and famished, following the Chaudière River toward Quebec, they found the last of the bateaux shattered and scattered along the riverbank after plunging over twenty-foot waterfalls. Men drowned or died when they could no longer be carried. Two men gave the rifleman John Henry a cup of greenish broth: "It tasted and smelled like it was a dog." It was, in fact, all that remained of Henry Dearborn's Newfoundland. He helped devour even the feet and skin.[13]

On November 3, the day after Fort St. John surrendered, Arnold sent back lifesaving livestock and supplies—along with specific orders. Anyone who had any provisions left was to let the livestock pass to the rear, where the weakest lagged behind. Soon, two birchbark canoes appeared, laden with cornmeal, mutton for the sick, even tobacco that he had purchased from the French Canadian *habitants*. After lunch, the restored army marched another twenty miles, in all covering thirty miles in a single day. For two days, Arnold paddled up and down the river, making sure all his men got fed.

At 10:30 p.m. on November 3, Arnold's army, down to 675 from the 1,080 men who had swung out of Cambridge fifty-one days earlier—40 percent of the army lost by death and desertion—and reeling like drunkards, staggered into the first French settlement, their bare feet leaving bloodstains on the snowy riverbank. But Arnold was too late to take the prize, Quebec, now heavily reinforced by land-hungry Scottish Highlanders rushed in from Newfoundland by Loyalist officers as well as by the tenant farmers of the land barons of New York. On November 11, as Arnold and his men tried desperately to commandeer enough Indian dugouts to attack the walled citadel, the *Adamant*, with Ethan Allen chained belowdecks, glided by, under full sail, just yards away from Arnold and his exhausted army. Arnold probably was unaware that, in their specially designed cage belowdecks, Allen and his thirty-two lice-covered fellow prisoners sat chained and shackled, shivering and starving, bound for England. And Allen may never have known how close his old rival Arnold had come to being able to rescue him.

NEWS OF ETHAN ALLEN'S capture and the conditions of his captivity spread rapidly. His fortitude was omitted while his rashness was noted. Philip Schuyler was able only to foresee grave damage as a result of Allen's lack of subordination. "I am very apprehensive of disagreeable consequences rising from Mr. Allen's imprudence," he wrote to the Continental Congress. With even less compassion, the Reverend Benjamin Trumbull, Puritan chaplain to the Connecticut troops besieging St. John, wrote that "this rash and ill-concerted measure of Colonel Allen" had badly damaged the American mission in Canada, "disheartening the army and weakening it and, in prejudicing the people against us, making us enemies and losing us friends." One English Canadian who had fought against Allen at Montreal thought the attack "has changed the face of things. . . . The Canadians before were nine-tenths for the Bostonians. They are now returned to their duty."[14]

Other revolutionary leaders were more sympathetic, however. When word of the harsh treatment of Allen and his fellow prisoners reached the Continental Congress in Philadelphia, the Virginia delegate Thomas Jefferson drafted a "Declaration on the British Treatment of Ethan Allen," aimed at the British and dated January 2, 1776:

> It is with pain we hear that Mr. Allen and others taken with him while fighting bravely in their country's cause, are sent to Britain in *irons*, to be *punished* for pretended treasons. . . . This question will not be decided by reeking ven-

geance on a few helpless captives, but by atchieving success in the fields of war. . . . To those who, bearing your arms, have fallen into our hands, we have afforded every comfort for which captivity and misfortune called. . . . Should you think proper in these days to revive antient barbarism, and disgrace our nature with the practice of human sacrifice, the fortune of war has put into our power subjects for multiple retaliation. . . . We have ordered Brigadier General Prescot to be bound in irons, and confined in close jail, there to experience corresponding miseries with those which shall be inflicted on Mr. Allen. His life shall answer for that of Allen, and the lives of as many others as for those of the brave men captivated with him.

Jefferson had last seen Allen standing before Congress a little more than six months earlier pleading for troops to invade Canada. A legal scholar, Jefferson here was echoing Washington's warning to Gage that the Americans would invoke the Roman doctrine of *lex talionis*—retaliation. Congress, in contrast to Schuyler and his circle, vowed to "shed blood for blood," Jefferson wrote, as "the means of stopping the progress of butchery."[15]

While Congress mulled a stronger protest to the British government over Allen's treatment, it decided for now to leave matters to General Washington, who continued his round of correspondence with Gage. Both commanders understood that, under the rules of war of the eighteenth century, the treatment of a prisoner was at the discretion of the commanding officer where he was captured. A key legal question was whether the rules of war extended to Allen's kind of guerrilla warfare, even though as a rebellious inhabitant of a colonial possession he was subject to the treatment accorded a common criminal. Allen was in effect the personal prisoner of Canada's governor-general, Sir Guy Carleton, who was determined to treat Allen and his comrades as common criminals, not prisoners of war.

Further compounding Allen's case was diplomacy. Having an army that took British soldiers prisoner did not mean British commanders could deal with the Americans as a belligerent military power. General Sir William Howe, the erratic and indecisive juggler of the olive branch and the saber who succeeded Gage in dealing with Washington, insisted that his prisoners were criminals under municipal law and, as such, were to be jailed, officers and enlisted men locked up together, as civil prisoners, regardless of rank, as civilians would be, in a common jail. Because American officers were considered criminals, they could expect no special privileges.

For British military commanders to treat American prisoners as prisoners of war would be tantamount to granting at least partial de facto diplomatic recognition, thus according the American government the status of a belligerent power. Congress and Washington recognized that their best, if not only, weapon to force the English to grant diplomatic and political recognition was British prisoners. To protect American prisoners in British custody, the American government, acting through General Washington, threatened retaliation against English soldiers in the revolutionaries' hands. Washington, backed by Congress, was making it clear that he would counter with force the British policy of treating the Revolutionary War as a domestic revolt. Under duress, Gage conceded some rights to American prisoners.

But Gage's successor, Howe, insisted, as had Gage at first, that officers had "no rank not derived from the King." Howe denied Allen's rank as an officer because his commission had come not from the king but from the rebel Congress. Howe believed that diplomatic disaster would follow for England if he acted or made any written declaration that could be construed as recognizing the independence of the rebelling Americans. Therefore, Howe refused to have any dealings with any American civil authority such as the Continental or state congresses that might be taken as tantamount to recognition of any American civil authority. Because he was forced to concede that there was a de facto military power that could take and hold prisoners, Howe would deal only with General Washington, and he and his regional commanders would communicate only through military channels.[16]

An alarmed Washington wrote to Schuyler on December 18, "I should have been very glad if Carleton had not made his escape," adding that he was "much concerned for Mr. Allen that he should be treated with such severity":

I beg that you will have the Matter and Manner of his treatment strictly inquired into, and transmit to me an Account of the same, and whether General Prescott was active and instrumental in occasioning it. From your letter and General Montgomery's to you, I am led to think he was: If so, he is deserving of our particular Notice & should experience some Marks of our Resentment for his Cruelty to this gentleman & his violation of the Rights of Humanity.[17]

That same day, Washington wrote to Howe:

Sir: We have just been informed of a Circumstance, which were it not so well Authenticated, I should scarcely think credible; It is that Col. Allan who with his small party was defeated & taken prisoner near Montreal, has been treated

without regard to decency, humanity, or the rules of War—
That he has been thrown into Irons & Suffers all the hardships inflicted upon common felons.

    I think it is my duty Sir to demand & do expect from
you, an *ecclaircisment* on this Subject. . . .[18]

SAILING ALL OBLIVIOUS through this military and diplomatic
tangle, Ethan Allen, shunted from ship to ship on his way to
almost certain execution in England, had been placed under the
authority of an English fur merchant, Brook Watson, a personal
friend of Sir Guy Carleton who would one day become the lord
mayor of London. Allen recognized Watson by sight as soon as
he boarded the *Adamant*: the wealthy merchant brought a party
of thirty of his New York Loyalist friends aboard the *Gaspee*
for a good laugh at his expense. Only a few months earlier, the
one-eyed Watson had visited Allen's office at Crown Point. The
Continental Congress had given Watson and two young *noblesse*
safe-conduct passes through the American lines with a large
cargo of furs bound for England and directed Allen to provide
transport down Lake Champlain to the border. Allen assigned
his brother Ira with a squad of men to escort Watson. Lieutenant Allen was "convinced in his own mind," he later wrote, "that
Mr. Watson (although he professed to be) was no friend to the
American Cause." Apprehending danger from Indians near the
Canadian line, Lieutenant Allen ordered his men "to new prime
their guns and be ready for the defense, at which Mr. Watson and
the two Frenchmen objected and attempted to seize their pistols."
After a brief struggle, young Allen put into the nearest shore and
deposited Watson, his assistants, and their precious cargo "in a
swamp three miles from any house." While Ira was still proud
of his youthful conduct three decades later when he penned his

memoirs, he had inadvertently contributed to his brother's ordeal at the hands of the vengeful Loyalist Watson.[19]

Coming aboard *Adamant* with Watson were the two leaders of the Iroquois Six Nations Confederacy, Colonel Guy Johnson, Britain's superintendant of Indian Affairs, and Chief Joseph Brant, both sailing to England to coordinate Indian military strategy with the British. Brook Watson, Allen remembered, proved "a man of malicious and cruel disposition" to his prisoners:

> A small place in the vessel, enclosed with white-oak plank, was assigned for the prisoners, and for me among the rest; I should imagine it was no more than twenty feet one way, and twenty-two the other. Into this place we were all, to the number of thirty-four, thrust . . . and provided with two excrement tubs; in this circumference we were obliged to eat and perform the office of evacuation, during the voyage to England; and were insulted by every blackguard sailor and tory on board, in the cruelest manner; but what is the most surprising is, that not one of us died in the passage. When I was first ordered to go into the filthy inclosure, through a small sort of door, I positively refused, and endeavoured to reason [with] Brook Watson . . . but all to no purpose, my men being forced in the den already. . . . [Watson] commanded me to go immediately in among the rest; he further added, that the place was good enough for a rebel, that it was impertinent for a capital offender to talk of honour or humanity; that any thing short of a halter was too good for me, and that that would be my portion soon after I landed in England. . . . About the same time a lieutenant among the tories, insulted me in a grievous manner . . . and spit in my face. . . . I sprang at him with both hands, and knocked him partly down. . . . [H]e got

under the protection of some men with fixed bayonets. . . .
Watson ordered his guard to get me into the place with the
other prisoners, dead or alive. . . . [W]e were denied fresh
water, except for a small allowance. . . . [I]n consequence
of the stench of the place, each of us was soon followed
with a diarrhoea and fever, which occasioned an intolerable thirst. . . . [I]t was so dark that we could not see each
other, and were overspread with body lice.[20]

Among the Loyalists on board was Colonel Johnson, son of
the former royal Indian commissioner, the late Sir William Johnson, and a member of the New York Assembly who had voted
for the Bloody Acts. He had called an Iroquois Confederation
conference at Oswego in July and won over four of the six tribes
to fight on the British side, ignoring Schuyler's blandishment.
Johnson had personally led the Caughnawaga Mohawks who
reinforced Carleton at Fort St. John and Montreal.
     Allen was developing a particular loathing for fellow Ameri-
cans who were taking the British side in the revolutionary struggle and transforming a war for independence into a bitter civil
war. The Loyalists aboard *Adamant*

behaved towards the prisoners with that spirit of bitterness, which is the peculiar characteristic of tories, when
they have the friends of America in their power, measuring
their loyalty to the English king, by the barbarity, fraud,
and deceit which they exercise towards the [prisoners].[21]

A British soldier taken prisoner by the American army a few
months later who saw Allen often at this time swore an affidavit
attesting to Allen's account, adding that Allen was emaciated and
jaundiced after a month's confinement in the ship's hold. Allot-

ted salted meat and a gill of rum (two ounces) a day, he "existed in this manner" for forty-five days of a lurching, rolling, heaving winter crossing of the North Atlantic until "the land's end of England was discovered from the mast head; soon after which the prisoners were taken from their gloomy abode, being permitted to see the light of the sun, and breathe fresh air, which to us was very refreshing."[22]

The next day, Allen clambered off the ship at Falmouth, wearing the same outfit of clothing he had been wearing for two months since he had donned it to cross the St. Lawrence:

> I happened to be taken in a Canadian dress, viz. a short fawn skin jacket, double-breasted, an under vest and breeches of sagathy, worsted stockings, a decent pair of shoes, two plain shirts and a red worsted cap; this was all the clothing I had, in which I made my appearance in England.

He was stunned to see crowds thronging the road climbing up from the waterfront to the massive, lowering sixteenth-century dungeon, high above the harbor, built by Henry VIII, an expert in such edifices who had sent three of his six wives to the axman's block. There Allen was to be confined until he was shipped to London for trial:

> Multitudes of the citizens of Falmouth, excited by curiosity, crowded together to see us, which was equally gratifying to us. I saw numbers of people on the tops of houses. . . . [T]he throng was so great, that the king's officers were obliged to draw their swords, and force a passage to Pendennis castle, . . . where we were closely confined, in consequence of orders from Gen. Carleton.

It had been more than six months since this American frontiersman had taken Ticonderoga, long enough for the news to spread all over England. In a day when there were sixteen newspapers spreading every scrap of intelligence gleaned from the leaked dispatches of the king's officers in America, Allen's fame had spread to the westernmost tip of England. In Cornwall, smuggling and defying the English government were ancient and honored customs, especially among the common people. Ethan Allen's outlaw image made him a folk hero in England.[23]

As ALLEN AND his manacled fellow American prisoners shuffled onto English soil a few days before Christmas 1775, "the rascally" Loyalist Brook Watson set out for London "in great haste," only to find he brought the British ministry less than welcome Yule tidings. Parliament was embroiled in a debate over the status of Allen and other American prisoners. Opposition to the American war was mounting steadily as news arrived with every dispatch ship of more British reverses. The Quebec Act was especially unpopular in England because it had established Roman Catholicism as an official religion in Canada at a time when it was still illegal in England. The ministry was finding it all but impossible to recruit British troops and was even considering hiring Russian mercenaries to fight their Americans. Trade with Americans, which normally accounted for nearly one-third of English commerce, was moribund, and thousands had been thrown out of work. British taxpayers were already groaning under the mountain of taxes left from the Seven Years' War. With Lake Champlain's fortresses lost, Boston besieged, Canada certain to fall, and two thousand prisoners already in American hands, pro-American members of Parliament were threatening to demand writs of habeas corpus for Allen and his fellow prisoners.

While the ministry mulled his fate, Allen and his compatriots were led up to the castle and confined together in "one common apartment" lined with bunks. Allen immediately requested pen and ink from the commander of the castle for the privilege of writing a letter ostensibly directed to "the illustrious Continental Congress." In his captivity memoir, Allen later reported, "This letter was wrote with a view that it should be sent to the ministry at London, rather than to Congress, with a design to intimidate the haughty English government and screen my neck from the halter."[24]

The letter had its desired effect: it was intercepted and forwarded to London to the American secretary, Lord George Germain, an anti-American nobleman in charge of prosecuting the war. "The prisoners from Quebec," Germain wrote as he forwarded a copy of Allen's letter to John Montagu, Earl of Sandwich, the first lord of the Admiralty, on December 27, "will occasion many difficulties. I wish the general had not sent us such a present."[25]

Whether to try Ethan Allen as a rebel and a traitor was a question made the more urgent by his proximity to Parliament. Allen later wrote that the minority in Parliament was arguing that the opposition of America to Great Britain was not a rebellion:

> "If it is," say they, "why do you not execute Col. Allen, according to law?" . . . But the majority argued, that I ought to be executed, and that opposition was really a rebellion, but that policy obliged them not to do it, inasmuch as the Congress had then most prisoners in their power. . . . [N]ecessity [was] restraining them [and] was rather a foil on their laws and authority, and they consequently disapproved of my being sent [to England]. . . .[26]

· · ·

On December 23, 1775, Thomas Pownall, secretary of the Board of Trade and Plantations, summoned the cabinet for a secret meeting at the London town house of Henry Howard, twelfth Earl of Suffolk and secretary of state for the Northern Department, which included the rebellious colonies, as well as the attorney general, Lord Edward Thurlow, the solicitor general, Alexander Wedderburn, and William Eden, undersecretary of state and head of the British secret service. The meeting was off the record but can be reconstructed from private letters. Wedderburn, a particular foe of American resistance, had presided two years earlier over the humiliating cashiering of Benjamin Franklin as deputy postmaster general in the wake of the Boston Tea Party. Pownall also summoned Lord Sandwich, whose aggressive searches and seizures of American ships had helped provoke the American Revolution.

That the assembled ministers had cause for alarm about American determination to retaliate on British prisoners stemmed from a report Howe had sent to Lord Dartmouth only the week before. According to a spy inside the Continental Congress, that body had resolved, as its response to the king's Proclamation of Rebellion, that retaliation would be its policy for any punishments inflicted by the British. Howe had also informed Lord Dartmouth that Washington was proposing an exchange of prisoners, but that he had refused until he received instructions from London. None of the assembled cabinet ministers doubted the legality of trying and executing Allen and other American prisoners as traitors. Lord Suffolk sharply attacked the leader of the pro-American faction in the House of Lords:

> The Duke of Richmond . . . says we brought over Ethan
> Allen in irons to this country, but were afraid to try him,
> lest he be acquitted by an English jury, or that we should

not be able legally to convict him. I do assure his grace that he is equally mistaken in both his conjectures; we neither had a doubt but we should be able legally to convict him, nor were we afraid that an English jury would have acquitted him, nor, further, was it *out of any tenderness to the man*, who, I maintain, had justly forfeited his life to the offended laws of this country.

But I will tell his grace the true motives which induced the administration to act as they did. We were aware that the rebels had lately made a considerable number of prisoners, and we accordingly avoided bringing him to his trial from considerations of *prudence*; from a dread of the consequences of retaliation; not from a doubt of his legal guilt, or a fear of his acquittal by an English jury.[27]

Ever a close observer of the current political scene, the man of letters Horace Walpole attributed the need for a secret Christmas recess gathering of the ministry to reconsider long-held British policy and accord the rebels the status of prisoners of war to the mood in Parliament and to the common people, a growing majority of whom now opposed continued fighting:

Bad news poured in from America. . . . The ministers were aground: they first thought of sending Hessians, Hanoverians, and even a large body of Russians—but found it would be too expensive or too unpopular. They were offered 3,000 Highlanders, but did not dare accept them. At last they thought of recalling Gage and the troops, and it was said to be carried in [the Privy] council but by one voice that they should not. At last, after several consultations, the Ministers determined to prosecute the war. . . .[28]

Ethan Allen's arrival in England had provoked a debate at the highest levels over British prosecution of the Revolutionary War.

Solicitor Alexander Wedderburn took on himself the assignment of offering the other ministers a solution. He had already met with Thurlow, the attorney general, he wrote to Eden:

> I am persuaded some unlucky incident must arrive if Allen and his people are kept here. It must be understood that Government does not mean to execute them, the prosecution will be remiss and the disposition of some people to thwart it, very active. I would therefore send them back, but I think something more might be done than merely to return them as prisoners to America.

According to a briefing by the secret service agent in Montreal who had escorted Allen and the other prisoners, Allen "took up arms because he was dispossessed of lands he had settled between Hampshire and New York in consequence of an Order in Council settling the boundary of these two provinces, and had balanced for some time to have recourse to ye rebels or to Mr. Carleton." The agent informed Wedderburn that Allen "is a bold, active fellow":

> I would then send to him a person of confidence with this proposal: that his case had been favorably represented to Government that the injury he had suffered was some alleviation for his crime, and that it arose from an abuse of an Order in Council which was never meant to dispossess the settlers in the lands in debate between the two provinces. If he has a mind to return to his duty, he may not only have his pardon from General Howe but a company of rangers and in the event if he behaves well, his lands returned on

these terms. He and his men shall be sent back to Boston at liberty. If he does not accept them, he and they may be disposed of as the law directs. If he shall behave well, it is an acquisition. If not, there is still an advantage in finding a decent reason for not immediately proceeding against him as a rebel.[29]

FOR THE MOMENT, Allen was to be held at Pendennis Castle. His treatment at Falmouth briefly improved. The ancient castle's youthful commandant sent him "every day a fine breakfast and dinner from his own table and a bottle of good wine." An aged officer sent him "a good supper." Allen continued to sleep in a bunk in a small, cramped apartment with the privates. There were to be no distinctions of rank. He and his men "were allowed straw" to pad their bunks. The privates also were well fed and, with Allen, "took effectual means to rid [them]selves of lice." On the surface at least, Allen seemed to be enjoying the respite at Pendennis Castle, a dank gray eminence built to ward off French invasions. As he put it, crowds came daily when he was allowed to take an hour's stroll under guard in the castle yard "out of curiosity to see" him before he could be hanged. He seemed not to realize that his reputation as a hero of the common man, if not the oppressed, had spread across the Atlantic and that he had become a romantic figure, a sort of a Robin Hood to an unpopular, high-taxing, and heavy-handed British government. "Gentle and simple" folk came to whisper to him, sometimes leaving presents. Someone he identified as a Temple, possibly John Temple, a former British customs official in Boston, "whispered in [his] ear" that bets were being laid in London that he "would be executed" and gave Allen a gold-guinea coin before hurrying away.

In the shadow of the gallows, Allen's spirits seemed to rise

when well-wishers came from fifty miles away to ask him questions. He attributed their interest to the taking of Ticonderoga, a
famous fortress, which so many English had died trying to conquer only a few years earlier. Released a little each day from the
small cell to the spacious green parade ground, he found "numbers of gentlemen and ladies were ready to see and hear [him]."
He decided to entertain them.

> One of them asked me what my occupation in life had
> been? I answered him, that in my younger days I had stud-
> ied divinity, but was a conjurer by passion . . . that I had
> conjured them out of Ticonderoga. . . . [T]he joke seemed
> to go in my favour. At one of these times, I asked a gentle-
> men for a bowl of punch, and he ordered his servant to
> bring it, which he did, and offered it me, but I refused
> to take it from the hand of his servant; he then gave it
> to me with his own hand, refusing to drink with me in
> consequence of my being a state criminal. . . . I took the
> punch and drank it all down at one draught, and handed
> the gentleman the bowl: This made the spectators as well
> as myself merry.[30]

Yet beneath the surface bonhomie, he later admitted, in his
stoical, after-the-fact rendition, that he could not tell whether he
would be spared or condemned by English politics. His ruminations on these questions provide the first examples of Allen the
philosopher, someone who invoked reason in thinking about life
and death. Like the Enlightenment philosophers whose work
revolutionized scholarship in the eighteenth century—and whose
writings he read avidly—Allen believed wholeheartedly in reason's power, and so, as a prisoner of war, he summoned reason
rather than religion to help him withstand his suffering. His

months of physical agony and psychological anguish were giving rise to a natural religion:

> I could not but feel inwardly extreme anxious for my fate, this I however carefully concealed from the prisoners, as well as from the enemy, who were perpetually shaking the halter at me. I nevertheless treated them with scorn and contempt; and having sent my letter to the ministry, could conceive of nothing more in my power but to keep up my spirits. . . .
>
> Such a conduct I judged would have a more probable tendency to my preservation than concession and timidity. This, therefore, was my deportment, and I had lastly determined in my own mind, that if a cruel death must inevitably be my portion, I would face it undaunted. . . . I reasoned thus, that nothing was more common than for men to die, with their friends round them, weeping and lamenting over them. . . . [A]s death was the natural consequence of animal life to which the laws of nature subject mankind, to be timorous and uneasy as to the event or manner of it, was inconsistent with the character of a philosopher or a soldier.[31]

BY EARLY JANUARY OF 1776, Lord Germain and the other cabinet ministers at Whitehall Palace had reluctantly concluded that Ethan Allen was so popular that no English jury would convict him, let alone condemn him to death. Germain later wrote to Lord Mansfield that Allen's actions "had the tacit approbation of the kingdom." The British ministry, especially Lord Germain, wanted him far away from the crowds maddening them more by the day. Germain's expedient solution was to send Allen and his fellow prisoners back to America for General Howe to hold until they could be exchanged on a case-by-case basis for prisoners of equal rank held by the Americans. Germain wrote to Howe to use Allen and the other prisoners "to procure the release of such of his Majesty's officers and loyal subjects [as] are in the disgraceful situation of being prisoners to the rebels."[32]

On January 8, barely two weeks after Allen had landed in England, his irons and those of his men were taken off—the result of a writ of habeas corpus filed in his behalf in London by English MPs opposed to the war. Before the actual writ could be served on prison officials at Pendennis Castle, Germain rushed orders to Falmouth to have Allen and his thirty-four cellmates hustled aboard the HMS *Solebay*, a frigate bound for Cork, Ireland. The privates were to be chained up and Allen was to be confined in the hold of yet another ship that was joining a great invasion fleet assembling to sail to the Carolinas. Unable to reinforce iced-over northern ports such as Boston and Quebec, the ministry had decided to besiege Charleston, where it expected support from large numbers of loyal Scottish Highlanders in the Carolina backcountry. Some forty warships had assembled at the Cove of Cork by the time the *Solebay* dropped anchor early in February.

When Allen was first taken aboard the frigate, its captain, assembling all the prisoners "in a sovereign manner ordered the prisoners, [Allen] in particular, off the deck, and never to come on it again; for said he, this is a place for gentlemen to walk." Allen was escorted down to the wet, dark cable tier, where he was shown his allotted corner amid hoops of rope and harnesses. He was already ill:

> I had taken cold, by which I was in an ill state of health. . . .
> I felt myself more desponding than I had done at any time
> before; for I concluded it to be a governmental scheme, to

do that clandestinely, which policy forbid to be done under
sanction of public justice and law.

Two days later, after he was able to shave and clean himself
as best he could, Allen decided to test the authority of the ship's
captain by going for a stroll on the deck. The captain railed at
Allen "in a great rage" and demanded, "Did I not order you not
to come on deck?" Allen reminded him that he had said it was "a
place for gentlemen to walk" and that he was Colonel Allen "but
had not been properly introduced to him." The captain replied,
"G——d damn you, Sir, be careful not to walk the same side of
the deck that I do."

Resistance always gave Ethan Allen renewed courage.[33]

WHEN NEWS SPREAD in Cork that Allen was on board the
Solebay, "a number of benevolently disposed" Irishmen who
sympathized with the American Revolution collected a fund
and "made a large gratutity of wines of the best sort, old spirits,
Geneva [gin], loaf and brown sugar, coffee, tea and chocolate,
with a large round of [corned] beef, and a number of fat turkeys."
Each of the thirty-three privates received "a suit of clothes from
head to foot, including an overcoat or surtout, with two shirts."

> . . . My suit I received in super-fine broadcloth, sufficient
> for two jackets, and two pair of breeches [and a] suit, eight
> fine Holland shirts and stocks ready made with a number of
> pairs of silk and worsted hose, two pair of shoes, two beaver
> hats, one of which was sent me richly laced with gold.

Loading a boat, two merchants sailed out to the *Solebay* while
the captain was ashore. A young lieutenant, the son of an admi-

ral, allowed them to bring aboard and unload their gifts, slipping Allen a small poignard, a dagger. Another "gentleman of Cork" sent him fifty gold guineas. Allen wrote that he decided to return all but seven guineas. He later used the money to buy medicine and pay the ship's doctor. Deeply moved by the Irish merchants' generosity, Allen dashed off a note of thanks: "Gentlemen: I received your generous present this day with a joyful heart. Thanks to God there are still the feelings of humanity in the worthy citizens of Cork towards those of their bone and flesh, who, through misfortune from the present broils in the empire are needy prisoners."[34]

His joy was to be short-lived. When Captain Symonds returned, he confiscated all the wine, liquor, and meats and, while consuming some of the wine himself, "swore by all that is good that the damned American rebels should not be feasted by the damned rebels of Ireland." Allen managed to conceal his new clothes, his gold pieces—and the dagger. Later, the captain relented somewhat and allowed the ship's tailor to make up the cloth he had been given into a suit of clothes. "I could then walk the deck, " Allen remembered, "with a seeming better grace."[35]

ALLEN SAILED FROM the Cove of Cork on February 12 aboard the *Solebay*, one of five men-of-war accompanied by forty troop and supply transports. Just before they sailed, his men were split up, divided among three men-of-war. Sailing south, the fleet ran into "a mighty storm," "which lasted near 24 hours without intermission." One of the men-of-war sprang a leak and had to turn back. He was shaken by his first experience of a storm at sea. "After the storm abated, I could plainly discern that the prisoners were better used for some considerable time."[36]

While Allen languished off the coast of Ireland, General

Washington, desperate for artillery to bombard the British and ward off any further counterattacks, dispatched a twenty-five-year-old bookseller named Henry Knox, his first artillery commander, to bring the cannon Allen had so daringly seized at Ticonderoga and Crown Point to the heights overlooking Boston. In the snows of a severe New England winter, Colonel Knox sorted through the weapons that Congress had ordered taken to the northern end of Lake George. He selected fifty-five guns weighing about sixty tons, including fifty-two field pieces, two short-barreled howitzers with a thousand-yard range, and fourteen mortars with a range of up to thirteen hundred yards. Hauling the guns and hundreds of heavy barrels of lead and flints onto bateaux, Knox and three hundred soldiers and civilians shoved out onto the lake. He then collected 160 oxen, several teams of horses, forty heavy-duty sleds, and a herd of cattle. Fifty miles farther south, they crossed the frozen Hudson River, the sleds spaced two hundred yards apart. Traveling over frozen ground and through deep snow, they crossed the Berkshires in mid-January, the teamsters using block and tackle to keep from losing a single gun as the unwieldy sleds slid down the steep slopes. When they reached Springfield, Massachusetts, on January 20, Knox rode ahead to Cambridge to supervise construction of gun carriages.

On the night of March 4, a work detail of 1,200 men and a covering force of 800 marksmen moved onto Dorchester Heights overlooking Boston and its harbor with a train of 360 oxcarts filled with the materials to make heavy fortifications. Firing artillery to drown out the noise of picks and shovels and axes, the work parties had by daylight built two forts and crammed them with the guns of Ticonderoga. British cannon could not elevate sufficiently to hit the new works. Unless the works could be eliminated, the British navy would have to withdraw from cannon range. Howe realized that his occupation of Boston was now untenable. Negotiating with Washington, he agreed not to put the town to the torch if Washington would allow him to withdraw unmolested. The British blew up Castle William in the harbor and evacuated 11,000 British army and navy personnel and 1,100 Loyalists, sailing on March 27 to Halifax at the end of an eight-year British occupation of the city. As they prepared to leave, heavy looting took place. Howe authorized the Loyalist Crean Brush, the man who had written the Bloody Acts of 1774 for the New York Provincial Assembly declaring Ethan Allen and seven Green Mountain leaders outlaws, to strip Boston of any clothing or other supplies that might benefit the Americans. But Brush's loot-laden brigantine *Elizabeth* was recaptured, and he fled to Halifax in a flotilla of fishing vessels crowded with Loyalists, their families, and whatever they could carry.

SAILING BY WAY of Madeira and Bermuda, the British fleet, ravaged by smallpox, two-thirds of its cargo of soldiers too sick to fight, arrived off Cape Fear, North Carolina, on May 3, 1776. Allen and all of his men except for two were reunited. One of the French Canadians had died during the passage from Ireland. Peter Noble, a Connecticut Yankee, would escape from the HMS *Sphynx* during the transfer to the frigate *Mercury*. As Allen put it, Noble "by extraordinary swimming got safe home to New England, and gave intelligence of the usage of his brother prisoners" to the Connecticut Assembly. The *Mercury* set sail on May 20, dropping anchor off Sandy Hook in the first week of June. Two New Yorkers whom Allen knew all too well came aboard to learn of English plans for the 1776 campaign: Governor William Tryon and Attorney General John Tabor Kempe.[37] A great British armada and the largest expeditionary force in English history had just sailed from England to invade New York that summer. Montgomery had been killed and Arnold seriously wounded in a failed attack on Quebec City on the last night of 1775. Despite the loss of Boston and a bungled attack on Charleston, South Carolina, that spring, Parliament now supported all-out war to extinguish the American Revolution, encouraged by Carleton's unexpected victory in Canada. Governor Tryon and Kempe were learning of their important new charge: to raise Loyalist legions to augment British invasion forces.

Remaining on the windward side of the deck, they ignored Allen, who stayed on the leeward side, designated for prisoners and subalterns. After their visit, Allen later wrote, his treatment once again deteriorated, his rations cut by two-thirds by a cruel "underwitted" captain as the *Mercury* sailed to Halifax. Leaving New York harbor on May 20, he did not arrive in Halifax until mid-June. By then, Ethan had been prisoner of war nine months, for all but two weeks confined in ships. His captors now put him in the Halifax jail with thirty-three other men, four of them American officers who, like him, were entitled to parole. He was to spend the next ten weeks in jail, growing "weak and feeble" and suffering from scurvy.[38]

In the months after Allen's departure from England, Lord North, the equivalent of prime minister, was becoming alarmed about the safety of so many British officers in American hands. In a series of lightning attacks, Washington would capture one thousand British and Hessian prisoners at outposts in Trenton and Princeton, New Jersey. Americans already held, among others, members of Parliament taken in the opening year of the Revolution. By this time, a pattern of expedient treatment was emerging on both sides. Parliament passed the North Act in March of 1776. Rather than risk American retaliation, it granted belligerent rights to Americans as prisoners without formally admitting the legitimacy of their revolutionary government. This grudging political concession was a vital victory for the Americans. It would be turned eventually into an effective tool in seeking de facto recognition of the Continental Congress as a legal entity after the signing of the Declaration of Independence in Philadelphia only two weeks after Allen arrived at the gates of Halifax's city jail.

But the exchange of prisoners became excruciatingly slow. The British declared each one to be exceptional, limited, and without prejudice to any other prisoner, each prisoner's exchange being only a temporary expedient taken by the military commander in whose jurisdiction the American rebel had been captured. When Washington complained to the British commander Howe about Allen's brutal treatment, Howe responded that Allen was not under his jurisdiction. Wherever Allen and his men were incarcerated at any given moment, only Sir Guy Carleton had control over Allen's eventual fate. And now Allen was in Nova Scotia, in Canada, where Carleton was still in command.

Even then, military commanders such as Carleton were supposedly making only informal, almost personal, arrangements for the exchange of each individual prisoner, implying no formal recognition or even formal negotiation between nations. Each exchange was a gentleman's agreement, relying on the personal integrity of each commander. This elaborate process condemned Allen to an indefinite imprisonment as he became the conspicuous knight-errant in an international game of military, political, and diplomatic chess.

TAKEN OFF THE *Mercury* in a harbor teeming with troopships and men-of-war about to set sail for the invasion of New York City, the sick men from Allen's company were sent to a military hospital. The Canadians still fit for duty were put to work in the citadel—and all of them escaped. Of Allen's original thirty-three fellow captives, only thirteen were still prisoners. As more of them escaped, Allen decided that escape would vitiate his claim to be an officer entitled to be exchanged. Allen was transferred to a prison sloop for six weeks and then, for the next ten weeks, locked up in the Halifax city jail in one large cell with only excrement tubs for furniture. For the first time since his capture, Allen had nearly enough to eat. Two of his old neighbors from Salisbury, now Loyalist refugees in Halifax, brought him "a good dinner of fresh meats every day, with garden fruit, and sometimes with a bottle of wine." With uncharacteristic understatement, Allen remembered the summer and fall of 1776 as a "time of consider-able distress." Despite his demands for "gentleman-like usage," he was ignored. He fell ill with jail fever—typhus—and lost his appetite. He "grew weaker and weaker, as did the rest." Also afflicted with a mild case of scurvy, he received some succor from a British doctor's mate who smuggled in some "smart drops" that arrested the disease. He was also losing weight: "the malignant hand of Britain had greatly reduced my constitution with stroke upon stroke." He had plenty of time to think about his transfor-mation from the hero of Ticonderoga to the depressed prisoner.[39]

On August 12, Allen managed to write to the Connecticut Assembly:

Halifax Jail

Honourable Gentlemen:

> ... *I greatly rejoice to hear that the States of America have declared for independency.* ... *I assure you that the English rascally treatment to me has wholly erased my former feelings of parent State, mother country, and, in fine, all kindred and*

friendly connexion to them. I have never asked better treatment
than what the laws of arms give to prisoners between foreign
nations; but instead of that, have been crowded into the most
filthy apartments of ships, among privates, where I have, almost
the whole of my time since taken, been covered with lice. . . . I
have been confined in the common jail of Halifax. . . . The pris-
oners have the liberty of the yard. . . .

For the first time, Allen was able to send back to Hartford
the names of the men captured with him. They included thirteen Canadians. One had died, the others were performing forced
labor "in the King's yard." Allen added, "I will lay my life on it,
were you to treat them as they have me, they would willingly have
exchanged us before. Now, we are destitute of cash, friends, &c.,
everything desirable."[40]

In October of 1776, Allen was transferred to a prison sloop
sailing to New York City, which had fallen to the British in
August. The North Act may explain a sudden amelioration of his
treatment during this voyage. The ship's captain, he later noted,
"met me with his hand, welcomed me to his ship, invited me to
dine with him that day, and assured me that I should be treated
as a gentleman, and that he had been given orders, that I should
be treated with respect by the ship's crew." The "unexpected and
sudden" transition "drew tears to my eyes." En route to New York,
another prisoner, the captain of a privateer, suggested that Allen
join in a plot to murder the British captain and crew and take
the £35,000 payroll on board to a friendly port. Allen refused.
He said he would defend the British officer with his life because
he and his fellow prisoners "had been too well used on board to
murder the officers." By this time, Allen's "constitution was worn
out by such a long and barbarous captivity."[41]

After more than a year of confinement at sea and ten months

since leaving Cork, Ethan Allen was back in the newly declared United States, a prisoner of war with no immediate prospect of freedom. In late October, he was transferred again, this time to the troop transport *Glasgow*. On November 2, a kindly British officer provided him with pen and ink to write a brief note to George Washington:

> *Sir*
>
> *Having procured the favour of Writing a few lines to your Excellency I chearfully embrace the opportunity and entertain fond hopes shortly to pay my compliments to your Excellency personally.*
>
> *The Kings officers encourage me that it will not be long before I am exchanged and I doubt not but that your Excellency will promote it, the more so as I have suffered a long and severe Imprisonment.... [I] have in great measure recovered my health. Provided a little cash could be sent me it would oblige your most obedient Humble Servant,*
>
> *Ethan Allen*

In a postscript, Allen informed Washington that Colonel Philip Skene, his onetime friend from Skenesborough Manor at the foot of Lake Champlain, was being exchanged that day. After another tantalizing month held captive on shipboard, on November 30, 1776, fourteen months after his capture, Allen was allowed to come ashore.[42]

FINALLY RELEASED FROM shipboard imprisonment on parole but restricted to Manhattan, Allen walked the streets of a New York City radically altered since his last stopover in June of 1775.

The town, inhabited by 25,000 a year earlier, now housed only 5,000 civilian New Yorkers (and those mostly Loyalists). It had been partially destroyed by a fire probably set by Americans as they retreated to New Jersey after their defeat at the Battle of Brooklyn Heights. Soon after midnight on September 21, 1776, a fire broke out in a tavern near Whitehall Slip, east of the Battery and, fanned by a strong wind, cut a swath across Bowling Green to Broadway, consuming entire blocks of houses and shops, finally burning itself out after destroying one-fourth of the buildings in the city and utterly wiping out the West Side. The fire left little shelter for Redcoats or civilians and less for the torrent of prisoners pouring in after the American defeat on Long Island. Informed of the blaze as he retreated across New Jersey, Washington had commented that "Providence or some good fellow" had struck the match.

As thousands of Loyalist refugees and runaway slaves sought the protection of the king's troops, many refugees pitched tents in "Canvass Town," a burned-over district west of Broadway. Captured field-grade officers (majors, colonels, and lieutenant colonels like Allen) were placed on parole of honor until they could be exchanged. They were free to find—and pay for—their own lodgings and food, able to walk the streets from dawn to sundown. Thirty American officers had found rented refuge at Liberty House, a large building on the west side of Broadway below Warren Street and opposite the common, today's City Hall Park. The house belonged to a Loyalist named Mrs. Carroll, a particular friend of General James Robertson, the British commandant of the occupied city. Liberty House recently had been the headquarters of Isaac Sears and the Sons of Liberty, its liberty tree cut down months ago and sawed up by British soldiers for firewood.

Strolling the streets in his newly tailored, Cork-donated blue silk suit and gold-laced hat, Allen, no doubt self-consciously, enfuriated Loyalists. One day near the end of November, "the famous Colonel Ethan Allen," as one fellow prisoner put it, stopped by for his first visit to Liberty House. John Adlum admired Allen's resilience and irrepressible spirit: "Colonel Allen was always a very welcome guest at our quarters. His manner of telling a story, his fund of anecdotes, his flashes of wit, and the force of his observations never failed of having an attentive and amused audience." Adlum remembered a December 1776 dinner when Allen's "history &c of his voyage to England &c and back again mixed with his observations and interlarded with anecdotes" kept the captive officers up "pretty late."[43]

Not everyone remained so entranced. Jabez Fitch of Norwich, Connecticut, a close friend of Benedict Arnold's, already bored with the endless attempts at entertainment at Liberty House, found Allen's storytelling irritating: "Colonel Allen came in and repeated to us again the story of his taking Ticonderoga and also many other of his adventures." In a posthumously published memoir, Alexander Graydon, a wealthy young Pennsylvania militia captain, wrote that he gradually warmed to Allen, describing him as "a robust, large-framed man worn down by confinement and hard fare." But he was now recovering his flesh and spirits:

A suit of blue clothes, with a gold laced hat that had been presented to him by the gentlemen of Cork, enabled him to make a very passable appearance for a rebel colonel. . . . I have seldom met with a man, possessing, in my opinion, a stronger mind, or whose mode of expression was more vehement and oratorical. His style was a singular compound of local barbarisms, scriptural phrases, and oriental wildness; and though unclassic and sometimes ungrammatical, it was highly animated and forcible. . . . Notwithstanding that Allen might have had something of the

insubordinate, lawless frontier spirit . . . he appeared to me
to be a man of generosity and honour. . . .

Graydon had earlier noted, "[S]hould [his] language be thought
too highly wrought, it should be remembered, that few have ever
more severely felt the hand of arbitrary power than Allen."

IN JANUARY OF 1777, the British provost marshal guards ferried Ethan Allen and some 300 prisoner officers over to Long
Island and placed them on parole in a string of small villages in
Kings County, whose entire population, mostly farmers who were
fourth- and fifth-generation descendants of seventeenth-century
Dutch colonists, was about 3,600. The largest village, Brooklyn,
boasted only a few score houses and a church. The county seat,
Flatbush, was even smaller. Allen was assigned to the tiny village
of New Lots, depicted by Jabez Fitch as "much more agreeable"
than Mrs. Carroll's Manhattan town house. Now New Lots Avenue in the East New York section of Brooklyn, the hamlet was
then just a string of a dozen farmhouses, two taverns, and a few
shops between meadows and mosquito-infested ponds. There,
with little money, Allen, billeted at 349 New Lots Avenue with
a fellow prisoner on the Dutch family farm of Daniel Rapelje,
would have to pay two dollars a week and survive on the local
fare, described by Fitch, who lived next door: clams, clams every
day and every way, fried or baked or cooked into a chowder and
invariably served with a side dish of suppuan, a porridge made up
of corn meal, milk, and molasses.

Under the terms of his parole, Allen had to remain within
New Lots Township and not "do or say anything contrary to the
interest of his majesty or his government." In good weather able
to walk and meet one another every day, the Brooklyn refugees

habituated taverns, especially Wyckoff's on the New Lots Road, where they could nurse a drink, smoke a clay pipe, play loo, or read newspapers, filtering the propaganda of Loyalist newspapers and speculating constantly about how the war was going and what their chances of being exchanged were.

IN JULY OF 1777, Allen was thrilled at the arrival of his brother Levi in New Lots, especially since Levi brought him £35 from the Connecticut Assembly. Allowing for runaway inflation, this would be about $2,000 in today's money, all that Ethan received in his nearly two years of captivity but enough to allow him to live modestly on parole. Levi came under a flag of truce. It was no secret he traded with the British and, using that leverage, had tried for nearly two years to find Ethan and help him. But Levi also brought Ethan his first news of home in nearly two years, and it was not good. Ethan's only son, Joseph, had just died of smallpox at age twelve. Zimri, too, had died, succumbing to tuberculosis. Mary and the other children, who had been living in Sheffield with Zimri, had gone to live with Ira in Arlington, where Remember Baker's widow and children also lived. Ira later wrote that Joseph had been "Enoculated for the Small Pox [and] when his Pock was about the Turn he got a Gun Privately & went to hunting Partridges, wett his feet took Cold was taken with a Rheumatick Payn [pneumonia] & dyed in three Days."[45]

News of Joseph's death devastated Ethan. Causing him sharper pain than his captivity, it came as a blow to "the tender passions of my soul, and by turn gives me the most sensible grief." When often dreaming of going home, "[I] had promised myself a great delight in clasping the charming boy in my arms," Ethan wrote to his brother Heman, "and in recounting to him my adventures. But mortality has frustrated my fond hopes, and with him my name expires—my only son, the darling of my soul." Ethan may have intended to spend more time with the boy, but he had been away from home so much of the time, hunting, policing Vermont's borders against the Yorkers, attacking one enemy or another, and paying in prison for his exploits, and now the boy was gone. Later that summer, Ethan wrote to Levi to thank him for bringing him money. He still was mourning his son's death, but he had not forgotten his wife and daughters. Levi was to watch over his family and see that his daughters went to school.[46]

WHILE HIS STRENGTH was returning, Allen had been growing uncharacteristically quiet, Fitch noted. On one stroll shortly after Allen learned of his son's death, he was in a "very Talkative Moode":

> When we came home we walked in Compy. with him. . . . [I]n our way some how we Introduc'd some Discourse on Moses's History of the early Ages of the World. . . . [M]ention was made of his Acct. of the universal Deluge, on which the Col. Reply'd that if [Moses] had been at that time on a certain height among the green Mountains (call'd by the name of Camel's Rump) he should not have been afraid to have given Defiance to all the Waters of Noah's Flood.[47]

AS HIS CONFINEMENT on Long Island dragged on into its eighth month, in April 1778, Allen, who had habitually ignored the sunset curfew, decided to ignore completely the terms of his parole. In his distinctive blue uniform and gilt-trimmed hat, he defiantly crossed over to Manhattan and wandered the streets. It had been three years since he had passed through the city on

his way back to Vermont after receiving his commission from the
Continental Congress. He could see all around him the consequences of civil war. For four miles, he saw nothing but British tents, gun emplacements, walls, and guard posts. As many
as eleven thousand American prisoners were crammed into
churches, warehouses, jails, and prison ships.

Allen visited the churches where the enlisted men were dying
in great numbers, as many as one hundred in a night: between the
Middle Dutch Church on Nassau Street and the North Dutch
Church on William Street, there were two thousand prisoners;
the Brick Church on Beekman Strreet had been turned into a
jail. The four hundred prisoners housed in the French Church on
Pine Street could not all lie down at once. They had long since
torn apart the pews, doors, windowsills, and molding to cook the
few ounces of rancid pork they were given each week. For three
months, they had eaten no meat at all. The Friends Meeting
House and the Presbyterian Church on Wall Street were serving as military hospitals. Kings College (present-day Columbia
University) and City Hall on Broadway were also packed with
prisoners. The city's new prison, the Bridewell, initially confined eight hundred prisoners. The unheated sugar warehouses
each held upwards of five hundred prisoners. By the time Allen
slipped over from Long Island, of nearly three thousand officers
and men captured when Fort Washington had surrendered only
eight months earlier, only eight hundred survived.

While military conventions were supposed to ensure that
officers on both sides would live comfortably in captivity, nothing
ensured the comfort of ordinary soldiers. Their fate was horren-
dous. As Allen now could see firsthand, thousands of prisoners
were suffering even worse treatment than he had. He learned for
the first time of the prison ships and the boats full of the dead. In
Wallabout Bay off the Brooklyn shore, the *Jersey*, a condemned,

rotting fifty-year-old decommissioned British man-of-war, held more than one thousand men and women belowdecks at a time. Fed spoiled provisions, they quickly became walking skeletons, dressed in rags and covered from head to toe with lice and their own feces from the resultant diarrhea. Racked by yellow fever, typhus, and dysentery, they died in their own bloody excrement and were buried a dozen at a time in shallow graves on the Brooklyn shore. Among the dead were African American, French, and Spanish prisoners.

As soon as he was able, George Washington finally sent a special envoy, Elias Boudinot, on an official inspection tour behind enemy lines in New York City to investigate accounts from American escapees about British brutality in their prisons. Commissary Joshua Loring, who had grown rich on misappropriated funds for rations, gave Boudinot unlimited access to the prisoners. At the Provost jail, the three-story former debtors' prison on the commons, Boudinot encouraged inmates to speak out about any abuses. They singled out Provost Marshal William Cunningham, testifying that he locked prisoners in a dungeon for weeks at a time without food as punishment for minor infractions of his rules and regularly beat them with his fists. Cunningham told Boudinot "with great insolence" that "every word was true," and "swore that [his power] was as absolute there as General Howe was at the head of his Army." Boudinot reported their plight to Congress, but prisoners continued to starve to death and had little hope of being released. The Provost prisoners were "wretched beyond description." The prisoners told Boudinot that, on hot summer days, the provost marshal used their excrement buckets to bring them drinking water, which they had to drink or die of thirst. Instead, many of them died of dysentery.[48]

• • •

WHEN HE RETURNED to Long Island, Allen began to get into arguments with Loyalists in taverns about what he had seen and heard. He knew he was violating the terms of his parole by leaving Kings County and taking the ferry over into Manhattan but he could no longer bear to sit out the war quietly. After one row on August 30, 1778, at Field's Tavern, a contingent of Redcoats came to Rapleje's house, searching for Allen. Jabez Fitch noted the next day in his diary, "I was busie at writing. . . . I perceived a file of men over at the next house, soon after which I was Inform'd that Col. Allen was Arrested, & carried off under a Strong Guard." His fifteen months' parole ending at bayonet point, Allen was ushered into New York's former City Hall, now the dreaded Provost jail. "I was apprehended . . . under the pretext of artful, mean and pitiful pretences," he later complained in his prison memoir. John Fell, another prisoner at the Provost, made a note of Allen's arrival in his diary: "Aug. 26. Ethan Allen brought to Provost from L.I. & confined below."[49]

"Confined below" meant that Allen had been taken down at bayonet point to the higher tier of a darkened dungeon where every new prisoner was held, usually for a week, in solitary confinement—Allen called it "lonely apartment"—with no food and no communication with anyone. It was Provost Marshal Cunningham's custom to visit the new prisoners each evening and personally beat them. Allen never wrote whether Cunningham beat him, but he did note how little he was fed. For the first two days in this "dark mansion of fiends," he was

denied all manner of subsistence either by purchase or allowance. The second day I offered a guinea for a meal of victuals, but was denied it. . . . [T]he third day I offered eight Spanish milled dollars for a like favour, but was denied, and all that I could get out of the sergeant's mouth, was, that by God he would obey his orders. I now perceived myself to be again in substantial trouble. . . .

And it came to pass on the 3d day, at the going down of the sun, that I was presented with a piece of boiled pork, and some biscuit, which the sergeant gave me to understand, was my allowance. . . .

John Fell, who would survive to become a congressman from New Jersey, made a note five days later: "Aug. 31. A.M. Col Allen brought into our room."[50]

Allen refused to be a model prisoner. He drilled a hole in the floor of his dungeon cell so that he could communicate with another prisoner who was being held in solitary confinement. He made a jailhouse friend this way, a Virginia navy captain named Edward Travis, a "gentleman of high spirits," whose personality matched Allen's: he "had a high sense of honor, and felt as big, as though he had been in a palace, and had treasures of wrath, in store against the British. In fine I was charmed with the spirit of the man."[51]

Allen was to remain a prisoner confined in the smelly, crowded cell with John Fell and twenty other ailing prisoners for the next nine months. He later tried to explain why his cellmate Fell was rapidly failing by December of 1777: "The stench of the gaol, which was very loathsome and unhealthy, occasioned a hoarseness of the lungs, which proved fatal to many who were there confined, and reduced this gentleman near to the point of death." Writing to Major General James Robertson, commandant of the city, he was able to arrange for Fell to be released from the jail and moved to a nearby house, where he began to recover. When Allen tried to organize a petition drive on behalf of all the Provost prisoners, he was overruled by three captive American generals. For his pains, Allen was once again consigned to a week in the dungeon.[52]

IN THE PROVOST jail, Allen heard the news of the great American victory at Saratoga. As he wasted his "very prime," he learned that his neighbors in Vermont had helped to destroy British General Sir John Burgoyne's northern invasion. He learned that his cousin and erstwhile rival Seth Warner had blunted a British attack at the Battle of Bennington. He learned that the French had signed a treaty of alliance with the Americans. He later wrote, "My affections are frenchified. . . . I glory in Louis the sixteenth, the generous and powerful ally."[53]

THE CHAIN OF unexpected events that finally led to Allen's exchange began on August 21, 1777, after a raid by Connecticut troops on Long Island Loyalist positions authorized by Samuel Holden Parsons, by then a general, went awry. Parsons, backed by Governor Trumbull, urged more frequent raids by whaleboat across Long Island Sound. Parsons sent Colonel Samuel Blachley Webb and sixty men to harass the Loyalists, but their boat came under heavy fire from a British sloop of war and ran aground, and they only joined the prisoners on Long Island. Webb's older brother, Joseph, was a wealthy merchant and Connecticut's commissary of prisoners. Webb visited New York City to negotiate the exchange of his brother, Jabez Fitch, and other Connecticut officers. In a dozen days he saw sixty prisoners buried. What he saw shocked him, and he reported it in detail to Governor Trumbull: "Unless something is immediately done, Newyork will be their Grave." Allen especially, sent off on orders from Trumbull and Parsons to take Ticonderoga and now in his third year of captivity, was becoming despondent. "He say's he's forgot—He's spending his Life, his very prime." Could a letter be sent on his behalf to General Washington? "Or what is to be done?"[54]

THE ANSWER CAME from George Washington, encamped with his army on the heights of Valley Forge, twenty-five miles west of British-occupied Philadelphia. Washington appointed four prisoner-of-war commissioners, including his aide-de-camp, Lieutenant Colonel Alexander Hamilton. The British commander, Howe, provided Hamilton with a pass to go through enemy lines to Germantown, where the talks took place. Hamilton carried Washington's authority to propose terms "on principles of justice, humanity and mutual advantage and agreeable to the customary rules and practice of war among civilized nations." But according to spies reporting to Hamilton, who also ran Washington's secret service, Howe was being replaced. France had signed a treaty of amity and alliance with the United States in February, and Hamilton questioned whether either commanding general, British or American, had the authority to make a binding agreement.

The talks took place between American and British lines at Newtown, in Bucks County. On April 11, 1778, Hamilton submitted seventeen "Questions concerning a Proposed Cartel for the Exchange of Prisoners of War." With Commissary of Prisoners Elias Boudinot, Hamilton coauthored "A Treaty and Convention for the Exchange and Accommodation of Prisoners of War," which became a model for future prisoner exchanges. It featured the principles and numerical values for exchanges. It began, "Those first captured shall be those first exchanged." Officers were to be exchanged for officers of equal rank. When that was impossible, "two or more inferior officers shall be given for a superior." The commander in chief was calculated to be worth 192 ensigns (second lieutenants today). If there remained any officers who could not be exchanged, five privates could be given for one ensign. Exchanges were to be made every two months. No officer or soldier was to be "thrown into dungeons" or any other kind of "unnecessarily rigorous confinement." Among the first to be exchanged were to be Major General Charles Lee and Lieutenant Colonel Ethan Allen. The treaty specifically banned transporting prisoners across the Atlantic for punishment.[55]

Realizing that he wouldn't be able to replace the thousands of troops the British had surrendered after the Battles of Saratoga the preceding autumn, Howe sent word that he was ready to exchange 790 prisoners held in Philadelphia, the only survivors of the more than 2,000 captured the preceding fall in the Battles of Brandywine and Germantown. He had already agreed on a partial exchange of officers on parole, rank for equal rank. Lee, a former British major appointed by the Continental Congress as Washington's second-in-command and captured early in the war during a dalliance with a tavern waitress in New Jersey, was to be exchanged for Richard Prescott, the British general who had meted out harsh punishment to Ethan Allen and then been captured when Montreal fell to the Americans. In mid-April 1778, as part of an exchange that included 59 American officers, 34 privates, and 3 surgeons, it was agreed that Allen was to be exchanged for Lieutenant Colonel Archibald Campbell, a member of Parliament whose ship had brought him to Boston after the British had evacuated the city and who had been held in filthy conditions in the Concord jail. For Allen, his exchange was a particular triumph. He had refused to try to escape, although all the men who had been captured with him had already escaped, except for two French Canadians who had died. But Allen insisted that he be treated as an officer appointed by the Continental Congress and therefore held a legal commission from a legitimate government. That he was exchanged for a member of Parliament must have seemed an even greater personal victory for the man who had been considered a contemptible wretch by so many New York aristocrats, Loyalists, and British cabinet ministers.

Allen had been held in the Provost jail from August 26, 1777, to May 3, 1778; in all, he had been a prisoner of the British for 952 days. Down to the last day, he had no idea of his fate:"I was taken out under guard, and conducted to a sloop." The vessel carried him through the Arthur Kill to Staten Island, where he was introduced to Colonel Campbell.

> [He] saluted me in a handsome manner, saying he was never more glad to see any gentleman in his life, and I gave him to understand that I was equally glad to see him, and was apprehensive that it was from the same motive. The gentlemen present laughed . . . and conjectured that sweet liberty was the foundation of our gladness; so we took a glass of wine together. . . .

A British ferry carried him to Elizabethtown Point, where Hamilton—and freedom for the first time in nearly three years— awaited him.[56]

Escorted across New Jersey by Colonel Elisha Sheldon and a troop of the Second Dragoons, Allen rode to the American camp at Valley Forge, where he was taken to the cream-colored fieldstone headquarters of General Washington and his staff, one of 284 temporary headquarters commandeered for Washington in the course of the eight-year war. Guards snapped to attention and, recognizing Hamilton, saluted. Passing down a narrow corridor, Hamilton ushered him into a crowded first-floor chamber, where as many as a dozen aides worked over maps and correspondence all day—then cleared away their desks and spread out at night on the floor, litter-like, to sleep head-first in front of the fireplace at night. In the next room, they found Washington: the one touch of home he allowed himself in his modest office was a Wilton rug from Mount Vernon. Washington, six feet four, courtly and unsmiling, robust in his navy blue dress uniform and his hair pulled back into a black-ribboned net, extended his powerful hand to the slightly smaller and now stooped Colonel Allen. The man Washington saw before him when he welcomed Allen into his cramped, high-spirited headquarters was forty years old, weak and haggard, his thick black hair all but gone, his blue Cork suit hanging loosely on him. But Allen remained unbowed as he offered to serve Washington once his health—"which was very much impaired"—was restored.

In the next few days, they met often. Back in Bennington a year later, when Allen penned his prisoner-of-war memoir, he was unable to tone down completely the immense pride he had felt in the company of Washington and the spit-and-polish officer corps he had assembled. "I was courteously received by gen. Washington, with peculiar marks of his approbation and esteem, and was introduced to most of the generals and many of the principal officers, of the army, who treated me with respect. . . ." Allen rode with Washington and his staff through a boulevard lined by Continental troops, freshly outfitted in new French-made uniforms and presenting French-made muskets, standing at attention beside 1,100 hastily constructed cabins, the officers saluting him with their sabers as he passed.[57]

After a few more days of rest and regaling, Allen rode west to York, to the Continental Congress's eighth temporary capital. He had impressed George Washington, who had done so much to try to ameliorate his suffering over the past months and years. After

Allen saluted one last time and left, Washington sat down and wrote to Congressional President Laurens to recommend Allen for promotion to full colonel:

> I have been happy in the [prisoner-of-war] exchange, and a visit from Lieut. Col. Allen. His fortitude and firmness seem to have placed him out of the reach of misfortune. There is an original something in him that commands admiration, and his long captivity and sufferings have only served to increase, if possible, his enthusiastic Zeal.

Standing before the Third Continental Congress, Allen could not help remembering the day nearly three years earlier when the Second Congress, hearing his jubilant recitation of the capture of Ticonderoga, had created the Green Mountain Regiment and placed him in its command. Adams, Hancock, and Jefferson had departed. Adams went to Paris to join Franklin in negotiations with European allies. Hancock and Jefferson left their delegations to govern their home states. Washington, who was being besieged by Europeans clamoring for generalships, was especially struck that Allen "does not discover any ambition for high rank." He was eager to return to *his* home state, to recover and take his place in governing the newly created republic of Vermont. Washington told Laurens he was sure that Congress would provide compensation for Allen's years of harrowing captivity and give him all the back pay that was "proper and suitable."[58]

ETHAN ALLEN's EFFECT on American prisoner-of-war policy proved long-lasting. His treatment set a precedent for future American wars, especially when it was cited in articles, books, and U.S. government reports four score and three years later as the Confederate South rebelled against the Union and both sides looked to Allen's ordeal as a precedent for how to treat, and not mistreat, prisoners of war; how to provide for their exchange; and how to think about the troublesome intersection of prisoner-of-war negotiations and diplomatic recognition of a state or a nation in rebellion. In the short run, Thomas Jefferson, as the governor of Virginia during the Revolution, used it as the pretext to retaliate on a high-ranking British prisoner, Henry "the Hair Buyer" Hamilton, deputy governor of Canada, who had offered bonuses for Indians to kill and scalp Virginia soldiers fighting in Illinois. Jefferson wrote to the British general William Phillips on July 27, 1779—four months after Allen's captivity narrative first came off the press in Philadelphia and reinvigorated flagging American morale—citing the "melancholy history" of "British cruelty to American prisoners" from "the capture of Colonel Ethan Allen" to "the present day" as justification for refusing to release Governor Hamilton on his parole of honor. In the long run, Allen's narrative of his own harsh treatment was a revolutionary act that helped to end the chivalric custom of releasing officers on parole until they were exchanged, whereas enlisted men were subjected to a different and crueler standard. His book revealed the fragility of the notion of honor in a civil war in which confiscation of property and revenge are principal motives. Fellow prisoners verified Allen's account of prison conditions and of his prisoner-of-war narrative. In editing Alexander Graydon's memoir, not published until 1846, John Stockton Littell comments, "His Narrative of his captivity is curiously written, but, is evidently, a faithful account." And no contemporary writer ever challenged it generally or in detail.[59]

Jefferson, who conducted the congressional investigation of the Canadian invasion and took a personal interest in Allen from the day he appeared before Congress, wrote that prisoners like him were paroled and their paroles honored by the British only until "some Tory refugee or other worthless person" suggested harsher treatment. Then they were "hurried to the Provost in New York." Jefferson urged Commissary of Prisoners Boudinot to inspect the Provost and found it a "common miserable jail built to confine criminals." Jefferson's strong and oft-quoted letters corroborated and added weight to the horror story that Allen was about to make public.[60]

For his part, Allen would always remain convinced that at least 10,000 Americans "fell a sacrifice to the relentless and scientific barbarity of Britain," to what he described in his own case as "malevolent cruelty." His estimate is remarkably conservative, according to modern research. The British, according to one recent study, imprisoned between 24,850 and 32,000 Americans in and around Manhattan alone during the war. Between 9,150 and 10,000 were held in the city's prisons, churches, and warehouses. Some 11,000 died in the abominable prison ships. Estimates of the total number who died, while imprisoned in New York City, range from 15,575 to 18,000—at least four times the toll of American Patriots killed in combat. Allen justifiably believed that the abuse of prisoners of war by their British captors had become a question not of international rules of war, or a reflection on the character of individual British officers and commanders, but an existential reflection of official British government policy itself.[61]

14.

"A Game of Hazard"

❋

BEFORE HE WAS strong enough even to put pen to paper, Ethan
Allen rode horseback all the way across five war-ravaged states.
Skirting British-occupied Philadelphia, hurrying through burnt-
out towns in New Jersey and around enemy-fortified New York
City, he passed through familiar landscapes in western Connecticut and Massachusetts before he came home to the new republic
of Vermont. On his way home after thirty-two months of brutal
incarceration, he immediately encountered a flash of dire news.
Accompanied by General Horatio Gates and his entourage and
then crossing into Connecticut, Allen rode swiftly to see his favorite brother, Heman, in Salisbury. Upon his arrival, he learned that,
only one week earlier, as Ethan received the accolades of the Third
Continental Congress in York, Pennsylvania, Heman, only thirty-
eight years old, had died of tuberculosis. Leading a company of
Green Mountain rangers in combat for a year after the attack on
Ticonderoga, he had contracted the disease during the eight-month

Canadian campaign. His health deteriorated after a spell of cold, rainy nights in the Taconic Mountains, where he helped Vermont and New Hampshire troops destroy a corps of Loyalist and German troops during the Battle of Bennington in August of 1777.

Heman's widow, Abigail, told Ethan that, on his last day, Heman asked to be helped up from his bed to a window to see one last time the green fields of Salisbury and to look down the road one last time to see whether Ethan, perchance, was coming. Very often, Heman had opened his home and his purse to Ethan and Mary and their children, crowding in their four children with his own, on occasion providing for a dozen Allens when Ethan was away hunting, fighting, or suffering in a British prison. The steadiest, most businesslike member of the flamboyant Allen clan, the trusted courier dispatched by the revolutionary leaders of New England to raise the alarm for the attack on Ticonderoga, he had accompanied Ethan on that first attack of the American Revolution. A quiet, shrewd diplomat, he later carried petitions to Philadelphia for Vermont's admission to the Continental Congress and knew, unlike his hot-tempered brother, when to back away rather than exacerbate the conflict with New York. Ethan already knew that his bachelor brother Zimri, who provided a home for their aged mother, had also died of tuberculosis, endemic in Vermont. More traumatized by these deaths than by his imprisonment, Ethan stayed in Salisbury only a few days, long enough to visit their graves and console Heman's widow. Robbed of farewells, helpless to ease their illnesses, the absent Ethan had lost two brothers and his only son in less than two years. Numbed by his grief, he left Salisbury and rode on north to Vermont, understandably alarmed by the news that his wife had developed a persistent cough.

· · ·

"Enfeebled," to use his own term, by his years in captivity, Allen, like any returning prisoner of war, faced major adjustments. During his long absence, the sweep of revolutionary events had radically changed circumstances in the Green Mountains. A new state in July of 1777 had declared itself born, independent of New York and New Hampshire, in the face of a massive British invasion down Lake Champlain. While Allen was wandering the country lanes of Long Island, the new state called itself New Connecticut until the Continental Congress informed its agent, Heman Allen, that the name had already been preempted by the Susquehannah Company of Connecticut for a proposed state in northeastern Pennsylvania. Allen's oldest friend, Dr. Young, then coined the name Vermont for the new republic, a corruption of the French for green mountain.

Arriving early in June of 1778 in Arlington, Allen found his wife and his three daughters living with his youngest brother, Ira. He had never before seen the youngest, three-year-old Maryann. Since Zimri's death, bachelor Ira, Mary, and the children had lived in a pitched-roof house along the Batten Kill the revolutionary government seized from a Loyalist who had fled to Canada. Allen's ambitious youngest brother had become the treasurer of the republic, its surveyor general, and, as Allen now learned, secretary of its governor's council, serving as the trusted adviser of Vermont's first governor, Thomas Chittenden. Allen's former Salisbury neighbor and onetime colonel of the Litchfield County militia, Chittenden, who had bought 10,000 acres of the Winooski Valley from the Allens' Onion River Land Company a few years before the Revolution, had fled south with his neighbors at the first British invasion in 1776. He lived and presided over council meetings in his confiscated home in the heart of the largely Loyalist village of Arlington. The governor's council, which also included Allen's old friend Jonas Fay of Bennington

and Allen's brother-in-law Timothy Brownson, was in session
when Allen, trailing a crowd of cheering children and neighbors
and appearing to be Vermont's Pied Piper, rode into Arlington.

Even before Allen could settle in for an evening with his family and his old friends, a courier arrived with a packet of dispatches
from General Gates at Albany. Gates forwarded a note from General Washington and, with it, the promotion to full colonel in the
Continental army. The congressional resolution accompanying
Allen's commission praised his "fortitude, firmness and zeal in the
cause of his country, manifested during the course of his long and
cruel captivity as well as on former occasions"—referring to his service at Ticonderoga and Montreal. A second resolution awarded
him a lieutenant colonel's back pay for his entire time in captivity.
Delighted, Allen wrote to Washington, Gates, and Henry Laurens, president of Congress, that he hoped to be fit for active duty
again after following a "regimane of Diet and Exercise."[1]

Handing his letters on June 9 to the waiting courier, Allen
rode the last nine miles to Bennington, escorted by Governor
Chittenden and his council. Farmers paused in their spring planting and women and children hurried to the roadside to wave and
cheer as the little cavalcade passed by, with a gaunt but beam-
ing Allen waving his beaver tricorn hat, his faded blue Cork suit
newly bedecked with a colonel's red sash. A triumphant celebration greeted him at Bennington. As a fourteen-cannon salute
echoed off Mount Anthony, half the town followed him to the
Catamount Tavern, where Allen settled into the familiar Council
Room and sipped punch from "the flowing bowl."

IN THE AUTUMN OF 1775, while Allen was taken prisoner in
his failed attack on Montreal and Benedict Arnold led a doomed
assault on Quebec, present-day Vermont provided the advanced

American base for the conquest of Canada. Convoys of bateaux glided past the new settlements heading north along Lake Champlain with reinforcements, supplies—and leaders of the Continental Congress. As the smallpox-riddled American army besieged Quebec City in the spring of 1776, Benjamin Franklin of Pennsylvania and three Marylanders, Samuel Chase, Charles Carroll (the wealthiest man in America), and his brother, John, soon to be the first Roman Catholic bishop in the United States, sailed north along the Vermont shore of Lake Champlain to organize the combined French Canadian and American forces.

Had they succeeded, Quebec would have become the fourteenth of the United States, but in May of 1776 the inevitable British counterattack devastated Vermont, which had been left virtually defenseless. Arnold, who led an assault on the lower town of Quebec, was seriously wounded and most of his troops captured; Richard Montgomery and all but one of his officers— the ever resilient Aaron Burr—were killed. Arnold besieged the walled city with the aid of 150 French Canadian volunteers and a single, portable thirty-two-pounder until a British fleet with thousands of Redcoats sent the Americans reeling back across the frontier into Vermont. Half of the 10,000 Americans who served in the Canada campaign were dead, victims of smallpox and the superstition of New England's leaders. In July of 1776, as the American colonies declared their independence from British rule and Ethan Allen languished in a Halifax jail, Vermont's fate was left undecided by Congress.

The first blue-water squadron of the Royal Navy, ten ships built in England, dismantled, and shipped on the decks of merchantmen, was assembled that October at St. John to carry an army of 4,000 Redcoats and 1,300 Germans. Accompanied by 400 native allies in long war canoes, the squadron swept down Lake Champlain, clashing in a five-day running battle with

Arnold's makeshift navy of sixteen vessels in the Battle of Valcour Island. People in Allen's Winooski River settlements fled south, Thomas Chittenden and his neighbors occupying abandoned farms in southern Vermont. Nineteen times during Allen's incarceration, the leaders of the Grants had met in "conventions" to ponder how to survive the British invasion, four times in Cephas Kent's tavern in Dorset, where, little more than a year earlier, they had voted to exclude Allen from command.

Virtually all delegates from towns east and west of the mountains agreed that they must constitute a separate government and then appeal to the Continental Congress for admission to the United States, which would entitle them to the protection of the Continental army. To try to make peace first with New York seemed fruitless. At the same Dorset conclave in July of 1775 that had chosen Seth Warner, the convention had voted overwhelmingly to perpetuate itself, to coordinate a common defense if invasion came, and to discuss their political options.

Forty-one delegates from thirty-two Green Mountain towns assembled for the third Dorset convention, on July 26, 1776. The delegates listened with deepening concern to Heman Allen's report of the rejection of the Grants' application for recognition by the Continental Congress in January. Even war seemed not to bring an end to the bitter factional hostilities. The New York delegates to Congress reacted hotly to the Grants' refusal to cooperate with the "Yorkers," as they called their sympathizers. They were supported by other provinces' delegations who feared the secession of the frontier parts of their colonies. Wisely, Heman withdrew the Grants' petition before it could come to a vote. At the July meeting at Dorset, Chitenden emerged as the leader of an independence movement, recommending "that application be made to the inhabitants of the Grants to form the same into a separate district"—outside the jurisdiction of the British Empire and the newly declared United States of America. At the fourth Dorset convention in September of 1776, delegates voted 49–1 to defend the United States "against the hostile attempts" of British invasion forces. At the same time, the convention pledged to condemn anyone who supported New York's claims to the Grants.[2]

Meeting at Windsor in the Connecticut Valley in its inaugural session in July of 1777, the first Vermont legislature subsumed the ten-year struggle over Grants land titles into the general struggle for independence from England. The same day, the Vermont convention dispatched Seth Warner to Albany to seek Philip Schuyler's pledge to defend Vermont against the British in the impending British counteroffensive while Chittenden, Ira Allen, and Dr. Jonas Fay of Bennington caucused with delegates from towns east and west of the Green Mountains. Holding out the sword of defiance toward the British and the olive branch to the Continental Congress, Vermont set up a provisional government. If the delegates were captured, they knew, they still could be hanged and drawn and quartered as rebels. What Ethan Allen had begun as legal opposition in court in Albany six years earlier, had grown by 1777 to become an independent state. Vermont thus was the first republic in the New World. Its first public building, in Manchester, was a jail to house active Loyalists.

To PIECE TOGETHER the revolutionary course that had transformed Vermont during his absence took Ethan Allen weeks. He learned that when the Continental Congress declared American independence, in July of 1776, it left the fate of the Grants undecided. It seemed as if the Vermonters had two enemies, not one. The revolutionary New York Assembly had decreed that all quitrents and fees formerly due to Great Britain or any of its colonies by settlers on the Grants were now due to the new state government of New York. Then, in September of 1776, fifty-eight delegates from Grants towns issued a call for independence from New York. The declaration they sent to Congress shrewdly noted that their "respectable frontier" shielded the borders of other states and could "muster more than five thousand hardy soldiers."[3]

A New York convention demanded that Congress restore the Grants to the control of New York. Vermont's petition seeking recognition as an independent state was again carried by Heman Allen and presented to Congress the next day. In Congress, the Vermonters heard themselves being called "defectors" and "insurgents." Shortly after Heman headed back to Vermont, allies in Congress and outside it in Philadelphia's radical committees, principally Thomas Young, mounted a campaign to win support for the Vermont petition. On April 21, 1777, the New York delegates fired off a report to Albany stating they were worried by Dr. Young's "address" to "the insurgents in our state." These "insurgents," the leaders of Vermont, had "taken the minds of several of the leading members of Congress."[4]

Then, in late June of 1777, as the British unleashed a second and stronger invasion down Lake Champlain, the Vermont convention reconvened at Windsor in the southeast corner of the Grants, where many of the landholders had already paid second or confirmatory grants to New York. After reclaiming the lake and retaking Fort Ticonderoga, the British army and navy controlled virtually all of Vermont west of the Green Mountains and north of a line running from Castleton through Rutland to Pittsford by the time Chittenden coauthored Vermont's constitution. The Windsor convention adopted a slightly modified version of the radical Pennsylvania constitution coauthored by Benjamin Franklin, Thomas Paine, and Thomas Young. Dr. Young had given Heman Allen a copy when he came to Philadelphia to petition

Congress again for admission in 1777. No longer, Young wrote to Vermont, would "New York Monopolizers" be able to hold power over Vermont's people.

When Congress learned that Dr. Young had urged Vermonters to set up their own government, delegates from New York and New Hampshire protested "this insolent Address, this incendiary production." Congress reacted hotly. Disallowing recognition of any government "to be established by the people styling themselves inhabitants of the New Hampshire Grants," it refused to use the word "Vermont," invented by Young, and labeled Young's remarks "derogatory to the honor of Congress . . . [tending] to deceive and mislead the people to whom they are addressed."[5]

The harsh reprimand, undoubtedly written by Ethan Allen's—and Vermont's—old nemesis, the New York delegate James Duane, came six days too late to affect Dr. Young. On June 24, while tending to sick and wounded revolutionary soldiers, Young died of typhus in a Continental army field hospital. Even after Young's death, Duane insisted on a public reprimand. "Compassion to his distressed family no doubt induced some of the Members to wish it to be passed over in silence," Duane wrote to Judge Robert R. Livingston. "You will observe however that it was of great Consequence to us to have this wicked production censur'd and exposd, and this point was finally carried in our favour after a Sharp Conflict." The judge and the lawyer, royal officials when Allen had stood before them fully six years earlier, were still attempting to cling to their land claims in Vermont. On his way home to Vermont, Allen had learned of another devastating loss—the death of the man who was his first intellectual mentor, his coauthor, and his drinking companion—the man who made Allen a skeptic and put a name to his idea of an independent state. To his grief over the death of his son and his broth-

ers he now added a deep sense of loss for Dr. Thomas Young, the
man who had inspired him.[6]

IT IS NOTEWORTHY that the Vermont constitution went further than any other state constitution in guaranteeing human
rights. The constitution's first article made Vermont the very
first American state to ban the slave trade and slave ownership,
advancing an original ideology. The somewhat contrarian philosophy of the state was reflected at the very beginning and this
distinctive way of thinking—somewhat libertarian with quite
different concerns from those of other, more established states
like New York, stemmed from the antiauthoritarian sensibility
found in its early inhabitants. The republic of Vermont's original
constitution also eliminated the property qualification for male
suffrage and provided compensation for private property taken
for public use. It broadened religious liberty, assuring security of
Protestants against civil disabilities on account of religion. Only
Vermont could police Vermont. Debtors could be arrested only
if the creditor could prove he is in danger of losing his debt. No
Vermonter could be "transported out of this State for trial, for any
offence committed within this State." No law could be enacted
hastily, and the acts of the governor and his council were to be
subject to review, restriction, and revision by a council of cen-
sors meeting every two years. It departed from the Pennsylvania
constitution, which banned continuous reelection of state officials
and multiple office holding; there were to be no term limits in
Vermont. It also provided for a strong governor who would rule
as "governor-in-council," and it gave the governor the power to
review all legislation proposed by the general assembly before its
passage. But the strongest language that Governor Chittenden

and his councillors added to Pennsylvania's prototype constitution condemned New York's pre-revolutionary royal government:

> The late Lieutenant Governor Colden, of *New-York*, with others, did, in violation of the tenth commandment ["Thou shalt not covet thy neighbor's goods"], covet those very lands; and by a false representation made to the court of Great Britain, in the year 1764, that for the convenience of trade and administration of justice, the inhabitants were desirous of being annexed to that [New York] government . . . which ever was, and is, disagreeable to the inhabitants.

The Vermont constitution specifically denounced New York's Governor Tryon for having passed the Bloody Acts of 1774, which included a steep fine and six months' imprisonment for anyone who refused to help a New York sheriff evict a Vermonter from his lands. The document furthermore condemned a succession of New York governors for regranting lands to "land jobbers in the government" and excoriated New York's assembly for empowering its supreme court of judicature to condemn to death Ethan Allen and the leaders of the Green Mountain Boys without trial. In July of 1777, after its assembly unanimously adopted its constitution at Windsor, Vermont's new government moved back across the mountains to the Catamount Tavern in Bennington, where Allen had planted the first seed of Vermont in 1770.[7]

MORE THAN THREE years had elapsed since Allen had led the Green Mountain Boys in their now legendary predawn attack on Fort Ticonderoga. The local fervor accompanying the raid now barely flickered. If Vermont needed anything, it was a spark of enthusiastic leadership to rekindle the revolutionary flame, guttering low after years of hardship, poverty, and near-starvation, always with British warships patrolling nearby on Lake Champlain and their Indian allies striking outlying settlements. Allen's homecoming offered a welcome patriotic release. A celebration renewed hope. The festivities ended, however, with a hanging, the first ever carried out in Vermont. David Redding was, like a significant minority of Vermonters, a Loyalist. He served with Burgoyne in a Loyalist unit during the 1777 Saratoga campaign. He stole powder, shot, and horses from the Continental army supply depot at Bennington for Loyalist dragoons in New York. He would undoubtedly have been hanged by New York's revolutionary government if he had been caught there, but he escaped prosecution by fleeing across the border into Vermont. Many of his Loyalist compatriots fled to Canada when Burgoyne surrendered after the Battles of Saratoga in autumn of 1777, but Redding stayed behind because he was trying to hold on to Vermont property granted him by New York.

Many of Vermont's Loyalists were spying for the British, operating networks based in New York City and Montreal and employing agents who were gathering intelligence all over Vermont. To his neighbors in close-knit Bennington, the newly arrived Redding was obviously a spy, and they accused him of stealing powder and muskets from the Continental army arsenal in Bennington. Patriots lived in constant fear of an armed uprising by their Loyalist neighbors. Redding's fate was never in doubt. For his "enemical conduct," Redding was scheduled to die on Bennington's new gallows on June 4, 1778. But at the last moment, his lawyer argued that the verdict was illegal because Redding had only been tried by a jury of six of his peers. The execution was postponed for a week so that Redding could have a new trial. The bloodthirsty crowd seemed determined to have its hanging anyway, and, because Bennington had no jail, it locked Redding under guard in the tack room of the Catamount Tavern.

To hold a new trial would require a prosecutor. Governor Chittenden solved the problem by appointing Allen the state's attorney. In a hasty jury trial "of a prisoner to be tried this day, for enemincal conduct against this, and said United States" conducted before the General Assembly in the Council Room of the Catamount Tavern, he had no trouble painting a picture of the growing Loyalist menace. He made it no secret that he had come to hate Loyalists. It was clear to him that the Loyalists were as much of a threat to the Revolution as the British. Reciting his own horrific experiences, Allen easily secured a conviction. At one o'clock on June 11, scarcely two weeks after his return, he emerged with a "guilty" verdict. A huge crowd thronged Bennington Green as much to see Ethan Allen as to witness the last agonal spasms of David Redding in the first execution in the new state's history.

A few days later, Allen wrote to the Continental Congress,

A Bill has Passed in the general Assembly of the State of Vermont, to Bannish Those Persons that are Judged by Certain Commissioners [Loyalists] . . . to the British lines . . . as they would be Equally Hurtfull to the Common Cause, in any Other state, as in this. The Inhabitants in these parts, are Determined to rid this Country of Tories, and to Confiscate their Estates, one of those Villains was hanged in this Place, the 11th Instant.[8]

BY THE TIME of Ethan Allen's exchange, the problem of Loyalists—called by Patriots "intestine enemies"—had transformed the Revolution into a civil war. In his weeks at Valley

Forge, before Congress and on horseback with American officers before he reached Vermont, he had no doubt learned of growing Loyalist activities in other states. By the end of the Revolution, the British, in addition to Loyalists enlisted in the British army and navy, had formed fifty-five regiments of Loyalist Provincial Corps, some 19,000 serving in their ranks. In all, nearly 50,000 Americans served under the royal standard, including 12,000 blacks. An estimated 500,000 of three million Americans, including about 20 percent of the white male population, were active Loyalists. In New York, this number included many tenant farmers who preferred to remain British subjects. Many of the Dutch farmers in New York and New Jersey preferred monarchy. In Pennsylvania, Germans and Quakers largely attempted to stay neutral, but when they failed, many of them sided with the British. When the British army evacuated Philadelphia, Pennsylvania hanged two Loyalists who had aided the British during their 1777–78 occupation of the city: some 5,000 Loyalist sympathizers trailed their coffins in a visually dramatic protest. Virtually all Anglican clergy fled America or joined Loyalist regiments as chaplains; many of their parishioners in Connecticut and New Jersey opposed the Revolution. Large numbers of Iroquois fought in support of British armies and were driven into Canada in a sustained campaign by General Washington.

After France joined the war on the American side early in 1778, the British, in a war of posts, concentrated their forces in coastal towns where they could be supported by their navy and increasingly relied on a supposed outpouring of Loyalist support when they struck out into the countryside or attacked other port towns. They also placed greater emphasis on recruiting more spies, on seeking to ascertain which Americans were disenchanted by the lagging course of the Revolution. In Vermont, Loyalists were regarded as a resource to be exploited, a solution to a desperate lack of cash with which to pay for the war against British invaders. Basically undefended after the fall of Fort Ticonderoga to the British in July of 1777, Vermonters had to raise an independent army to protect their own settlements. But there was no public treasury, no time for taxation, no chance to borrow.

At a late-night session at the Catamount Tavern, the dejected members of the governor's council sat silently until Governor Chittenden rose at his place and gave his most impassioned speech:

> We have sent a dispatch requesting aid of New Hampshire. But how can we expect they will do anything till we do something for ourselves, 'till they know whether they will find among us more friends to feed and assist than enemies to impede them. . . . I submit to you, gentlemen, whether it is not now high time to act. . . . If we can't vote taxes, we can contribute towards raising a military force. . . . Let us show the world that [we] can be *men*. I have ten head of cattle, which, by way of example, I will give for the emergency. But am I more patriotic than the rest of you here and hundreds of others in the settlements? My wife has a valuable gold necklace. Hint to her today that it is needed and, my word for it, tomorrow will find it in the treasury of freedom. But is *my* wife more spirited than yours and others? Gentlemen, I wait your propositions.[9]

At the next morning's meeting, a sleepless Ira Allen suggested that the Vermont government appoint agents to seize and sell the personal and real property of Loyalists, including their livestock, crops, clothes, household goods, and farm equipment. This would not only raise cash but also discourage Loyalist recruiting. Overnight, Vermont rallied the resources to support its own army—and Chittenden was able to keep his cows and his wife her coveted necklace.

ETHAN ALLEN BECAME the governor's unelected counselor the day he returned to Vermont. He admired the understated style of "One-Eyed Tom" Chittenden, as he was called by the Vermont farmers who reelected him governor nineteen times. For one thing, Allen liked the fact that Chittenden never flaunted his authority. He was frugal and preferred to dress, speak, and act like a plain farmer—which often fooled the pretentious. According to one persistent Vermont legend, he owned one dress coat, which could be worn either side out. One side was scarlet: he had worn it as a Connecticut militia colonel under the British and then ex officio as captain general of the Vermont militia. The other side was dark blue, worn when he was presiding over a meeting or simply minding his own business. He sported no wig and no powder, a plain white stock at his throat if any, and an unadorned vest, even though he owned a rare silver pocket watch and monogrammed silver vest buttons and late in life walked with the assistance of a gold-headed cane.

One day shortly after Allen came home, a uniformed British courier rode up to Chittenden in Arlington while he was feeding his hogs. As the Englishman dismounted, so the story goes, he carelessly handed the bumpkin the reins of his horse and inquired if His Excellency Governor Chittenden was at home. The farmer said yes. The British officer strode to the front door and banged on it. He asked the woman who answered whether he might see her husband. She replied that he already had: he was the fellow the Englishman was using for a hitching post. Chittenden accepted the mortified officer's apologies, and had a good laugh.

Describing the same encounter a century and a half later, the Vermont writer Dorothy Canfield Fisher told the story of a fancily dressed English rider who found his path blocked by a large hay wagon. A farmer sat on its fresh-cut cargo. The visitor rode up alongside and asked the farmer, "Can you tell me where His Excellency Governor Thomas Chittenden lives?" The farmer, casting his eye over the braided tricorn hat, the brilliant blue coat, and lace ruffles and shining gold buttons, replied, "I'm going there. Follow me." The wagon bumped along slowly on the rutted dirt road and finally creaked into a barnyard. The farmer jumped down from the hay wagon, dusted off his trousers and said, "I'm Governor Chittenden. What can I do for you?"[10]

IN THE SPRING OF 1778, when Allen came home to Vermont, hunger gripped the state as the result of the British invasion during the preceding summer's harvest. The years of clear-cutting the forests to produce timber and potash had also deprived much of the land cover and food for its game. The woods were often silent now, and it was too dangerous to range very far to hunt. During the bitter winter of 1777–78, while Allen shivered in the Provost jail in New York City, Vermonters suffered an accumulation of hardships. Many towns and farms were sacked and burned by combined forces of Redcoats, Loyalists, and Indians during two British invasions. Two autumns of war made it impossible to harvest crops. Driven from their homes, many Vermonters were destitute of grain, for either food or seed. The governor's council prohibited, under heavy penalties, the transportation of any wheat, rye, corn, flour, or meal out of state without a permit.

AS THE EXCITEMENT over Allen's return subsided, he took his place at the governor's council table in Arlington as a matter of daily routine. Chittenden and his councillors invited him to attend their sessions. As the lawmakers pondered bills for regulating the Sabbath, paying bounties for destroying wolves, and confiscating Loyalists' farms, Allen told them his stories, and they, in turn, repeatedly toasted his health. It was almost like the good old days, only more complicated. Sixteen towns along the east bank of the Connecticut River were petitioning to break away from New Hampshire on the grounds that citizens on the west side of the White Mountains could not afford to travel to the new state capital at coastal Portsmouth for legal business and that river towns were left undefended during raids by the British, the Loyalists, and the Indians.

Only a few days after Allen's homecoming, a petition from Eleazar Wheelock, president of Dartmouth College in Hanover in the Connecticut River valley, lay on the table in the house Governor Chittenden had confiscated in Arlington. Three months earlier, the Vermont Assembly, acting on the request of the sixteen New Hampshire towns that they be annexed and taken under Vermont's protection, had agreed to the annexation. Dartmouth College had thereby become the first college in Vermont, a notion that appealed to Allen. At the moment, Wheelock was asking to be appointed justice of the peace for Dresden, the part of Hanover owned by the Dartmouth corporation, and was seeking approval to appoint an assistant justice. Allen made himself, as in the old days, spokesman for Vermont's government. He wrote to Wheelock on June 14, 1778, that his request appeared to him "reasonable."

For now, writing to the Reverend Wheelock, Allen was circumspect. He was getting only an inkling of the complexity of the question, and he stalled for time. The Vermont Assembly probably would not be ready to take up the annexation in its September 1778 session, he wrote Wheelock. Not until the spring 1779 session would it be "the Most Proper, to Determine upon so Copious a Matter." Meanwhile, Allen promised his own personal protection for the college and its students, many of them young Indian men. He would use his "Influence that this Assembly, Take the College under their Patronage, and Invest Your self with Civil Authority, in the Manner you Desire." Not only did he vow that Vermont would protect Dartmouth College, but he assured Wheelock, "In all things, I will Exert my Self to Strengthen your hands."[11]

APPOINTED BY CHITTENDEN and confirmed by the general assembly as brigadier general in charge of Vermont's 500-man militia, Allen inspected the defensive perimeter of the new state. A northern line of blockhouses dotted the landscape from Vergennes east through Rutland and Pittsford: the northern two-thirds of the state was left defenseless for the duration of the war. Attempts to hold any town farther north had proven futile. At Shelburne, overlooking Lake Champlain ten miles south of the Winooski River settlements, farmers had fled south before Burgoyne's army in the autumn of 1777. They had returned the next spring to harvest their winter wheat crop, accompanied by fifteen Vermont militia, who occupied a nearby blockhouse. A Loyalist neighbor skated to the British fort at Crown Point and, on March 12, led a party of British regulars and Indians to Shelburne. Two wheat buyers were killed as they slept by an open window at the house of Major Pierson, the community leader. His house in flames, Pierson led his men to the blockhouse, where the Vermonters were able to fight off their attackers, killing the British captain, the Indians' leader, and ten Redcoats, while losing just three of their own number in all.

Allen made his headquarters at Castleton, where he could watch British warships that patrolled the lake unmolested. He turned over the defense of the frontier blockhouses to his third cousin, Captain Ebenezer Allen, who had joined him in the attack on Ticonderoga, served with the Green Mountain Regiment in Canada, and narrowly missed freeing Ethan at Montreal. Ebenezer was now a captain in the militia regiment of Vermont rangers and commanded the forts at either end of the defensive line at Vergennes and Pittsford. It was from Ebenezer that Ethan probably learned of the fate of Major John Brown, who had abandoned Ethan's forces at Montreal after proposing the attack in the first place. Brown had led his men to reinforce Montgomery at St. John. In 1777, after Burgoyne's army swept south toward Saratoga, Brown led a behind-the-lines ranger action with Ebenezer as his second-in-command. They destroyed two hundred boats on Lake Champlain and at the north end of Lake George that the British were relying on in case they had to retreat to Canada. Brown and Allen then succeeded in capturing Mount Defiance and its guns overlooking Fort Ticonderoga. Ebenezer and his men held Mount Defiance, cutting off Burgoyne's rear guard, taking forty-nine Redcoats prisoner, and freeing the officers' black slaves. Once again, Brown backed away from attacking the British, losing the last opportunity to recapture Fort Ticonderoga intact before the British could demolish it. Soon afterward, Brown was killed in an Iroquois ambush of a force sent by Schuyler to reinforce the besieged Americans at Oswego.

ONCE THE ASSEMBLY adjourned, Allen turned to Vermont's straitened finances. Seizure of estates of Loyalists who had fled to Canada had, for a year, financed Vermont's defense and its regiment in the Continental army, but after the initial seizures, the money all but dried up. It was Allen's idea now to confiscate the property of Loyalists who had *not* fled. His bitterness toward the Loyalists unabated, he prodded the assembly until it adopted his plan and appointed five commissioners of confiscation—including Allen himself.

Personally leading the movement to drive out the Loyalists, he raided the town of Dorset with his Vermont militiamen near the British lines first. It was there, at Cephas Kent's tavern, that the white-haired town leaders of Vermont had rejected him as commander of *his* regiment. Could he forget this as he rounded up suspected Loyalists and herded seventeen "wicked Tories" toward Albany. Writing to New Hampshire Congressman Elisha Payne, he also confided that by eliminating Loyalists from Vermont, he was expelling another ancient enemy, the "New York Malcontents" who "greatly infested" pro–New York Cumberland County. "These inimical persons are Yorkers as well as Tories," he told Payne. Free only a few weeks from captivity, Allen blamed his harshest treatment on Loyalist Americans and was opportunistically lumping Loyalism with refusal to recognize Vermont or its authority.[12]

Immediately after David Redding's execution, Allen, clearly not interested in reconciliation, convinced the governor's council and the assembly that the confiscation of Loyalist properties was still not being prosecuted vigorously enough. Obviously, not all of the Loyalists had fled. Many continued to live on the east side of the mountains on lands chartered or confirmed by New York grants. In Allen's view, to be pro–New York was to be pro-British, potentially a spy for the British. Vermont's policy of confiscation, Allen argued, needed to be expanded to include these left-behind Loyalists. The Banishment Act of 1778 established confiscation boards in each county to hear and decide charges of disloyalty among citizens of Vermont. From October 1778 to

February 1779, Allen and his fellow commissioners seized and sold thirty-three farms or tracts of land in Bennington County alone. In 1779, 158 persons in twenty-four towns east of the Green Mountains lost their properties by confiscation.

The bulk of revenue of these courts came from absent or dead Loyalists. Of 60,000 acres claimed by the late Crean Brush, author of the Bloody Acts, Vermont confiscated and sold off 40,000 acres. Samuel Peters fled to London; Vermont confiscated 56,000 acres. James Rogers declined the rank of general of militia of three counties claimed by New York in Vermont, a commission offered by the New York Provincial Congress; he joined the British and forfeited 47,000 Vermont acres. The former Green Mountain Boy Justus Sherwood fled after the Battle of Valcour Island in October 1776 and became a major in the Loyalist Queen's Rangers, served as a scout in Burgoyne's 1777 campaign and lost most of his Loyalist company at the Battle of Bennington. He also lost 13,000 Vermont acres. And the New Yorker William Smith, future chief justice of Quebec, later claimed £26,000 worth of confiscated Vermont land. At the first public sale of confiscated lands, Ira Allen, perpetuating the family's ability to accumulate large parcels of land, put in a bid of £200 for 150 prime acres of Burlington land confiscated from the Loyalist William Marsh. Ira had once surveyed the choice land himself.

Passing a new Act of Banishment in 1779, the Vermont Assembly, at Ethan Allen's urging, created a court where Loyalists could defend their property. Allen directed the court. The income derived from selling the properties these boards confiscated provided £190,000, more than all other sources of public revenue combined, and left Vermont free of Revolutionary War debts. As a result, Vermont did not have to tax its loyal citizens until 1781, one cause of the Allens', and the new government's, great popularity.

Acting as the spokesman for Vermont's government, Allen became the Bennington County judge of the court for confiscations, Vermont's most active and profitable, seizing the property of "any person or persons charged with being guilty of any inimical treacherous or treasonable conduct or conspiracies against this and the Independent States, within and for the County of Bennington." Not always the most ethical of leaders, he took advantage of being empowered to select the other judges. Doing in Vermont what he most derided in New York, Allen raided the home of Asa Baldwin, the wealthiest man in Dorset, seizing the man and confiscating his property. In Manchester, William Marsh's lands fell forfeit: Allen bought 150 choice acres in Burlington at the confiscation auction. He also had a new source of income, receiving one guinea a day in hard money from the proceeds of auctioning confiscated estates.

For it is really a game of hazard between whig and tory. The whigs must inevitably have lost all, in consequence of the abilities of the tories, and their good friends the British; and it is no more than right the tories should run the same risk, in consequence of the abilities of the whigs.[13]

As head of the Bennington Board of Confiscation, Allen convicted eight "inimical persons" in his first two weeks of service. They had to leave Vermont immediately with what little they could carry—and Allen personally escorted them to Albany. New York's revolutionary governor, George Clinton, demanded that Allen turn them over to him, but George Washington refused. All of the male "wicked Tories" whom Allen herded south were packed off to military custody at West Point. The prisoners complained to Governor Clinton that they were not Loyalists at all but New Yorkers. To Allen, it was all the same, and Washington was increasingly hostile to suspected Loyalists. Under cover of the Revolution, Allen was determined to drive the Yorkers, at last and forever, out of Vermont.[14]

ETHAN ALLEN BECAME, however, a little too good at ferreting out Loyalists. The scent soon led to his own brother Levi. A merchant, Levi had given up a lucrative fur-trading business at Detroit to throw in with Ethan and his brothers' deer-skin-tanning scheme in Salisbury. He had remained personally loyal to Ethan, even if he was considered a Loyalist. He had traveled to Washington's headquarters in Cambridge, to the Connecticut Assembly in Hartford, and to Halifax to plead for Ethan's exchange. He had brought Ethan the cash that bought him food while paroled in New York. But Levi, who, according to his writings as well as his erratic behavior, appears to have been mentally unstable, didn't take politics, or anything else, very seriously, tried to swindle his brothers Ethan and Ira out of large tracts of land. Ethan came to call Levi "that accursed rogue" and that "Goddam devilish Tory." Levi unquestionably was a Loyalist, and he was openly cynical about the course of events in Vermont: "I boast not of loyalty. . . . Nor have I in the least concerned myself with Revolutionary principles. There are in all governments the 'ins' and the 'outs' at Court. The latter are ever grumbling."

After shouldering a musket with Ethan in the attack on Ticonderoga, Levi had turned to making money, not war, plowing his profits from trade into Vermont real estate. Moving to Dutchess County, New York, he became a Yorker, in Ethan's eyes. On one business trip, he was seized by Connecticut revolutionaries and jailed for six months for trading with the British on

Long Island, a practice that had once benefited brother Ethan. He had hardly left a Yankee jail and was en route to British-occupied Florida when he learned that his own brother was confiscating his lands. He stopped to write a blistering denunciation that his brother read in the *Connecticut Courant*:

> Can this be the man for whom so many were ready to drop a tear while he endured chains and captivity for his oppressed country? Or is he no sooner at liberty than, unmindful of his benefactor, like the serpent in the fable, he would sting him to the heart? .... Can he forget my voyage to Halifax, afterwards to New York, and the insults, imprisonments and sufferings sustained . . . merely to restore him to his country and friends?[15]

Stunned and embarrassed, Ethan sputtered and swore, "But, God damn it all, under cover of doing favors for me, when a prisoner at New York and Long Island, he was holding treasonable correspondence with the enemy!"

The fight escalated, and Levi called Ethan a liar, challenging his older brother to a duel. "I have no doubt he would have fought me," Levi later wrote, "but all his friends jointly put in their argument that Levi was only mad," and Ethan laughed off the challenge.[16]

On his way back from depositing eight Loyalist prisoners at Albany, Allen met with his youngest brother, Ira, in Salisbury to settle their brother Heman's tangled estate. Heman had willed them jointly one-half his shares in the Onion River Land Company, leaving the other half to his widow, Abigail, but because of wartime business constraints, his months away in combat, and his long illness, he had left his business affairs in disarray. Nearly everybody in Connecticut seemed to owe Heman Allen money. Heman bequeathed Ethan and Ira the 20,000 acres of undeveloped land in northern Vermont, but it was behind British lines. Yet, so confident was Ethan of ultimate American victory that he continued to buy and sell lands behind enemy lines. A 300-acre share in Tinmouth fetched one hundred times the dollar an acre Ethan had paid for it before the war.

Ethan had moved his family back to his farm in Sunderland when he'd come home from imprisonment. There, alone with the children during Ethan's frequent absences on government business, Mary found that her cough was worsening. Ethan began to divide his days between governor's council meetings and, for the first time since his capture three years earlier, spending long hours writing under his own roof with his family.

FOR YEARS, THE major grievance among the Connecticut Valley towns and other settlements in every colony west of the Allegheny Mountains had been unequal representation by legislatures, invariably based in the east, closer to the Atlantic Coast, where the first settlements were planted. As late as 1774, only 46 of 147 towns in New Hampshire were represented in the colonial assembly. When the British Proclamation of 1763 closed the frontier to further settlement, settlers were funneled up the Connecticut River valley into the western region of New Hampshire, yet no town in Grafton County, the area in the southwest that included Dartmouth, the home of Dartmouth College, had been admitted to the legislature. Added to the burdens of cost and time it took to go to court over poor mountain roads was the growing feeling of disenfranchisement and the virtual impossibility of being protected from British and Indian raids from Quebec. As in most of backcountry America, taxation without representation was here more than a political slogan.

After three years of unsuccessfully seeking representation in the newly created New Hampshire Assembly, sixteen towns voted at a convention in Hanover to unite with Vermont. Like many of the settlers of western New Hampshire, Dartmouth's president, the Reverend Eleazar Wheelock, and his adherents believed that New Hampshire's new state government merely perpetuated control by seaboard interests in Portsmouth and Exeter and ignored the needs of territories further inland. A College Party based in Hanover, supported by some landowners in southeastern Vermont towns along the Connecticut River, wanted to form a union of towns on both sides of that river and create a new state with its capital in Hanover. Their propagandists argued that the Connecticut River valley towns on both shores could not be satisfactorily governed by either New Hampshire or New York. Since the Revolution had abolished British jurisdictions and vacated the Crown's boundary decision of 1764, the valley towns, the College Party contended, were in a state of nature and could form their own government.

When the Vermont towns, by large majorities, approved the annexation of the sixteen New Hampshire towns in their annual town meetings in March 1778, they forced the Vermont Assembly to accept the towns on June 11. Allen at first derided the would-be architects of a separate Connecticut Valley state as "imbeciles," but he was clearly alarmed by the annexation movement. He feared that, if it succeeded, it would reduce the republic of Vermont to little more than a narrow strip of land between the Green Mountains and Lake Champlain. He was also certain that New Hampshire would oppose the separatist movement with force of arms. That he was correct in assuming that New

Hampshire leaders were also alarmed is evident from a letter that New Hampshire Congressman Josiah Bartlett wrote to New Hampshire President Meshech Weare in early August. While he blamed the secession movement on the "condescending" manner of the new state of New Hampshire toward the valley citizens, Bartlet still considered Vermont part of New Hampshire. The New Hampshire grants, he wrote, "fell into the snare laid for them by New York." New York was still pressing its claim to Vermont, and Vermont needed New Hampshire's support in Congress if it wanted statehood. Now the New Hampshire state government would surely join New York in opposing Vermont. That Allen was also "banishing" New Yorkers as Loyalists, Bartlett wrote, was being "loudly Complained of" by New York.[17]

As Allen rode home from imprisonment, Bartlett was one of his traveling companions and the two became fast friends, but now Bartlett was spreading New Hampshire's protest to other New England delegates in Congress and "some others." Over a month's time, Bartlett started referring to "the nominal state of Vermont" in correspondence back home to New Hampshire. His fellow congressmen advised him to bring the matter before the entire Congress. In the ensuing debate, Bartlett wrote to Weare, "Every person who Spoke on the Subject Severely Condemned the Conduct of the Revolted Towns of Vermont." Congress scheduled a special session to debate the controversy on August 18, but an unforeseen emergency forced a one-day postponement.[18]

THE OVERTHROW OF royal government in New York had only led to a few new riders on the old hobbyhorse of Vermont land titles. The latest New York governor to menace Vermont was the unforgiving and pertinacious George Clinton, who had chaired the committee that wrote the Bloody Acts and would always consider Allen an outlaw. He was now trying to assert the jurisdiction of the new state of New York over Vermont. In ten years, Vermont's population had increased tenfold, making the prize of cultivated farmland even more attractive. Clinton issued a proclamation, offering to confirm the titles of all lands that had actually been settled in exchange for Vermont's acknowledgment of New York's jurisdiction. In addition, he offered to rescind the Bloody Acts. Sharpening his quills, Allen pointed out that this law, like all the old New York laws, had died a natural death along with the end of royal rule:

> In the lifetime of this act, I was called by the *Yorkers* an outlaw, and afterwards by the *British* was called a rebel. . . . I humbly conceive, that there was as much propriety in the one name as the other. . . . I verily believe, that the king's commissioners would now be as willing to pardon me for the sin of rebellion, provided I would afterwards be subject to *Britain*, as the [New York] legislature, provided I would be subject to *New-York* . . . I must confess, I had as leave be a subject to the one as the other. . . .[19]

Breaking into prose, Allen attacked New York's claims in the *Connecticut Courant*. His aggressive narrative defense of Vermont's rights, the pamphlet-length *An Animadversory Address to the Inhabitants of the State of Vermont*, derided Governor Clinton's "folly and stupidity" for writing "romantic proclamations" that were "calculated to deceive woods people." He knew that Vermont's "woods people" always snapped up his heated prose. When Clinton opened his copy of the *Courant*, he was infuriated, barely able to restrain himself from leading a military force to attack Vermont. He fumed at Allen's "impudence and treason." The public vituperation between these two founding fathers delighted British officials, who wrote home to London that the rivalry might be turned to His Majesty's benefit. The Loyalist secret agent Andrew Elliott reported to London that "Governor" Allen would "be superior to Clinton" unless the Continental Congress sent troops into Vermont in support of New York.[20]

AS THE DEBATE in Congress over Vermont statehood loomed, Vermont needed a diplomat, someone who had the stature and the respect of members of Congress. Chittenden appointed Allen as Vermont's official agent to the Continental Congress. He was to be part diplomat and part lobbyist, with the power to negotiate. The title of agent was familiar to many congressmen: Benjamin Franklin had long served as the agent for American colonies to Parliament in London. Chittenden and his "junto" rightly believed that, if anyone could win Vermont's admission to the Union, it was Vermont's best emissary, Ethan Allen.

What may have precipitated Allen's appointment was a letter to Chittenden from New Hampshire's president, Meshech Weare, formally protesting Vermont's annexation of the sixteen towns. Chittenden was in high dudgeon. Weare addressed him as "Hon. Thomas Chittenden, Esq." instead of "Governor" because, Weare was insisting, Vermont hadn't been recognized as a state. The towns' secession, Weare argued, made as little sense as if Boston were to secede from Massachusetts or Hartford from Connecticut and then transferred their allegiance to New Hampshire. While the letter infuriated Chittenden, Allen had the imagination to see a way to use Weare's protest as a bargaining chip in Congress.

Between the intransigence of New York and the threat of military intervention if New Hampshire persuaded the Continental Congress that Vermont had illegally seized its towns, Allen saw an opening that, he persuaded Vermont's leaders, could lead to statehood after all. Scarcely three months after his release as a haggard, enfeebled prisoner of war, he rode some three hundred miles on horseback in ten days over rutted roads from southern Vermont down through the familiar Berkshire Hills of Massachusetts and Connecticut, crossing the Hudson at Fishkill, skirting British lines as he swung west into Pennsylvania and down the Post Road.

As was his custom, with his new appointment and with his latest anti–New York screed in hand, he rode to Hartford and personally delivered it to the press of Watson and Goodwin in Hartford. As he waited for Watson to run off enough copies for him to blanket Congress, Allen made a side trip to Salisbury and sold a 300-acre Vermont farm for £1 an acre, pocketing enough cash to pay the printer and advance his travel expenses. Ira awaited him at Heman's house, where they decided to bring suit for a £5,000 bill for flour their brother had sold a merchant. Ethan and Ira now were the only surviving partners in the Onion River Land Company. Ethan remained sales manager, even if, for the rest of the war, much of its holdings were behind enemy lines. Ira, meanwhile, vastly increased the company's inventory by accepting grants of land along the Canadian border from Governor Chittenden in lieu of salaries for his Vermont offices.

ON THE MORNING of September 19, 1778, congressmen made their way on horseback and on foot through the denuded streets of Philadelphia to Independence Hall for a critical debate on the Vermont problem. As Allen rode down Second Street into the square mile of redbrick that once again was the new nation's capital, he could see the most visible scar of British occupation: all the trees cut down from streets that now only bore symbolic names—

Pine, Walnut, Chestnut, Cherry—to provide firewood, barracks, and barricades for the British the preceding winter. Everywhere in the Quaker city, he could see guard boxes and sentry posts, most notably around Independence Hall. What he found inside was hardly encouraging. New Hampshire's delegates had laid the petitions and correspondence between the breakaway towns and Vermont before the entire Congress, which was sitting as the committee of the whole. It was to be decided that very day, and he could hear only criticism of Vermont.

Stalling for time, Allen maneuvered quickly. He took Josiah Bartlett aside before Congress could convene and before the doors could be locked for the executive session, keeping him out. He assured Bartlett that he, too, personally opposed the annexation. Bartlett seemed pleased to find that Allen agreed with New Hampshire's position, and Allen now felt he would have New Hampshire on his side when the debate shifted to New York's opposition to Vermont statehood. Allen implored Bartlett not to press Congress for immediate action until he had a chance to rush back to Vermont and confer with his assembly when it reconvened in three weeks. He assured Bartlett that the assembly would rescind its vote and disclaim any annexation of New Hampshire territory. If that failed, Allen said, he would personally petition Congress to block the annexation at that time and personally deliver the petition to Congress and use all his influence to prevent anything as unjust as this union. Confidently, Bartlett wrote to Weare, "He informs me the vote [in the Vermont Assembly] was past by a Small majority soon after his Return home. . . . He [said he] will use Every other means in his power to procure New Hampshire Redress against So unjust and impolitic a measure." Here, Allen was equivocating. Even though the vote in the Vermont Assembly had been close, the vote in the individual town meetings had been overwhelmingly in favor of annexation.

Bartlett also assured Weare that Allen would "immediately write to you & inform you what the Assembly Shall Do" whether "they Rescind it or not." Allen also had promised he would "write to our Delegates here [in Philadelphia] or Come himself [to New Hampshire] in Case their assembly Does not Renounce their Connection to those Towns." Allen's direct, persuasive approach won over Bartlett, who had by now learned that other congressmen wanted to seek a peaceful settlement. "At this critical time," Bartlett told Weare, he decided not to exercise New Hampshire's prerogative and press the whole Congress for action against Vermont.[21]

But Allen was not relying entirely on New Hampshire's good will. He may have learned from Bartlett that New York's delegates to Congress had written to Governor Clinton to send a committee to New Hampshire to consider what joint action the two states should take against Vermont. Bartlett recommended to Weare that New Hampshire steer clear of any such action, "as the Claim of New York to the whole of Vermont, in my opinion, is not better founded than is the Claim of New Hampshire." He warned against lumping the annexation controversy with "the old Dispute" of who owned the New Hampshire Grants. With Bartlett neutralized at least for the moment, Allen busily blanketed Congress with copies of his *Animadversions* against New York's claims and buttonholed the president of Congress, Henry Laurens, who remembered well the emaciated prisoner of war now reincarnated as a diplomat. In confidence, Laurens assured Allen that, if Vermont dissolved the union with the sixteen towns, he had no objection to Vermont becoming a state and taking its place in Congress.

Allen's first triumph as Vermont's agent to Congress came at a cost—to him personally. When some friendly members of Congress introduced a resolution to give him an active-duty commission in the Continental army with a full colonel's pay, a New York delegate, Gouverneur Morris, moved that the rank be only a brevet, or temporary, grade, which carried lower pay, and blocked a field commission. "He would certainly have had the Commission," Morris wrote to Governor Clinton, "if I had not learnt that he hath lately interfered" by opposing "the authority of the State of New York." Morris wrote Clinton that Vermont had "debauched" the annexed towns. He saw to it that Allen's pay would be only $75 a month in badly depreciated Continental money—if and when Allen could collect it at all. That gave Allen one more reason to despise New York.[22]

IT MAY BE surprising to learn that Ethan Allen never held an elective office. He was the man who was associated by most of his contemporaries, inside and outside Vermont, American, French, British, or Loyalist, as the epitome of the Vermonter, the champion of the woods people he organized, led, and fought to keep independent, even if the majority of woods people didn't share his ability at land speculations that actually created some dissonance between his public image and his personal character. The town fathers either loved or hated him, but they all realized that it was Allen who was the most recognizable and, by many, respected Vermonter. The Green Mountain Boys who were willing to risk their lives and their homesteads had elected him their leader, their colonel commandant, but it was Allen who never accepted elective political office, and when he once had a narrow brush, refused to meet the terms required of him, because it meant going against his idea of freedom.

After his hero's homecoming, the people of the town of Arlington elected him their delegate to the Vermont Assembly on Freeman's Meeting Day in September of 1778. He was away at the Continental Congress when the men of Arlington enthusiastically elected him. When he returned to Vermont, Allen declined the office. The town's freemen then called a special town meeting and chose Matthew Lyon, Allen's adjutant in the attack on Fort Ticonderoga, to serve in his stead, but Lyon's record was blemished by a court-martial after a charge of cowardice when he abandoned the stockade at Jericho as the British approached in 1776. Lyon was acquitted by a court-martial over which Allen presided. The disputatious "Spitting Lion" would one day win the distinction of becoming the only American elected to Congress from three different states. At first representing Vermont, he would fight a duel with fireplace tools on the floor of Congress, then distinguish himself as the only congressman jailed under the Alien and Sedition Acts. When the assembly voted in October 1778 to disqualify Lyon, Chittenden asked Allen to fill the seat temporarily. Allen hesitated, then agreed, but when it came his turn to take the oath of office in Windsor's Congregational meetinghouse, where the assembly was in session, and he learned that he would have to acknowledge the divine inspiration of the Bible and the Puritan creed, Allen refused, making himself ineligible to serve in the assembly.

Allen would attend all of the assembly's sessions anyway for many years, even serving ex officio as militia commander on several key legislative committees. His suggestions cropped up everywhere: when Governor Chittenden decided there should be a state seal, Allen urged that it should contain a tree and a cow. According to local legend, Chittenden drew the great walnut tree he could see out his commandeered window in Arlington. Since Allen could not in good conscience serve as a town representative, to legitimize his participation in Vermont government at all levels the assembly voted him the rank of brigadier general of militia. He retained his rank of colonel in the Continental army, establishing the enduring tradition that the head of the Vermont

National Guard carried both ranks, a generalship at home and a colonelcy on national business.

ALLEN'S REPORT OF his mission to the Continental Congress set off a debate that raged for ten days in October of 1778. Unless the assembly rescinded its annexation of New Hampshire towns, the entire political and military power of the United States would be unleashed against Vermont. As he stood facing a barrage of questions, Elisha Payne, a delegate from Cardigan, one of the towns, asked Allen whether the New Hampshire congressmen had agreed to urge their assembly to support Vermont in its fight against New York if Vermont agreed to rescission. A flushed Allen responded, "Yes, they did, upon honor." Still, there was no motion to dissolve the annexation. Instead, an assembly committee wrote up a justification for annexation to send to New Hampshire's assembly. Allen's promise to Bartlett of a speedy rescission drifted away as seven and then eight days produced only more committees threatening to draft letters to New Hampshire and Congress.

Exasperated, Allen finally hit upon a stratagem to outflank opponents in the assembly. When the assembly formed yet another committee to divide the state into four counties, Allen went to work out of doors. On Wednesday, October 21, a motion to leave the counties as they were passed by a 35–26 vote, the sixteen towns included in the minority. Clearly, Allen had mustered more than a three-to-one margin of the original forty-five towns' representatives. When a motion was introduced to include the sixteen New Hampshire towns in Cumberland County, across the river, it failed by a 33–28 vote. The same lopsided majority defeated a final motion to form the sixteen towns into a separate county. Allen's strategy had triumphed, leaving Vermont intact.

Settling into his Bennington house for the winter of 1778,

Allen finished writing his first attack on New York and its claim to the lands of Vermont since his return from captivity. On December 28, after riding across the mountains to Sharon, he intercepted a postrider with instructions to ride quickly to the printshop of Watson and Goodwin, printers of the *Connecticut Courant*, in Hartford with the manuscript of An *Animadversory Address to the Inhabitants of the State of Vermont*:

> *Gentlemen*
>
> *I send you by Mr Auldin the Post an Answer to Governor Clinton's Proclamation which I Expect you will Insert in your Courant you will Correct the Spelling and make proper stops I Desire you would send me by the Post which comes to Arlington Eight Dozen of the Papers without fail.—Col. Samuel Elmoor [sic] will send you the Cash by the Post as well for Inserting the answer as for the Eight Dozen Papers Extraordinary pray you do not fail as this is of Importance to the State of Vermont to have a Circulation Thro, the Chanel of Your Paper.*[23]

As WINTER SNOWS grounded Ethan Allen in Arlington in January of 1779, he sat down day after day to work on a narrative of his years of captivity at the hands of the British. He reserved his harshest condemnation for the Loyalists who had made his suffering greater at so many junctures, naming the Americans who treated him far worse than the English, whom he often praised as gentlemen. Chief among his nemeses was the merchant Brook Watson, who had consigned Allen and his men to a foul, freezing box in irons belowdecks on the *Gaspee* as they sat in the St. Lawrence and crossed the Atlantic, and who would shortly become lord mayor of London. He pillorized the former Crown officials of New York who had claimed Vermont lands before the war and then, as Loyalists, saw to it that Allen nearly starved to death during a month in irons as a man-of-war delivered him to a jail cell in Halifax; he vilified Loyalists on Long Island who had thrown him into the dungeon at the Provost jail in New York City after he dared to witness the wretched conditions that other prisoners of war were enduring.

During his congressional visits to Philadelphia, Allen became aware that his old rival, now Major General Benedict Arnold, the military governor of Philadelphia, was coddling the capital city's Loyalists. Allen resented that Loyalists could thrive so soon after collaborating with the British during their occupation of the city. To Allen, Arnold especially seemed disloyal, but he soon pieced together the narrative of Arnold's success since their respective abortive attempts to conquer Canada.

After Allen sailed beyond Arnold's ability to rescue him opposite Quebec in November of 1775, Arnold was seriously wounded when he stormed the walled city, yet he was able to maintain a feeble siege until reinforced by nearly ten thousand New England troops. Twice superseded in command, when both generals and half their uninoculated men died of small-pox, Arnold was left to lead a pell-mell retreat from Canada with a large British army, sent from England, close on his heels. Building a makeshift navy in the summer of 1776, he fought a British naval squadron to a standstill at the Battle of Valcour Island but was again passed over for promotion and once again resigned. Washington coaxed him back into uniform to reinforce Philip Schuyler's defenses in northern New York as the British once more invaded down Lake Champlain. In a pair of battles near Saratoga, Arnold blunted the British advance in a reckless charge against a Hessian redoubt, shattering British morale— and receiving a second and crippling bullet wound in his right leg. Unable to sit on a horse, Arnold was given the rear-area post of Philadelphia's military governor.

There, cash-strapped after his merchant fleet rotted at the dock in New Haven, Arnold turned to investing in privateering vessels and opened a store where he sold captured British goods. Always living well beyond his income, he fumed as congressmen visited him at mealtimes, even as they refused to pay him five years in back wages. At the same time, he attended dancing assemblies frequented by Loyalists. At one, he met Peggy Shippen, eighteen-year-old daughter of a former British judge. Arnold's very public courtship and lavish marriage angered revolutionary leaders, who untimately accused him of eight counts of malfeasance and non-feasance in office. When Washington, preoccupied with fighting the British, did not respond to Arnold's demands for his support and allowed Arnold's court-martial, with his wife's assistance he opened up an eighteen-month clandestine correspondence with the British secret service. The two ambitious men who had heroically charged together through the wicket gate at Fort Ticonderoga in the opening days of the long war had followed sharply different trajectories, reflecting the divergent paths of the Revolution.

BETWEEN LOBBYING CALLS and days of debates in Independence Hall, Ethan Allen delivered the manuscript of his captivity narrative to Philadelphia's best printer, Robert Bell, who had set the type for the Declaration of Independence. Allen was enormously gratified when his memoir first appeared serialized in the *Pennsylvania Packet* and then as the book *A Narrative of the Captivity of Colonel Ethan*. An immediate success, Allen's narrative riveted a populace still at war and instilled a patriotic feeling into a beleaguered people. As Allen became a symbol of triumph over captivity, his book was reprinted eight times before the Revolution was over and then became one of the most widely read books during the first half of the nineteenth century. In 1780, eight new editions came off the printing presses in Philadelphia, Boston, Salem and Newburyport, Massachusetts, and Norwich, Connecticut, where its publisher was Governor Jonathan Trumbull, the man who had launched Allen on his military career four years earlier and followed it ever since. As the historian Edwin G. Burrows has put it, "No one before Allen had given the reading public a full-length, firsthand, blow-by-blow account of what it was like to be caught and held by the enemy." In fact, Allen's classic captivity narrative became the second best-selling book of the American Revolution, after Tom Paine's *Common Sense*. No one familiar with Allen or the conditions he described ever refuted his version of events. His narrative inspired Philip Freneau, who was America's leading eighteenth-century poet, after reading Allen's slender memoir, to pen his epic poem *The British Prison-Ship*. Together, the two works rekindled the flagging determination of many Patriots, identifying the Loyalists as the Patriots' implacable foes as well as revealing in detail the monstrously inhumane British policy toward their prisoners of war.[24]

STIRRED BY THE SPECTER of a civil war inside Vermont, Allen turned next to literary combat against New York. He had fresh cause to unsheath his pen when he learned that New York's latest governor, George Clinton, had written to Pelatiah Fitch, a friend in the pro–New York southeast of Vermont, urging armed resistance to Vermont's authority in the lower Connecticut Valley towns, which preferred to be part of New York, regardless of the geographical barriers imposed by the Green Mountains and western Vermont. Clinton either was forgetting natural obstacles or was supremely confident that a weakened Vermont would ultimately, entirely be part of New York. At least for the past year, Clinton had made no secret of his confidence that the Continental Congress would concur in his wisdom. He had, in fact, written a proclamation and sent it to Congress, urging it to come to some decision, blaming Vermont for the controversy, and warning that their intransigence would soon bring on a civil war.

Allen recognized Clinton's campaign as a serious threat to Vermont's survival, and he saw the danger that infighting between states could pose to the outcome of the Revolution. He set to work composing a response to Clinton and Vermont's ancient rivals in New York that encompassed the entire frontier controversy and included documents dating back to the English chartering of New York in 1664. In part, he recapitulated his 1774 *Brief Narrative*, but he then went much farther, in both its more sarcastic tone and its exhaustive content, writing *A Vindication of the Opposition of the Inhabitants of Vermont to the Government of New-York, and of Their Right to Form an Independent State*. The governor's council had only expected a pamphlet; Allen wrote a 178-page book that he personally delivered to all the members of the Continental Congress and sent to every general in the Continental army and state militias.

In a thumb-in-the-eye call to action, Allen opened fire:

One reason why this [New York] government have not already destroyed the inhabitants of the *New-Hampshire* grants, with fire and sword, is their want of ability.... The common people in the government, are universally of opinion that the inhabitants [of the Grants] have a good right to those lands, and should not be molested in the peaceable enjoyment of them.... [W]hen laws in their original design and administration [have] degenerated from the good ends for which laws and government were instituted, terminating in the ruin and destruction of the society it should secure and protect, from the same principles, viz. self-preservation, the subjects are obliged to resist and depose such government.[25]

Allen made no distinction between New York's royalist leaders under British government and Clinton and his revolutionary colleagues:

The government of *New-York* make the greatest outcry against her sister colonies, taxing them with intrusion, violence and encroachment and, at the same time, are flagrantly more guilty of the same avaricious, unjust, and hostile wickedness. . . .[26]

Chiding New York's governor for the legalistic language he used to argue New York's case, Allen made it clear that he could see a class element to the revolutionary struggle. He was blunt about the need for farmers to be on an equal footing with wealthy speculators and land barons in a true revolution:

Labouring men that support the world of mankind, are obliged to form their judgments of the jurisdiction of governments by the common received opinions of mankind they are conversant with.[27]

Allen's line of reasoning would resonate better with his New England neighbors, he believed. Yet one barrier he could not easily overcome: the absence of a single printer, of a single printing press, in Vermont left him at the mercy of weather and season to get his message into print where he could counteract the effusions of New York's press. The nearest presses were at

Hartford, Connecticut, or Exeter and Portsmouth, across the Green Mountains and the White Mountains from the seat of Vermont's government. They were under the control of the New Hampshire government and not available for such a revolutionary publication.

Help came from an unexpected quarter. Eleazar Wheelock, president of Dartmouth, was equally worried that eastern New Hampshire would continue to exploit western New Hampshire's attempt to be annexed by Vermont unless the college had a printing press. The eastern interests were pouring out what he considered propaganda from a press only eighty miles away, propaganda that would "wholly defeat the desire as well as the purpose of the College" unless a printer and a press could be brought across the mountains. "Pray don't fail," he wrote to the trustee Benjamin Pomeroy in Connecticut.[28]

In June, only a few weeks after Allen's exchange, the Reverend Wheelock sent his son, the Continental army lieutenant colonel John Wheelock, to Connecticut, where Governor Trumbull offered to help him find a printer and a press. By mid-July of 1778, a press and a printer had been located, but there were unexpected delays in getting it to Dartmouth. The press was the one brought from England in 1638 by Stephen Daye shortly after the founding of Harvard College, where it printed the first hymnbook in America, the *Bay Colony Psalmody*, as well as the first Indian Bible. After long service at Harvard, it was sold to the Green family in Connecticut. So rare were printing presses in war-torn New England that a 150-year-old press was still coveted. The Green family of printers now promised to send the Daye press to Dartmouth College. (It resides today in the Vermont Historical Society Museum in Montpelier.) At the time, however, a few obstacles remained. On July 16, Timothy Green wrote the Reverend Wheelock that delivering the heavy press and its lead fonts would have to wait a while longer. "One of the oxen is lame," Green explained, "and the cart is unfit." Alden Spooner, the printer Green had hired to set up the press in Hanover, would be able to leave Norwich as soon as the ox recovered and the printer returned from a privateering mission at sea.[29]

By the autumn, ox and press were en route to the wilderness campus and the printer safely ensconced in the basement of Dartmouth Hall in Hanover. At Ethan Allen's insistence, the Vermont General Assembly appointed Judah Paddock and Alden Spooner as official printers for the state of Vermont. In the next year, no one kept them busier than the eager Allen, who rushed the publication of *Vindication* so much that wet ink smeared its final pages. He then stuffed copies into his saddlebags and rode off once again to demand that the Continental Congress admit Vermont to the Union.

15.

"A Hook in the Nose"

❊

WHEN FRANCE ENTERED the American Revolution in 1778 after the American victory at Saratoga, the war was transformed from being primarily a land war to being a worldwide naval war. The British held on to strong posts in Quebec, Halifax, and New York City but shifted to a strategy of defensive war coupled with diplomacy and espionage. From the headquarters of Sir Henry Clinton in New York City, the British secret service, headed by Major John André, was working to detach disgruntled Americans from their loyalty to the Continental Congress. On March 30, 1780, Ethan Allen was riding down the high street in Arlington, Vermont, when a man in the garb of a farmer galloped up and handed him an envelope. While the man waited, Allen tore open the seal and quickly scanned the letter. Waving the messenger off, he nudged his horse toward the home of Governor Chittenden, where he had been going for the council's daily working meeting. "Within ten minutes," he later wrote to the Continental Congress, he had turned the envelope over to the governor.[1]

At first glance, Chittenden might have been offended: the letter was addressed to "Governor Allen" by Colonel Beverley Robinson of the King's American Regiment, a Loyalist unit based in New York City. Robinson, a high-ranking Loyalist working closely with the British secret service, was already deeply involved in clandestine negotiations with Benedict Arnold to betray West Point and its garrison. Robinson wrote to Allen, "I have often been informed that you & most of the Inhabitants of Vermont, are opposed to the wild and chimerical scheme of the americans; in attempts to separate this Continent from Great Britain & to Establish an Independt State of their own. . . ." Perhaps inadvertently, Robinson was acknowledging the existence of Vermont by referring to its chosen name, while Congress and neighboring states still insisted on nebulous circumlocutions.

Not the first New York land baron to offer Allen a bribe, this time more than a horse and a little cash, the Loyalist leader was writing secretly to offer to make Allen a Loyalist general if he would take "an active part [in] embolding the Inhabitants of Vermont in favour of the Crown." How this must have echoed James Duane and James Tabor Kempe's bid, a decade earlier, for Allen's aid in evicting settlers from their New Hampshire–granted lands or, five years earlier, from royal officials during his incarceration in England. Each bribe offer lefthandedly acknowledged Allen's preeminence as the leader of the people of Vermont. Now, in return for Allen's support, Vermont could "obtain a separate Government under the King & constitution of England." Allen could, if he accepted Robinson's offer and won the certain approval of British commander in chief, Sir Henry Clinton, from Loyalist regiments "under such officers as you shall Recommend." The letter implied that Allen would be placed at the head of a new royal province's government and have all his land grants confirmed by the king. If Allen took the offer as an insult, the Loyalist leader asked only that he allow the courier to "return in safety." If he went along with the scheme and Clinton balked, "the matter shall be buried in oblivion between us."[2]

Allen later said that he at once grasped that here was an opportunity to neutralize the continuing threat to Vermont from British ships and Loyalist and Indians raiding parties that continued, year after year, to attack all along the shores of Lake Champlain and deep into its river valleys. At the same time, to appear to play along with Colonel Robinson might bring pressure on the Continental Congress to recognize the importance of continued Vermont support at a time when the Revolution appeared to be stalemated. Robinson's remarkable letter arrived at a propitious moment, as Ethan, not averse to playing both sides against the middle, could see. The governor's council had just received another stinging rebuke from the Continental Congress. Many members, swayed by intransigent New York delegates, insisted that, even by entertaining the annexation of towns in New Hampshire, Vermont had subverted the unity of the United States. Although towns in New Hampshire and along the upper Hudson had sought annexation to Vermont to assure protection against British raiders from Canada, Congress and the governments of both New Hampshire and New York were blaming Vermont and were less likely than ever to admit Vermont to the Union. Surrounded by enemies, Allen was ready for a new line of attack. He urged Chittenden and his half dozen other councillors to keep quiet about Robinson's letter while they considered the possibilities for exploiting it.

About one o'clock on the hot afternoon of May 31, 1780, Keziah Taylor, seven, and her sister Betsey, five, wandered into the dense forest around her family farm in Sunderland. Three hours later, their anxious father, Eldad, knocked on the door of neighbor Ethan Allen's cottage: would he join a search party? At dusk, some one hundred men clambered into the underbrush, bearing torches and blowing hunting horns as they searched fruitlessly all night. The next day, more men and women came from nearby towns. By the third day, about seven hundred men, some from Massachusetts and New York, joined the desperate round-the-clock effort. That afternoon, milling around Taylor's farmhouse, the weary rescuers were debating calling off the hunt when Allen leapt onto a stump and berated them. They were parents. How could they think of leaving the children "perishing with hunger and spending their last strength in crying for their father and mother"? Allen vowed he would go on searching until he found the girls or died trying. Who would join him? Instructing the men to march an arm's length apart, he told them not to fire a gun until they found the "lost girls." Four hours later, a captain of the Green Mountain Boys discovered the girls asleep under a tree, unharmed. They had survived on berries.[3]

THE BRITISH HOPED, by bribe and espionage, to lure Vermont back into the British Empire, thus driving a wedge between New York and New England; at the same time, they set out to prevent another American attack on Canada from the Hudson River forts, where George Washington was now basing the bulk of his army. In Quebec Province, General Frederick Haldimand, the Swiss-born former second-in-command to General Howe, had become governor-general of Canada, replacing Sir Guy Carleton, who had been superseded for failing to retake Lake Champlain and its forts in the 1776 campaign. Each year, from his base in Montreal, Haldimand launched attacks down both shores of the lake. Convinced by his spies that a combined Franco-American force would try to liberate French-speaking Quebec and add it to the United States, Haldimand maintained bases at Fort Ticonderoga, Crown Point, and Ile aux Noix, five miles inside Canada, and sent raiding parties of ever greater strength against Vermont. Haldimand worried that Allen and his Green Mountain militia,

> once united with Congress, would be very formidable enemies, having been from their early contests with their neighboring province continually in arms. . . . They are in every respect better provided than the Continental troops, and in their principles more determined. [They are] ready to a man to turn out upon the first alarm with provisions upon their backs. . . . [They] have always made me anxious to prevent the Union [with the United States] they seem so bent upon accomplishing.[4]

There had been sporadic raids ever since the first British invasion of 1776. As Burgoyne's army marched south in 1777, Indians raided into Vermont's northern valleys, burning houses, barns, and crops on isolated farms and taking men and boys as prisoners to Montreal's jails.

Shortly after Allen's appointment as brigadier general and before he could build up supplies and enlistments, Haldimand decided to launch an attack on the Allens' settlements in the Winooski Valley. A combined force of Loyalists and Mohawk Indians broke up after squabbling. Their July 28 raid "only destroyed some barns and a couple of mills upon the lower part of the Onion River," Haldimand reported to Secretary of State Germain in London. He explained that his next target would be settlements from Crown Point to Ticonderoga that could supply provisions for an American army attacking Quebec from the south. Haldimand intended to destroy those farms after hauling the hay north on shipboard to feed the king's horses.[4]

In late September, Benedict Arnold's plot to turn over West Point to the British and, with it, Washington and his visiting suite of generals collapsed when Major André, appointed by Clinton to head his secret service, ignored Clinton's instructions and was captured in civilian clothes behind American lines with detailed schematics of West Point and reports on troop strengths hidden in his unmistakable English boot. By this time, Colonel Robinson had sent copies of his original letter of enticement to Allen, and twice more the governor's council had decided to shelve them. Within the next month, Haldimand unleashed two devastating British raids on Vermont. In the first, on October 16, a British force of regimental strength that included some three hundred Mohawks descended on the widely scattered farmsteads along the White River, destroying dozens of homes and barns, killing livestock, and burning the town of Royalton. Of the four settlers killed, the Indians speared two men in revenge for the killings of two Indians before the war.

Obviously demonstrating the consequences of ignoring Colonel Robinson's blandishments, only one week later the British attacked again, in even greater force. On October 24, Colonel Christopher Carleton, a nephew of Sir Guy Carleton who adopted the Indian lifestyle, bore Mohawk tattoos, painted his face, and married an Indian woman, attacked Vermont with a mixed force of a thousand troops, including Loyalists, Hessians, and a hundred Mohawks. War canoes flanked two men-of-war, the *Lady Maria* and the *Carleton*, named after the major's aunt and uncle, as the flotilla sailed south, attacking settlements and gathering prisoners as it went, and sending them north to the Montreal jail. By the time Carleton reached Fort Ticonderoga, forty Vermonters shivered under a tent on the *Lady Maria*'s deck. On November 6, Carleton's force reached Otter Creek and destroyed all the buildings and supplies below Middlebury Falls. It next attacked up Otter Creek, burning cabins and seizing seven settlers at Weybridge who had not heeded warnings of the attack. At Panton, it destroyed the home of Peter Ferris, a Quaker who had bought his lakefront land from the Allens. While their home burned, Ferris and his son, deer hunting across the lake, were captured when they returned. Four more prisoners were taken at New Haven. In all, Carleton shipped off fifty-one prisoners to Canada: en route, a handful managed to escape, including Allen's brother-in-law Israel Brownson, who had served with him at Ticonderoga and Montreal and once before been a British prisoner. (Brownson was either the luckiest or the unluckiest man in Vermont: thrice a prisoner of war, he was shot thirteen times during the Revolution and survived.) In all, Carleton's raiders destroyed seven buildings and "four month's provisions for 12,000 men," he reported to Governor Haldimand.[5]

As if strategically timed to coincide with Carleton's raid, the arrival of a British cutter in East Bay off Castleton four days later signaled the onset of two years of secret negotiations between Ethan Allen and a British spy who was a former member of the Green Mountain Boys. Representing Haldimand, Lieutenant Colonel Justus Sherwood of the Queen's Rangers landed at the Mills, a frontier outpost of Vermont's militia four miles west of the Castleton blockhouse, under a flag of truce with a "drum, fife and two men." Before he was blindfolded and led to Colonel Samuel Herrick's quarters, Sherwood, as he later reported to Haldimand, calculated that the troop strength at the outpost was a mere three hundred. A former Green Mountain Boy who had left his farm at New Haven on the Lake Champlain shore and fled to Canada during the 1776 British invasion, he had formed a Loyalist corps and commanded it in the battles at Saratoga. Agent 008 in the British secret service, he supervised all British intelligence activities in Vermont, running a network of spies based in Montreal. Allen certainly knew this.

When Herrick "demanded my business," Sherwood wrote, "I informed him I was sent by Major Carleton to negotiate a cartel for the exchange of prisoners." More importantly, Sherwood carried dispatches from General Haldimand to Allen and Vermont Governor Chittenden. Herrick told Sherwood that "General Allen commanded at Castleton and that my dispatches should be forwarded without delay." The next day, October 29, 1780, Sherwood noted in his journal, he "had an interview with General Allen." After breakfast, they "removed to Major [Isaac] Clark's house":

> General Allen summoned a council of ten field officers and informed them that I was sent to negotiate a cartel for exchange of prisoners but as he found that my instructions was [sic] somewhat discretionary he desired, previous to entering on business to have a short conference with me by himself that he might clearly understand my ideas and assist me in explaining my business to them. To this they consented.

Sherwood reported to General Haldimand,

> I walked out with him and after much conversation informed him that I had some business of importance with him, but before I communicated it must request his honor as a gentleman that, should it not please him, he would take no advantage of me nor ever mention it while I remain in the country. He said he would if it was no Arnold plan

to sell his country and his own honor by betraying the trust reposed in him.

Sherwood also reported that he told Allen "that General Haldimand was no stranger to their disputes with the other states" and that "His Excellency was perfectly well informed of all that had lately passed between Congress and Vermont and of the fixed intentions of Congress never to there being a separate state." From Allen's "common character," Congress was only duping the Vermonters and waited for a favorable opportunity to crush them, that this was a proper time for them to cast off the Congress yoke and resume their former allegiance to the king of Great Britain:

> General Allen observed that the proposals so far had not the weight of a straw with him, that he was not to be purchased at any rate, that he had been offered a lieutenant colonel's commission while in captivitiy which he refused . . . but that since the proposals seemed materially to concern the whole people of Vermont whose liberties and properties for a number of years past was much dearer to him than his own life, he should take them into very serious consideration. He then said we must go in as we had already been too long together.

Allen and Sherwood had "another short conference that evening" and the next day, October 30. Sherwood "conversed with him till 2 o'clock free of any restraint" and told him, "I had brought written proposals with me and had secreted them but could procure them if he thought proper. He advised me to let them rest."

In his lengthy report, long overlooked by American historians, Sherwood summarized "our several conferences."

General Allen says he finds himself surrounded by enemies on every side, the most inveterate is New York; that
he is heartily weary of war and wishes once more to devote
himself to his philosophical studies . . . that nothing short
of the same tyrannical proceedings from Congress towards
Vermont which Congress at first complained of suffering
from Great Britain . . . should ever cause him to deviate
from the cause. . . .

Allen would consider a truce and a prisoner exchange, and
would listen to further suggestions by Haldimand just so long as
Haldimand would propose "no damned Arnold plan to sell his
country and his honor by betraying the trust reposed in him."[6]

Yet he then dangled the intelligence that Vermont would
soon publish a manifesto that it would "declare herself a neutral
power," cease sending troops and supplies to support the Continental army, and "invite all people to a free trade with her."
Allen promised to send his brother Ira and Major Daniel Fay to
negotiate the prisoner cartel. Meanwhile, for his part, Sherwood
promised there would be no further British attacks on Vermont
or the northeastern frontier of New York during their negotiations. Should New York attack Vermont, the British would have
a force ready to protect Vermont. In that extremity, Allen would
"expect to command his own forces." But "Vermont must be a
government separate from and independent of any other province
in America."[7]

THE CEASE-FIRE THAT Allen had arranged with the British
command in Canada under the guise of an exchange of prisoners
of war prevented any further British attacks on the shores of Lake
Champlain for the next three years. He seems not to have enter-

tained any question whether Governor Chittenden and the other Vermont leaders he let in on the secret compact would repudiate it or chastise him for it. Allen was never more confident that he spoke for Vermont. Indeed, Carleton's raid had already convinced Chittenden and the other members of the executive council that they could no longer ignore British overtures. When another copy of Robinson's March 30 letter arrived under flag of truce, the governor's council, aware of intense espionage taking place all around them, decided to keep entirely secret all meetings and correspondence with the British while they carried out private talks that might provide leverage in pursuing admission to the Continental Congress over New York's adamant objections. Now, as a result of Haldimand's overtures, Allen was able to drag out, until war's end, the secret negotiations for a cartel to exchange all Vermont prisoners of war incarcerated in Montreal for the Loyalist and British prisoners held in the Windsor jail. All this time, Allen, through his trusted intermediaries Ira Allen and Daniel Fay, led Haldimand and his seconds to believe that the citizens of the republic of Vermont would, in due time and after careful preparation, return to their allegiance to the king. Concomitantly, in an attempt to win the support of any sympathetic New Yorkers, Allen insisted that the truce include northern New York. As they dragged their feet and leaked to spies for Washington and the Continental Congress that they were considering rejoining the British, the Allens became the principal negotiators with Sherwood in talks on shipboard at the British base off Crown Point and at Loyal Fort on Ile aux Noix, inside Canada, where Ira met twice with the chief British negotiator, Justus Sherwood.

Allen appears to have been sincere in negotiating a prisoner exchange as well as hoodwinking the British and manipulating congressional support, but a prisoner exchange by the Americans without the authorization of George Washington had become

impossible. The British accused the Americans of violating a surrender agreement signed by Benedict Arnold and a British officer
near Montreal during the Canadian campaign of 1776. Washington refused to allow Allen to trade prisoners taken by Major
Brown and Captain Ebenezer Allen when the Vermont regiment
took British works at Fort Ann and atop Mount Defiance, overlooking Ticonderoga, during the Saratoga campaign of 1777.
Washington insisted on his firm policy that prisoners held far
longer must be exchanged first and then rank for rank. He would
go only so far as to write to Haldimand to protest the "close and
rigorous confinement of suffering" Vermonters and demand that
officers be sent to New York City for exchange "in the due order
of their capture."[8]

BY JULY OF 1781, Washington was already planning his joint
attack with the French army and navy on British forces under
Cornwallis that had backed into a trap on the Yorktown Peninsula of Virginia, where he would appeal futilely for support by the
lethargic Clinton. After three weeks of fruitless talk between Ira
Allen and Joseph Fay at Ile aux Noix with Sherwood, Haldimand
was growing suspicious. He declared that he would give the Vermont leaders until October, when the Vermont General Assembly reconvened, to come to an agreement and meet British terms,
or he would send in his army and force a decision. Meanwhile,
Allen was spreading persistent rumors of the secret negotiations
to induce the Continental Congress to act. He was so successful
that George Washington, unnerved by Benedict Arnold's defec-
tion to the British and egged on at first by New York's General
Philip Schuyler, began to believe that Ethan Allen was indeed
a traitor and a spy and authorized Schuyler to try to arrest him.
This ruled out further visits by Allen to the Continental Con-

gress, which took him through New York. Washington actually sent to Vermont a spy, the same Ezra Hickok whom Allen had sent into Fort Ticonderoga the day before his famous attack. Hickok apparently reassured Washington about the true nature of Allen's bold gambit.

Finally, fear that Vermont and its combat-seasoned troops would accept the British offer prompted a congressional committee to recommend admitting Vermont to the confederation. On that news, a Vermont delegation led by Ira Allen hurried to Philadelphia, but by the time it arrived, it found Congress astir over captured British documents that revealed the Crown's intention to regain Vermont. Congress, also alarmed that Vermont had recently annexed corners of northern New York and Massachusetts, once again reversed itself and refused to reconsider Vermont's status until it shed all of its annexations.

For three years, the Machiavellian Ethan Allen had been playing a dangerous game, going back and forth between the British and the Continental Congress, letting each know only part of his dialogue with the other, all the time keeping Vermont on its independent course. After this latest failure to win congressional approval, Allen urged Haldimand to be patient. He confided that the Vermont General Assembly would refuse Congress's conditions for recognition. On Allen's recommendation and the junto's redoubled assurances, Haldimand prepared a proclamation confirming the terms of reentry, including confirmation of Vermont land titles, free trade with Canada, and the protection of the British army. To Allen's mind, Washington's refusal to exchange prisoners taken from the independent republic of Vermont gave him the justification he needed for Vermont to continue its own independent negotiations with Haldimand for prisoner exchanges. His negotiations finally did succeed, even without Washington's cooperation, in winning a general exchange of prisoners between

Vermont and the British. In the summer of 1781, the prisoners seized during the October 1780 raids went home.

When he at length successfully negotiated the basis for present and future exchanges, Allen wrote to Colonel Carleton, in command of the British-held fort at Crown Point, that he was pleased that "the present Cartel respects Vermont." That mattered mightily to Allen, and, at times, he must have wavered as Congress and all the surrounding states rebuffed Vermont. He was well aware that such an agreement between Haldimand and Vermont meant not only that Vermonters captured by the British could expect to be returned to their families after suffering captivity for far less time than he had but also that, as Washington must know, it was tantamount to British recognition of Vermont as an independent state. Only the British, it seemed, would acknowledge Vermont's sovereignty, its independent existence.[9]

But Allen remained cautious. Even to his old friend General John Stark, who had led Vermont and New Hampshire troops to victory in the Battle of Bennington, he refused to spell out all his dealings: "The transactions of this State in making a truce with the British" would be made plain in a manifesto at some indefinite future date. Until then, "people must be content" with "conjectures." He added bluntly, "I am at a loss to form an Idea what the people of the United States would have Vermont to do."[10] Twice, Congress had promised to admit Vermont to the Union, only to renege when New York threatened to secede from the confederation and pull its troops out of the Continental army. So much of Vermont's difficulty in gaining statehood obviously was coming from New York. In March of 1781, Allen argued to Samuel Huntington, president of Congress, that he personally had a "Sincear Attachment to the cause of my Country" but that "Vermont has an Indubitable Right to agree on terms" for a truce with England so long as "the United States Persist in Rejecting her Application for a Union with them."[11]

AFTER THE DEFEAT of the British army at Yorktown in October of 1781 all but ended any fighting, Allen broke into print again, spelling out, in *The Present State of the Controversy*, that he doubted, now that the Revolutionary War was drawing to a close, that Congress would "rouse the whole confederacy and destroy Vermont." This was "as unlikely as that the tail of the next comet will set the world on fire." By mid-June of 1782, Allen was writing to General Frederick Haldimand, the British commander in Canada, that Congress's latest refusal to admit Vermont into the Union "has done more to awaken the common people to a Sense of their Interest and resentment of their Conduct" than all the years of open opposition by New York. Congress "by their own act declare that Vermont does not and shall not belong" to the Union. "I Shall do Every thing in my Power to render this State a British province."[12]

But did Allen mean it, or was he only wedging the door open for future ties between Vermont and Canada? Had he ever meant it? By this time, Haldimand suspected that Allen and his damnable Vermonters had outwitted the British, by promises and foot dragging, shielding Vermont from British invasion for the past five years. Cornwallis had surrendered, and Guy Carleton was preparing the British evacuation from the United States. The British government once believed that its Loyalist informants were accurate when the Anglican Reverend Charles Ingles wrote, "It would not be difficult to bring over Allen."[13]

The British spymaster in Vermont, Agent 008, Captain Justus Sherwood, Allen's old friend in the Green Mountain Boys who had personally led secret negotiations at Crown Point, believed that Allen would lead a Vermont army to attack Albany, but that it would be "a work of time." That time had dragged on, as first Ethan, then Ira and Ethan, and then only Ira met infrequently with Sherwood, eventually confining their meetings to the Ile aux Noix. Ethan and Ira scrupulously turned over written communications to the governor's council, but when the general assembly was not kept abreast of the talks, some delegates began to doubt that Ethan had been able to avert further invasions by "a hook in the nose." Tired of the political wrangling, Allen resigned as brigadier general of the Vermont militia.[14]

EVER SO SLOWLY, the British authorities came to realize that Allen and his junto were equivocating. Haldimand was the first to express his doubts about Allen—"I am assured by all [Loyalist spies], that no dependence can be had in Him," he wrote as early as 1780. "His character is well-known and his Followers . . . are a collection of the most abandoned wretches that ever lived, to be bound by no Laws or Ties." Sherwood wrote to Haldimand in February 1781 that either Allen was "sincere" and the plot to join Vermont to Canada was "drawing to a favorable conclusion much faster than I ever expected, or he is a most subtle, designing fellow." Haldimand finally ran out of patience and warned that he was preparing an invasion of Vermont in October of 1781, but then he learned that Cornwallis and the southern British army had surrendered at Yorktown. As he waited for further instructions from England, tens of thousands of Loyalists began to flee to Canada, to England, to Caribbean islands. Finally, Frederick Haldimand realized that he had been duped.[15]

BETWEEN 1778, WHEN he was released from captivity, and 1784, Ethan Allen served as commander in chief of Vermont's militia, unelected member of its assembly, chief diplomat to the Continental Congress and the New England states, close personal adviser to Governor Chittenden, and ex officio judge of Vermont's court of confiscation. The war hero, the counselor of state, he became the public face of Vermont, inside and outside the republic. All bluster and dash on the surface, Allen was all the while careful to urge Governor Chittenden to grasp any opportunity to correspond over the heads of the Vermont government and the Continental Congress, directly with General Washington. Congress deliberated on Vermont's admission to the Union again in August 1781 and, this time, only New York voted its continued opposition.

By 1781, many Vermonters in the Connecticut Valley were becoming disenchanted with the Allens, Chittenden, and the Arlington Junto, especially their inability to ward off British attack, above all after Carleton's raid and a bloody raid on Royalton, more than halfway across the state. By then, New York and Massachusetts both were claiming that Vermont belonged under their jurisdiction, rendering Congress incapable of any decision on Vermont's right to statehood. Meanwhile, the New Hampshire towns along the Connecticut River once again were demanding to join Vermont, this time opposed by Vermont towns along the river whose leading landowners remained loyal to New York and were eager to escape the domination of the Arlington Junto. In the summer of 1782, the Vermont Assembly responded in force, sending Allen with four hundred militia across the mountains in a raid on Guilford in Windham County, where two sets of officials had been contesting control for several years. Allen declared martial law in the name of the Vermont legislature and demanded back taxes. Anyone who did not swear allegiance to Vermont would have to leave for New York.

• • •

FINALLY DETERMINED TO break the impasse, General Washington, dealing secretly through military couriers from his base at New Windsor on the Hudson, was supplying Chittenden with the resolutions of Congress. On January 1, 1782, he wrote again from Philadelphia on his way north from his final victory at Yorktown. Chittenden had used the pretext of a letter congratulating Washington on his great victory to spell out the "essence of the dispute." Washington wrote back privately, chastising the Vermonters for what was obviously, to him, their land-grabbing ploy:

> Now I would ask you candidly, whether the Claim of the people of Vermont, was not for a long time confined solely, or very nearly, to that tract of Country [called Vermont and] the late extension of your Claim upon New Hampshire and New York, was not more of a political Manoeuvre than one in which you conceived yourselves justifiable. . . . [Y]our late extension of Claim [has] rather diminished than increased the number of your Friends. . . . [I]f such extension should be persisted in, it will be made a common cause. [It is] a loss of too serious a nature not to claim the attention of many people.
>
> There is no calamity within the compass of my foresight, which is more to be dreaded, than a necessity of coercion on the part of Congress. . . .[16]

Washington, who knew that Governr Clinton was chomping at the bit to attack Vermont, then wrote privately to General Philip Schuyler, some of whose lands Vermont had annexed. Schuyler, prodded by one son-in-law, Colonel Alexander Hamilton, and turning a deaf ear to further arguments of another son-in-law, James Duane—Hamilton's law preceptor—now openly swung his support to Vermont's independence. Washington told Schuyler that he had shown this "private" letter "to a number of [his] friends, members of Congress and others. . . . Perhaps it may have some effect upon the leaders of Vermont." Washington was also writing to other rivals of Vermont's leaders in New York. He bluntly warned Governor George Clinton that the majority of New Englanders, especially among his officers, supported state-hood for Vermont.

Almost as soon as they heard from Washington in February of 1782, Allen met with the Arlington Junto, which authorized Governor Chittenden to send a resolution of the general assembly racing south to Washington's headquarters. Vermont had decided, after all, to return once and for all to its former boundary lines. In addition, Vermont was sending Ethan Allen and three other "agents" to the Continental Congress "to negotiate the admission of the state of Vermont into the confederation of the United States."[17]

ABOUT NINE MONTHS after Allen's return to Vermont in 1778, the Allens' fourth daughter, Pamelia, was born early in 1779. Mary Brownson Allen had suffered greatly during Ethan's imprison-ment, probably doubting at times that even her Ethan was strong enough to survive. His recovery had been remarkably swift: by July 15, 1778, only two months after his return, he could write to Horatio Gates from Albany, where he had gone on business, "I am now in a State of Perfect health." Unfortunately, Mary was not. She had long complained about chest pains. For the next four years, as Ethan came and went—to Philadelphia, to Connecticut, to Boston, to Poughkeepsie—Mary stayed home with the children. It was the longest time they ever shared together, living in a deep valley, her small, square, clapboarded house surrounded by tall, dark evergreens. Even while sick, she was always expected to care for a large group of people. And although her three grown daughters supported her, she was constantly kept busy by two babies, brothers, in-laws, her husband, and a friend or two of his, talking politics and punch. Ethan must have noticed the coughing spells as they lasted longer. Then Mary became bedridden and, in June of 1783, worn out at age fifty, she died of tuberculosis. There is no written record of Ethan's reaction, although some people thought he wrote the lines of lachrymose verse that appeared in the next *Vermont Gazette*. But he must have been moved. A few days later, he sold Mary's brother Gideon a right—some 350-odd acres—on the Heroes, the two islands in northern Lake Champlain granted to the Allens and the Green Mountain Boys. He charged Gideon only one shilling. The customary price was £50.[18]

WHAT LIFTED ETHAN Allen's spirits amid so much sickness, unhappiness, and uncertainty was his lifelong habit of writing. Encouraged by the popularity of his captivity memoir and provided with enough cash from royalties to buy himself not only land but leisure, he penned long pep talks for his neighbors in the Green Mountains. By 1784 he was signing himself, in letters to Ira, "From the Philosopher." During one of his visits to Philadelphia in 1781 to charm and arm-wrestle members of the Continental Congress, he tracked down the widow of his old friend Dr. Thomas Young and, en route back to Bennington, he found her living in poverty with her five children on her family's farm in Dutchess County, New York. He brought home to Vermont the opening chapters of the deistic work they had begun in collaboration two decades earlier. It is unimaginable that he did not help her with some of the cash he received from his book. He did, in fact, find a job for Young's son in Vermont's government and petitioned the Vermont Assembly for a sizable land grant for the children of the man who helped to draft the Pennsylvania model of Vermont's constitution and gave the state its name, but the general assembly turned him down.

For three winters, writing consumed much of Allen's time. In the winter and spring of 1782, he began to write a volume of rational philosophy, the first deist work published in America (although Allen still insisted he couldn't be quite sure he was a deist):

> In the circle of my acquaintance (which has not been small) I have generally been denominated a Deist, the reality of which I have never disputed, being conscious I am no Christian, except mere infant baptism makes me one; and as to being a Deist, I know not, strictly speaking, whether I am one or not, for I have never read their writings; mine will therefore determine the matter. . . .[19]

In his 1785 work, the 477-page *Reason, the Only Oracle of Man*, Allen attacked conventional Christianity and all other forms of revealed religion, labeling them a "torrent of superstition." The historian T. D. Seymour Bassett has written that Allen was "against superstition, miracles and anything that violated natural law" and believed "in the rationalism of common sense, immortality, morality and progress."[20] In what became known as "Ethan Allen's Bible," he employed his special brand of ridicule to mock the idea that the devil was turned loose on two innocent young people in the Garden of Eden, "just out of the mold" and "destitute of learning or instruction, having been formed at full size in the space of one day, and consequently void of experience." At least God could have given them a bodyguard of angels. He heaped special scorn on superstition and on the clergy, beginning with Moses, "the only historian in the circle of my reading, who has ever given the public a particular account of his own death." Allen had never understood how full-grown, otherwise intelligent people could take the Bible seriously. He blamed this, too, on the clergy. Writing at the end of a revolution that was changing every other fact of life in America, he claimed that "priest craft is being discredited at roughly the rate of fifty percent per annum."

Allen attacked dogmatic religion and supernaturalism in general, positing, instead of this "dreary" system, a natural religion based on the use of reason. "As far as we understand nature, we are become acquainted with the character of God, for the knowledge of nature is the revelation of God":

> If we form in our imagination a compendious idea of the harmony of the universe, it is the same as calling God by the name of harmony, for there could be no harmony without regulation, and no regulation without a regulator, which is expressive of the idea of a God.

Morality, he argued, came not from the Bible "but from the fitness of things." It was not the exclusive domain of Christians and certainly did not require predestination. From his studies, Allen also found morality "interspersed through the pages of the Koran." According to him, morality "is founded on eternal right" and does not require the revealed words of Scripture:

> Reason therefore must be the standard, by which we determine the respective claims of revelation. . . . [I]f reason rejects the whole of those revelations, we ought to return to the religion of nature and reason. . . . Preposterously absurd it would be, to negative the exercise of reason in

religious concerns, and yet be actuated, by it in all other
and less occurrences of life.

He refused to espouse the dark visions of the hell's-fire-and-
brimstone orthodox Puritanism: "God is infinitely good; . . .
therefore there cannot be an infinite evil in the universe."[21]

As Allen explained to his close friend and attorney, Judge
Stephen Bradley, he was trying to debunk the central Calvinist
doctrine of predestination by negating its linchpin, original sin.
Writing to Bradley from Bennington on September 7, 1785, as
he waited for his book to come off the press, he argued against
the fundamental Christian doctrine that human beings have been
perpetually tainted by the sin of Adam and the never-ending
"Vindictive displeasure of Almighty God for it":

On the Christian scheme, God was Criminal, Judge, &
Executioner, and thus having wrought an everlasting
Righteousness, imputed it to a certain Elect number, of
favourites, and doomed the residue of the human race, to
Everlasting wo[e] and perdition. . . .
    I Fancy sir, you will be diverted when you read the
12th Chapter, it rips up, and overturns the whole notion
of Jockeying, alienating, transferring, or imputing of Sin,
or Righteousness, from one person to another, and leaves
all mankind accountable, for their own moral agency. This
is fatal to the Ministerial Damnation Salvation, and their
merchandize thereof.

Attacking the clergy with as much reckless abandon as he had
Ticonderoga or Montreal, he took on Protestants and Catholics
alike:

In order to carry on this Priestcraft, the Clergy must invalidate the law of Nature, Reason is represented as Carnal, and depraved, and the natural State, a condition of mankind, to be damnable, to make way for their mysteries, insperations, and pious frauds, and thus most of the Human race, have been miserably Priest-ridden.

To remedy the human species, from this Ghostly Tyranny (as far as in me lay,) was the Object of my writing, the Oracles of Reason, an Object worthy of Genl Allen, whatever his success may be.[22]

Reason, he contended, had to replace reliance on miracles.

Allen's self-described "compendious system of natural religion" was, according to the family genealogist John L. Barr, an amalgam of "English Deism, Spinozan naturalism," and "what would later become known as New England Transcendentalism."

ALLEN WAS NOT entirely prepared for the violent reaction to his book. For six months, his manuscript languished in the Hartford print shop that had turned out so many of his earlier writings quickly. The printer obviously hesitated to print something so anticlerical in Puritan-dominated Connecticut. Fetching it back, Allen sold large quantities of land and pressed his debtors to pay up scarce hard cash so that he could pay the Bennington printer Anthony Haswell, to run off fifteen hundred leather-bound copies. He sent off the first forty copies to influential friends, including one to his former captor, the new governor-general of Canada, Lord Dorchester (the former Sir Guy Carleton).

To Benjamin Stiles of Woodbury, Connecticut, his former partner in the failed lead mine in Northampton, Massachusetts, he wrote,

As to my philosophy. . . . The curiosity of the public is much excited, and there is a great demand for the books, they will in all probability reach Woodbury, in the course of the winter. In one of them you read my very soul, for I have not concealed my opinion, nor disguised my sentiments in the least, and however you may, as a severe critic, censer [sic] my performance, I presume you will not impeach me with cowardice. I expect, that the clergy, and their devotees, will proclaim war with me, in the name of the Lord, his battles they effect to fight, having put on the armour of Faith, the sword of the Spirit and the Artillery of Hell fire. But I am a hardy Mountaineer, and have been accustomed to the dangers and horrors of War, and captivity, and scorn to be intimidated by threats, if they fight me, they must absolutely produce some of their tremendous fire, and give me a sensitive scorching.[23]

Allen sent a copy to Paris to the French *philosophe* Hector St. John de Crèvecoeur, whom he had met in Philadelphia. Crèvecouer had farmed in Dutchess County in upstate New York not far from Bennington. At first unsympathetic to the Revolution and targeted as a Loyalist, he fled to France, forced to leave behind his American wife and their three children. In Paris, he published his classic commentary on "the new man," *Letters from an American Farmer*. He returned to America as France's vice consul general and discussed philosophy several times with Allen during Allen's frequent visits to Philadelphia as Vermont's agent, lobbying Congress for statehoood. During his absence from America, Crèvecoeur's American wife died, and his three children were being raised as orphans. When he returned to France again after the American Revolution, his book a success, he took his place in the salon of his close friend, the influential Comtesse d'Houdetot, an ideal position for introducing the work of *his* friend Ethan Allen.

To Crèvecoeur in Paris, Allen wrote,

> I am not so vain as to imagine that my theology, will afford any considerable entertainment, to the enlightened mind of M^r. S^t. John, or to any learned Gentlemen in France. Yet it is possible, that he or they, may be Somewhat diverted, with the untutored logic, and Sallies of a mind nursed principally, in the Mountanious wilds of America. And since it is the almost universal foible of mankind, to aspire to something, or other, beyond their natural, or acquired abilities, and as I feel the infection I desire, that M^r. S^t. John, would lay the oracles of Reason, before the royal academy. . . .

Allen added that "the Clergy in this County, reprobate the work, and anathematize the writer of it!"[24]

In September of 1785, three years after he began to write *Reason*, Allen advertised it in Haswell's *Vermont Gazette*. The Reverend Timothy Dwight, soon to be president of Yale College, later summed up the Puritan theologian's view of *Reason* as the "Contemptible plagiarism of every hackneyed, worn-out, half-rotten dogma of the English deistical writers. . . ."

> When it came out, I read as much of it as I could summon patience to read. Decent nonsense may possibly amuse an idle hour, but brutal nonsense can only be read as an infliction of penal justice. The style was crude and vulgar, and the sentiments were coarser than the style. The arguments were flimsy and unmeaning, and the conclusions were fastened upon the premises by mere force.[25]

While Dwight characterized *Reason* as "the first attack on Christianity," not everyone agreed. Vermonters who applauded "Ethan Allen's Bible" rarely commented on it, except Tom Paine, who had been a boon companion of Thomas Young and had met Allen in Philadelphia after arriving from England in 1775 and many times later when the Vermonter came to lobby Congress for statehood. Paine had found a sinecure as secretary to the congressional Committee on Foreign Affairs. He was aware of the work, which anticipated by ten years his *The Age of Reason*.

Some twentieth-century historians believed that Paine borrowed heavily from Allen's *Reason*. The biographer John Pell quoted John E. Henry, the historian of Benedict Arnold's march to Quebec: "Long after the publication of Allen's book, which had fallen into oblivion even with its readers, that vile reprobate, Thomas Paine . . . filched from Ethan Allen the great body of his deistical and atheistical opinions. . . ." As the Reverend Nathan Perkins, a Congregational missionary touring Vermont while on leave from his parish in Connecticut, wrote in his journal, "About one quarter of the inhabitants and almost all of the men of learning [are] deists." Basing his impressions on visits to about two dozen households, Perkins traveled 150 miles to the edge of settlements on the west side of the mountains and back in forty-seven days. "I have rode more than 100 miles and seen no meeting house!" he wrote from Governor Chittenden's farm in Williston. A disgruntled Perkins recorded that the governor gave him only a dollar and that Mrs. Chittenden made him dine with the farmhands. Perkins came away from his Vermont sojourn with a jaundiced view of its populace:

> People pay little regard to ye Sabbath, hunt & fish on that
> day frequently. Not more than 1-6 part of the families

attend family prayer. About 1-2 would be glad . . . to support public worship & yᵉ gospel Ministry. The rest would chuse to have no Sabbath—no ministers—no religion—no heaven—no hell—no morality.

Touring the Vermont frontier on a sabbatical from his Hartford congregation, Nathan Perkins recorded in his journal that he was appalled to find every stripe of Protestant, Jew, Catholic, Quaker, deist, and agnostic, for a Calvinist such an intolerable diversity in a New England state. He did not grasp the central point that Vermont's religious diversity was, as the historian Bassett has phrased it, "central to the understanding of successful resistance to New York's political and Congregationalism's religious authority."[26]

The historian Robert E. Shalhope found that Allen's longest work had a lasting effect outside Vermont:

In this book, the most radically democratic of all his works, Allen supported a natural religion resting upon man's reason rather than the revealed religion based upon the Bible and the hierarchy of ministers that held sway throughout New England. In place of a fearsome Calvinistic deity, Ethan offered a benevolent god who allowed each person, through the use of intelligence and conscience, to judge between right and wrong. In essence, Allen democratized religion, just as he had democratized all other social and politcial aspects of his culture. Unlike his earlier publications, however, his attack upon the Bible predictably brought the wrath of clergymen down upon his head.[27]

Unfortunately for Ethan Allen, many of the citizens of Bennington, where he had lived for most of his years in Vermont, were horrified at the book that Allen penned in the hip-roofed house right next door to the Congregational meetinghouse. (The house was demolished in the early nineteenth century to make way for an extension to the graveyard.) While some town historians claim that it was a bolt of lightning, possibly hurled from heaven, that set fire to the five hundred uncirculated copies of *Reason*, others are certain that Haswell, who was just launching his own printing business, was so thoroughly terrified by the irate indignation of the town's Congregationalists that he himself burned the rest of the pages in his own fireplace. Only the forty copies Allen had already shipped and some he had at home escaped the flames. Whatever actually happened, Allen began to think it was time to move away from Bennington as soon as he could find a way. By then, however, he had another motive, to some in Vermont more scandalous than his theological skepticism.

16.

"Clodhopper Philosopher"

❊

In the years just after the Revolution, a depression in trade in America caused growing political discontent as well as economic hardship. With the public credit destroyed by huge war debts and the loss of British and French gold, currency was in free fall. Disbanding the army had produced widespread unemployment. The reimposition of Britain's Rule of 1756 restricting trade to Canada and the British Isles to "English goods in English bottoms," the Confederation teetered on the brink of collapse. Competition between states sharpened. New York demanded a customs duty on every boatload of firewood from New Jersey vital to fueling and heating New York City. Pinched New Jersey boatmen put pressure on their legislature to tax New York for the lighthouse and plot around it on Sandy Hook that belonged to New York City. Connecticut exacted heavier customs duties on imports from Massachusetts than on those from Great Britain.

As thousands of New Englanders poured into Vermont, more

than tripling the population in a decade, the newcomers often ran up bills and faced lawsuits, the courts filling with debt cases and attorneys who came to harvest them. By 1786, the assembly was receiving a torrent of petitions complaining of court costs and legal fees. One unpopular Bennington lawyer who had moved up from Princeton was called "Jersey Slick." Early in 1786, Vermonters, reflecting a sensibility that had already begun, were petitioning the legislature to have lawyers expelled and debts canceled. By the mid-1780s, no one seemed to have any money. Most people sought extensions from creditors.

Ethan Allen was away then, seeking an extension from a creditor, the Hartford firm of Hudson and Goodwin, printer of a pamphlet he had coauthored six years earlier, offering to repay the debt in cattle he had raised and asking for more time—a commonplace request in cash-strapped post-revolutionary America. Like those of most Vermonters, Allen's creditor wouldn't wait. Barzillai Hudson wanted the full amount and wanted it immediately. Allen's attorney was Stephen R. Bradley, a young Yale-educated Revolutionary War veteran who had emigrated from Massachusetts during the war, quickly rose to colonel of the Green Mountain Regiment, and was one of the first admitted to the Vermont bar. When Allen's case came up, Bradley argued before the court that he didn't owe Hudson, because the signature on the note wasn't in his handwriting. Furious, Allen interrupted Bradley. He hired Bradley to get an extension, not to lie for him. "That is a true note," he told the crowded court. "I signed it, I'll swear to it, and I'll pay it. I want no shuffling, but I want time." The judge approved the extension.[1]

"I am drove almost to death for money," Allen wrote to his brother Ira. While he owned thousands of acres of Vermont land, nobody had the money to buy it. For three weeks, Ethan went from courthouse to courthouse in Connecticut and Vermont, juggling judgments. He didn't even have enough cash to pay the property taxes on three tracts of land in the Heroes that the Onion River Land Company had sold and he would have to refund their entire purchase price if he couldn't come up with fifteen dollars. He asked his cousin Ebenezer, who was operating a tavern and a ferry on South Hero, to stall for time. "We are rich poor Cursed rascals By God," Allen told Ira.[2]

All over Vermont, by late summer of 1786, farmers facing foreclosures were desperately trying to block foreclosure hearings and forced sales. That August, two hundred farmers had milled outside the Rutland County courthouse as the Vermont Supreme Court deliberated debtors' cases. Haswell's *Vermont Gazette* reported that they were "manifesting appointed resentment" and cursing lawyers as "banditti" and "pickpockets." Although the *Gazette* reported that "nothing of a riotous or unlawful nature took place," the crowd warned both lawyers and judges to "take notice how you impose upon those who have passed thro' the wilderness and endured fire, famine and the sword [to obtain] their own rights." The crowd continued to menace the lawyers until a hundred Vermont militia arrived to break it up.

The economic distress continued well into the fall. In October, angry crowds harassed surveyors trying to lay out town lines and lots in the Northeast Kingdom, a mountainous region full of squatters. The mobs included settlers whose land titles had been clouded by earlier surveys, some made by Surveyor General Ira Allen. Two weeks later, in Windsor, thirty armed men, wielding guns, bayonets, swords, clubs, and deadly farming implements, attempted to keep the county courts from opening. From October 31 to November 13, mobs clashed with Windsor County sheriff's deputies, only dissolving when six hundred Vermont militia arrived. Four days later, another riot broke out when the Rutland County court reconvened. A "considerable number" of men carrying bludgeons petitioned the court to adjourn. When the judges refused, one hundred protesters, led by Colonel Thomas Lee, stormed the courthouse and "in a most insolent manner began to harangue and threaten the court." The next day, the mob took the judge and the sheriff prisoner. Calling themselves Regulators, the term first heard on the North Carolina frontier in the early 1770s, they seized the courthouse and called for reinforcements. When one hundred and fifty Vermont militia arrived the next day, the mob evacuated the courthouse but lingered nearby. The militia arrested the leaders of the protest, among them a Vermont assemblyman who was fined heavily and expelled from the legislature. But two days later, another angry crowd, some two hundred strong, surrounded the local colonel's house, demanding to know what would happen to the prisoners. He assured them that the rumor that they were being mistreated in jail was false, and the crowd broke up.[3]

AS THE CRITICAL YEAR of 1787 began, Captain John Marshall of Virginia wrote to a former Revolutionary War comrade in arms, with an air of despair hanging over veterans like themselves. On New Year's Day, the future chief justice of the United States Supreme Court wrote to General James Wilkinson, "All is gloom in the Eastern states." Massachusetts, where the fuse of the Revolution had been lit only a dozen years earlier, was now, wrote Marshall, "rent into two armed factions." A civil war between armed and embittered frontier farmers, many of them veterans, and Boston politicians and merchants loomed not only in Massachusetts but also as far south as North Carolina. Currency and land speculators were in control of state legislatures.

As two private Massachusetts armies formed to march against each other, Marshall worried that he could get very little accurate news from New England, but he feared that "an appeal to force

has, by this time, been made to the God of Battles." Marshall
had himself wintered, often hungry, with George Washington at
Valley Forge. He feared that the rebellion on the New England
frontier would spread south through the Appalachian backcountry and destroy the fragile fabric of the young American confederation. "Such violent, bloody dissension as this so-called Shays
Rebellion casts a deep shadow over the new nation," Marshall
wrote Wilkinson. "I fear we may live to see another revolution."[4]

Other former Revolutionary War leaders shared Marshall's
forebodings. The thirteen newly independent states, economi-
cally impoverished, were behaving more like warring nations
than members of the same victorious confederacy. Marshall was
embarrassed to write that he had even been unable to obtain a
passport for General Wilkinson to cross the Potomac River from
Maryland to Virginia on his way to Kentucky. In Vermont, Allen
wrote to Frederick Haldimand, Canada's governor general, offering to supply beef cattle to British troops garrisoning Quebec
Province. Haldimand wrote back and apologetically declined
Allen's offer because British policy on "free trade" with the republic of Vermont was unclear. The Allen brothers nonetheless were
already exporting to Canada lumber taken from the Winooski
Valley on a huge raft. Levi Allen had set up a business in St.
Jean-sur-Richelieu, and Ira was supplying him from the Vermont
side. But their notes and drafts were being refused by Canadian
merchants. Often, the only way debts could be paid was by barter. One bill introduced into the Vermont Assembly called for
merchants to accept cattle as currency, a measure that the Allens,
who were raising cattle, supported.

As the economic crisis deepened, George Washington
and other revolutionary leaders conferred at Mount Vernon and

decided to call a convention at Annapolis, Maryland, for the autumn of 1786. The conference, attended by representatives of six states, ended abruptly when news arrived that debt-ridden farmers in the Berkshire Mountains on the New England frontier, on Vermont's southern border, had rebelled. When the Massachusetts state government tried to collect taxes to pay the interest on bonds issued to pay the state debts and bought by wealthy Boston merchants, widespread tax foreclosures ensued. A high percentage of the region's farmers, no longer able to pay tax collectors, now faced eviction with their families from their farms. The rebels, as Massachusetts politicians quickly denominated them, were especially bitter because the Massachusetts legislature had adjourned on July 8 without heeding their plea to issue paper money or to pass "stay" laws that would halt foreclosures on farms and homes. At a town meeting at Worcester on August 15, discontent boiled over into angry calls for action that led to a Hampshire County convention of some fifty towns at Hatfield a week later.

In a tense gathering, town delegates condemned the Massachusetts Senate, the lawyers, the high costs of obtaining justice, the entire tax system, and the lack of paper money. While the conventioneers advised against the use of force, armed violence broke out. One week after the Hatfield convention, on August 31, an angry crowd of armed men prevented the judges and court officers at Northampton to sit; another week and protesters closed the September session of courts at Worcester. The same anger that had fueled the Revolution was now aimed at the new sitting government. Crowds barred judges and lawyers from entering the courthouses at Concord and Great Barrington, chasing away the sheriffs and stopping the sheriffs' sales. Near panic, Governor James Bowdoin dispatched six hundred militiamen to guard the Massachusetts Supreme Court in Springfield.

On both sides, the situation was threatening to snowball out of control. At Springfield on September 26, 1786, Daniel Shays, a destitute farmer who had attained the rank of captain in the Revolutionary army and since held town offices in Pelham, gathered about 600 men who were armed with flintlocks and were ready to fight. Confronting an inferior state militia, the veterans forced it to back away. The supreme court fled. In panic, Secretary of War Henry Knox reported with wild exaggeration to Congress, to George Washington, and other former Revolutionary War leaders that Shays commanded 10,000 to 15,000 men and that they were besieging the federal arsenal at Springfield. Civil war appeared imminent. Thoroughly alarmed at reports that the armed rebels were about to seize cannon from the Springfield arsenal, Congress did the one thing it had clear-cut authority to do under its governing Articles of Confederation. On October 20, it voted to raise an army, even if it did it on tenterhooks. Congress authorized the secretary of war himself, three-hundred-pound Henry Knox, to raise 1,340 men, ostensibly to serve against the Indians. But Knox was able to gather recruits for the federal force only so slowly that they never saw combat.

The taxpayers' revolt suffered a severe setback with the capture of one of its organizers, Job Shattuck, on November 30, but, as snow blanketed the Berkshires, Captain Shays gathered his own army of about 1,200 men in November and December. The day after Christmas, he marched them to Springfield on the Connecticut River to join forces with other insurgents under the command of Luke Day. They aimed to intimidate a small militia force already guarding the federal arsenal. Their march thoroughly alarmed Governor Bowdoin, who now called up 4,400 men and put them under the command of the veteran General Benjamin Lincoln. Authorized for one month, it was the largest armed force mustered in the United States since the Revolution. The mayhem produced by the rebellious militia threatened to undo the very existence of the new government.

The insurgent leaders Shays and Day made the classic mistake of keeping their forces divided by the Connecticut River as they rushed toward Springfield and attempted to scatter the arsenal's guard before Lincoln could reinforce it. When Shays proposed a joint attack, Day sent him a note, insisting that he could not attack for another two days. The note was intercepted. Shays pressed on, confident that Day would strike simultaneously. The Shaysites marched uphill within one hundred yards of the arsenal before the arsenal's gunners unleashed a volley of cannon fire. Four rebels dropped dead; the rest broke and ran. When Lincoln arrived with his army of mercenaries, he pursued Day, splitting off his force as Day fled into the hills of New Hampshire. Hard marching all night, Lincoln and his army surprised Shays at dawn on February 4 at Sheffield, where they captured 150 of the insurgents. Many of them, like Shays and his aides, disappeared across the Vermont border to seek refuge in Bennington. In the next few months, facing arrest for treason, some 4,000 Shaysites and their families sold their belongings and fled to Vermont.

Shays's Rebellion thoroughly alarmed many Americans who were worried that the fragile Union was on the verge of collapse. Shays's escape into Vermont threatened to ignite another tinderbox of rebellion. One expert on Vermont's land laws and its tempestuous relations with neighboring states was Alexander Hamilton. He had closely followed Vermont's claims for independence from New York as aide-de-camp to Washington before becoming a member of the New York Assembly. He was one of the Continental officers supporting Vermont's request to join the Continental Congress. Increasingly, he opposed Governor Clinton's belligerent insistence that New York militia be mobilized to crush resistance in Vermont and force it back to its claimed status as part of New York.

EVEN AS VERMONTERS touched off armed resistance to debt collections and mortgage foreclosures at frontier courthouses in the Green Mountains, Ethan Allen turned his attention to another smoldering revolt in the Wyoming Valley of northeastern Pennsylvania. Before the Revolution, hundreds of settlers, including his father, Joseph, had bought land from the Susquehannah Company in the Pocono Mountains. After the war, in yet another example of the feebleness of diplomacy between states under the Confederation, Pennsylvania laid claim to the region and insisted that the Wyoming Valley settlers did not hold clear title to the lands unless they repurchased them—exactly as New York had done in Vermont before the Revolution. Irate settlers appealed their plight to Congress. On December 30, 1782, a five-man congressional tribunal had met in Trenton, New Jersey, and ruled unanimously that the disputed lands belonged to Pennsylvania because its territory was contiguous. Without waiting to settle individual claims, the Pennsylvania Assembly had approved plans to evict the Connecticut settlers.

In desperation, some of the Wyoming Valley settlers turned to that legendary defender of local autonomy—Ethan Allen of Vermont. Shays's Rebellion convinced the Wyoming Valley settlers that Allen and his rough-riding Green Mountain Boys could be "particularly serviceable" in their cause by striking terror into the hearts of lawyers and lawmakers in Philadelphia. Allen's presence in the Poconos along with some of his Boys might coerce Pennsylvania to negotiate. To lure Allen, they offered him the two commodities he loved the most, land and command. He declared that the Wyoming Valley cause—"our cause"—was "just." Writing from Vermont, he promised to fight to the death the "avaricious men [who] make interest their God." On his advice, the Wyoming Valley settlers procured guns and ammunition and recruited four hundred Connecticut settlers waiting for the arrival of their leader, the "head doctor from the North with his glister pipe" (a glass device used, when heated, for giving an enema) to purge the Pennsylvania government. But first Allen warned a Connecticut delegate to Congress that he intended to "speedily repair to Wyoming with a small detachment of Green Mountain Boys to vindicate" their claims. Confident that Congress could hardly respond quickly enough, Allen rode into Pennsylvania on April 27, 1786, boasting to a crowd "that he had formed one new state" and now would do it again "in defiance of Pennsylvania." One anxious official reported to Philadelphia that "since [his] arrival every idea of submission to the laws of Pennsylvania has vanished."[5]

In the spring of 1786, Philadelphians were reading a broadside reminiscent of Allen's rhetoric before he led his Boys to seize Fort Ticonderoga a decade earlier. He scorned Congress's "tribunal of land monopolizers." Addressing "the court of conscience, of the people at large," he declared that the Wyoming settlers— and he now counted himself one of them—"will not tamely surrender our farms, orchards, tenements, neighbors, and right to soil to a junto of land thieves." He threatened to "smoke it out at the muzzle of the firelock." Did Philadelphia's "pious legalists" believe that the farmers had fought the Revolution in vain, only for Pennsylvania and Congress to "cram their laws down our throats"? As panicky rumors of the approach of an army of Green Mountain Boys flew through the streets of Philadelphia, the state legislature hastily convened inside Independence Hall. Terrified lawmakers, declaring that "bandittis [are] rising up against law and good order in all quarters of our country," regarded Ethan Allen and Daniel Shays as part of the same lawlessness that threatened to destroy the Union.[6]

In two brief visits to the Wyoming Valley of Pennsylvania, Allen managed to jolt Pennsylvania's legislature into confirming the Connecticut settlers' claims to their lands—including his twelve rights (about 4,000 acres)—and forming their settlements into a separate Pennsylvania county. On April 30, Allen, his letter dripping with scorn, wrote from the Wyoming Valley to Connecticut's governor, Matthew Griswold, that two days earlier he had

> arrived to the Hostile ground, and found a territory which has been distressed by Britons, Tories, Savages, and the more Savage and avaricious land-jobbers (I had almost said Government) of Pennsylvania. Every exertion of Government, in its consequences, has hitherto been attended with cruelties. . . . Law, Order, and Government, are the Hobby Horses of the Pennsylvanians, with which they . . . design to dispossess the Connecticut Settlers, and obtain and accumulate to themselves, their lands and labours.

Allen reported that, two years earlier, the Pennsylvania secretary of state, Brigadier General John Armstrong, had been sent with an armed force to "quiet the disturbances" in the Wyoming Valley "and parley between them." The settlers agreed to surrender their weapons to Armstrong's militia or he "would shoot them dead." Armstrong then arrested the settlers. Jailed for high treason against Pennsylvania's government, they were acquitted after a jury trial.[7]

In the short run, Allen's personal intervention in Pennsylvania and Shays's Rebellion in Massachusetts had the combined effect of electrifying discontented frontiersmen all up and down the Appalachian Mountain frontier. At Mount Vernon, George Washington became convinced that the rebellion would spread into a full-scale resumption of the Revolution. He feared that "levelers" were triggering agrarian reforms that would reapportion wealth and produce a schism of social classes in the new country—something Ethan Allen knew how to exploit. Washington's estate had already dwindled by half, because of currency depreciation and wartime and postwar British curtailment of trade. On a tour of his frontier lands in western Pennsylvania, Washington was unable to collect rents from his tenant farmers, most of them Revolutionary War veterans who had served under him, and instituted eviction proceedings against them in Fayette County court. Returning to Mount Vernon, he wrote to James Madison, "We are fast verging to anarchy and confusion."[8]

AFTER GENERAL BENJAMIN LINCOLN scattered the Shaysites in western Massachusetts in early February 1787, Governor Bowdoin decided to hunt down and punish the rebels who had fled across the border to Vermont. He called on the governors of neighboring states to arrest the "malcontents." The governors of Connecticut and New Hampshire promised to cooperate. New York's Governor Clinton marched with three regiments of militia to reinforce Lincoln. Twice, Lincoln called for Vermont's Governor Chittenden, whose government was closest to the rebellion, to help. Chittenden promised to see what he could do. Vermont's white-haired legislators dreaded being dragged into the war with their neighbor even as they sought their neighbors' support for their petition for statehood. Some Vermonters thought that promises to intervene in Massachusetts would actually increase Vermont's support in Congress. A scant majority of the Vermont legislature voted to disavow Shays's Rebellion. At the end of February 1787, after Shays fled to Vermont, Chittenden issued the assembly-drafted proclamation warning citizens not to "harbor, entertain or conceal" Shays and the three other rebel leaders—who were camping, at Chittenden's invitation and with his personal protection, on the Arlington farm right next door to Chittenden's.[9]

But Vermont's waffling only led worried leaders in New York and Massachusetts to believe that Vermonters were planning, once again, to annex the rebellious border regions of both states. In Boston, Governor Bowdoin heard that hundreds of Shaysites were massing near Ethan Allen's homestead in the Winooski River valley. Allen, even though he was a significant landholder, openly sympathized with the Shaysites. When Bowdoin sent Major Royall Tyler, General Lincoln's aide-de-camp, to demand that Governor Chittenden turn over Shays for Tyler to bring him back for trial, Allen met with him in Rutland against the backdrop of a made-to-order gathering of protesters. Fresh from his triumph in Pennsylvania, Allen harangued the crowd about the evils of Massachuetts' iniquitous leaders, including Bowdoin, Lincoln, and the Adamses. Those who "held the reins of government in Massachusetts [are] a pack of damned rascals and there is no virtue among them," he bellowed. Allen appears to have pledged to Tyler that Vermont would not be used as a base for any Shaysite attack on Massachusetts. The Vermont Assembly refused Tyler's demand that they turn over the Shaysite leaders and agreed only that Govenor Chittenden would issue his proclamation. Tyler carried orders to return empty-handed if his life appeared threatened. Author of *The Contrast*, the first play written and produced in the United States, Tyler knew a good exit line: he decided to leave Vermont, at least temporarily. A few years later, he returned to Vermont to practice law and became a justice on its supreme court. In August of 1787, when

Vermont militia caught "two notorious offenders" with horses they had stolen from Massachusetts, Allen took the opportunity to write to Tyler:

> Such persons who are criminals and have acted against law and Society in general and have come from your State to this we send back to you. . . . Others who have only taken part with Shayes we govern by our laws so that they do not, and dare not make any inroads or devastation in the Massachusets.

Allen did not mention that, five months earlier, Daniel Shays had sent two fellow insurgents, Luke Day and Eli Parsons, to Allen to offer him the command of a "revolutionary army" to carry on the struggle.[10]

In the meantime, in the months before the Constitutional Convention convened in Philadelphia in May, Alexander Hamilton led a personal crusade in the New York Assembly to end the twenty-year-old confrontation with Vermonters. He introduced a bill directing the states' congressional delegates to support independence for Vermont. "Vermont is in fact *independent*," he contended, "but she is not confederated." He understood Ethan Allen's shrewd efforts to exploit Shays's Rebellion. "Is it not normal for a free people, irritated by neglect, to provide for their own safety by seeking connections?" Vermont had turned first to the British, now to Shays. New York must finally settle the controversy. "They are useless to us now," he said of Vermonters, "and if they continue as they are, they will be formidable to us hereafter." The New York Assembly agreed, but the Senate, where Governor Clinton and Allen's old nemesis James Duane held sway against Hamilton and his father-in-law, Philip Schuyler, refused. In the end, Allen's moderate stance during Shays's Rebellion and his refusal of its command won over a majority of New York law-makers. By keeping Vermont neutral, Allen finally won a quarter-century-long struggle. New York at last abandoned its fight to claim Vermont. Four years later, in 1791, Vermont paid New York patentees of lands in Vermont a mere $30,000 for clear land titles. This removed the last obstacle for Governor Clinton to sign off, endorsing Vermont's admission to the Union.[11]

Hamilton's support in New York struck Allen like a lightning bolt, coming just when Shays was offering him command of a revolution. Allen had to choose between the independence for Vermont he had pursued for more than twenty years or a brief adventure that might end on the gallows. He chose statehood for his beloved Vermont. Publicly, he "contemptuously refused" Shays's offer of command and ordered him and his lieutenants to leave Vermont. (Of course, Allen had no intention of expelling Shays; in fact, Shays and his aides stayed put in the governor's side yard even as four thousand Shaysites and their families fled across the border from Massachusetts and settled in Vermont.) Hamilton had long ago helped the prisoner-of-war Allen escape from brutal confinement in New York's Provost jail by arranging his exchange. Now he gave Hamilton the political victory he needed. Allen would not live to see it, but Hamilton, four years later, helped usher Vermont into the Union as the fourteenth state.

IN THE WINTER OF 1784, about six months after Mary Brownson Allen died, the Vermont Assembly convened in Westminster in the Connecticut Valley. As usual, Allen attended at Governor Chittenden's invitation. His close friend and lawyer Stephen Bradley had built a sprawling house in Westminster and took in lodgers to help pay for it. Two women, Margaret Schoolcraft Brush Wall and her young niece Frances Montresor Brush

Buchanan, rented several rooms while they located lands left to them by Mrs. Wall's late husband, the Loyalist Crean Brush. Onetime claimant of sixty thousand acres of Vermont lands who had drafted the Bloody Acts a decade earlier, Brush had committed suicide after Vermont confiscated virtually all of them.

When Margaret Schoolcraft married Brush in 1766, she brought to the marriage six-year-old Frances Montresor. Fanny, as she became known, was her sister Anna's illegitimate daughter by Captain John Montresor, the Swiss military engineer and mapmaker in the British army whose bogus travel diary led Benedict Arnold's army astray in the Maine woods in 1775. When Crean Brush died, Fanny stood to inherit any of his land that Vermont hadn't confiscated, as much as twenty thousand acres. When the Revolution ended, Fanny's aunt, now remarried to Patrick Wall and living in Boston, brought her to Westminster to see what lands they could salvage and sell.

Allen, forty-five, was, quite simply, mesmerized, when he first saw the twenty-four-year-old Fanny. It was, after all, not uncommon for older widowers to marry younger women then: Benedict Arnold was twice Peggy Shippen's age. Twenty years earlier, Allen had married a woman six years older than him. Fanny Montresor was all that Mary Brownson had not been: physically beautiful, sensitive and vivacious, accomplished in music, fluent in French, and a notable botanist in addition to having a lot of money, which clearly Mary never had. Ethan, still wearing his forest green brigadier general's uniform, was the commanding figure of a military officer that Fanny had always responded to. In the drab northern woods, the flamboyant General Ethan Allen was encountering a lady of New York fashion. Each had weathered tempestuous lives. Ethan would soon learn, if he didn't already know, that Fanny's aunt, who survived three husbands, had forced her illegitimate niece Fanny to marry, at sixteen, a British navy officer who left her pregnant when he was killed in a sea fight with an American privateer. Ethan didn't care, as they said then, a fig about her past life. In fact, he quite readily abandoned reason when he first saw her at a party at his good friend Stephen Bradley's house in Westminster during the February session of the Vermont Assembly some six months after Mary Brownson Allen died.

According to the kind of persistent Vermont legend that sounds more like thigh-slapping nineteenth-century Vermont humor than history, Ethan may have heard about Fanny for the first time in a local tavern—almost all Ethan Allen stories are somehow connected to a tavern and a flowing bowl—from the tavern's owner, a friend of Ethan's, who said he had quipped with Fanny a few days earlier, "If you marry General Allen, you will be the queen of a new state."

Stephen Bradley was entertaining judges at breakfast on February 9, 1784, when he heard the bells of a sleigh stop at his door. Allen strode in and knocked the snow off his boots. Bradley invited him to join the judges who had gathered to smoke their long clay pipes in the drawing room. The general declined. He preferred to cross the hall and meet the ladies having their breakfast. Fanny was dressed in a morning gown when he came in. She promptly told him that proper gentlemen didn't make social calls so early in the morning. Ethan apologized, but explained that he was on military business and had to leave for Bennington at once.

Then, the story goes, Ethan blurted out, "If we are to be married, now is the time." Apparently nonplussed, the young widow put down the cracked decanter she was dusting and said slowly, softly, "Very well, but give me time to put on my Joseph [coat]." A few minutes later, they crossed the hall arm in arm to the parlor, where the men, still smoking their glowing long pipes, were startled to see Fanny on the general's arm. "Judge Robinson," Ethan said to his old friend Moses Robinson, "this young woman and

myself have concluded to marry each other and to have you per-
form the ceremony."

"When?" asked Judge Robinson.

"Now," replied Ethan. "For myself I have no great opinion of
such formality, and from what I can discover, she thinks as little
of it as I do. But as a decent respect for the opinions of mankind
seems to require it, you will proceed."

"General, this is an important matter," said the judge. "Have
you given it serious consideration?"

"Certainly," Ethan replied, turning to Fanny. "But I do not
think it requires much consideration."

The ceremony was as swift as Ethan's and Fanny's recognition of each other's passion. While it cannot be gainsayed that
Allen was aware of her reputed means and social standing, and
she aware of his popularity, it was evident that this was a marriage based on initial attractional love, rather than mere conve-
nience. When Judge Robinson asked Ethan whether he promised
to live with Fanny "agreeable to the laws of God," Ethan glanced
out a window for a moment. "The law of God as written in the
great book of nature? Yes." When the ceremony was over, Ethan's
hired man, the freed slave Newport, lugged out Fanny's portmanteau and guitar case and put them in the back of Ethan's sleigh.
Wrapping his bride in a great bear rug, he snapped his bullwhip
over the horses' heads, and to the jingling of sleigh bells, the newlyweds raced off across the Green Mountains.[12]

ETHAN AND FANNY ALLEN enjoyed the best five years of
their tempestuous lives together, first in the shadow of the Bennington Congregational meetinghouse, where Ethan still rented
the large hip-roofed house, and then, after Ethan dissolved the
Onion River Land Company, in a modest 24-by-36-foot two-

story frame house Ethan had his brother Ira arrange to build on Ethan's 1,400-acre share of choice intervale land overlooking the Winooski River in the town of Burlington. Nine people, including Fanny's son, Ethan's three daughters, two farmhands—Newport and William Stewart (who had been tomahawked and taken prisoner with Ethan at Montreal)—and a woman servant, filled the small clapboard house with din, music, laughter. Stewart, a former Green Mountain Boy and surveyor's assistant for the Onion River Land Company, had charged into Fort Ticonderoga with him. When someone had tried to attach the impoverished Stewart's musket for nonpayment of a small debt, Allen had come to his rescue in court and then given him a lifetime job as a farmhand.

The first year on Allen's idyllic farm, Fanny gave birth to a girl. They named her Frances Margaret after her mother and great aunt: this Fanny Allen later studied French in Montreal, converted to Catholicism, and became the first American-born nun. (A hospital in Vermont is named after her.) Subsequently, a boy, whose name is unrecorded, died of whooping cough as an infant. A son named Hannibal survived. Ethan was ecstatic to have a son again: he named him, reflecting his interest in classical military history, after the great Carthaginian conqueror who came over the Alps in winter to attack the mighty empire of Rome. A second living son he named Ethan Voltaire Allen, whose namesake's writings Allen had learned enough French, with Fanny's help, to read and admire, especially now that, like Candide, he had turned his back on politics. Aided by Fanny, he kept up his correspondence with Hector St. John de Crèvecoeur. At Crèvecoeur's request, Allen had obtained for him Vermont citizenship so that his American-born son could inherit his French patrimony. To win the favor of Louis XVI, Allen, at Crèvecoeur's suggestion, gave French place-names to towns he founded on Allen's land: Vergennes after the foreign minister who talked the indolent king into an alliance with the infant United States that saved the American Revolution; Calais on the Canadian border after the Channel port; Danby after the French naval commander whose fleet invaded New England's waters in the French and Indian War. Allen honored his friend St. John de Crèvecoeur by naming the timber-rich town of St. Johnsbury in Vermont's Northeast Kingdom after him.

Borrowing a page from Voltaire's *Candide*, Allen cultivated his own philosophizing gardens by continuing to write. He began to sign his letters, self-mockingly, "Clodhopper Philosopher." After the uproar that greeted his *Reason*, he wrote a long appendix, which was not published for eighty years. At the time of Shays's Rebellion, amid the constitutional crisis over the failure of the Articles of Confederation to unite the former British American colonies, Allen had grave doubts about Vermont's ever joining the United States. He could never forget all the years of border warfare with the state of New York, which had obstructed Vermont's efforts to join the Union for so long even while Vermont provided a military and diplomatic buffer against further British invasion. More importantly, he knew that Vermonters recoiled at heavy taxation and feared that they would have to pay a share of the United States' heavy load of unpaid Revolutionary War debts if they joined the Union now. Unlike other states, Vermont had paid for its share of the war and for troops it sent to the Continental army with the proceeds of confiscated Loyalist lands. To have to pay again would be an egregious reminder of New York's long-ago demand that New Hampshire grantees pay a second time for their land. This had, after all, been the cause of forming the Green Mountain Boys and fighting a dangerous guerrilla war with a rebel's death noose hanging over his head.

By the winter of 1789, a new U.S. government had been formed after a Constitutional Convention in Philadelphia unattended by delegates from Vermont, which was still unrepresented in national government. In its dozen years as a republic, Vermont thrived, its population doubling and redoubling since the Revolution. Allen no longer played an active role in politics, but his influence was pervasive. He loved returning to farm life. He told his friend Stephen Bradley that he was planning to cultivate some 350 acres of "choice River Intervale" and upland, meadows "interspersed with the finest of wheat land and pastureland." He had picked out the land two decades earlier: it was "by nature equal to any tract of land of the same number of acres that I ever saw." At first, he was cultivating an ambitious 40 acres. There was not enough hay to feed his cattle during the drought year of 1788. The same three-year drought created grain shortages and food riots in Paris and would, a few months later, lead to the storming of the Bastille and the French Revolution. At almost exactly this moment, newly elected U.S. senators and congressional representatives were casting their ballots as electors to choose, inevitably and unanimously, George Washington as the first president.[13]

After such a stormy life, Ethan Allen died quietly, his sudden death failing to match the action and drama that had marked so much of his life. In the bitter cold February of 1789, he set out across frozen Lake Champlain with a sledge to borrow hay from his third cousin Ebenezer, who had settled at the southern tip of South Hero Island. That night, after word flashed through the Heroes that Ethan Allen was coming, the Green Mountain Boys crowded into Ebenezer's tavern. The stories, the rum punch toasts, the songs lasted well into the early hours of morning. As Newport drove the loaded sledge slowly across the frozen lake, he noticed that Allen had become unusually silent. The last thing Allen mumbled was how dark the trees looked in the early morning light. Then he slumped over, falling into the arms of his freed slave. By the time they reached Allen's homestead, it was plain that Allen had lapsed into a coma, apparently after suffering a stroke. Ira and his wife, Jerusha, Fanny and their children, the servants and the farmhands crowded into the small house as Ethan Allen, quietly and without regaining consciousness, died the next day. He was only fifty-one. It was February 12, 1789, one week after Washington was elected the first president of the United States and exactly twenty years before another poor boy, Abraham Lincoln, would be born in Kentucky, on the latest frontier.

When the Reverend Ezra Stiles, then the president of Yale College, heard that Allen had died, he wrote in his diary, "13th Instant died in Vermont the profane and impious Deist General Ethan Allen, author of the *Oracles of Reason*, a book replete with scurrilous reflexions on Revelation. . . . And in Hell he lift up his Eyes being in Torments."[14]

Afterword

WHILE ETHAN ALLEN'S DEATH was undramatic and lacked ceremony, Vermonters were determined not to let go quietly. His funeral, as a result, was enormous. The Green Mountain Boys, his friend Governor Thomas Chittenden, the assembly, and 10,000 of the roughly 80,000 citizens of the republic of Vermont glided over the icy roads to Ira Allen's house in Colchester, across the river from his homestead, for a civil funeral that contrasted with the religious ceremonies of so many of his Revolutionary peers. Allen had helped to make the United States an independent nation and Vermont an independent republic. He had fought off anyone who tried to weaken it, and now a stunned Vermont populace braved a frigid winter wind to escort his body through a tattoo of cannon and musket salutes to the cemetery atop Colchester Hill, overlooking a frozen Lake Champlain and his beloved Winooski Valley. There, Ethan Allen was buried in what has become a shrine for travelers for more than two centuries. A

plain marble slab resting on a granite foundation bore an inscription, long since obliterated, testifying to the enigma so many had
found in him:

> The corporeal part of General Ethan Allen rests beneath
> this stone, the 12th day of Feb., 1789, aged 51 years. His
> spirit tried the mercies of his God, in whom alone he
> believed and strongly trusted.

On a hilltop overlooking the Winooski River, in Burlington's Green
Mountain Cemetery, stands a pillar that supports a statue bearing
his likeness. It depicts him looking much like a Napoleonic-era
hussar. At its base, these words are etched in stone:

> Wielding the pen as well as the sword, he was the saga-
> cious and intrepid defender of the New Hampshire Grants
> and the master spirit in the arduous struggle which resulted
> in the sovereignty and independence of this state.[1]

Four years later, as the Age of Reason came to its sanguinary
climax during France's Reign of Terror, the Reverend Nathan Perkins, echoing the imprecation of the Reverend Stiles, stopped by
the hilltop graveyard in Burlington and denounced Ethan Allen
as he stomped on his grave. From their pulpits, the New England
clergy—from Chestnut Hill to Bennington—attacked Allen and
his rational religious views, making no distinction between deism
and atheism as they demonized him. The obloquies continued,
year after year, acting only to ensure Allen's elevation to the status of frontier rebel and folk hero, a man who spurned the siren
call of America's new aristocracy, its upper classes, despite being
offered a seat at their table, instead preferring a farm and a cabin
on its fertile frontier.

Five years after Allen died, the Reverend Lemuel Hopkins, the pastor of the Congregational Church in Bennington, penned a second epitaph for him, which he titled "On General Ethan Allen," ending with this punchline:

> One hand is clench'd to batter noses,
> While t'other scrawls 'gainst Paul and Moses

With Allen's death, a rapprochement of sorts between Vermont and New York finally seemed more likely. Accordingly, commissioners from the republic of Vermont, selected by the Bennington lawyer Isaac "Jersey Slick" Tichenor, met with commissioners selected by New York's Governor Clinton. After thirty-five years of acrimony, after the longest border war in American history had kept Vermont out of the Union and almost driven it back into the smothering fold of the British Empire, the commissioners negotiated a final settlement. Vermont agreed to pay $30,000 to buy off the New York land claimants. Among them was James Duane, the first mayor of New York City, a U.S. district court judge at the time of settlement. In the end, Duane relinquished any claim to Vermont lands. His heirs received $2,629.21.[2]

The way was then clear for Vermont statehood. In 1791, two years after Allen's death, in a special session called by President George Washington, the U.S. Senate admitted Vermont to the Union. And two months later, already weary of the new nation's politics, Thomas Jefferson, the man who, as the first secretary of state, wrote the necessary documents for Vermont's statehood, came to Vermont on vacation with his closest friend, James Madison, more celebrated as the author of the Bill of Rights. They drove through New York in a tall black glass-enclosed carriage made at Monticello by Jefferson's slaves and driven by his French-trained slave, chef, and body servant, James Hemings, the half brother of Jefferson's dead wife, Martha.

In his journal, Madison noted sharp differences between the citizens of the two neighboring states. On the New York side of the border, threadbare tenant farmers still living in seedy rented cottages tilled the soil on the great manors of Philip Schuyler and other Hudson River magnates, whose acreage was increased by the addition of lands confiscated from the departed Loyalists. The New York tenant farmers still were afraid to improve their farms for fear the landlord would evict them and re-rent at higher rates. Coming into the valley that Ethan Allen first saw a quarter of a century earlier with his cousin Remember, Madison noted in his palm-sized journal that now there were houses that were larger, more substantial, more "closely settled" than he had seen in New York, handsomely situated on 50- to 200-acre tracts that were owned outright by farmers whose "fields were full of corn and potatoes, flax to make linens, wheat and closer and half a dozen grass crops for feeding livestock." The settlements in the Valley of Vermont, Madison wrote, filled "seven or eight [miles] of a fine fertile vale separating two ridges of low mountains . . . rich and covered with sugar maple and beech."

The Virginia travelers discovered that a young couple could emigrate from Massachusetts or New Jersey to the Vermont frontier, buy land and clear it, build a house and barn, and be mortgage-free within five years. In a hundred-mile north–south swath between Lake Champlain and the Green Mountains, they discovered a "champagne country," the fields of wheat waving in the shore breeze. According to the first U.S. census, Vermont had the highest yield per acre of wheat.[3]

Lake Champlain, they observed, was full of commerce, with sloops carrying barrels of potash, and enormous rafts, made of timbers to be dismantled and sold in Montreal. Although the British were still boycotting all trade with the original thirteen states, thanks to Ethan Allen's subtle diplomacy, only Vermont was benefitting from America's first free exchange of trade with its northern neighbor. Allen did not live to show off the state that he had fought to carve out of the British Empire. The republic of Vermont was, in fact, so much his handwork. But Jefferson and Madison clearly noted the progress, admiring what they saw.

Resilient and irrepressible, Ethan Allen was a determined populist and creative leader. A man possessing more contradictions than folklore has suggested, he was both a successful and self-serving businessman and a farmer. A philosopher on horseback, he was, however, resolute in his belief in building a new kind of state on the intrinsic value of the land owned and worked by people of modest means. He fought all his life the tyranny of intolerance, insisting on the separation of church and state and championing the right to speak out freely against both. His reputation as the original Green Mountain Boy survived the counterattacks of an enraged Puritan clergy. He left no portrait from life: no portrait painter could make a living on the New England frontier. Eventually, family members described him to an artist, or there would be no image of him today.

There was no statue to honor him until the Civil War, and then a swashbuckling granite figure finally graced the rotunda of the Capitol in Washington and the foyer of the Vermont capitol in Montpelier as well as his hilltop family graveyard in Burlington. His prisoner narrative, which chronicles his rank sufferings, kept on selling, going through sixty editions before the Civil War. It even remains in print today. Invoking his memory, twice as many Green Mountain Boys per capita went south and died as in any other state in the North. They streamed down from their hill farms and crowded onto trains and steamboats to go south and fight and die at Gettysburg and Andersonville in their struggle to preserve the Union. While no one could equate their suffering to that of the slaves, their numbers strongly suggest that they were sensitive to the sufferings of others, memorializing their own flights to New England's, and America's, first frontier.

Acknowledgments

WHEN I MOVED to Vermont a quarter century ago to begin to write biography, a name I encountered almost immediately was Ethan Allen. His name was on ships, schools, a military firing range, and furniture, but he was almost never mentioned alone: it was usually "Ethan Allen and the Green Mountain Boys." He was depicted as a hard-drinking, brawling, hair-triggered, uneducated country bumpkin: part Davy Crockett, part Paul Bunyan, and two parts Jack Daniels. Gradually, I met people who had a more complicated view of the state's founding father, and I want to thank a few of them. The late John Buechler, special collections librarian at the University of Vermont, told me right away I should look into the Haldimand negotiations: they were the key not only to Allen but to the early history and character of the state. Ethan Allen Hitchcock Sims, Allen's great-great-great-grandson, came to a talk I gave and told me his ancestor was a serious philosopher. My son, Christopher, wrote his senior thesis at Princeton University on the links between the treatment of prisoners of war in the American Revolution and the Civil War, citing the brutal treatment of Allen by the British. That led me to read Allen's own narrative of his thirty-four-month captivity. Studies I had already made of Benedict Arnold, George Washington, Alexander Hamilton, Thomas Jefferson, and Thomas Chittenden all seemed to touch on this elusive mountain man.

The path soon led to archival research. I wish to thank the late Whitfield J. Bell, librarian of the American Philosophical Society; Peter Carini at the Rauner Special Collections Library at Dartmouth College; Jeffrey D. Marshall, research director in the Wilbur Collection at the University of Vermont; Vermont State Archivist Gregory Sanford; Nick Westbrook at Fort Ticonderoga; Kevin Graffagnino, director of the William L. Clements Library of the University of Michigan; and the patient library staffs at St. Michael's College and at Champlain College, especially Marie Kascus and Tammy Poquette. My student assistant, Samantha Snow, gave invaluable help. Visits to the manuscript reading rooms of the Morgan Library, the New York Public Library, the New-York Historical Society, and Princeton University Library all yielded important pieces for the emerging mosaic of Allen's life and times on the Revolutionary War–era New England frontier. The courtesy of librarians makes the biographer's work feasible. I want to thank the staff at St. Anne's College at Oxford University for granting me a corner in which to continue my research on the British ministry's decisions on how to deal with Allen and his captured comrades on English soil. But without the generous hints of vigilant fellow researchers of the period, I would have missed important leads: Thomas Fleming told me about Washington's reaction to Allen when the released prisoner came to Valley Forge, and he vetted my account of the Battle of Bunker Hill; John Nagy told me the British

secret service rank of Allen's go-between in the Haldimand negotiations and helped identify the spies Allen sent into Fort Ticonderoga the night before the famous attack. David Donath, director
of the Woodstock National Historic Park, dusted off his graduate
school notes on the Reverend Solomon Palmer. For years Professor
David Bryan as well as Joyce Huff and Daniel O'Neil, directors of
the Ethan Allen Homestead in Burlington, Vermont, gave me valuable help. Beal Hyde, descendant of Remember Baker, guided me to
the site of Baker's brutal death.

I owe special thanks to the late Professors Lawrence Stone
and Arthur Link of the graduate faculty of Princeton University,
who encouraged and aided me as I made an awkward transition
from investigative journalist to historian, and to Professor Edmund
Sears Morgan of Yale University, who urged me to carry on with
my first attempt at biography during a colloquium at Princeton.

My daughter, Lucy, helped me find key documents at Dartmouth and in the New York Public Library, then acted as reader as
she used her fine editorial skills to help me weed and prune my first
draft. My wife, Nancy Nahra, lent me her poet's ear for language
as I read to her, as I always have, long passages of the all-too-rough
draft. This book has been a six-year undertaking that might never
have been completed without her help and encouragement and that
of my close friend, Dr. John W. Heisse Jr., who first read the entire
manuscript and found a way to tell me what he didn't like about it.
Several eminent historians closely read and generously commented,
among them Thomas Fleming, John Ferling, Thomas Wermuth,
and Randolph Roth. I am in their debt.

But all of my research would remain in notebooks if Deborah
Grosvenor, whom I am fortunate to have as my literary agent, had
not brilliantly vetted my proposal before delivering me to the hands
of the editorial master craftman who knows more American his-

tory than I ever will, and how best to express it—my editor at Norton, Robert Weil. His patient and capable assistant, Philip Marino, has helped to make it possible for me to meet all Bob's deadlines, and the incomparable copyediting of Otto Sonntag has polished the pieces of the mosaic until, I hope, the real Ethan Allen emerges from the shadows where he has too long dwelled.

NOTES

Preceding the numbered notes in most of the chapters are background subjects, each with sources that were found especially valuable and pertinent. Full particulars of each work cited are given in the bibliography.

The following abbreviations are used in the citations:

AA	Peter Force, ed., *American Archives*
ABF	*The Autobiography of Benjamin Franklin* (ed. Labaree)
ANB	*American National Biography*
BA	Benedict Arnold
BF	Benjamin Franklin
CHS	Connecticut Historical Society
DAR	Davies, ed., *Documents of the American Revolution*
DCL	Dartmouth College Library
DHNY	O'Callaghan, ed., *Documentary History of New York*
EA	Ethan Allen
EAC	Duffy et al., eds., *EA and His Kin: Correspondence*
FTM	Fort Ticonderoga Museum
FTMB	*Fort Ticonderoga Museum Bulletin*
GW	George Washington
IA	Ira Allen
JA	John Adams
JCC	*Journals of the Continental Congress*
JH	John Hancock
LAP	Levi Allen Papers, University of Vermont
LDC	Smith et al., eds., *Letters of Delegates to Congress*
LOCO	Library of Congress Online

ND	Clark, ed., *Naval Documents of the American Revolution*
NHA	New Hampshire Archives
N-YHS	New-York Historical Society
NYPL	New York Public Library
PAC	Public Archives of Canada
PCC	Papers of the Continental Congress
PGW	*Papers of George Washington*
PS	Philip Schuyler
PTJ	*Papers of Thomas Jefferson*
PUL	Princeton University Library
RM	Richard Montgomery
SA	Samuel Adams
TC	Thomas Chittenden
TJ	Thomas Jefferson
TP	Thomas Paine
TY	Thomas Young
UVA	Alderman Library, University of Virginia
UVM	University of Vermont
VH	*Vermont History*
VHS	Vermont Historical Society
VMHB	*Vermont Magazine of History and Biography*
VSA	Vermont State Archives
VSP	*Vermont State Papers*
WF	William Franklin
WLCL	William L. Clements Library, University of Michigan
WMQ	*William and Mary Quarterly*
WW	*Writings of Washington*

CHAPTER 1: "A SINCERE PASSION FOR LIBERTY"

Attack on Fort Ticonderoga: EA, *Narrative of Colonel Allen's Captivity*, ed.
Pell; Pell, *EA*; Randall, *BA*; *ND*, vol. 1; French, *Taking of Ticonderoga*;
Commager and Morris, *Spirit of 'Seventy-Six*, 97–105; Fiske, *Critical
Period in American History*; Force, ed., *AA*; Fischer, *Paul Revere's Ride*;
Stiles, *Literary Diary*; SA, *Writings*; JA, *Diary and Correspondence*; *PTJ*,
vol. 1; TP, *Common Sense*; *Jesuit Relations*, vol. 72; Metzger, *Quebec Act*;
Neatby, *Quebec*; Headley, *Chaplains and Clergy*; Lanctôt, *Canada and
the American Revolution*; Reynolds, *Guy Carleton*; Hatch, *Thrust for
Canada*.

1. Commager and Morris, 90–91.
2. SA, May 15, 1764, in "Instructions of the Town of Boston to Its Representatives in the General Court," MS, Boston Public Library.
3. Gage to Conway, Dec. 31, 1765, quoted in Fischer, 38.
4. Gage to Barrington, Nov. 12, 1770, quoted in Fischer, 38–39.
5. Gage to Hillsborough, Oct. 31, 1768, quoted in Fischer, 40.
6. Fischer, 96.
7. Pitcairn quoted in Stiles, *Literary Diary*, 1:604–5.
8. JA, *Diary and Autobiography*, 3:314.
9. TJ to Wm. Small, May 7, 1775, in *PTJ*, 1:165–67.
10. BF to David Hartley, May 8, 1775, in *LDC*, 1:335–36.
11. TP, *Common Sense*, Jan. 1776.
12. GW to Wm. Fairfax, May 31, 1775, in *WW*, 3:291–92.
13. *JCC*, May 16, 1775.
14. Quoted in *Jesuit Relations*, 72:391–92; Stiles, quoted in Metzger, 102.
15. Metzger, 103.
16. Neatby, 148.
17. James Warren, "Suffolk Resolves," in Commager and Morris, 54.
18. "Letter from a Gentleman at Pittsfield to an Officer at Cambridge," May 4, 1775, *AA*, 4:507.
19. EA, *Narrative*, 5.
20. Ibid., 6–7.
21. According to the folklorist Benjamin A. Botkin, Israel Harris, one of the Green Mountain Boys present at the time, recounted Allen's exact words to his grandson, the University of Wisconsin historian James D. Butler. See Botkin, *A Treasury of New England Folklore*, rev. ed. (New York: American Legacy Press, 1965).

CHAPTER 2: "THE ROUGHEST TOWNSHIP IN CONNECTICUT"

Ethan Allen's Family Origins: Barr, *Genealogy of EA;* O. P. Allen, *Allen Memorial.*

The Antinomian Crisis: Heimert and Delbanco, eds., *Puritans in America*; Morgan, *Puritan Family*; D. H. Hall, *Antinomian Controversy*; Holifield, *Theology in America*; Stone, *Family, Sex, and Marriage*; Underdown, *Revel, Riot, and Rebellion*; Camden, *Elizabethan Woman*; C. Hill, *Society and Puritanism*; L. B. Wright, *Middle-Class Culture in Elizabethan England*; Huber, *Women and the Authority of Inspiration*; Randall and Nahra, "Anne Hutchinson," in *American Lives*, vol. 1.

The Great Awakening: Heimert and Delbanco, eds., *Puritans in America*; Heimert and Miller, eds., *Great Awakening*; Morgan, *Puritan Family*; Morgan, *Genuine Article*; Stout and Onuf, "James Davenport and the Great Awakening"; Miller, "Half-way Covenants"; Goen, *Revivalism and Separatism*; Zeichner, *Connecticut's Years of Controversy*; Gaustad, *Great Awakening in New England*; Chauncy, *Seasonable Thoughts*; Butler et al., *Religion and American Life*; P. Miller, *Jonathan Edwards*; Winslow, *Jonathan Edwards*; Tracy, *Jonathan Edwards*; Holifield, *Theology in America*; Gipson, *British Empire*, vol. 3; Buckley, *Place Called Paradise*.

1. Frank Shuffleton, "Thomas Hooker," *ANB*.
2. Stone, 102.
3. Heimert and Delbanco, 155.
4. Randall and Nahra, *American Lives*, 1:11–20.
5. Heimert and Delbanco, 154–55.
6. Ibid., 156; Morgan, *Puritan Dilemma*, 141–42.
7. Stone, 102.
8. Quoted in Heimert and Delbanco, 160.
9. Quoted in Morgan, *Puritan Dilemma*, 149.
10. Hugh Peter, quoted in Feintuch, 469.
11. Stone, 367.
12. Underdown, 39.
13. "Nathan Cole's Spiritual Travels," in Heimert and Miller, 183–86.
14. *ABF*, 175.
15. J. Edwards, quoted in Dudley and O'Neill, 235.
16. Chauncy, *Seasonable Thoughts*, 96, 106.
17. *Boston Evening Post*, April 11, 1743.
18. Stout and Onuf, 557.
19. Chauncy, *Seasonable Thoughts*, 36–37, 366.
20. Heimert and Delbanco, 409.
21. Gale to Ingersoll, quoted in Bushman, *From Puritan to Yankee*, 248.
22. Ezra Stiles to Leverett Hubbard, Sept. 21, 1766, MS, New Hampshire Historical Society *Collections*.
23. Morgan, *Genuine Article*, 24.

CHAPTER 3: "I EXPERIENCED GREAT ADVANTAGES"

Cornwall, Connecticut: EA, *Reason*; Gold, *Cornwall*; Starr, *Cornwall*; Dwight, *Travels in New England*, vol. 2; Dexter, *Yale Graduates*; Szatmary, *Shays' Rebellion*; Gipson, *British Empire*, vol. 3; Belknap, *History of New Hampshire*, vol. 3; Pell, *EA*.

EA in French and Indian War: "Capt. Moses Lyman's Co.," in *CHS Collections*, 9:247.

1. Palmer, quoted in Dexter, 1:387.
2. Dwight, *Travels*, 2:260.
3. EA, preface to *Reason* (1784 edition).
4. IA to Samuel Williams, June 6, 1795, in *EAC*, 2:443.
5. EA, *Reason*, 99.
6. Pell, *EA*, 7.

CHAPTER 4. "ANY FURNACE FOR MAKING STEEL"

French and Indian War: Pell, *EA*; Randall, *GW*; Randall, *Little Revenge*; Randall and Nahra, "Teedyuscung," in *American Lives*, vol. 1.

Palmer Controversy: Dexter, *Yale Graduates*, vol. 1; Pell, *EA*; Hawks and Perry, eds., *Documentary History of the Protestant Episcopal Church*.

1. Randall and Nahra, 21–30.
2. Declaratory Act of 1766, in Pickering, ed.
3. Gipson, 3:225.

CHAPTER 5. "A TUMULTUOUS AND OFFENSIVE MANNER"

Forbes and Allen Forge: Pell, *EA*; Schallenberg, "Charcoal Iron"; Heyrman, *Commerce and Culture*; Rasmussen, "Wood on the Farm."

Thomas Young and Deism: Pell, *EA*; Hawke, "Dr. Thomas Young"; Caldwell, "The Man Who Named Vermont,"; Edes, "Memoir of Dr. TY"; *Transactions of the Colonial Society of MA*; Morais, *Deism in Eighteenth-Century America*; C. Wright, *Beginnings of Unitarianism in America*; Holmes, *Faiths of the Founding Fathers*.

Smallpox Inoculation: Henderson, "Smallpox and Patriotism"; Middlekauff, "Cotton Mather," in *ANB*; Warden, *Boston*; Randall, *Little Revenge*.

Postwar Connecticut: Gipson, *British Empire*, vol. 3; Randall, *BA*; Gipson, *Jared Ingersoll*.

Palmerite Controversy: Hawks and Perry, eds., *Documentary History of the Protestant Episcopal Church*, vol. 2; Dexter, *Yale Graduates*, vol. 1.

1. Morgan, *Genuine Article*, 25–27.
2. Pell, 11.
3. Jellison, 8.
4. Ibid.
5. Hawke, "Dr. TY," 9–11.
6. GW to Francis Hopkinson, quoted in Britt, 177–78.
7. Quoted in Hawke, 10.
8. Ibid., 11.
9. EA quoted in Pell, *EA*, 16.
10. IA to Sam. Williams, June 6, 1795, in *EAC*, 2:443.
11. EA, preface to *Reason*.
12. BF to Thomas Hopkinson, [October 16, 1746], *Papers of Benjamin Franklin*, ed. Leonard W. Labaree et al. (New Haven: Yale University Press, 1950–), 3:84–88.
13. *ABF*, 113–14.
14. TJ to JA, April 11, 1823, *WTJ*, 1466.
15. Holmes, 49.
16. Quoted in Randall, "WF," in *Loyalist Americans*, 63.
17. *Connecticut Gazette*, quoted in Gipson, *Jared Ingersoll*, 115, 155.
18. Ethan Allen Papers, 1:431–34, Henry Stevens Collection, VSA.
19. *Tousley v. Heman and EA*, Salisbury Justice Records, 1:25, Aug. 1764.
20. Hawke, 12.
21. Ibid.
22. Ibid., 12–13.
23. Ibid., 8.
24. Salisbury Justice Records, 1:3, Sept. 1765.
25. Ibid., 1:11, Oct. 1765.
26. Ibid., 1:27, Oct. 1765.

CHAPTER 6. "THE GREATEST HASSURDS OF HIS LIFE"

Northampton Sojourn: Nobles, *Divisions throughout the Whole*; Nobles, "Breaking into the Backcountry"; Buckley, *Place Called Paradise*; Trumbull, *History of Northampton*, vol. 1; Marsden, *Jonathan Edwards*.
New Hampshire Grants: Gipson, *British Empire*, vol. 3; Jones, *Vermont in the Making*; Randall and Nahra, *TC's Town*; Shalhope, *Bennington*.

1. Quoted in Burrows and Wallace, 204.
2. Edwards, quoted in Buckley, ed., 95; Marsden, 298–99.
3. Burrows and Wallace, 199; F. L. Engelman, "Cadwalader Colden and the

New York Stamp Act Riots," *WMQ*, 3d ser., 10 (Oct. 1953): 511; Nash, *Urban Crucible*, 58; Anderson, *Crucible of War*, 678–79.

4. Colden to Board of Trade, Sept. 26, 1763, MS, Colden Letter Books, 2:106, N-YHS.
5. Order in council, July 20, 1764, *DHNY*, 4:574.
6. H. Schuyler to Colden, *DHNY*, 4:575–76.
7. Wentworth to Colden, *DHNY*, 4:576.
8. Randall, *BA*, 56–57.
9. IA to Sam. Williams, June 6, 1795, in *EAC*, 2:443.
10. Dwight, quoted in Thompson, *Independent Vermont*, 2.
11. Hall, *EA*, 15.
12. Quoted in Pell, *EA, 18*.
13. Champlain, 164.
14. Quoted in Randall and Nahra, *TC's Town*, 49.
15. Hemenway, 2:889.
16. John Wentworth to Lord Hillsborough, Dec. 4, 1771, MS, Wentworth Letter Book, NHA.

CHAPTER 7: "NO BETTER THAN PEDDLERS"

Jurisdictional Struggle: Jones, *Vermont in the Making*, 132–223; Shalhope, *Bennington*, 52–69; Pell, *EA*, 28–29; Randall, *Little Revenge*, 208–50; Burrows and Wallace, *Gotham*; *DHNY*, vol. 4.
Onion River Company: Jones, *Vermont in the Making*, 196–200.
Green Mountain Boys: Shalhope, *Bennington*; Thompson, *Independent Vermont*; Jones, *Vermont in the Making*; Pell, *EA*.
Evictions from the Grants: Shalhope, *Bennington*; Jones, *Vermont in the Making*; Hamlin and Baker, *Supreme Court*; Thompson, *Independent Vermont*.

1. *DHNY*, 4:558–60
2. Burroughs and Wallace, 222.
3. Journal of Major Walter Rutherford, MS, James Duane Papers, N-YHS.
4. Colden to Board of Trade, Sept. 26, 1763, Colden Letter Books, 2:106, MS, N-YHS.
5. Order-in-council of July 20, 1764, *DHNY*, 4:574–75.
6. Quoted in Mark, 135.
7. Shelburne to Moore, April 11, 1767, *DHNY*, 4:589–90.
8. Wilbur, *IA*, 1:vii.
9. Colden to Board of Trade, Feb. 8, 1769, in Coll. N-YHS, 9:232–37.
10. "Affidavit of Breakenridge and Robinson," Feb. 14, 1770, *DHNY*, 4: 617–19.

11. Ibid.; Shalhope, 72–73.
12. Colden, "Proclamation," Dec. 19, 1769, *DHNY*, 4:615–16.
13. Petitions, Oct. 18 and 19, 1769, Papers of the Continental Congress (PCC), 1774–89, National Archives, Washington, D.C., microfilmed as M247, r47, i40, VI, pp. 38–47, and M247, r47, i40, VI, pp. 29–31.
14. Belknap, *History of New Hampshire*, 3:192.
15. Wentworth to Wm. Bayard, Feb. 23, 1769, in Jones, 210.

CHAPTER 8: "GODS OF THE HILLS"

New York Eviction Trials: Pell, *EA*, 28–33; Jellison, *EA*, 31–38; Gipson, *Jared Ingersoll*; Alexander, *Revolutionary Conservative*; Thompson, *Independent Vermont*; *DHNY*, vol. 4; Jones, *Vermont in the Making*; Hamlin and Baker, *Supreme Court*; Shalhope, *Bennington*; Kierner, *Traders and Gentlefolk*; Upton, *Loyal Whig*; Lustig, *Privilege and Prerogative*; H. Hall, *History of Vermont*; Crary, "American Dream"; Sparks, *Library of American Biography*, 240–42; DePuy, *EA*.

1. Quoted in Hamlin and Baker, 1:356.
2. EA, *Vindication*, 5.
3. B. J. Lossing, "EA and the Green Mountain Boys," *Harper's New Monthly Magazine* 102 (Nov. 1858): 742; DePuy, 148–50; Pell, 32–33; Jellison, 37; IA, *History*, 24; Van der Water, 82–83.
4. Hall, "Journal of James Duane, July 4, 1770, in Alexander, *Revolutionary Conservative*, 76 n. 34.
5. EA, *Brief Narrative*, in EA and IA, *Collected Works* (hereafter cited as *Works*), 1:25.
6. Ibid.
7. Breakenridge petition, Feb. 22, 1770, PCC, in m247, r47, i40, VI, pp. 51–54.
8. Dunmore to Board of Trade, March 6, 1771, *DHNY*, 4:676.
9. Wentworth to Tryon, Dec. 14, 1771, *DHNY*, 4:671–72.
10. Dunmore, Nov. 1, 1770, *DHNY*, 4:661–63.
11. Ibid., Feb. 27, 1771, 4:687.
12. Ibid., 4:690.

CHAPTER 9: "THE LAW OF SELF PRESERVATION"

EA as Outlaw: Pell, *EA*, 34–65; Jones, *Vermont in the Making*; Shalhope, *Bennington*; Thompson, *Independent Vermont*; EA and IA, *Works*, 1:113; *DHNY*, vol. 4.

1. Randall, *Little Revenge*, 136.
2. Levi Allen Papers, MS, Wilbur Coll., UVM.
3. Charles Hutcheson to Duane, Sept. 10, 1771, Duane Papers, N-YHS.
4. Quoted in P. D. Nelson, *William Tryon*, 111–12.
5. *DHNY*, 4:763–64.
6. Reproduced at Pell, *EA*, 42.
7. *Connecticut Courant*, March 24, April 21 and 28, June 2, and July 7, 1772.
8. EA, *Vindication*, 6.
9. EA to Skene, quoted in Pell, *EA*, 45–46.
10. James Duane Papers, N-YHS.
11. Wentworth to Wheelock, Jan. 29, 1771, quoted in Chase, *History of Dartmouth College*, 435–36.
12. EA to Tryon, June (?) 1772, *VSP*, 25–28.
13. *Connecticut Courant*, June 9, 1772.
14. Tryon to the Inhabitants of Bennington, Aug. 11, 1772, *DHNY*, 4:793–94.
15. Ibid.
16. IA, *Autobiography*, 18.
17. Ibid., 44.
18. Pell, *EA*, 59.
19. IA, *Autobiography*, in Wilbur, 40–43.
20. TC quoted in *TC's Town*, 43.
21. Pell, *EA*, 59–60.
22. IA, *Autobiography*, 43.
23. *DHNY*, 4:859–73.
24. EA to Crean Brush and Sam. Wells, May 19, 1774, in *EAC*, 1:16.
25. *DHNY*, 4:891–93.
26. EA to Oliver Wolcott, March 1, 1775, in *EAC*, 1:18.

CHAPTER 10: "IN THE NAME OF THE GREAT JEHOVAH"

Attack on Ticonderoga: Pell, *EA*; Randall, *BA*; EA, *Narrative*; French, *Taking of Ticonderoga*; Commager and Morris, *Spirit of 'Seventy-Six*, 97–105; *ND*, vol. 1.

1. Gen. Frederick Haldimand to Tryon, Sept. 19, 1774, *Canadian Archives*, Report, 1887, xii.
2. BA to Albany Comm. of Safety, May 3, 1775, MS, Copley Library.
3. E. Mott to Mass. Prov. Cong., May 11, 1775, *ND*, 1:315–16.
4. EA, *Narrative*, 8.

5. Lt. Jocelyn Feltham to Gen. Thomas Gage, June 11, 1775, in Commager and Morris, 101; B. A. Botkin, *A Treasury of New England Folklore*, rev. ed. (New York: American Legacy Press, 1965).
6. Feltham to Gage, June 11, 1775, in Commager and Morris, 101.

CHAPTER 11: "THOU BOLD BLASPHEMER"

Lake Champlain 1775 Campaign: *ND*, vol. 1; Randall, *BA*, 87–114; Pell, *EA*; *AA*, 4th ser., vol. 3; Fleming, *Now We Are Enemies*.

1. Feltham to Gage, June 11, 1775, in Commager and Morris, 102.
2. EA to the Treasurer of Connecticut, May 12, 1775, in *EAC*, 1:23.
3. BA to Mass. Comm. of Safety, May 11, 1775, in *ND*, 1:312–13.
4. EA to Jonathan Trumbull, May 12, 1775, in *EAC*, 1:22–23.
5. EA to the Albany Comm. of Corres., May 11, 1775, in *EAC*, 1:20.
6. EA, *Narrative*, 11; BA to Mass. Comm. of Safety, May 14, 1775, in *ND*, 1:330.
7. John Brown to Mass. Comm. of Safety, Aug. 14, 1775, in *AA*, 4th ser., 3:135.
8. EA to Montreal merchants, May 18, 1775, in *EAC*, 1:25–26.
9. EA to Noah Lee, May 25, 1775, in *EAC*, 1:28.
10. EA to the Connecticut Assembly, May 26, 1775, in *EAC*, 1:29–30.
11. EA to Continental Cong., May 29, 1775, in *EAC*, 1:31–33.
12. *JCC*, June 1, 1775.
13. BA to Mass. Comm. of Safety, May 19, 1775, MS, Copley Library.
14. Wm. Gilliland to Continental Cong., May 29, 1775, in *AA*, 4th ser., 2:731.
15. EA et al. to Continental Cong., June 10, 1775, in *ND*, 1:647.
16. BA in Regimental Memorandum Book, MS, FTM.
17. Fleming, *Now We Are Enemies*; Randall, *Little Revenge*, 341–46.
18. JA to AA, June 10, 1775, in *LDC*, 1:465.
19. Randall, *Little Revenge*, 293–94.
20. *JCC*, June 23, 1775.
21. JH to N.Y. Provincial Cong., June 24, 1775, in *AA*, 4th ser., 2:1076.
22. Hawke, *Paine*, 31; *American Magazine*, June 1775;
23. Hawke, "Dr. TY," 17; Edes, "Memoir," 38–39; TY to John Lamb, Oct. 4, 1774, Lamb Papers, N-YHS.
24. SA to TY, Oct. 17, 1774, in SA, *Writings*, 3:130.
25. BA to JH, July 11, 1775, in *ND*, 1:862.
26. William Smith, *Diary*, April 29, 1775, quoted in Burrows and Wallace, 224.
27. EA and Seth Warner to Eliphalet Dyer and Silas Deane, July 4, 1775, in *EAC*, 1:41.

28. PS to the President of Cong., July 10, 1775, NYPL, Schuyler Papers, Letter Book 1775–76, 52.
29. PS to Daniel Fay, July 10, 1775, quoted in Lossing, *Life and Times of Philip Schuyler*, 1:363.
30. Wm. Marsh to PS, July 16, 1775, *Journals of the New York Provincial Congress*, 1:72.
31. July 20, 1775, in *EAC*, 1:45–46.
32. EA to Trumbull, Aug. 3, 1775, in *EAC*, 1:47.
33. IA, quoted in Wilbur, *IA*, 1:67.
34. Quoted in C. E. Crane, 130.

CHAPTER 12: "I HAD NO CHANCE TO FLY"

Invasion of Canada: Lanctôt, *Canada and the American Revolution*; EA, *Narrative*, 12–23; Jellison, *EA*, 121–42; Pell, *EA*, 116.
Attack on Montreal: Pell, *EA*, 115–21; Jellison, *EA*, 143–56; Randall, *BA*; Lanctôt, *Canada and the American Revolution*; Hatch, *Thrust for Canada*, 1–20; Bush, *Revolutionary Enigma*, 27–55; Reynolds, *Guy Carleton*, 59–66.

1. GW to PS, Aug. 20, 1775, in Middlekauff, *Glorious Cause*, 300–301.
2. PS to GW, Aug. 31, 1775, in *PGW*, 1:394–95.
3. PS to JH, *JCC*, July 12, 1775.
4. EA, *Narrative*, 13.
5. Samuel Mott to Gov. Trumbull, Oct. 6, 1775, in *AA*, 4th ser., 3:973.
6. Ibid., 3:973–974.
7. EA, *Narrative*, 14.
8. EA to RM, Sept. 20, 1775, in *EAC*, 1:51–52.
9. EA, *Narrative*, 14–15.
10. Ibid., 15.
11. "Extract of a Letter from Quebec dated Oct. 25, 1775," *AA*, 4th ser., 3:1185–87.
12. EA, *Narrative*, 15–22.

CHAPTER 13: "YE SHALL GRACE A HALTER"

Ethan Allen, POW: Pell, *EA*, 120–34; EA, *Narrative; PGW*, vols. 1 and 2; *WW*, vols. 11, 19, and 21; Burrows, *Forgotten Patriots*; Dandridge, *American Prisoners*; Metzger, *Prisoner of the American Revolution*; O. Anderson, "Treatment of Prisoners"; Lord Dorchester Papers, WLCL; Wharton,

Revolutionary Diplomatic Correspondence; Bowman, *Captive Americans*; Bowman, "Pennsylvania Prisoner Exchange Conferences"; *NDAR*; Curtis, *Tracts on the Exchange of Prisoners*; T. S. Anderson, *Command of the Howe Brothers*; Burrows and Wallace, *Gotham*; Wertenbaker, *Father Knickerbocker Rebels*; *DAR*, vol. 12; Fleming, *Now We Are Enemies*; Nelson, *General Sir Guy Carleton;* Ferling, *Almost a Miracle*, 102–5.

1. GW to Thomas Gage, Aug. 11, 1775, in *PGW*, 1:289.
2. Gage to GW, Aug. 13, 1775, in *PGW*, 1:301.
3. EA, *Narrative*, 25.
4. EA to Richard Prescott, Sept. 25, 1775, in *EAC*, 1:52–53.
5. EA, *Narrative*, 26–27.
6. Ibid., 27.
7. Ibid., 28.
8. PS to GW, Aug. 27, 1775, *AA*, 3:442.
9. RM to Janet Livingston Montgomery, Sept. 12, 1775, MS, Edw. Livingston Coll., PUL.
10. Randall, *BA*, 148–50.
11. Ibid., 168–75.
12. Ibid., 178.
13. Ibid., 186.
14. PS to JH, MS, Letter-book for 1775–76, NYPL.
15. TJ, Jan. 2, 1776, *PTJ*, 1:276–77.
16. Gage to GW, Aug. 13, 1775, in *PGW*, 1:301.
17. GW to PS, Dec. 18, 1775, in *PGW*, 2:578.
18. GW to Wm. Howe, Dec. 18, 1775, quoted in Crockett, *Vermont*, 2:249–50.
19. IA quoted in Wilbur, *IA*, 1:64–65.
20. EA, *Narrative*, 32–35.
21. Ibid., 32.
22. Ibid., 35.
23. Ibid., 36.
24. Ibid., 39.
25. Ibid., 38; Germain to John, Earl of Sandwich, Dec. 27, 1775, in Barnes and Owen, eds., *Private Papers of Earl of Sandwich*, 1:86.
26. EA, *Narrative*, 37.
27. Suffolk, reprinted in Wharton, 2:289n.
28. Horace Walpole, entry of June 23, 1775, *Last Journals*, 1:467.
29. Wedderburn to Wm. Eden, Dec. 27, 1775, VHS, Stevens facsimiles, 5:462.
30. EA, *Narrative*, 42–43.
31. Ibid., 40–41.
32. Germain to Mansfield, Aug. 6, 1776, in *DAR*, 12:176–77.

33. *EA, Narrative*, 45–46.
34. EA to the Gentlemen of Cork, Jan. 24, 1776, in *EAC*, 1:54–55.
35. EA, *Narrative*, 53.
36. Ibid., 52.
37. Ibid., 57–58.
38. Ibid., 58–59.
39. Ibid., 67–68.
40. EA to Conn. Assembly, Aug. 12, 1776, in *EAC*, 1:59–60.
41. EA, *Narrative*, 69–72.
42. EA to GW, Nov. 2, 1776, in *EAC*, 1:61–62.
43. John Adlum, quoted in Burrows, 61.
44. Graydon, 243, 242.
45. IA to Samuel Williams, June 6, 1795, in *EAC*, 2:443.
46. EA to Heman Allen, June 4, 1777, MS, Ethan Allen Papers, Henry Stevens Collection, VSA; EA to Levi Allen, July 27, 1777, in *EAC*, 1:71.
47. Fitch, quoted in Huguenin, 115.
48. E. Boudinot to John Adams, May 20, 1778, Boudinot Papers, Historical Society of Pennsylvania.
49. Huguenin, 117; EA, *Narrative*, 97; Fell, quoted in Burrows, 94.
50. EA, *Narrative*, 97–99; Burrows, 94.
51. EA, *Narrative*, 98.
52. Ibid., 102.
53. Ibid., 120.
54. Samuel Blachley Webb to Trumbull, quoted in Burrows, 103.
55. Randall, *Alexander Hamilton*, 166–67.
56. EA, *Narrative*, 121–22.
57. Ibid., 123.
58. GW to Laurens, May 12, 1778, in *WW*, 11:381.
59. Graydon, 243–44.
60. TJ to William Phillips, July 22, 1779, *PTJ*, 3:44–49.
61. EA, *Narrative*, 93.

CHAPTER 14: "A GAME OF HAZARD"

EA Returns to Vermont: Pell, *EA*, 135; Jellison, *EA*, 195–202; EA, *Works*, vol. 2; *ND*, vol. 10; *LDC*, vol. 10; Randall and Nahra, *TC's Town*; R. N. Hill, *College on the Hill*; D. F. Hawke, *Paine*; *EAC*, vol. 1; *WW*, vols. 19–20.

1. EA to GW, May 28, 1778, in *EAC*, 1:78.
2. Randall and Nahra, *TC's Town*, 60.
3. Ibid., 63.

4. Hawke, "Dr. TY," 27.

5. Ibid., 28; N.Y. delegates to president of N.Y. Convention, April 21, 1777; Wm. Duer to Robert R. Livingston, July 9, 1777, in Burnett, ed., 2:336, 410; Edes, 48; Caldwell, 297.

6. Duane to R. R. Livingston, June 28, 1777, in *LDC*, 7:260–61.

7. *VSP*, 242, 244–46.

8. In council, June 9, 1778, *VSP*, 239–40; EA to Henry Laurens, June 17, 1778, in *EAC*, 1:81.

9. TC in *TC's Town*, 71–72.

10. Ibid., 52.

11. EA to Eleazar Wheelock, June 14, 1778, in *EAC*, 1:80, and MS, DCL.

12. EA to Elisha Payne, July 11, 1778, in *EAC*, 1:82.

13. See *EAC*, 1:83, n. 2. The author is indebted to the editors of the *Correspondence of EA and His Kin* for their careful research into confiscation in Bennington County. The quotations are from Jellison, 198, and DePuy, 251.

14. EA to Elisha Payne, July 11, 1778, in *EAC*, 1:82.

15. *Connecticut Courant*, March 2, 1777.

16. Quoted in Jellison, *EA*, 203.

17. Josiah Bartlett to Meshech Weare, Aug. 4, 1778, in *LDC*, 10:388.

18. Sept. 26, 1778, in *LDC*, 10:693–94.

19. EA, *Vindication*, 22.

20. Quoted in Pell, *EA*, 160.

21. Bartlett to Weare, Sept. 26, 1778, in *LDC*, 10:693–95.

22. Gouverneur Morris to George Clinton, Sept. 27, 1778, in *LDC*, 10:703.

23. EA to Watson and Goodwin, Dec. 28, 1778, MS, Morgan Library.

24. Burrows, 161.

25. EA, *Vindication*, 159–60.

26. Ibid., 132.

27. Ibid., 139.

28. E. Wheelock to Benj. Pomeroy, March 30, 1778, MS, DCL.

29. T. Green to E. Wheelock, July 16, 1778, MS, DCL.

CHAPTER 15: "A HOOK IN THE NOSE"

Haldimand Negotiations: Pell, *EA*, 185–220; Randall and Nahra, *TC's Town*; Wilbur, *IA*, 1:148–291; Sherwood, *Journal of an Expedition*; McIlwraith, *Sir Frederick Haldimand*; *PAC*, Haldimand Papers, reels 88–93; Wardner, "Haldimand Negotiations"; Richardson, "Chief Justice William Smith"; Van Doren, *Secret History*.

NOTES 555

Philosopher: Pell, *EA*, 226–28; Jellison, *EA*, 299–334; EA, *Reason*; Williamson, *Vermont in Quandary*; Shalhope, *Bennington*; Shapiro, *EA*; Wardner, "Journal of a Loyalist Spy."

1. EA to Samuel Huntington, March 9, 1781, in *EAC*, 1:109–10.
2. Beverley Robinson to EA, March 30, 1780, in Haldimand Papers, PAC, reel 88, ser. B175, BM 21835.
3. *Burlington Sentinel*, March 10, 1849; Thompson, *Independent Vermont*, 400; Holbrook, *EA*, 140; Jellison, *EA*, 192.
4. Haldimand to Germain, Oct. 15, 1778, MS, Germain Papers, WLCL
5. C. Carleton to Haldimand, Nov. 14, 1778, Haldimand Papers, PAC.
6. Justus Sherwood to Haldimand, Oct. 26, 1780, "Journal of an Expedition to Negotiate with the State of Vermont," Haldimand Papers, PAC, reel 88, ser. B180. BM21840.
7. Ibid.
8. GW to Haldimand, Aug. 30, 1780, in *WW*, 19:473–74;
9. EA to C. Carleton, Nov. 4, 1780, in *EAC*, 1:105.
10. EA to John Stark, Dec. 7, 1780, *EAC*, 1:106–7.
11. EA to Samuel Huntingdon, March 9, 1781, in *EAC*, 1:109–10.
12. EA to Haldimand, June 16, 1782, in *EAC*, 1:130–31.
13. Charles Inglis, Dec. 12, 1778, MS, Riker, Memoria, vol. 15, 4–5. NYPL.
14. Justus Sherwood to Haldimand, Feb. 2, 1781, PAC.
15. Haldimand to Henry Clinton, Aug. 13, 1780, quoted in McIlwraith, *Sir Frederick Haldimand*, 208–10.
16. GW to TC, Jan. 1, 1782, in *WW*, 23:420–21.
17. GW to PS, quoted in Randall and Nahra, *TC's Town*, 82.
18. EA to Horatio Gates, July 15, 1778, in *EAC*, 1:83–84.
19. EA, preface to *Reason*.
20. Bassett, *The Gods of the Hills*, 19.
21. EA, *Reason*, 7, 59, 100.
22. EA to Stephen Bradley, Sept. 7, 1785, in *EAC*, 1:181–82.
23. EA to Benj. Stiles, Nov. 16, 1785, in *EAC*, 1:184.
24. EA to Crèvecouer, March 2, 1786, in *EAC*, 1:190–92.
25. Dwight, *Travels*, 2:283–84.
26. Bassett, "Intolerant Vermonters," in *We Vermonters*, 137.
27. Shalhope, *Bennington*, 187; EA's great-great-grandson and family historian, the late Ethan Allen Hitchcock Sims, maintained that Allen was "really a transcendentalist." Quoted in *Burlington (Vt.) Free Press*, Nov. 12, 2010.

CHAPTER 16: "CLODHOPPER PHILOSOPHER"

Shays's Rebellion: Pell, *EA*, 249–51; Minot, *History of the Insurrection*; Sanford, "Rutland Court Riots"; *EAC*, 1:235–45; Randall, *AH*, 317–27; Szatmary, *Shays' Rebellion;* Richards, *Shays's Rebellion*; Royall Tyler Papers, VHS.

Wyoming Valley Venture: EA, *Works*, 2:95–101; Pell, *EA*: 249–56; Randall, *AH*, 323–26; Freeman, *GW*, 6:15; Oliver Wolcott Sr., Papers, CHS; Pickering Papers, Mass. Historical Society; Cabell Gwathmey Papers, UVA; Nevins, Allan, *American States.*

1. EA quoted in Pell, *EA*, 257.
2. EA to IA, Aug. 18, 1786, in *EAC*, 1:205.
3. *Vermont Gazette*, Feb. 28, 1786; Aug. 28, 31, 1786; DePuy, 425.
4. John Marshall to James Wilkinson, Jan. 1787, MS, LOCO.
5. Hamilton to Franklin, March 24, 1786, in Boyd and Taylor, *Susquehannah Company*, 8:313.
6. Julian P. Boyd, "A Rare Broadside by EA," in PUL.
7. EA to Matthew Griswold, April 30, 1786, in *EAC*, 1:197–98.
8. GW to JM, Jan. 1782, quoted in Freeman, *GW*, 6:15.
9. TC, Feb. 27, 1787, in *VSP*.
10. EA, MS, Royall Tyler Papers, VHS.
11. Alexander Hamilton, "Remarks," Feb. 8, 1787, in Syrett, ed., *Papers*, 4:115–18.
12. Pell, *EA*, 244–45; F. J. Fairbanks, "The Other Parish," in Hemenway, 5:588; Holbrook, 210–13.
13. EA to Bradley, Nov. 16, 1787, in *EAC*, 1:249–50.
14. E. Stiles, *Literary Diary*, entry for Feb. 12, 1789.

AFTERWORD

1. Lossing, 1:164.
2. *DHNY*, 4:1024. The first post-revolutionary mayor of New York City, Duane served as a U.S. district court judge from 1790 until his death, in 1797. Only then were the funds distributed, his relatives receiving $2,621.29, the third-largest share.
3. JM quoted in Randall and Nahra, *Forgotten Americans*, 115–16.

BIBLIOGRAPHY

Abbott, Wilbur C. *New York in the American Revolution*. New York: Scribner's Sons, 1929.

Adams, Samuel, *Writings*. Edited by Harry Alonzo Cushing. 2 vols. New York: G. P. Putnam, 1904–08.

Ahlstrom, Sydney. *A Religious History of the American People*. New Haven: Yale University Press, 1972.

Ainslie, Thomas. *Canada Preserved: The Journal of Captain Thomas Ainslie*. Edited by Sheldon S. Cohen. New York: New York University Press, 1968.

Albers, Jan. *Hands on the Land: A History of the Vermont Landscape*. Cambridge: MIT Press, 2000.

Albion, Robert G. *Forests and Sea Power: The Timber Problem of the Royal Navy, 1652–1862*. Cambridge: Harvard University Press, 1926.

Aldrich, Lewis Cass, ed. *History of Bennington County, Vermont*. Syracuse: D. Mason, 1889.

Aldrich, Lewis Cass, and Frank R. Holmes, eds. *History of Windsor County, Vermont*. Syracuse: D. Mason, 1891.

Aldridge, A. Owen. *Thomas Paine's American Ideology*. Newark: University of Delaware Press, 1984.

Alexander, Edward P. *A Revolutionary Conservative: James Duane of New York*. New York: Columbia University Press, 1938.

Alexander, John K. "Forton Prison during the American Revolution: A Case Study of British Prisoner of War Policy." *Essex Institute Historical Collections* 103 (1967): 365–89.

Allen, Ethan. *An Animadversory Address to the Inhabitants of the State of Vermont*. Hartford: Watson and Goodwin, 1778.

———. *A Brief Narrative of the Government of New-York Relative to Their Obtaining the Jurisdiction of That Large District of Land Westward from the Connecticut River*. Hartford: Watson, 1774.

————. Letter. In "Mr. James Morrison and the Montreal Merchants at the Time of the American Invasion." *Canadian Antiquarian and Numismatic Journal* 3 (1847): 13–15.

————. *A Narrative of Colonel Ethan Allen's Captivity*. Edited by John Pell. New York: Georgian Press, 1930.

————. *A Narrative of Colonel Ethan Allen's Captivity*. Introduction by John Pell, illustrated by Will Crawford, 1988.

————. Papers. Wilbur Collection, Special Collections. Bailey/Howe Library, University of Vermont.

————. *Proceedings of the Convention of New Hampshire Settlers*. Hartford, 1775. In *Records of the Governor and Council of the State of Vermont*. Edited by E. P. Walton. 8 vols. Montpelier: Poland, 1873–80, 2:491–500.

————. *Reason, the Only Oracle of Man*. New York: G. W. Matsell, 1836.

————. *A Vindication of the Opposition of the Inhabitants of Vermont to the Government of New-York*. Hanover, N.H.: Alden Spooner, 1779.

Allen, Ethan, and Jonas Fay. *A Concise Refutation of the Claims of New Hampshire and Massachusetts Bay to the Territory of Vermont*. Hartford: Hudson and Goodwin, 1782.

Allen, Ethan, et al. *The Present State of the Controversy between the States of New York and New Hampshire on the One Part, and the State of Vermont on the Other*. Hartford: Hudson and Goodwin, 1782.

Allen, Ira. *The Natural and Political History of the State of Vermont*. London: J. W. Myers, 1798.

Allen, Orrin P. *The Allen Memorial*. Palmer, Mass.: Fiske, 1907.

American National Biography. Edited by John A. Garraty and Mark C. Carnes. 24 vols. New York: Oxford University Press, 1999.

Anderson, Fred. *Crucible of War: The Seven Years' War and the Fate of Empire in British North America, 1754–1766*. New York: Knopf, 2000.

————. *The War That Made America: A Short History of the French and Indian War*. New York: Viking, 2006.

Anderson, Olive. "The Treatment of Prisoners of War in Britain during the American War of Independence." *British Institute of Historical Research* 28 (1955): 63–83.

Anderson, S. Axel, and Florence Woodard. "Agricultural Vermont." *Economic Geography* 8 (1932): 12–42.

Anderson, Troyer Steele. *The Command of the Howe Brothers during the American Revolution*. New York: Oxford University Press, 1936.

Appleby, Joyce, ed. *Thomas Paine: Common Sense and Other Writings*. New York: Barnes & Noble Classics, 2009.

Armbruster, Eugene L. *The Wallabout Prison-Ships, 1776–1783*. New York, 1920.

Austin, Aleine. *Matthew Lyon: "New Man" of the Democratic Revolution.* University Park: Pennsylvania State University Press, 1981.

———. "Vermont Politics in the 1780's: Emergence of Rival Leadership." *Vermont History* 42 (1974): 140–54.

Bailyn, Bernard. *Ideological Origins of the American Revolution.* Cambridge: Harvard University Press, 1967.

Bancroft, George. "Mr. Bancroft's Letter on the Exchange of Prisoners during the American War of Independence." In *Tracts on the Exchange of Prisoners.* New York: n.p., 1862.

Barber, J. W., and Henry Howe. *Historical Collections of the State of New York.* New York, 1841.

Barck, Oscar T. *New York City during the War for Independence.* New York: Columbia University Press, 1937. Reprint, Port Washington, N.Y.: Friedman, 1966.

Barker-Benfield, G. J. "Anne Hutchinson and the Puritan Attitude toward Women." In *Portraits of American Women from Settlement to the Present.* New York: St. Martin's Press, 1991.

Barnes, G. R., and J. H. Owen, eds. *Private Papers of John, Earl of Sandwich, First Lord of the Admiralty, 1771–1782.* 4 vols. London: Navy Records Society, 1932–38.

Barnes, Melvin. *A Circular or Short Biography of Colonel Ebenezer Allen. . . .* Grand Isle, Vt.: privately printed, 1851.

Barr, John L. *Genealogy of Ethan Allen.* Burlington, Vt.: Ethan Allen Homestead Trust, 1991.

Bassett, T. D. Seymour. *The Gods of the Hills.* Montpelier: Vermont Historical Society, 2000.

Beardsley, Ebenezer E. *History of the Episcopal Church in Connecticut.* 2 vols. New York, 1865

Becker, Carl. *History of Political Parties in the Province of New York, 1760–1776.* Madison: University of Wisconsin Press, 1960.

Beebe, Lewis. "Journal of a Physician on the Expedition against Canada, 1776." *Pennsylvania Magazine of History and Biography* 49 (1935): 321–61.

Belknap, Jeremy. *History of New Hampshire.* 3 vols. Boston, 1791.

Bigelow, Edwin, and Nancy Otis. *Manchester, Vermont, 1761–1961: A Pleasant Land among the Mountains.* Reprint, Manchester: Rod and Reel Publishing Co., 1981.

Blake, J. B. "The Inoculation Controversy in Boston." *New England Quarterly* 25 (1952): 489–506.

Blow, David J. "Ethan Allen's Burlington Home, 1787–89." *Chittenden County Historical Society Bulletin* 13 (April 1978).

Bonomi, Patricia U. *A Factious People: Politics and Society in Colonial New York.* New York: Columbia University Press, 1971.

Bowman, Larry G. *Captive Americans: Prisoners during the American Revolution.* Athens: University of Ohio Press, 1976.

———. "The Pennsylvania Prisoner Exchange Conferences, 1778." *Pennsylvania Historical Review* 45 (1978): 257–69.

Boyd, George Adams. *Elias Boudinot: Patriot and Statesman, 1740–1821.* Princeton: Princeton University Press, 1952.

Boyd, Julian P. "Attempts to Form New States in New York and Pennsylvania, 1786–1789." *Quarterly Journal of the New York Historical Society* 12 (1931): 257–70.

Boyd, Julian P., et al., eds. *Papers of Thomas Jefferson.* 21 vols. Princeton: Princeton University Press, 1950–2009.

Boyd, Julian P., and Robert J. Taylor, eds. *The Susquehannah Company Papers.* 11 vols. Wilkes-Barre and Ithaca: Wyoming Historical and Geological Society, 1930–1971.

Brady, James E. "Wyoming: A Study of John Franklin and the Connecticut Movement into Pennsylvania." Ph.D. diss., Syracuse University, 1973.

Brault, Lucien. "Anglo-Canadians pro-rebelles pendant la Révolution Américaine." *Bulletin des Recherches Historiques* 44 (1938): 343–44.

Bremner, Robert H., ed. *Children and Youth in America: A Documentary History.* 3 vols. Cambridge: Harvard University Press, 1970–74.

British Headquarters Papers. William L. Clements Library, University of Michigan, Ann Arbor.

Britt, J. S. "Lessons for Martha's Children." *Virginia Cavalcade* 35 (1986): 172–83.

Brown, Richard Maxwell. "Back Country Rebellions and the Homestead Ethic in America, 1740–1799." *In Tradition, Conflict, and Modernization: Perspectives on the American Revolution*, edited by R. M. Brown and Donald Fehrenbacher. New York: Academic Press, 1977.

Brown, Wallace. *The Good Americans: Loyalists in the American Revolution.* New York: William Morrow, 1969.

———. *The King's Friends: The Composition and Motives of the American Loyalist Claimants.* Providence: Brown University Press, 1966.

Brunhouse, Robert L. *The Counter-Revolution in Pennsylvania, 1776–1790.* Harrisburg: Pennsylvania Historical Commission, 1942.

Brush, Crean. Papers, 1763–1775. Wilbur Collection, Special Collections, Bailey/Howe Library, University of Vermont.

Bryan, David. *A Nun for Two Nations: The Life of Sister Fanny Allen, RHSJ, 1784–1819.* Privately printed, n.p., n.d.

Brynn, Edward. "Vermont and the British Emporium, 1765–1865." *Vermont History* 45 (1977): 5–30.

Buckley, Kerry W., ed. *A Place Called Paradise: Culture and Community in Northampton, Massachusetts, 1654–2004.* Northampton: University of Massachusetts Press, 2004.

Bumsted, J. M. "Revivalism and Separatism in New England: The First Society of Norwich, Connecticut as a Case Study." *WMQ*, 3d ser., 24 (1967): 588–612.

Burnaby, Andrew. *Travels through the Middle Settlements of North America in the Years 1759 and 1760.* London, 1775. Reprint of 2d 1775 ed., Ithaca, N.Y.: Great Seal Books, 1960.

Burnett, Edmund C., ed. *Letters of the Members of the Continental Congress.* 8 vols. Washington, D.C.: Government Printing Office, 1921–36.

Burrows, Edwin G. *Forgotten Patriots: The Untold Story of American Patriots during the Revolutionary War.* New York: Basic Books, 2008.

Burrows, Edwin G., and Mike Wallace. *Gotham: A History of New York City to 1808.* New York: Oxford University Press, 1999.

Bush, Martin H. *Revolutionary Enigma: A Reappraisal of General Philip Schuyler of New York.* Port Washington, N.Y.: Kennikat Press, 1969.

Bushman, Richard L. *From Puritan to Yankee: Character and the Social Order in Connecticut, 1690–1765.* Cambridge: Harvard University Press, 1967.

Butler, Jon, et al. *Religion in American Life: A Short History.* New York: Oxford University Press, 2003.

Cahill, Robert Ellis. *The Old Irish of New England.* Peabody, Mass.: Chandler-Smith, 1985.

Caldwell, Renwick K. "The Man Who Named Vermont." *Vermont History* 26 (1958): 204–300.

Calhoon, Robert M. *The Loyalists in Revolutionary America, 1760–1781.* New York: Harcourt Brace Jovanovich, 1973.

Callahan, North. *Flight from the Republic: The Tories of the American Revolution.* Indianapolis: Bobbs-Merrill, 1967.

Calloway, Colin G. "The Conquest of Vermont: Vermont's Indian Troubles in Context." *Vermont History* 52 (1984): 161–79.

———. *Dawnland Encounters: Indians and Europeans in Northern New England.* Hanover, N.H.: University Press of New England, 1991.

———. *The Western Abenakis of Vermont, 1600–1800.* Norman: University of Oklahoma Press, 1990.

Camden, Darroll. *The Elizabethan Woman.* Houston: Elsevier, 1952.

Cameron, Kenneth W. *The Papers of Loyalist Samuel Peters.* Hartford: Transcendental Books, 1978.

Carleton, Sir Guy. *Papers*. Wooster, Ohio: Bell & Howell Micro Photo Division, 1980.

Carmer, Carl L. *The Susquehanna*. New York: Rinehart, 1955.

Caron, Ivanhoe. "Les Canadiens français et l'invasion américaine de 1774–1775." *Mémoires de la Société Royale du Canada*, 3d ser., 23 (1929): 21–34.

Carpenter, Dorr Bradley. *Stephen R. Bradley: Letters of a Revolutionary War Patriot and Vermont Senator*. Jefferson, N.C.: Macfarland, 2009.

Cavendish, Sir Henry. *Debates of the House of Commons in the Year 1774*. London, 1792. Reprint, New York: Johnson Reprint Co., 1966.

Champlain, Samuel de. *Voyages en Nouvelle-France*. Edited by Eric Thierry. Paris: Cosmopole, 2004.

Chase, Frederick. *A History of Dartmouth College and the Town of Hanover, New Hampshire*. 2 vols. Cambridge: Harvard University Press, 1891.

Chauncy, Charles. *Seasonable Thoughts on the Present State of Religion in New England*. Boston, 1743.

Chipman, Daniel. *Memoir of Thomas Chittenden*. Middlebury: privately printed, 1849.

———. *Reports of Cases Argued and Determined in the Supreme Court of the State of Vermont*. Middlebury: D. Chipman & Sons, 1824.

Chittenden, Lucius E. *Exercises Attending the Unveiling of a Statue of General Ethan Allen, July 4, 1874*.

Clark, L. D. "Vermont Lands of the Society of the Propagation of the Gospel in Foreign Parts." *New England Quarterly* 3 (1930): 279–96.

Clark, Solomon. *Antiquities, History and Graduates of Northampton*. Northampton: Gazette Publishing Co., 1882.

Clark, William Bell. *Naval Documents of the American Revolution*. 10 vols. Washington, D.C.: Government Printing Office, 1964–73.

Coke, Daniel P. *The Royal Commission on the Losses and the Services of the American Loyalists*. Edited by Hugh E. Egerton. Oxford, 1915. Reprint, New York: Arno Press, 1969.

Collier, Christopher. *Roger Sherman's Connecticut*. Middletown, Conn.: Wesleyan University Press, 1971.

Colonial Dames of America. *Ancestral Records and Portraits*. 2 vols. Baltimore: Grafton, 1910.

Commager, Henry Steele, and Richard B. Morris, eds. *The Spirit of 'Seventy-Six: The Story of the American Revolution as Told by Participants*. New York: Harper & Row, 1967.

Conforti, Joseph A. *Jonathan Edwards, Religious Tradition, and American Culture*. Chapel Hill: University of North Carolina Press, 1995.

Connecticut (colony). *The Public Records of the Colony of Connecticut, 1636–1776.* Edited by J. H. Trumbull et al. 15 vols. Hartford: Brown and Parsons, 1850–90.

Connecticut Historical Society. *Collections.* Hartford: published for the Society, 1860–90.

———. *Public Records, 1776–1818.* 17 vols. Hartford: published for the Society, 1894–1919.

Continental Congress. *Journals of the Continental Congress, 1774–1789.* Edited by Worthington C. Ford et al. 34 vols. Washington, D.C.: Government Printing Office, 1904–37.

Cothren, William. *History of Ancient Woodbury, Conn.* 2 vols. Bowie, Md.: Heritage, 1992.

Countryman, Edward. "Consolidating Power in Revolutionary America: The Case of New York, 1775–1783." *Journal of Interdisciplinary History* 6 (1976): 645–77.

———. *A People in Revolution: The American Revolution and Political Society in New York, 1760–1790.* Baltimore: Johns Hopkins University Press, 1981.

Cousins, Norman, ed. *"In God We Trust:" Religious Beliefs and Ideas of the American Founding Fathers.* New York: Harper, 1958.

Crane, Charles Edward. *Let Me Show You Vermont.* New York: Knopf, 1937.

Crary, Catherine. "The American Dream: John Tabor Kempe's Rise from Poverty to Riches." *WMQ,* 3d ser., 14 (1957): 176–95.

———. *The Price of Loyalty: Tory Writings from the Revolutionary Era.* New York: McGraw-Hill, 1973.

Crocker, Henry. *History of the Baptists in Vermont.* Bellows Falls, Vt.: Gobie, 1913.

Crockett, Walter Hill. *Vermont, the Green Mountain State.* 5 vols. New York: Century, 1921.

Cronon, William. *Changes in the Land: Indians, Colonists, and the Ecology of New England.* New York: Hill and Wang, 1983.

———. "Roger Sherman and the New Hampshire Grants." *Vermont History* 30 (1962): 211–19.

Cruikshank, E. A. "The Adventures of Roger Stevens: A Forgotten Loyalist Pioneer in Upper Canada." *Proceedings of the Ontario Historical Society* 33 (1939): 11–38.

Curtis, George T. "The Exchange of Prisoners in the American Revolution." In *Tracts on the Exchange of Prisoners.* New York: n.p., 1862.

———. "Report on Exchange of Prisoners during the American Revolution."

Curwen, Henry. *Ethan Allen and the Publishers.* In *Massachusetts Historical*

Society Proceedings 5 (1860–62). Reprint, Brattleboro, Vt.: Stephen Greene, 1973.

Dabney, William M. "After Saratoga: The Story of the Convention Army." In Charles Metzger, *The Prisoner in the American Revolution*. Chicago: Loyola University Press, 1971.

Dandridge, Danske. *American Prisoners of the Revolution*. Charlottesville: University of Virginia Press, 1911.

Dangerfield, George. *Chancellor Robert R. Livingston of New York, 1746–1813*. New York: Harcourt, Brace, 1960.

Dann, John C., ed. *The Revolution Remembered: Eyewitness Accounts of the War of Independence*. Chicago: University of Chicago Press, 1980.

Davies, K. G., ed. *Documents of the American Revolution, 1770–1783*. Colonial Office Series. 21 vols. Dublin: Irish University Press, 1972–81.

Davies, William. *Report of Commissioners for Settling a Cartel for the Exchange of Prisoners*. Philadelphia, 1779.

Davis, Kenneth S. "In the Name of the Great Jehovah and the Continental Congress." *American Heritage*, October 1963, pp. 66–77.

Dean, Leon W. *The Admission of Vermont into the Union*. Burlington, Vt.: Vermont Historical Society, 1941.

Del Papa, Eugene M. "The Royal Proclamation of 1763: Its Effect upon Virginia Land Companies." *Virginia Magazine of History and Biography* 83 (1975): 406–11.

Denio, Herbert W. "Massachusetts Land Grants in Vermont." *Proceedings of the Colonial Society of Massachusetts* 24 (1920): 35–59.

Dennis, Donald D. "The Deistic Trio: A Study of the Central Religious Beliefs of Ethan Allen, Thomas Paine and Elihu Palmer." Ph.D. diss., University of Utah, 1978.

DePauw, Linda Grant. *Founding Mothers: Women in America in the Revolutionary Era*. Boston: Houghton Mifflin, 1975.

———. *Four Traditions: Women of New York during the American Revolution*. Albany: New York State American Revolution Bicentennial Commission, 1974.

DePuy, Henry W. *Ethan Allen and the Green Mountain Boys of '76*. New York: J. C. Derby, 1854.

Dexter, Franklin Bowditch. *Biographical Sketches of the Graduates of Yale College*. 6 vols. New York: Holt, 1885–1919.

———, ed. *Literary Diary of Ezra Stiles*. New York: Scribner's Sons, 1901.

Dillon, Dorothy R. *The New York Triumvirate: A Study of the Legal and Political Careers of William Livingston, John Morin Scott, and William Smith, Jr.* New York: Columbia University Press, 1949.

Dionne, Narcisse-E. "L'Invasion de 1775–1776." *Bulletin de Recherches Historiques* 6 (1900): 132–40.

Dolin, Eric James. *Fur, Fortune, and Empire: The Epic History of the Fur Trade in America.* New York: Norton, 2010.

Douglas, Elisha P. *Rebels and Democrats: The Struggle for Equal Political Rights and Majority Rule during the American Revolution.* Chapel Hill, N.C.: Institute of Early American History, 1955.

Doyle, William. *The Vermont Political Tradition.* Rev. ed. Montpelier, Vt.: Leahy Press, 1999.

Duane, James. *Narrative of the Proceedings Subsequent to the Royal Adjudication.* New York: Holt, 1773.

Dudley, William, and Teresa O'Neill, eds. *Puritanism: Opposing Viewpoints.* San Diego: Greenhaven, 1994.

Duffy, John J., et al., eds. *Ethan Allen and His Kin: Correspondence, 1772–1819.* 2 vols. Hanover, N.H.: University Press of New England, 1998.

Dunn, Mary Maples. "Saints and Sisters: Congregational and Quaker Women in the Early Colonial Period." *Atlantic Quarterly* 30 (1978): 582–601.

Durfee, Eleazar, and D. Gregory Sanford, eds. *A Guide to the Henry Stevens Sr. Collection at the Vermont State Archives.* Montpelier: The Archives, 1989.

Dwight, Timothy. *Travels in New England and New York.* Edited by Barbara M. Solomon. 4 vols. Cambridge: Harvard University Press, 1969.

East, Robert A., and Jacob Judd, eds. *The Loyalist Americans: A Focus on Greater New York.* Tarrytown: Sleepy Hollow Restorations, 1975.

Eddis, William. *Letters from America . . . from 1769 to 1777, Inclusive.* London, 1792.

Edes, H. H. "Memoir of Dr. Thomas Young." *Transactions of the Colonial Society of Massaachuetts* 11 (1906): 2–54.

Egnal, Marc. "The Economic Development of the Thirteen Continental Colonies, 1720–1775." *WMQ*, 3d ser., 32 (1975): 191–222.

———. *A Mighty Empire: The Origins of the American Revolution.* Ithaca: Cornell University Press, 1988.

Elliott, Emory. *Power and the Pulpit in New England.* Princeton: Princeton University Press, 1975.

Elwood, Douglas. *The Philosophical Theology of Jonathan Edwards.* New York: Columbia University Press, 1960.

Encyclopedia of New England: The Culture and History of an American Region. Edited by Burt Feintuch and David H. Watters. New Haven: Yale University Press, 2005.

"Ethan Allen." In *Encyclopedia of the American Enlightenment*, edited by Mark G. Spencer. 2 vols. New York and London: Continuum, 2011.

Fennelly, Catherine. "Riots of 1742." *Pennsylvania Magazine of History and Biography* 92 (1968): 306–19.

Ferling, John E. *Almost a Miracle: The American Victory in the War of Independence.* New York: Oxford University Press, 2007.

Fischer, David Hackett. *Paul Revere's Ride.* New York: Oxford University Press, 1994.

———. *Washington's Crossing.* New York: Oxford University Press, 2004.

Fiske, John. *The Critical Period of American History.* Boston: Houghton Mifflin, 1888.

Fleming, Thomas. *Now We Are Enemies: The Story of Bunker Hill.* New York: St. Martin's Press, 1960.

———. *1776: Year of Illusions.* New York: Norton, 1975.

Flick, Alexander. *Loyalism in New York during the American Revolution.* New York, 1901. Reprint, New York: Arno Press, 1969.

Foner, Philip S., ed. *Complete Writings of Thomas Paine.* 2 vols. New York: Citadel Press, 1945.

Force, Peter, ed. *American Archives: Consisting of a Collection of Authentic Records, State Papers, Debates, and Letters . . . .* 4th ser., March 7, 1774–July 4, 1776, 6 vols. 5th ser., July 4, 1776–Sept. 3, 1783, 3 vols. Washington, D.C., 1837–46 and 1848–53.

Franklin, Benjamin. *The Autobiography of Benjamin Franklin.* Edited by Leonard W. Labaree. New Haven: Yale University Press, 1965.

Freeman, D. S. *George Washington: A Biography.* 7 vols. New York: Scribner's, 1948–57.

French, Allen. *The First Year of the Revolution.* New York: Octogon Books, 1968.

———. *The Taking of Ticonderoga in 1775: The British Story.* Cambridge: Harvard University Press, 1928.

Fruchtman, Jack. *Thomas Paine and the Religion of Nature.* Baltimore: Johns Hopkins University Press, 1993.

———. *Thomas Paine, Apostle of Freedom.* New York: Four Walls Eight Windows, 1994.

Gallagher, John J. *The Battle of Brooklyn, 1776.* New York: Sarpedon, 1995.

Gaustad, Edwin S. *The Great Awakening in New England.* New York: Harper, 1957.

Gerlach, Don R. *Philip Schuyler and the American Revolution in New York, 1733–1804.* Lincoln: University of Nebraska Press, 1964.

———. *Philip Schuyler and the Growth of New York, 1733–1804.* Albany: Office of State History, 1968.

Gipson, Lawrence Henry. *The British Empire before the American Revolution.* 12 vols. New York: Knopf, 1936–70.

———. *Jared Ingersoll: A Study of American Loyalism in Relation to British Colonial Government.* New Haven: Yale University Press, 1920.

Goebel, Julius, Jr. "The Courts and the Law in Colonial New York." In *Essays in the History of Early American Law,* edited by David H. Flaherty. Chapel Hill: University of North Carolina Press, 1969.

Goebel, Julius, Jr., and T. R. Naughton. *Law Enforcement in Colonial New York: A Study in Criminal Procedure, 1664–1776.* New York: Commonwealth Fund, 1944.

Goen, C. C. *Revivalism and Separatism in New England.* New Haven: Yale University Press, 1962.

Gold, Theodore S. *Historical Records of the Town of Cornwall.* Hartford: Case, Lockwood, and Brainard, 1904.

Goodrich, John E. "Immigration to Vermont." *Proceedings of the Vermont Historical Society* (1907–08): 65–86.

Gordon-Reed, Annette. *The Hemingses of Monticello: An American Family.* New York: Norton, 2008.

Graffagnino, Kevin, ed. *Ethan and Ira Allen, Collected Works.* 3 vols. Benson, Vt.: Chalidze, 1992.

Graham, Ian C. C. *Colonists from Scotland: Emigration to North America, 1707–1783.* Ithaca: Cornell University Press, 1956.

Graydon, Alexander. *Memoirs of His Own Time: With Reminiscences of the Men and Events of the Revolution.* Philadelphia: Lindsay and Blakiston, 1846. Reprint, New York: New York Times, 1979.

Graymont, Barbara. *The Iroquois in the American Revolution.* Syracuse: Syracuse University Press, 1972.

Great Britain, Royal Commission on Historical Manuscripts. *Commission Report on American Manuscripts in the Royal Institution of Great Britain.* 4 vols. London, 1904–09.

Gruber, Ira. "America's First Battle: Long Island, August 27, 1776." In *America's First Battles, 1776–1965,* edited by Charles Heller and William Stofft. Lawrence: University of Kansas Press, 1986.

———. *The Howe Brothers and the American Revolution.* New York: Atheneum, 1972.

Hall, Benjamin Homer. *History of Eastern Vermont, from Its Earliest Settlement to the Close of the Eighteenth Century.* New York: G. P. Putnam Sons, 1857.

Hall, Donald D., ed. *The Antinomian Controversy, 1636–1638: A Documentary History.* Middletown, Conn.: Wesleyan University Press, 1968.

Hall, Henry. *Ethan Allen: The Robin Hood of Vermont.* New York: Appleton, 1892.

Hall, Hiland. *History of Vermont from Its Discovery and Its Admission into the Union.* Albany: Munsell, 1868.

Halleck, Henry Wager. *Elements of International Law and Laws of War.* San Francisco, 1866.

Hamlin, Paul M., and Charles E. Baker. *Supreme Court of Judicature of the Province of New York, 1691–1704.* New York: New-York Historical Society, 1959.

Handlin, Oscar. "The Eastern Frontier in New York." *New York History* 18 (1937): 50–75.

Harrington, Virginia. "The Colonial Merchant's Ledger." In *History of the State of New York*, vol. 2, *Under Duke and King*, edited by Alexander C. Flick. New York: Columbia University Press, 1933.

Hatch, Nathan O. *The Democratization of American Christianity.* New Haven: Yale University Press, 1989.

Hatch, Robert M. *Thrust for Canada: The American Attempt on Quebec, 1775–1776.* Boston: Houghton Mifflin, 1979.

Hawke, David Freeman. "Dr. Thomas Young: 'Eternal Fisher in Troubled Waters.'" *N-YHS Quarterly* 54 (1970): 6–29.

———. *Paine.* New York: Harper & Row, 1974.

Hawks, Francis L., and William Stevens Perry, eds. *Documentary History of the Protestant Episcopal Church in the United States of America.* New York: James Pott, 1863.

Headley, Joel Tyler. *The Chaplains and Clergy of the Revolution.* New York: Scribner, 1864.

Heimert, Alan, and Andrew Delbanco, eds. *Puritans in America: A Narrative Anthology.* Cambridge: Harvard University Press, 1985.

Heimert, Alan, and Perry Miller, eds. *The Great Awakening.* Indianapolis: Bobbs-Merrill, 1967

Hemenway, Abby Maria. *The Vermont Historical Gazetteer.* 5 vols. Montpelier, Vt., 1867–91.

Henderson, H. James. *Party Politics in the Continental Congress.* New York: McGraw-Hill, 1974.

Henderson, Patrick. "Smallpox and Patriotism: The Norfolk Riots, 1768–1769," *Virginia Magazine of History and Biography* 73 (1965): 413–24.

Heyrman, Christine Leigh. *Commerce and Culture: The Maritime Communities of Colonial Massachusetts, 1690–1750.* New York: Norton, 1984.

Higginbotham, Don. *The War of American Independence: Military Attitudes, Policies, and Practice, 1763–1789.* New York: Macmillan, 1971.

Hill, Christopher. *Society and Puritanism in Pre-Revolutionary England.* New York: Schocken Books, 1964

Hill, Ralph Nading. *The College on the Hill: A Dartmouth Chronicle.* Hanover: Dartmouth Publications, 1964.

———. *The Winooski, Heartway of Vermont.* New York: Rinehart, 1949.

Himelhoch, Myra. *The Allens in Early Vermont.* Introduction by T. D. Seymour Bassett. Barre, Vt.: Star Printing, 1967.

Hindle, Brooke, ed.. *America's Wooden Age: Aspects of Its Early Technology.* Tarrytown: Sleepy Hollow Restorations, 1975.

Hoffman, Ronald, and Peter J. Albert, eds. *Sovereign States in an Age of Uncertainty.* Charlottesville: University Press of Virginia, 1981.

Holbrook, Stewart Hall. *Ethan Allen.* Portland, Ore.: Binfords & Mort, 1958.

Holifield, E. B. *Theology in America: Christian Thought from the Age of the Puritans to the Civil War.* New Haven: Yale University Press, 2003.

Holmes, David L. *Faiths of the Founding Fathers.* New York: Oxford University Press, 2006.

Hoyt, Edwin P. *The Damnedest Yankees: Ethan Allen and His Clan.* Brattleboro, Vt.: Stephen Greene, 1976.

Huber, Elaine C. *Women and the Authority of Inspiration: A Reexamination of Two Prophetic Movements from a Contemporary Feminist Perspective.* Lanham, Md.: University Press of America, 1985.

Huguenin, Charles A. "Ethan Allen, Parolee on Long Island." *Vermont History* 25 (1957): 103–25.

Hurst, James Willard. "Alexander Hamilton, Law Maker." *Columbia Law Review* 78 (1978): 483–547.

Isham, Edward Swift. "Ethan Allen, A Study in Civic Authority." *Proceedings of the Vermont Historical Society* (1898): 27–103.

Jefferson, Thomas. *Writings.* Edited by Merrill D. Peterson. New York: Library of America, 1984.

Jellison, Charles. *Ethan Allen: Frontier Rebel.* Syracuse: Syracuse University Press, 1969.

Jenkins, Kathleen. *Montreal, Island City of the St. Lawrence.* Garden City, N.Y.: Doubleday, 1966.

Jennings, Francis P. "Anthropological Foundations for American Indian History." *Reviews in American History* 7 (1979): 486–93.

———. "The Indian Trade of the Susquehanna Valley." *Proceedings of the American Philosophical Society* 110 (1966): 406–24.

———. *The Invasion of America: Indians, Colonialism, and the Cant of Conquest.* Chapel Hill: University of North Carolina Press, 1975.

Jesuit Relations, Letters from Missions. Edited by Reuben Gold Thwaites. 73 vols. Cleveland: Burrows Brothers, 1896–1901.

Johnson, William Samuel. Diary and Correspondence. MS in Connecticut
    Historical Society.
Johnston, Henry P. *The Campaign of 1776 around New York and Brooklyn.* New
    York, 1878. Reprint, New York: Da Capo Press, 1971.
————. *Record of Service on Connecticut Men in the War of the Revolution.* Hart-
    ford, Conn.: Case, Lockwood and Brainard, 1889.
Jones, Matt B. *Vermont in the Making, 1750–1777.* Hamden, Conn.: Archon
    Books, 1968.
Jones, Thomas. *History of New York during the Revolutionary War.* 2 vols. New
    York: New-York Historical Society, 1879.
Journals of the Continental Congress, 1774–1789. Washington, D.C.: Library of
    Congress, 1929–32.
Kaminski, John P. "Adjusting to Circumstances: New York's Relationship
    with the Federal Government, 1776–1788." In *The Constitution and the
    States: The Role of the Original Thirteen in the Framing and the Adoption of
    the Federal Constitution,* edited by Patrick Conley and John P. Kaminski.
    Madison: University of Wisconsin Press, 1988.
Keane, John. *Tom Paine: A Political Life.* Boston: Little, Brown, 1995.
Kierner, Cynthia A. "Landlord and Tenant in Revolutionary New York: The
    Case of Livingston Manor." *New York History* 70 (2001): 133–52.
————. *Traders and Gentlefolk: The Livingstons of New York, 1675–1790.* Ithaca:
    Cornell University Press, 1992.
Kim, Sung Bok. *Landlord and Tenant in Colonial New York: Manorial Society,
    1665–1775.* Chapel Hill: University of North Carolina Press, 1978.
————. "A New Look at the Great Landlords of Eighteenth-Century New
    York." *WMQ,* 3d ser., 27 (1970): 581–614.
Klein, Milton. *The American Whig: William Livingston of New York.* New York:
    Garland, 1990.
Klingle, Philip. "King's County During the American Revolution." In *Brooklyn
    USA,* edited by Rita S. Miller. New York: Columbia University Press, 1979.
Knollenberg, Bernhard. *Origins of the American Revolution, 1759–1766.* New
    York: Macmillan, 1960.
Kouwenhoven, John Atlee. *The Columbia Historical Portrait of New York.* Gar-
    den City, N.Y.: Doubleday, 1953.
Kowalski, Gary. *Revolutionary Spirits: The Enlightened Faith of America's
    Founding Fathers.* New York: Bluebridge, 2008.
Labaree, Leonard W. *Royal Instructions to British Colonial Governors.* 2 vols.
    New York: London: Appleton-Century, 1935.
Lanctôt, Gustave. *Canada and the American Revolution, 1774–83.* Toronto:
    University of Toronto Press, 1967.

Landesman, Alter F. *A History of New Lots: Brooklyn to 1877.* Port Washington, N.Y.: Kennikat Press, 1977.

Leder, Lawrence H. "The New York Assembly Elections of 1769: An Assault on Privilege." *Mississippi Valley Historical Review* 49 (1962): 675–82.

Lemisch, Jesse. "Listening to the 'Inarticulate': William Widger's Dream and the Loyalties of American Revolutionary Seamen in British Prisons." *Journal of Social History* 3 (1969): 1–28.

Lincoln, Charles Z. *The Colonial Laws of New York from the Year 1664 to the Revolution.* 5 vols. Albany, N.Y.: J. B. Lyon, 1894.

Lossing, Benson J. *Pictorial Field Book of the American Revolution.* 2 vols. New York: Harper Brothers, 1860.

Love, William DeLoss. *Colonial History of Hartford.* Chester, Conn.: privately published, 1974.

Lustig, Mary Lou. *Privilege and Prerogative: New York's Provincial Elite, 1710–1776.* Madison, N.J.: Fairleigh Dickinson University Press, 1995.

Maier, Pauline. *From Resistance to Revolution: Colonials Radicals and the Development of Colonial Opposition to Britain, 1765–1776.* New York: Knopf, 1972.

Main, Jackson Turner. *The Social Structure of Revolutionary America.* Princeton: Princeton University Press, 1965.

Mark, Irving. *Agrarian Conflicts in Colonial New York, 1711–1775.* New York: Columbia University Press, 1940.

Marsden, George M. *Jonathan Edwards: A Life.* New Haven: Yale University Press, 2003.

Mather, Frederick G. *The Refugees of 1776 from Long Island to Connecticut.* Albany, 1913. Reprint, Baltimore, Md.: Clearfield, 1995.

McBride, Kevin A. "The Source and Mother of the Fur Trade: Native-Dutch Relations in Eastern New Netherland." In *Enduring Traditions: The Native Peoples of New England,* edited by Laurie Weinstein. Westport, Conn.: Greenwood Press, 1994.

McCaughey, Elizabeth P. *From Loyalist to Founding Father: The Political Odyssey of William Samuel Johnson.* New York: Columbia University Press, 1980.

McCusker, John J. *Money and Exchange in Europe and America, 1600–1775: A Handbook.* Chapel Hill, N.C.: Institute of Early American Studies, 1978.

McIlwraith, J. N. *Sir Frederick Haldimand.* London: Oxford University Press, 1926.

McNamara, Patrick. "'By the Rude Storms of Faction Blown': Thomas Jones a Long Island Loyalist." *Long Island Historical Journal* 7 (1995): 178–90.

Meacham, Jon. *American Gospel: God, the Founding Fathers, and the Making of a Nation.* New York: Random House, 2006.

Metzger, Charles H. *The Prisoner in the American Revolution*. Chicago: Loyola
University Press, 1971.

————. *The Quebec Act: A Primary Cause of the American Revolution*. New
York: U.S. Catholic Historical Society, 1936.

Middlekauff, Robert. *The Glorious Cause*. New York: Oxford University Press,
1982.

Miller, Perry. "The Half-way Covenants." *New England Quarterly* 6 (1933):
676–715.

Miller, Perry, and Thomas H. Johnson, eds. *The Puritans*. 2 vols. New York:
Harper & Row, 1963.

Miller, Rita S. *Brooklyn, USA*. New York: Columbia University Press, 1979.

Miner, Charles Abbott. *History of Wyoming in a Series of Letters to His Son,
William Penn Miner*. Philadelphia, 1845.

Minot, G. R. *History of the Insurrection in Massachusetts*. Worcester, Mass.:
Isaiah Thomas, 1788.

Montresor, Captain John. *A Map of the Province of New York with Part of Pennsylvania and New England*. . . . London, June 10, 1775.

Moore, Frank. *Diary of the American Revolution from Newspapers and Original
Documents*. 2 vols. New York: Washington Square Press, 1860.

Morais, Herbert M. *Deism in Eighteenth Century America*. New York: Columbia University Press, 1934.

Morgan, Edmund S. *The Genuine Article: A Historian Looks at Early America*.
New York: Norton, 2004.

————. *The Puritan Dilemma: The Story of John Winthrop*. Boston: Little,
Brown, 1958.

————. *The Puritan Family: Essays on Religion and Domestic Relations in
Seventeenth-Century New England*. Boston: Boston Public Library, 1944.

————. *The Stamp Act Crisis*. Chapel Hill, NC: Institute of Early American
History, 1953.

————. *Visible Saints: The History of a Puritan Idea*. New York: New York University Press, 1963.

Nahra, Nancy, ed. *When the French Were Here*. Burlington, Vt.: Queen City
Press, 2010.

Nash, Gary B. *The Urban Crucible: Social Change, Political Consciousness, and
the Origins of the American Revolution*. Cambridge: Harvard University
Press, 1980.

Neatby, Hilda. *Quebec: The Revolutionary Age, 1760–1791*. Toronto: McClel-
land and Stewart, 1966.

Nelson, Paul David. *General Sir Guy Carleton, Lord Dorcester: Soldier-Statesman of Early British Canada.* Madison, N.J.: Fairleigh Dickinson University Press, 2000.

———. *William Tryon and the Course of Empire: A Life in British Imperial Service.* Chapel Hill: University of North Carolina Press, 1990.

Nelson, William H. Nelson. *The American Tory.* Oxford: Clarendon Press, 1961.

Nevins, Allan. *The American States during and after the American Revolution, 1775–1789.* New York: Macmillan, 1927.

Nobles, Gregory H. "Breaking into the Backcountry: New Approaches to the Early American Frontier, 1750–1800." *WMQ*, 3d ser., 46 (1989): 641–70.

———. *Divisions throughout the Whole: Politics and Society in Hampshire County, Massachusetts, 1740–1775.* New York: Cambridge University Press, 1985.

Norton, Thomas Elliott. *The Fur Trade in Colonial New York, 1686–1776.* Madison: University of Wisconsin Press, 1974.

Oberholzer, Emil. *Delinquent Saints: Disciplinary Action in the Early Congregational Churches of Massachusetts.* New York: Columbia University Press, 1956.

O'Callaghan, E. B., ed. *Documentary History of the State of New-York.* Vol. 4. Albany: Charles van Benthuysen, 1851.

Olson, Allison Gilbert. *Anglo-Amerian Politics, 1660–1775: The Relationship between Parties in England and Colonial America.* New York: Oxford University Press, 1973.

Onderdonk, Henry, Jr. *Revolutionary Incidents of Suffolk and Kings County.* Port Washington, N.Y.: Kennikat Press, 1970.

Pachter, Marc, and Frances Wein, eds. *Abroad in America: Visitors to the New Nation, 1776-1914.* Reading, Mass.: Addison-Wesley, 1976.

Paine, Thomas. *The Age of Reason.* Edited by Philip S. Foner. Secaucus, N.J.: Citadel Press, 1974.

———. *Common Sense.* Philadelphia, 1776.

Peckham, Howard H. *The Colonial Wars, 1689–1762.* Chicago: University of Chicago Press, 1964.

Pell, John. *Ethan Allen.* Boston: Houghton Mifflin, 1929.

Pemberton, Ian. "Justus Sherwood, Vermont Loyalist, 1747–1798." Ph.D. diss., University of Western Ontario, 1972.

Perkins, Nathan. *Narrative of a Tour through the State of Vermont.* Woodstock, Vt.: Elm Tree Press, 1920.

Pickering, Danby, ed. *Great Britain: Statutes at Large [from 1225 to 1867].* London: C. Bathurst, 1869.

Pope, Robert G. *The Halfway Covenant: Church Membership in Puritan New England.* Princeton: Princeton University Press, 1969.

Potter, Janice. *The Liberty We Seek: Loyalist Ideology in Colonial New York and Massachusetts*. Cambridge: Harvard University Press, 1983.

Puls, Mark. *Samuel Adams: Father of the American Revolution*. New York: Palgrave Macmillan, 2006.

Purvis, Thomas L. "Origins and Patterns of Agrarian Unrest in New Jersey, 1735 to 1754." *WMQ*, 3d ser., 39 (1982): 600–27.

Randall, Willard Sterne. *Alexander Hamilton: A Life*. New York: HarperCollins, 2003.

———. *Benedict Arnold: Patriot and Traitor*. New York: William Morrow, 1990.

———. *George Washington: A Life*. New York: Henry Holt, 1998.

———. *A Little Revenge: Benjamin Franklin and His Son*. Boston: Little, Brown, 1984.

———. *The Proprietary House at Amboy*. Trenton, N.J.: Whitechapel, 1975.

———. *Thomas Jefferson: A Life*. New York: Henry Holt, 1993.

Randall, Willard Sterne, and Nancy Nahra. *American Lives*. 2 vols. New York: HarperCollins, 1996.

———. *Forgotten Americans*. Reading, Mass.: Addison-Wesley, 1998.

———. *Thomas Chittenden's Town: A Story of Williston, Vermont*. Burlington, Vt.: Queen City Press, 1998.

Rasmussen, Wayne D. "Wood on the Farm." In *America's Wooden Age: Aspects of Its Early Technology*, edited by Brooke Hindle. Tarrytown: Sleepy Hollow Restorations, 1975.

Reports of Cases Argued and Determined in the Supreme Court of the State of Vermont. Middlebury, Vt.: D. Chapin and Sons, 1824.

Reubens, Beatrice G. "Pre-emptive Rights in the Disposition of a Confiscated Estate: Philipsburg Manor, New York." *WMQ*, 3d ser., 22 (1965): 435-56.

Reynolds, Paul Revere. *Guy Carleton: A Biography*. New York: William Morrow, 1980.

Riccards, Michael P. "Patriots and Plunderers: Confiscation of Loyalist Lands in New Jersey, 1776–1786." *New Jersey History* 86 (1968): 14–28.

Richards, Leonard L. *Shays's Rebellion: The American Revolution's Final Battle*. Philadelphia: University of Pennsylvania Press, 2003.

Richardson, A. J. H. "Chief Justice William Smith and the Haldimand Negotiations." *Proceedings of the Vermont Historical Society* 9 (1941): 84–114.

Rife, Clarence W. "Ethan Allen: An Interpretation." *New England Quarterly* 2 (1929): 561–84.

Riker, James, Sr. *The Annals of Newtown in Queens County, New York*. New York, 1852. Reprint, Lambertville, N.J.: Hunterdon House, 1982.

Ritchie, Carson I. "A New York Diary of the Revolutionary War." In *Narratives of the Revolution in New York*. New York: New-York Historical Society, 1975.

Rugg, Harold Goddard. "The Dresden Press." *Dartmouth Alumni Magazine* 12 (1920): 798–814.

Rutland, Robert A. *The Birth of the Bill of Rights, 1776–1791.* Chapel Hill, N.C.: Institute of Early American History, 1955.

Sabine, Lorenzo. *Biographical Sketches of the Loyalists of the American Revolution.* 2 vols. Boston: Little, Brown, 1864.

Sachse, William. *Colonial Americans in Britain.* Madison: University of Wisconsin Press, 1956.

Schallenberg, Richard H. "Charcoal Iron." In *America's Wooden Age: Aspects of Its Early Technology,* edited by Brooke Hindle. Tarrytown: Sleepy Hollow Restorations, 1975.

Schaukirk, Ewald G. *Occupation of New York City by the British.* New York, 1887. Reprint, New York: New York Times, 1979.

Schecter, Barnet. *The Battle for New York: The City at the Heart of the American Revolution.* New York: Penguin, 2003.

Scull, G. D., ed. *The Montresor Journals.* New York, 1882.

Serle, Ambrose. *The American Journal of Ambrose Serle, 1776–1778.* Edited by E. H. Tatum Jr. San Marino, Calif.: Huntington Library, 1940.

Shalhope, Robert E. *Bennington and the Green Mountain Boys: The Emergence of Liberal Democracy in Vermont, 1760–1850.* Baltimore: Johns Hopkins University Press, 1996.

Shapiro, Darline. "Ethan Allen: Philosopher-Theologian to a Generation of American Revolutionaries." *WMQ,* 3d ser., 21 (1964): 236–55.

Sherwood, Justus. *Journal of an Expedition.* In *Report on the Canadian Archives,* compiled by Douglas Brymner. Ottowa: Maclean, Roger, 1883.

Smith, Donald A. "Legacy of Dissent: Religion and Politics in Revolutionary Vermont." Ph.D. diss., Clark University, 1981.

Smith, Paul Hubert, et al., eds. *Letters of Delegates to Congress, 1774–1789.* 26 vols. Washington, D.C.: Government Printing Office, 1976–2000.

Smith, William. *An Examination of Connecticut Claims to Lands in Pennsylvania.* Philadelphia: J. Cruikshank, 1774.

———. *Historical Memoirs from 12 July 1776 to 25 July 1778.* Edited by William H. W. Sabine. New York, 1958. Reprint, New York: New York Times, 1969–71.

Snyder-Grenier, Ellen M. *Brooklyn! An Illustrated History.* Philadelphia: Temple University Press, 1996.

Sparks, Jared. *The Library of American Biography.* Vol. 1. New York: Harper and Brothers, 1839.

Spaulding, E. Wilder. *His Excellency George Clinton: Critic of the Constitution.* New York: Macmillan, 1938.

———. *New York in the Critical Period, 1783–1780*. New York: Columbia University Press, 1932.

Sprague, William B., ed. *Annals of the American Pulpit*. 9 vols. Philadelphia: 1858.

Squires, James D. *Granite State of the United States: A History of New Hampshire from 1623 to the Present*. Vol. 1. New York: American Historical Co., 1956.

Starr, Edward C. *A History of Cornwall, Connecticut*. Cornwall, Conn.: Tuttle, Morehouse, and Taylor, 1926.

Stiles, Ezra, *The Literary Diary of Ezra Stiles*. Edited by Franklin Bowditch Dexter. 3 vols. New York: C. Scribner, 1901.

Stokes, I. N. Phelps, comp. *The Iconography of Manhattan Island, 1498–1909*. 6 vols. New York: R. H. Dodd, 1915–28.

Stone, Lawrence. *The Family, Sex, and Marriage, 1500–1800*. New York: Harper & Row, 1979.

Stout, Harry, and Peter Onuf. "James Davenport and the Great Awakening in New London." *Journal of American History* 70 (1983): 556–78.

Strickland, William. *Journal of a Tour in the United States of America, 1794–1795*. Edited by J. E. Strickland. New York: New-York Historical Society, 1971.

Syrett, Harold, ed. *The Papers of Alexander Hamilton*. 27 vols. New York: Columbia University Press, 1961–87.

Szatmary, David P. *Shays' Rebellion: The Making of an Agrarian Insurrection*. Amherst: University of Massachusetts Press, 1980.

Thomas, Isaiah. *The History of Printing in America*. 2d ed. 2 vols. Albany, 1874.

Thompson, Charles Miner. *Independent Vermont*. Boston: Houghton Mifflin, 1942.

Thompson, Zadock. *History of the State of Vermont from Its Earliest Settlement to the Close of the Year 1832*. Burlington, 1832.

Tiedemann, Joseph S. "Patriots by Default: Queens County, New York, and the British Army, 1776–1783." *WMQ*, 3d ser., 43 (1976): 35–63.

Tracts on the Exchange of Prisoners. 4 vols. New York, 1862.

Tracy, Patricia J. *Jonathan Edwards, Pastor: Religion and Scoeity in Eighteenth-Century Northampton*. New York: Hill and Wang, 1980.

Trumbull, James Russell. *History of Northampton*. 3 vols. Northampton, Mass.: Gazette Printing Co., 1902.

Underdown, David. *Revel, Riot, and Rebellion: Popular Culture in England, 1603–1660*. Oxford: Clarendon Press, 1985.

Unger, Harlow Giles. *John Hancock, Merchant King and American Patriot*. Hoboken: John Wiley, 2000.

United States. Naval History Division. *Naval Documents of the American Revolution*. 10 vols. Washington, D.C.: Government Printing Office, 1964–73.

Upton, L. F. S. *The Loyal Whig: William Smith of New York and Quebec.* Toronto: University of Toronto Press, 1969.

Van der Water, Frederic F. *The Reluctant Republic: Vermont, 1724–1791.* New York: John Day, 1941.

Van Doren, Carl. *Secret History of the American Revolution.* New York: Viking, 1941.

Van Tyne, Claude H. *The Loyalists in the American Revolution.* New York: Macmillan, 1902.

Vermont. *Constitution of the State of Vermont.* Montpelier, 1852.

Vermont State Papers. Middlebury: Copeland, 1823.

Virtual Reference Library. Haldimand Papers Digital.

Waldman, Steven. *Founding Faith: Providence, Politics, and the Birth of Religious Freedom in America.* New York: Random House, 2008.

Wall, Alexander J. "New York and the Declaration of Independence." In *Narratives of the Revolution in New York.* New York: New-York Historical Society, 1975.

Walpole, Horace. *Last Journals of Horace Walpole during the Reign of George III from 1771–1783.* Edited by John Doran. 2 vols. London: J. Lane, 1910.

Ward, Christopher. *The War of the Revolution.* Edited by John R. Alden. 2 vols. New York: Macmillan, 1952.

Warden, Gerard. B. *Boston, 1689–1776.* Boston: Little, Brown, 1970.

Wardner, Henry Steele. "Haldimand Negotiations." In *Birthplace of Vermont: A History of Windsor to 1781.* New York: Scribner's 1927.

———. "Journal of a Loyalist Spy: Justus Sherwood." *Vermonter* 28 (1923).

Warnock, James. "Thomas Bradbury Chandler and William Smith: Diversity within Colonial Anglicanism." *Anglican and Episcopal History* 57 (1988): 272–97.

Washington, George. *The Papers of George Washington.* Edited by Philander Chase et al. Revolutionary War Series. 20 vols. to date. Charlottesville: University of Virginia Press, 1985–.

———. *The Writings of George Washington.* Edited by Worthington Chauncey Ford. 14 vols. New York: G. P. Putnam, 1889–93.

Washington, Ida H., and Paul A. *Carleton's Raid.* Weybridge, Vt.: Cherry Tree Books, 1977.

Weld, Ralph Foster. *Brooklyn Is America.* New York: Columbia University Press, 1950.

Wertenbaker, Thomas J. *Father Knickerbocker Rebels.* New York: C. Scribner's, 1946.

We Vermonters: Perspectives on the Past. Edited by Michael Sherman and Jennie Versteeg. Montpelier: Vermont Historical Society, 1992.

Wharton, Francis, ed. *Revolutionary Diplomatic Correspondence of the United States*. 6 vols. Washington, D.C.: Government Printing Office, 1889.

Whiteman, Maxwell. *Copper for America: The Hendricks Family and a National Industry, 1755–1939*. New Brunswick: Rutgers University Press, 1971.

Wilbur, James Benjamin. *Ira Allen, Founder of Vermont, 1751–1814*. 2 vols. Boston: Houghton Mifflin, 1928.

Williamson, Chilton. *Vermont in Quandary, 1763–1825*. Montpelier, Vt.: Vermont Historical Society, 1949.

Winslow, Ola Elizabeth. *Jonathan Edwards, 1703–1758: A Biography*. New York: Macmillan, 1940.

Winthrop, John. *The Journal of John Winthrop*. Edited by Richard S. Dunn et al. Cambridge: Harvard University Press, 1996.

Woodward, Florence May. *Town Proprietors in Vermont: The New England Town Proprietorship in Decline*. New York: Columbia University Press, 1936.

Wright, Conrad. *The Beginnings of Unitarianism in America*. Boston, 1955. Reprint, Hamden, Conn.: Archon Books, 1976.

Wright, Louis B. *Middle-Class Culture in Elizabethan England*. Ithaca: Cornell University Press, 1965.

Young, Alfred F. *The Democratic Republicans of New York*. Chapel Hill, N.C.: Institute of Early American History, 1967.

Young, Thomas. *Some Reflections on the Disputes between New York, New Hampshire and Col. John Henry Lydius of Albany*. New Haven: B. Mecom, 1764.

Zeichner, Oscar. *Connecticut's Years of Controversy, 1750–1776*. Hamden, Conn.: Archon Books, 1970.

INDEX

ABOUT THE AUTHOR

Born in Philadelphia, Willard Sterne Randall is the author of thirteen books, including six biographies, and a former investigative reporter who won the National Magazine Award for Public Service from Columbia Graduate School of Journalism.

After graduate studies in history at Princeton University, Randall turned to writing biographies. He has written award-winning books about Benjamin Franklin, Thomas Jefferson, George Washington, Alexander Hamilton, and Benedict Arnold. His *Benedict Arnold: Patriot and Traitor* was a finalist for the *Los Angeles Times* Book Prize and was a Notable Book of the *New York Times*. The American Revolution Round Table conferred its highest honor, the Award of Merit, on Randall. Randall has appeared on the *Today Show*, NBC's "One on One," C-Span, PBS, and the History Channel. A contributing editor to *American Heritage* and *MHQ: The Quarterly Magazine of Military History,* he has twice participated in C-Span's Rating of Presidential Leadership. A Fellow of the Vermont Academy of Arts and Sciences, he is currently Distinguished Scholar in History and Professor at Champlain College and Visiting Professor of History at John Cabot University in Rome. He lives in Burlington, Vermont, with his wife, Nancy Nahra.

B   Randall, Willard
ALL   Sterne.

           Ethan Allen.

$18.95

DATE			
		DISCARD	

TAYLOR